1776 REWIND

The Great Awakening is Revolutionary:
A memoir of actual letters written
to fight for the soul of our nation.

HASSAN BARTLEY (SONNY B.)

ARCHWAY
PUBLISHING

Archway Publishing books may be ordered through booksellers or by contacting:

Archway Publishing
1663 Liberty Drive
Bloomington, IN 47403
www.archwaypublishing.com
844-669-3957

ISBN: 978-1-6657-2453-1 (sc)
ISBN: 978-1-6657-2713-6 (e)

Library of Congress Control Number: 2022913187

Print information available on the last page.

Archway Publishing rev. date: 09/09/2022

This book is dedicated to my wife and children, my mother, my mother-in-law, Mrs. Billie and Mrs. Youngblood.

CONTENTS

PREFACE

I grew up in an era where communism and the cold war was taught in our schools; as a result, we would come to understand the effects it had on the world and the detriment to its own people. Tyrannical governments ruling with an iron fist, and anyone resisting would receive a blow from that fist. Many would suffer and many more would be murdered under the strong arm of dictatorship. Here is a headline showing us the horrors of communism, titled, "100 years of communism- and 100 million dead." Subtitle, "The Bolshevik plague that began in Russia was the greatest catastrophe in human history." Here is a quote from the first paragraph of that article posted, "Armed Bolsheviks seized the winter palace in Petrograd- now St. Petersburg- 100 years ago this week and arrested ministers of Russia's provisional government. They set in motion a chain of events that would kill millions and inflict a near-fatal wound on western civilization." This article was published by the Wall Street Journal on November 6, 2017, and written by David Satter. It's strange to see, not long ago, the liberal media actually publishing real news. It's unfortunate, like the mainstream media, academia has become complicit in the cover-up of communism as they glamourize and highlight the seemingly "Good Parts" of socialism while indoctrinating our children with ideals that has nothing to do with education. Before communism can take root, there has to be societal Marxism implemented causing 'Wokeism' into culture to create turmoil justifying a hostile governmental takeover. However, I believe a nation can easily be brought down through the ineffectiveness of the church and the breakdown of the nuclear family. Look around to see decades of decay to godly principles and the family. Remove God and there goes the family and then your love for the country.

Can you see the turn of events here in America? If you can't, it's because of the 'Information War' explained here in my book. Or maybe because of the fear mongering distraction of

Covid-19 (Wuhan virus), a curable virus. That too, would cause one to become blind to what's going on in our nation because of the 'Information War.' How do you seize a nation, first you indoctrinate, then you project fear into society and lastly control the information going out to the citizens with 24/7 propaganda and rhetoric; moreover, create a 'Cancel Culture' to all others defying the narratives. "How else do you get blacks and whites to riot? "You feed them racism and you make it a steady diet." That's an excerpt from my poem, 'Look to a Nation.'

We who are awake see the effects of indoctrination and cancelation. We were told by the mainstream media for almost a year as we saw chaos with our own eyes that the riots were "Mostly Peaceful." During those 'Mostly Peaceful protest, BLM/Antifa would burn the American flag, while yelling, "Death to America, Bring in Communism." If this isn't a very serious problem to you, then you are part of the problem, and this would be an example of controlling the minds of the masses Malcolm X spoke of. Ill-informed citizens have injected an unpatriotic culture into our society, and it must be stopped. The media, combined with the political cesspool on Capitol Hill is destroying the very foundation of our country. Those of us who are awake, must awaken those who are under the mesmerizing spell of the zombie media apocalypse. The fight is right now. We can no longer afford to sit on our hands and watch from the sidelines, because that mindset is what put us in the predicament we see today. We have to go back to the constitution that our forefathers left us as a backup plan against tyranny. 'We the People' have to get into this war because there isn't any calvary coming, WE ARE IT!!! 1776REWIND!!!

FREDERICK DOUGLASS REPUBLICAN; INTRODUCTORY

Oddly enough, the very last writing will become the first presentation of my book. Why is this? An explanation will be rendered as you read the entire introduction. It will serve as a threefold purpose: 1) To introduce the tone and reasoning for a memoir of actual letters sent out to save the future of our nation; 2) How American citizens with multiple backgrounds can get involved with the 'Great Awakening' to overthrow tyranny; 3) And to aquatint you to the new revolutionary constitutional party movement called 'The Frederick Douglass Republican.' My writings have one common goal and it's simple; **SAVE THE SOUL OF OUR NATION**. The media, politicians, elected officials, foreign influences, organizations, corporations, professional sports, academia, governmental agencies, Hollywood, music industry, Big Tech., Big Pharma, fake woke individuals, and clergy are only called out for their hypocrisy and supporting knowingly or unknowingly the Marxist and global agenda (The Great Reset). In other words, corruption has taken control of every facet of life in America, but I'm here to sabotage the expectations of the enemy with the help of God almighty. I believe most would agree, we've been sold a bill of goods, we've been hoodwinked, bamboozled, and we've been swindled. I see the handwriting on the wall, it says Communism and I'm furious at politicians that have sold out our country to the highest bidder, and for their own personal gain. Needless to say, the gig is up, and they can no longer distracted me with the entertainment of professional sports, ESPN, Disney theme parks, nor with the mesmerizing spell of the deceitful and manipulative media (mainstream and locally across the country). Neither can they depend on my reliance to the controlled oppositions like FOX News, Newsmax and Bill O'Reilly.

My writings have evolved and grown with me as I constantly take a stroll down memory lane. Remembering how my beloved America used to be and how did we get to a very crucial crossroad today, that would hold the very existence of the United States in its hands. In bewilderment, asking myself the rhetorical question, HOW DID WE GET HERE AND WHY WOULD ANYONE WANT TO TURN ON THEIR COUNTRY? When I say evolved, I mean as I learned, the state of my thinking and writings would mature over time. Ironically, I began writing in April 2020 and I would write my last writing in 2022 of April. So, you can imagine the disparities over a two-year unintended project. My thought of this beautiful but insane world created by Marxist would change drastically as current events poured in each day. I could hardly keep up as I wrote because of the hysteria in our nation, while being inspired to counteract with my letters, writings and poems.

I love to write so that ordinary Americans like myself can relate; therefore, I lay my heart on the table for the world to examine its transparency, honesty, boldness and love for God, Family and Country, because anything else would be a travesty we already experience each day. I'm a real and genuine person with a disdain for people with facades, because I refuse to put on an act; what you see, is what you get. All of my writings are inspired by God, so if there's something you disagree with, take it up with Him, Lol. So, step into my shoes and take this journey with me, not as a black American but as an American. America the beautiful, a delightful melting pot of all colors, creeds and nationalities. No one person or group above another but equal in the eyes of God according to the Declaration of Independence. A historical document that ties us all together as one nation under God who gives life, liberty and the pursuit of happiness.

We are reliving 1776, defying a tyrannical government, sounds familiar? However, we are fighting enemies more deadly than ever: the invisible enemy and the enemy controlling the information. 2020 and January 6 would prove to us just how diabolical and sinister this scheme is. It's not a bloody war with guns and missiles but it leads to blood in the streets among its own citizens. It's a battle for the minds of the masses. I believe Malcolm X guides us to the detriment of a disingenuous Marxist media and Big Tech. controlling the information in his quote, "The media's the most powerful entity on earth. They have the power to make the innocent guilty and to make the guilty innocent, and that's power, because they control the minds of the masses." 'The Information War,' I believe should be coined as World War III, because it's that destructive and divisive to an already volatile society on the brink of a racial collapse with an entire nation heading for its demise. The elites know this, which is why the 'Cancel Culture' was created and why we have to support independent media outlets and 'Truth Social,' giving us truthful news as is, without a spin or an agenda. We have to be direct and proactive in our approach to wake-up the masses who are still in a coma.

Exit stage left, people are fleeing the democratic party. Why? Because they associated them to being a wolf. We know who they are, and they make no apologies for it. They are anti-life, anti-God, they don't want school choice, unpatriotic, they hate the Constitution, and they say they are most tolerant, but disagree with them and you will see the collusion of evil at work. There is so much more about the democratic party, but I'll stop there. Exit stage right, patriots are questioning their status as a republican. Why? Because they are a wolf in sheep's clothing. In my opinion, are the worst of the two parties. Why do I say this? Because the republican party appears as an angel of light. They have hidden behind conservative values and Christian principles. So, I say cast the stone at the party you believe has the worst transgression. If you say both, it wouldn't hurt my feelings. However, if you take a moment and examine what I just said, it will become clear who's more guilty of playing the devil's advocate. Again, we know what we get in the democratic party: Marxism, division and stealth oppression of the black race. It's in plain sight for those of us who are truly awake and see the media as a shield for the democratic party. It's blatantly obvious which platform they embrace because the democratic party and the media are identical twins as they use identity politics to gain leverage to obtain power. In addition, on the other hand, republicans seized the opportunity to take advantage of the hard-working patriots living the American dream, as we put our trust in them to care for our country. Instead of republicans standing up for the American people, they stand on the sidelines with their hands in their pockets as they watch the atrocities transpire right before their eyes, as they cheer-on the opposition in secrecy. I'm sorry to break the news to you folks, but there isn't any calvary coming, we're it (We the People).

Before the 2020 mostly peaceful protest, PLAN-demic and treasonous election, by the way, we call that a trifecta, a perfect storm; I must admit, I was driving the republican bus and would run anyone off the road that didn't want to get on board of that republican train. Boy how naive and foolish I was, but at least I'm willing to admit my transgressions and right the wrong. I thought like every other American that we truly had a two-party system. I was flabbergasted and sickened when I saw and realized a collaboration of international and domestic treason of an obvious stolen election. In addition, if you believe that a very unpopular guy in the basement beat President Trump by getting more votes than President Obama, then I have some ENRON stock to sell you. This was inconceivable and a terrifying breach to our Republic as democrats and the media twin denied such a notion as the republicans went silent, while cheering in the grandstand. This should've disturbed ALL AMERICANS, no matter your status, rather you are a democrat, republican, independent or libertarian, we were all defrauded. I don't care how anyone felt or feel about President Trump, we all should want a fair and honest election. If this is allowed to stand, all of our votes are meaningless and worthless as the dollar bill backed by the Central Banks. My God, the crime families have nothing on the political cesspool on Capitol Hill, it is the biggest racket and clown show the world has ever seen as the mainstream media continue to bring in the clowns. In which, I believe is an appropriate time to insert this quote, "When a clown moves into a palace, he doesn't become king. The palace becomes a circus." -Turkish Proverb

How do we fix the corrupt deep state system? There are very good organizations out there I believe are doing a great job fighting to save the soul of our nation, but I can only vouch for one because I am an Ambassador for Freedom for CCDF-USA (County Citizens Defending Freedom) founded by Mr. Steve Maxwell. I am so grateful to him for paving the road to fix our nation county by county, which is an extraordinary concept in my opinion. 'We the People,' taking back our country. I am partial to the CCDF-USA for four reasons: 1) Again, I am a member; 2) Anyone can become an Ambassador of Freedom, no matter your party affiliation; 3) You must at least acknowledge God as our creator; 4) You have to be a patriot to our country. However, what sealed the deal for me is, number 3 and 4 are deal breakers if you don't believe in God and have no love for the United States of America. REASON: We the People cannot win this nation back without God, IT IS AN IMPOSSIBILITY!!!, because of the powers of darkness we're up against. Furthermore, why would you join something that is Pro-America if you don't love the country, will someone tell that to Olympian's that despise our country? If you are very concerned with where our country is headed, very concerned about election integrity, appalled at the indoctrination of our children in the educational system, and believe that dark money and under the table deals by our elected officials is a detriment to our country, then CCDF-USA is the perfect place to get involved saving out nation. You can become a huge asset by becoming an advocate to the CCDF-USA with your time and/or donations to help sustain the enduring process it's going to take to win back and keep our country. Donate to your county, your county closest to where you live, or at the national level. Wherever your money is directed, it will support the grassroots earnestly working to reclaim our nation one county at a time.

Who was Frederick Douglass? He was an abolitionist, wrong. Okay, you're not exactly wrong. If you're like me, that's all I learned in school and I am ashamed to say, but is that my fault? Or is it the negligence of a 99.99% predominantly black public high school I attended? I am 52 years old, and I am now realizing how much the educational system has failed us all. Then it happened, I was at a CCDF-USA training session when I heard a proud black American citizen who loves God, family and country named K. Carl. He calls himself a Frederick Douglass Republican. What??? I know, you're probably asking the same question, why is he referring to himself as a Frederick Douglass Republican? When Frederick Douglass was only an abolitionist; so, I thought. Well, the brother broke it down and it would change my life forever; as a result, I purchased his book entitled, Frederick Douglass Republicans, subtitle, The movement to re-ignite America's passion for liberty, co-authored by K. Carl Smith and Dr. Karnie C. Smith Sr. I would purchase his book for me, my mother and 3 oldest children. That's 5 books for those of you who were keeping count. I was told by some of my colleagues who heard K. Carl speak before, that I was in for a treat. I had no idea how much!!! He educated me on who Frederick Douglass really was and that he was much more than an abolitionist. He was a pioneer for the black race, a constitutionalist and a trailblazer for all Americans to take note of and learn from, especially citizens today. He advised not one, but five presidents, that's remarkable, because that is unheard of regardless of what century we're in. That's just one example to describe a constitutionalist that loved his country. Don't believe me, get his book and book him for your next event, I promise, you won't be disappointed. Amazing, Amazing, Amazing. Hello, my name is Sonny B., and I am a Frederick Douglass Republican. **1776REWIND!!!** May God Bless America, Sonny B.

THE PUBLISHER II

Greetings Publisher,

I met the wonderful, intriguing Mrs. Youngblood, an 85-year-old white female and longtime RNC representative at a black voices for Trump meeting here in Jacksonville, FL. I fell in love with her warm personality, friendliness, but frankness. We hit it off the first time I met her; it was if I'd known her my whole life. She read some of my writings and told me how much she enjoyed them. I told her I was writing a book; As I said this, I saw the excitement in her eyes and heard the confidence in her voice as she told me she would be the first to buy my book. This would give me the inspiration I needed to move forward.

Now, let me tell you a little bit about myself. I am a proud black American citizen of this great nation. I am a 51-year-old father of (6) six wonderful children with my lovely wife of 22 years. I'm a retired fireman of the Jacksonville Fire/Rescue Department and chef desiring to open my first restaurant in the near future. I was thoroughly enjoying cooking at the prestigious hotel located on the beach when covid-19 hit. I was laid-off at the end of March 2020, this outcome would soon begin my journey of writing.

I started mowing yards at the age of 10, I basically had a job all my life. This was the first-time being home without a job in over 41 years. Well, I thought to myself, this is a time to enjoy my family to the fullest without any employment in the way. Then George Floyd happened. I watched the chaos, lawlessness and mayhem in the streets of America.

Our economy was wrecked by the Wuhan virus, I believe because of political reasons. The real problem wasn't that it was happening, because Americans are resilient. The real issue was the chaos allowed to happen. The lunacy was applauded by democratic politicians and the media would regard the protest as mostly peaceful, as we watched burning buildings in the background; As one democratic mayor would put it, "it's a summer of love." Therefore, I became outraged and poised to do something. Listen, I stand against injustice, but I do not condone injustice for injustice, because it never brings about a solution. Now, in light of the election, I am dumbfounded at the massive voter fraud of our election process. I don't care what side of the isle you're on, rather it be a democrat, republican, independent or libertarian; If a certain political party or foreign countries can manipulate the outcome of an election with obvious fraud and deceit, all Americans should be furious. Because if this were allowed to go unpunished, our republic is DEAD, and America as we know it, is DONE!!! I believe I'm one of millions of Americans fed up with the hypocrisy of the WOKE radical progressives, which is why I write with heart and passion. I have my children's future to protect from those who want to see our country come to its demise. The Cuban born American, Maximo Alvarez who fled from Cuba during the reign of Fidel Castro, made a profound statement during the RNC convention in DC, he said, "If we lose our Republic in America, there is nowhere else to go"; he said this with tears in his eyes. Again, this is why I fight because I know what's at stake.

I've always been a writer, but never gave any thought of writing a book. I was sort of ushered into my first writing in the form of a poem, titled," Look to a Nation." My second writing was a letter to Mayor Curry, Sheriff Williams, 79 black pastors and the whole city council, regarding the cancelation of the RNC convention in Jacksonville. My letter was given to Eye on Jacksonville; As a result, founder of Eye on Jacksonville wanted me to become a guest writer for her column. I gladly accepted and the rest is history.

Again, in my idleness, I was made to see the assault on our Republic, constitution, values, patriotism, and freedoms of the United States of America. Therefore, I kept writing, on a quest to join in the fight to save America from the liberal socialist that despise our country and president.

With all that being said, I believe I have all the material needed for a book completion. This is a new adventure for me; Even though I've read articles about publishing, I still feel like a novice. I found a few publishers from the books I've read of: Thomas Sowell, Candace Owens, Jesse Lee Peterson, and Larry Elder, or just listen to from time to time. I've been told I sound just like the said names just mentioned, which is the reason why I found a few of their publishers. Which leads me to my million-dollar question, what are the next steps for getting my book published? My book is unique in itself, it's not written in standard novel or book form with chapters. It is made up of actual letters sent out about serious issues plaguing our country, inspired writings, and poems. My writings are filled with a roller coaster ride of emotions put on paper. Although my book is untitled, it speaks to the American patriots of our nation to: Be polite but fearless, courageous and bold, while having the same tenacity of the anarchist and savages without the violence. Thank you for your attention to this matter, I look to hear from you soon.

May God bless America,
(Sonny B.)

LOOK TO A NATION
By Sonny B.

The Civil War was a war between brothers
Who bled on both sides
For a cause that should've since long died
So I say leave the monuments
For the world to see
As a reminder of what happens when we disagree
In hopes to learn not to repeat history
Blacks fought in this war
It could land them back with the slave master
Knew if they lost the war
It would be a monumental disaster
Police brutality no I don't condone,
But reality is I'm more likely to be murdered by my own
Police brutality so loud we can't hear the sound!
Of Black on Black blood cryin out from the ground
Why no outrage when we kill each other?
Is it because the media sees it as ok to kill your brother?
Naw that just don't fit the bill
A black man taken down by a white man

Yeah that's more of a thrill

So you censor my voice and agree with another

While you recklessly divide a nation of all colors

All lives do matter, black, white, yellow and red

We are all God's children so can we put this issue to bed?

We say the justice system is broken

And Blacks get more time

The fix is simple

Just don't do the crime

Am I the only Black man that can see this?

We getting sold out by Judas' kiss

Will somebody define racism PLEASE!!!

Media tryin to infect our minds with a sick disease

Are you tellin me we're worse off in the future?

And our pain compares to Dr. Luther?

Wake up my brother before it's too late,

Before we destroy the whole human race

Can we admit there are issues on all sides?

Let's band together so this nation can truly thrive

Take a slave out of chains and out of the cotton fields

Tell a man he's a victim and watch what it yields

Anger, rage now he's back in a cage

Imprisoned in his mind only to be enslaved

How do you get young minds both black and white to riot?

You feed them racism and make it a steady diet

Make blacks oversized with malice and hate

And shame the whites with guilt by saying they have the same trait

Kaepernick, Lebron James oh yeah and Kyrie too,

We pander to these three

And dare me to disagree

If I disagree I will have to pay

Or give an apology on the very next day

I used to get away from fake news by watching ESPN

Now politics in sports have become the new trend

Is that equality?

Seems one sided to me

And this is what we callin free speech?

You kneel to the flag
You disrespect the Anthem
White lives died, black lives died
We all had a loss
And before you made your millions
It came at a cost
If we could remain as a child
So innocent, so mild
Pure in heart without ever being defiled
Go ahead ask a child what do you see?
I only see a person that's a friend of me
Look again don't you see his color?
No I see a person that's like a brother
The Good Book tells us
There's nothing new under the sun
Everything we see today has already been done
So love your neighbor as yourself
And please don't tell a lie
We can't run from the truth
It's a word we can't deny
It's not a race issue
But an issue of the heart
But you can't understand this, because we've grown too smart
So, what is the answer to undo this MESS?
By LOOKING TO A NATION, that says God Bless!!!

LETTER TO CITY COUNCIL, MAYOR AND SHERIFF OF JAX

Greetings,

I am a proud Black American citizen of this Great Nation. I'm also a law abiding, tax paying citizen of our wonderful city. I have been following the coverage of the RNC ever since it was announced that the Convention was coming to Jacksonville. Therefore, I tuned into the online coverage of the City Council meeting this morning. I wanted to see the response of each member and the silence of each member (staying silent and neutral says a lot as well.)

I understand that the Convention has been cancelled and I would like to end with this message to everyone on the City Council, Mayor, and Sheriff. The two incidents I'm about to mention happens all across America towards Trump supporters. "Liberals say they want tolerance until you have a different opinion than them." That's a quote from Congresswoman Debbie Lesko of Arizona's 8th Congressional District in response to a Bath and Body Works manager yelling F Donald Trump at a customer for wearing a pro-Trump face mask in the store.

Second incident: The Denver police department might tell you that they were not told to stand down by a Democratic mayor at a pro-police event a few days ago as Michelle Malkin was viciously attacked by Black Lives Matter/Antifa thugs, but they can't deny the assault caught on video with NO response from the police department. I remind you, this was a pro-Police event. This is appalling and absurd. I must say if this is the cowardice, gutless, heartless attitude of the Denver police department, then I do agree with the BLM/Antifa democratic Thugs, they should defund and dismantle a department of spineless human beings.

This is why I am no longer a part of the democratic party. Conservative, law abiding citizens are despised, ridiculed, assaulted, ostracized and made to apologize, but lawless renegades are given concessions and allowed to run the town granted by democrats and excused and applauded by Fake News. This seems one-sided to me; I thought all Americans were protected under the Constitution of the First Amendment? No, you are only protected if you agree with the far-left Liberals agenda.

There were 79 Black Pastors who signed a petition under the guise of safety. Why no concern for the safety of the city during the protest that almost progressed into a riot but didn't because of the leadership of the mayor and the sheriff's office. I wonder if the tables were turned and the DNC convention was coming to Jacksonville; would there have been a negative reaction from: Ju-Coby Pittman, Garrett L. Dennis, Brenda Priestly Jackson, Joyce Morgan, Randy Defoor, Ronald B. Salem and Tommy Hazouri.

Back to the 79 Black Pastors; there are many problems in the Black community, mostly self-inflicted that has plagued the Black community for decades. Yet, a signed petition to halt the RNC from coming to Jacksonville was a top priority. I can see why the Black community never gets any better. On November 3rd President Donald Trump will maintain his Presidency, and that's what you're really afraid of. I am of the silent majority, but silent no more.

May God Bless America,
Sonny B.

LETTER TO 79 BLACK PASTORS

Greetings,

I am a proud Black American patriot. I heard about, then I read about 79 Black Pastors petitioned to the mayor to halt hosting RNC convention on grounds of safety. This is comical, a joke and downright hilarious. Which one of you petitioned to the mayor about halting the protest here in Jacksonville. In the name of George Floyd's death? None because I didn't see a headline. When you talk safety, you mean safety from Covid-19? Each of you are going on hypotheticals that someone may get sick or gravely ill. When in fact the safety of people in other cities were actually threatened and many lives loss as a result of the protestors and rioting. No hypotheticals here. Innocent people did die because of the rioting. Does the safety of those people matter? You are Pastors. You're supposed to be concerned about all people, right? No not a peep. Instead, these criminals were applauded, by mainstream media, democratic politicians, Al, Jessie, major corporations, Hollywood and Professional athletes for chaos mayhem and lawlessness.

A White man killing a Black man. This is the real issue here, right? Blacks getting slaughtered at the hands of other Blacks all across America, but not a sound from Black Pastors. You might say, "You're wrong. I cry loud about Black-on-Black homicide. "Apparently, it's not loud enough to get the fake news media's attention, because I have never seen a headline that says, "79 Pastors outraged about the epidemic of Black-on-Black homicide across the country. I agree, no one should die the way George Floyd did at the hands of a cop. This act is vastly disproportionate to Black-on-Black homicide, but no outrage by anyone, especially 79 Black Pastors.

So, what is this petition all about? I'll tell you. I begin with a hate and a disdain for the president because the media told you to. President Trump has done more for the Black community than President Obama ever thought about. He has done prison reform (just in case you didn't know Blacks are a minority in the free world, but a majority in prisons and jails), poured millions into inner cities across the country where Blacks mainly dwell, and before this Covid-19 madness, the Black unemployment rate was at an all-time low, doing his best to defund Planned-Parenthood (an organization responsible for aborting of over 350,000 Black babies a year) to name a few. Quit listening to Fake news for a minute and seek the truth about President Trump and the democratic party for yourselves. Listen I do not like politicians, but you have to get on either side. This is why I became a republican, I'm not saying they're perfect by any means; however, the Republican party, is pro-life, pro-tradition family, and pro-school choice to name a few. These things are important to me and vital to a country's survival because of values. The democratic party is the polar opposite, ant-life, anti-traditional family, anti-God and anti-school choice to name a few. If you are on the side of the Democratic party, you are supporting politicians who are heavily against what you say or at least supposed to believe as Pastors.

Has anyone of you thought about what God thinks about the party you are representing? According to the article, there were only Black Pastors involved. If this was not about race or one-party affiliation, why are there only Black Pastors involved? There are many self-inflicted problems that have plagued the Black community for decades and halting a convention from coming to town is a priority? It's no wonder why the Black community never gets any better all across America with this type of mentality each of you possess.

Lastly, let's just be honest. It's about the RNC convention. If there were some grave concerns over people coming to the city causing possible Covid-19 outbreaks, Orlando opening up its theme parks should have people crying bloody murder. Not a peep. I will say that if you're that concerned about the spread of Covid-19 while the Convention is here, STAY HOME!! A few days shouldn't be a problem. After all we were shut in at home for over THREE MONTHS. You have time to prepare, the Convention is weeks away. So, sit in your recliners and listen to Fake News tell you how evil and racist the president is. I want to end with a news alert that the Fake News won't tell you: Racism comes in all colors!!! And God doesn't like it in any race of people.

May God Bless America,
Sonny B.

WHY I BECAME A REPUBLICAN

Let's go back some years to a little classroom in 7th grade with economics being the subject. My economics teacher would be fired today because of the information shared with his students. He taught us about the instability of international trade and the corruption of our government among other things. I believe this was the beginning of my journey into politics.

When you are Black, I believe it is an unwritten rule that you're a democrat at birth. This is what it is, so accept it. Well, I am the unique one. Let's just say I don't like politicians, democrats or republicans. I felt politicians divided America with their differences of opinion, but had one common goal, that is to benefit themselves. Therefore, at the age of 19, I changed my affiliation from democrat to independent. I realized in a hurry that I had even less power as a voting citizen, because I couldn't vote in the primaries. So, I did my due diligence and researched for myself to find out the platform of both parties. I soon realized that among the two evils, the republican Party's ideals and values at least leaned towards issues I hold dear. I noticed the republican's voting habits on a consistent basis were conservative. Almost 100% of republicans voted issues in favor of pro-life, pro-traditional family, pro-God, and pro-school choice. This of course won me over. Therefore, I changed my affiliation from independent to the republican party. I have to say this. There was once a time when you had a moderate to slightly left-leaning democrats. However, presently democrats have become far left, Marxist, socialist, and anti-American liberals.

George Floyd's death exposed just who the democrats really are. They hijacked the Black Lives Matter cause for their own agenda; that is to dismantle the values, Constitution,

Republic, and patriotism of the United States of America. I wasn't born when prayer was taken out of school and was too young when the Cross and Ten Commandments were removed from all federal buildings. Nonetheless, I saw the handwriting on the wall. The rioting was heading down a slippery slope. I saw a democratic mayor threatening law-abiding citizens with jail time for wanting to go back to work to feed their families but said nothing to rioters and criminals. I saw a democratic mayor calling the riots a 'Summer of Love.' I saw the democratic cities and states stand by while their cities were burned to the ground. All the while, the fake news mainstream media celebrated and applauded these renegades for destroying cities, livelihoods and even lives. The media reveal to us whose side their on by covering for these democratic cities instead of holding them accountable.

There's an old saying, "Fool me once, shame on you. Fool me twice, shame on me." The democratic party has fooled the black church and the black community time and time again and draw white America in with white guilt of the past and inflated racism of the present. Every time there are midterm elections for an election year all the democrats have to do is call republicans racist, white supremacist, and cry social injustice. Black America falls for it every time, because they fail to see the clear signs of very democratic poor policies that harm all Americans, especially the black community. However, a huge reason the black community is so blind is that the fake news media helped do a great job of keeping Americans ill-informed.

I saw a mayor and governor shun help from the Trump Administration because of disdain and hate for the president. Because of hate, democrats would rather cut off their nose to spite their face and disregard the needs and safety of American people under their leadership. I want to say, I wasn't born yesterday and I'm now old enough to understand exactly what's going on. My children's future is at stake, and I will not stand by and allow the democrats to dismantle America without a fight. This is why I became a republican and a Man on FIRE!!!

WHY I VOTED TRUMP (REPUBLICAN PARTY)
Letter to a relative

I would like to start off by saying, why do you stick with the democratic party? But first, let me tell you why I voted for Trump, or should I say, voted for the republican party? Because it's not about a person, it's about the candidates' platform. I believe we can agree, during any election, we can rip apart both democrat and republican candidates until we are blue in the face. Therefore, despite Trumps flaws, we can agree all candidates on both sides of the isles have flaws, hang-ups, and sins, because we live in an imperfect and fallen world, but the only difference with Trump, Trump wasn't a career politician. That alone drew my attention towards him, to start paying attention to what he was saying and not what the media wanted me to think about him. Then I realized, he didn't need or want money from the lobbyist; Therefore, he couldn't be controlled or manipulated, unlike career politicians.

Let me make this clear, I do not like politicians, which is why at the age of 19, I went from democrat to independent. I soon realized, I had less power, because I couldn't vote in the primaries. Therefore, I did my due diligence, to find out which party represented what I believe in as a Christian; As a result, my endeavors led me to the republican party. Case in point, republicans are: pro-life, pro-God, pro-traditional family, pro-America and pro-school choice/vouchers.

I texted you two links, one with a NY Post article about some of the things Trump did for the black community and a letter/article I wrote to Mayor Curry, Sheriff Williams, and entire city council about not defunding JSO. Two YouTube raps by Bizzle, that explains a list of issues, if you listen to his lyrics. I hope you read and listened in its entirety, because it was a great start of telling why I vote the way I do.

Let me continue, President Trump asked for the black vote, he didn't assume like the democratic party does every election year, because I'm black, I'm supposed to automatically vote democrat. Make me at least think you care about me as a person and not just another vote. These actions towards the black race came after Trump became president; However, it proves once again why I voted for Trump. He invited into the oval office, Black: Pastors, leaders, conservative activists, law enforcers, entertainers and entrepreneurs, to get their thoughts on how to improve the black community. Not to mention, he started 'Operation Legend,' named after the black 4-year-old toddler killed as a result of the rioting. Legend was one of nine (9) children killed as a result of the riots; the ages ranged from 1 to 14 years old. While the media and democrats are ignoring the chaos and lawlessness on the streets, President Trump is remembering the innocent soul's loss to racist BLM/Antifa rioting.

Democrats are no longer moderate; they have swayed to the far-left socialist scale. This socialist mentality is led by Bernie Sanders and AOC, who are also pushing for a green new deal that would bankrupt America. Before the Wuhan virus, the economy under Trump was thriving, with black unemployment at an all-time low. Trumps foreign policies has caused peace treaties and fair-trade deals, that hold foreign countries accountable for fair treatment of the U.S. financially.

I also, realize the Marxist mainstream media is an extension of the democratic party, thus the reason for only negative coverage on Trump and never about any of his accomplishments. This is why I hate the media, they paint the picture they only want you to see, to make you think the way they want you to. Here is a quote from Malcolm X, I believe best describes the media: "The media's the most powerful entity on earth. They have the power to make the innocent guilty and to make the guilty innocent, and that's power, because they control the minds of the masses." End quote.

Finally, I end with this, President Trump's inaugural speech, sealed the deal for me; As a result, I knew I chose the right candidate for president. It went like this, as I set the stage. Daddy Bush, The Clinton's, Son Bush, The Obama's, the whole republican party and the one or two democrats that had the decency to attend, they were all sitting behind Trump. Trump, turns and point at those just mentioned behind him, and says, these people have failed the American people, he turns back to the camera and look to the American people and says, but I am giving the power back to the American people. I believe we want the same thing, a sovereign nation under God and the Constitution of the United States of America. I don't believe you want socialism for our country, but that is where the democratic party is taking us, pushed by the media. You, like many others are mesmerized under the spell of the

Marxist mainstream media. They are the enemy of the people, by playing identity politics: Blacks against whites, homosexuals against the church, Jews against Muslims, we can match them up however we please, but they still yield the same result, Socialism; All backed by China, Ukraine, and George Soros a multi-billionaire Hungarian American that vowed to turn our country into Socialism. The Bush's, The Clinton's, the Obama's, CIA, FBI, DOJ, FDA, CDC, and the WHO, to name a few, they are all in on it, the destruction of this nation; that's how the phrase came about, 'drain the swamp'. If you didn't know, Trump initiated the human trafficking operation. There are a lot of top indictments coming down of some serious crimes, thus the reason why the deep state, wants him out of office to put a stop to it. This political cesspool of corruption is so much bigger than us, this is why they want the citizens of America to fight against one another, to take the focus off the corruption. If they can divide, they can conquer. Please, search for yourself to find the truth, I will say the search engines like Google, and social media with their cancel culture and censoring, don't make it easy; However, if you really want the truth, God will reveal the truth, if you sincerely want truth. Love you, and may God bless America.

INFORMATION WAR

LET ME TAKE YOU ON A JOURNEY OF HOW I BECAME AN INFORMATION WARRIOR! In 2019, I retired as a Fireman of Jacksonville, it took courage, determination, commitment, proper planning and hard work to finally get to the point of retirement. While employed with the JFRD, I became interested in food and found out I really enjoyed cooking. I became so enamored with the preparation of food, I wanted to attend culinary school and make it a permanent career after retirement. So, I used my own hard-earned money to pay for my education to attend FCCJ, now FSCJ's Culinary School of Arts. Getting an education would catapult me into catering as a side job and working as a line/prep cook in many popular kitchens in Jacksonville, Amelia Island and Ponte Vedra Sawgrass to earn extra money for my family and to gain kitchen experience working in restaurants. After retirement, I took a temporary sabbatical to refresh from 41 years of working and to enjoy some time with the family undisturbed from any outside sources. After about 4 months, I found employment in a very popular restaurant in Sawgrass. I was enjoying cooking, finally I could focus all of my attention on cooking fulltime. I was living the American dream as a black American. No oppression, systematic racism, white privilege, or white supremacy could hold me down, because I am not a victim. This country affords us all, the opportunity to succeed, no matter your color. Will there be obstacles? Absolutely! However, good things come with a price, so BLM supporters of a Marxist, racist movement, quit complaining, stop making excuses, get off the couch and work for what you want and stop looking for hand-outs.

I just mentioned nothing could hold me down. Well, March 23, 2020, would bring my dreams to a halt with Covid-19 (Wuhan virus). Not to mention, I was approved at the Riverside market to sell my desserts. Also, I eventually wanted to own my own restaurant. I was enjoying life, until the virus came and took that all away. Now, this is systematic corruption from a deep state system that will hold you down, you'll understand what I mean later on in this article as you read on. Devastation was the likely story for many hard-working law-abiding citizens across the country and even the world. For the first time in 41 years, I was without employment. Like every other American, I was working to provide for my family and would unwind with the entertainment of Hollywood, sports and ESPN. However, in the midst of all of the distractions, I always knew there was something evil lurking in the waters of Capitol Hill. I just didn't realize how sinister, until all employment and all entertainment came to a standstill. Recent exposure of Fauci's 'Gain of Function', would seal the government's doom in my eyes, because they are not to be trusted. However, I believe the virus was a blessing in disguise, satan meant it for evil, but God meant it for good. As I sat idle, I became keen in my awareness as the 2020 chaos and mayhem transpired right before our very eyes. Riots of destruction was called mostly peaceful protest by the media. This would bring me to the realization, that we were in an information war. WOW, the media is the bullhorn, also they're the political gangster's (Democrats/Republicans) hitman to keep the American people in the dark and ill-informed on major issues in our country, as politicians play the political game with American lives. So, I guess you can say, like everything else made and owned in this country by the Chinese Communist Party (CCP), you can say, I was made in China, SO DON'T GET ANGRY AT ME!!!, because the Wuhan, China virus made me. This would set me on FIRE, and on a journey to find truth, and justice with actual letters written to: ESPN, NBA, NFL, local and state governmental officials, governmental officials across the country, police departments, POTUS (Trump), and U.S. Supreme court, to name a few. I saw where our country was headed, and I wanted to preserve the American dream for my children and the generations to come. Therefore, I put my dream on the back burner to get into this fight to help save America. IF YOU ARE OBLIVIOUS TO WHAT'S HAPPENING IN OUR COUNTRY, IT'S BECAUSE WE ARE IN AN INFORMATION WAR!!!

Looking back at my letter to the FDA, CDC, and NBC, just generally speaking, I realize some people don't agree with me on the dangers of the experimental Covid vaccines and that's ok. I give you a pass, especially if you've already taken the jab. Why do I say this? Because taking the Covid vaccine is like flying in an airplane, once you're in the air, you're committed. Therefore, I can understand the anxiety that may come about from a foreign substance being injected into your body, unassured of short or long-term effects. So, I empathize with you. I understand, hearing anything else, other than positive news about the vaccines, would make anyone fearful and defensive, because it's human nature. In addition to, no one wants to believe that they have been duped, hoodwinked, bamboozled or lie to, because we pride ourselves on being able to sniff out a con-artist and a swindler. With that being said, THERE IS A CURE FOR COVID-19!!! I know firsthand, because I contracted the virus. I was treated with: Ivermectin and budesonide, drugs demonized by the corrupt three letter agencies and the mainstream media. Not to mention, these are safe, FDA approved prescriptions. Therefore, there is no need for a vaccine. We are in an information war to keep this news from the public, because if the majority of the citizens would've found out about the cure, there wouldn't have been a "pandemic" (SCAMDEMIC)!!!

THIS IS WHAT MAKES THE INFORMATION WAR SO DEADLY!!! People are generally loving, caring and trusting. We tend to trust those closest to us: clergy, family, friends, local news, doctors, coaches and teachers. Then we become a little more trusting and we venture out into national news, academia (colleges and universities), and government. However, I believe these three entities take advantage of our innocence, trust and occupied time, especially the media. They seek to indoctrinate each of us from the time we learn how to walk as a child; In hopes, that it will flow into adulthood. Now we began to form distant relationships with people we feel are credible and trustworthy; As a result, they shape our lives, thinking and decisions we make. Think about it, CNN, MSNBC, and FOX are a mainstay, we are inundated with disinformation: in our homes, hotel rooms, doctor's offices, fitness gyms, airports, barber shops and restaurants. They vow for our attention until we lay down our heads at night. Do you think this is intentionally done? Listen, all the networks and cable companies are owned by 6 entities with the same mindset and controlled and/or funded in some way by the CCP, to make sure we think the way they do. This is how operation mockingbird went into action. It's been scientifically proven, if humans hear a story often enough and hear it repetitiously from every network (local and nationally), they can control the minds of the masses. I think Malcolm X gave us a clear understanding about the media when he said, "The media's the most powerful entity on earth. They have the power to make the innocent guilty and to make the guilty innocent, and that's power, because they control the minds of the masses."

When will we realize, they're all in on the hostile communist takeover? (The Media, government, academia, major corporations, professional sports, Big Tech, social giants, Hollywood and Big PHARMA are all in on the takedown of America). So why would you trust any of them? Case in point, the FDA and the CDC have been telling the American people that the experimental vaccines (shots) are safe, and ivermectin is deadly. The media is the bullhorn, so they run the story 24/7 that the Covid vaccines are safe, and proven treatments, like: ivermectin, hydroxychloroquine and budesonide that are given to treat Covid patients by thousands of frontline doctors, are dismissed by the media as drugs that are either fatal, have severe side effects or are ineffective. They are programing you for what they want you to believe, because they know you trust them. This is how you know that

Capitol Hill and the mainstream media have the same agenda, because they speak the same language. The same news outlets across the country, that say Covid vaccines are safe, are the same news outlets pushing the narrative that America is a racist nation. So why should you believe them? Because you trust them, and they know it, which is why, they can push a 24/7 narrative of massive racism of MANUFACTURED RACISM CASES LIKE: Jussie Smollett, Covington Catholic students in DC, and Bubba Wallace. Again, the fake news media pushed this narrative until the patriots found out they were lying and being disingenuous to the American people. Fake news gave no apologies for this divisive lie, they just move on to the next lie, because they know you are naïve, gullible and trusting.

Brandon Straka was a staunch liberal drawn into the propaganda, and an avid viewer of news anchors like: Anderson Cooper, Don Lemon, Joe Scarborough and Joy Reid, until he found out they were lying to him; As a result, he started the hashtag walk away from the democratic party movement, he was able to confiscate a huge following. There is no accountability to call the media out for their intensions to fraud the citizens of this nation, because the news outlets are on the same team, and politicians are too busy swimming in their political cesspool. However, the exception to the rule are the independently patriotically owned media outlets, bloggers, podcasters, doctors and journalist telling the American people the truth. While the media gangsters continue on with their scandalous agenda to change the face of America, to usher in the new world order. Our only recourse is to walk away, to not allow fake news to have influence over us. Of course, this is easier said than done, because anyone defying the political cesspool on Capitol Hill, the deep state, the elites and exposing fake news, big tech, social giants and big pharma for being complicit in the scandal: are Canceled, Censored, Attacked, Demonized, Assaulted and Doxed (Just ask Tucker Carlson and Andy Ngo). Sadly to say, some have even loss their lives for proclaiming the truth and exposing the lie. The most disheartening thing is, the unpatriotic so-called citizens are the ones doing the political mob boss's biddings to invoke harm, both physically and mentally, because they have bought into the communist agenda.

BLM/Antifa destroyed cities across the country for over a year, the media never demonized it; Yet, somehow, one day on January 6th was an insurrection??? PLEASE WAKE UP FROM THE LIE!!! The same BLM/Antifa thugs, during a year of chaos, burned the American flag, while yelling out, "Death to America, bring in Communism," this is a foretelling of what's to come, if we don't take a courageous stand. Don't take my word for it, go and do your own research on Marxism and you will find that America has almost completed the laws of Marxism, just about every point made in Karl Marx's teachings are coming to fruition, and it must be stopped.

ALERT!!! WE ARE IN AN INFORMATION WAR!!! No one wants a bloody war with tanks, guns and explosives. However, I believe a war with the tongue can be more deadly; I believe, the chaos, destruction, civil disobedience, and unlawfulness throughout 2020, bears witness to my statement. Here are two quotes from Su Tzu's 'The Art of War' of how he perceived war should be, (1) "The supreme art of war is to subdue the enemy without fighting." (2) "The greatest victory is that which requires no battle." In 1956 Russia's Communist leader Nikita Khrushchev said, "We will take America without firing a shot. We do not have to invade the U.S. We will destroy you from within." What do you think, he meant by this? Turn off fake news, and look around you and you will see, America has been infiltrated by foreign foes, provoking Americans to destroy ourselves through identity politics, as immoral policies are made in our government against our constitution. Our tyrannical government is giving America up to foreign foes, piece by piece. The media knows this, but they choose to cover it up. While the citizens fight one another, sounds familiar (CIVIL WAR)? Blue vs Red, Left vs Right, patriotic vs unpatriotic, democrat vs republican, donkey vs elephant, conservatives vs socialists liberals, LBGTQ vs the world, black vs white, police vs blacks, citizens vs illegals, and vaccinated vs unvaccinated. I believe you have the point by now. They divide, we fight one another, and they conquer!!!

I was talking to a friend when I mentioned the cover-up of 9/11. He was astonished with disbelief because he could not fathom anyone being that evil, and certainly not our government. I asked this same gentleman a question, why was our presidential election shut down for the first time in history? Trump had a substantial lead before we went to bed, and we would wake up to a Biden lead. This was election fraud personified, even Ray Charles could see. Now we know why they needed the lockdown and fear of a curable virus. To dictate and manipulate the laws, to induce fraudulent mail-in ballots. The elites needed Trump out of the way because he was draining the swamp. Therefore, the Wuhan virus was used to assist and facilitate the election fraud, while simultaneously hiding the cure from us, and locking down the nation. This was meant to destroy our economy, and bankrupt the country, to commence globalism. This same friend asked, why would they keep a cure away from the American people? He continued on to say, they would just allow all of the deaths, knowing about a cure? And our government knew 9/11 was coming and allowed all those deaths to happen? I said to him, I know, it's a lot to try and wrap your head around, how can anyone be that sinister? I say this to everyone in disbelief, and to those that refuse to believe. I point them to the ID channel, I tell them to watch it, just for a day and you will see how violent one human being can be to another. Not to mention, this is a channel showing some of the most, brutal, horrific, murderous, diabolical and heinous crimes of all times and currently going on in our nation. These violent acts are not just from serial killers and thugs, but ordinary everyday people, whom we put our trust in: They are our neighbors, co-workers, family, clergy, friends, doctors, lawyers, coaches, etc., etc. … By the way, the first murder recorded in the bible, was a brother slaying his own blood brother because he was envious of him. I am reminded of a scripture out of the Holy bible, (Jeremiah 17:9) "The heart is deceitful above all things and desperately wicked: who can know it?" If our hearts aren't given over to God, we are likely to do anything.

Lastly, I write to combat against the information war, to spread truth and expose the propaganda and lies of fake news (Enemy of the People). We are at a very crucial point in our country, we're at the very precipice of a dictatorship. If you care anything about the future of America, turn off fake news and do your own research. I promise, if you search with a sincere heart and unbiased, open mind, you will find the truth; As a result, you will respect my words and despise the words of the mainstream media. However, regardless of the naysayers, I will continue to stand and be vigilant in this fight to help to restore all that has been stolen. Like Nehemiah, I will cry aloud at these renegades posing as Americans. Nehemiah was a man well off and comfortable in a distant land when he heard his country was in shambles; As a result, he went to see about his country and to restore the wall that protected the Israelites from their enemies. While restoring the wall of his original country that was destroyed by the enemy. He would speak to those same enemies that criticized and taunted him for restoring the wall, by saying, "I'm doing a great work, so that I cannot come down." (Nehemiah 6:3). I'm willing to die for what I believe, which is: love of God, family and country. So, will you join the patriots in this fight? 1776(REWIND) Because, if we lose our freedom to totalitarianism, then we are dead already, because there would be no reason to live.

May God bless America,
Sonny B.

LETTER TO PRESIDENT TRUMP

Greetings Mr. President Trump,

I am a proud Black American, who wanted to say thank you for all you are doing for this country. I have six beautiful children with my lovely wife. I am a retired fireman of Jacksonville, Florida. While employed as a fireman, I became a chef because I love to cook. As a result, owning a restaurant became a long-time dream of mine. However, I have put my dreams on hold in lieu of a concern for my children's future. I cannot really enjoy one of the many freedoms this country affords us all. That is, the American dream to become and be anything you set your mind to, of course with the help of God. What do I mean when I say I can't enjoy my dream? I can't be comfortable with the fact that if my child wanted to wear MAGA paraphernalia in public to support your presidency they will be attacked, ostracized, ridiculed, assaulted, punished by employers, called coon and Uncle Tom, censored by social media, embarrassed by fake news media, and their privileges cut off by PayPal and Go Fund Me among other vengeful things the far left socialist can think of.

However, if my children chose to wear paraphernalia of the corrupt, evil Democrats in public, they would be praised by all just mentioned. The Democratic party is very afraid of black Americans realizing the Democrat's true colors. I don't mean the colors of red, white, and blue, but Black and White colors of terrorism, the colors that push a Marxist and Anti-American agenda. I refuse to continue to be silent, because I am fed up with decades of political corruption and lawlessness allowed to run amok. The way George Floyd was killed,

I will be the first to say that no human should die this way, no matter your color. However, trying to vindicate a death, should never bring forth total chaos and lawlessness in our country, but it did, and that wasn't the worse of it. The chaos and lawlessness were applauded, praised, and excused by Democratic states, fake news media, colleges, major corporations, sports and Hollywood. True Americans should have been ashamed, embarrassed, and appalled at the display of these renegades.

I get it now. If you divide a nation, you conquer it. The death of a black man once again has been hijacked by the far-left liberals. Just cry racism and social injustice to stir up outrage in the black community, because that's all the Democratic party has; along with failed policies and destruction of our nation. The Democratic party is losing the black vote and they know it, this is why their polices are so lenient on illegal immigrants, mail in ballots and no voter ID. The Democratic party is losing a large majority of black votes; therefore, they have to find another means of getting you out of office so that the Deep State can gain its power once again.

How do you disrespect someone with the highest office in the country with no regard and arrogance from: Fake news, major corporations, Hollywood, professional athletes, musicians, rappers and politicians, of a president that's so American? People who are Un-American and people who I am ashamed to call citizens of the United States of America. True Americans speak and exemplify solidarity, sovereignty, virtues, respect, honor, protection, capitalism and patriotism, everything that unites us as Americans.

I watched and listened to your inaugural speech; I believe it resonated with most Americans. In that moment I definitely knew America made the right choice. Mr. President, when you said," these people behind me have failed the American people." You then turned and looked to the American people and said, "but I am giving the power back to the American people." Behind you was: the Republican party, the one or two Democrats that had some decency to at least show up, the Clinton's, the Obama's and both Bush families. Calling them all out left no doubt in my mind you were the perfect pick for this country. However, almost four years later, the establishment still doesn't understand how you got into office. Their political arrogance leaves them CLUELESS!

Mr. President, those that are awake realize again what's at stake on November 3rd. I can't reiterate it enough to everyone who will listen, the Democrats want no voter ID and mail in ballots to steal the election. The Democrats are using the (PLAN)demic to orchestrate their diabolical scheme, but God will not allow it. We prayed to God that He would deliver America from the eight years of Democratic rule, because another 4 to 8 years of democratic power would've destroyed our country. Again, we prayed that God would send someone to save America, who He sent was so unassuming; but God always send those who are unassuming but have a tender and willing heart. People look at the outward appearance, but God ALWAYS looks at the HEART.

In conclusion, every moment evil is trying to bring you down; the prayers of true Christians are undergirding your life with courage to withstand all of the demonic attacks.

I have with this letter, an original poem and writing I wrote to explain and give an answer to the woes of our Nation. They are titled: Look to a Nation and Land of the Free.

We thank you Mr. President, your family and administration for your courage and hard work to serve the American people (those who are awake and even those who are ill-informed).

WWG1WGA

May God bless America,
Sonny B.

BLACK VOICES FOR TRUMP

I know each of us have a story of why we became a Republican. If I asked everyone about their story, I believe each one would be unique but also telling. However, I can guarantee each account would hold in it family and friends who are narrow minded, who walk with blinders on. They only see the world with tunnel vision seen through the lens of the corrupt fake news media. We've lost friends and relatives because of a difference of opinion. I bet you, your story is like mine, you try to disagree agreeable, but derogatory and vicious names are launched towards you from the other side. You're left alone, wondering what just happened, I was only trying to show them the truth. It's been said a deceived person doesn't know their deceived because they're deceived, make sense, right? The fools we are, every time we are enlightened from an article of the truth other than fake news, like women in an abusive relationship, you say to yourself, it's going to get better, I know they will change, as soon as I give them this bit of truth I just learned. You quickly realize, I just made the same mistake again and again and again. Until you finally understand, there are some battles not worth fighting if you're going to win the war; or did you really finally understand or did they tell you to quit it with the politics and leave me alone. Now I believe you get it, they say to you, please don't clutter my mind with the truth. I've come to know that the truth, truly does hurt. Especially to a person who has closed his mind to other suggestions and opinions. I've found that this is a bad place to be in, when you only focus on two subjects: racism and social injustice. You say to yourself, yes there is racism and injustice, but does it just come from white America? Then you say to yourself, is racism and injustice that prevalent, that vast? That it's so bad in 2020, black people are worse off than the civil rights movement and slavery times? I'm sorry you're never going to make me believe that, when you have so many ungrateful black multi-millionaires even billionaires. When most of them made their millions by the opportunities given by white America. I said in one of my writings, "If our ancestors had the same opportunities we have today, they all would've become billionaires." What do we do with the opportunities? We squander our money and leave nothing for the next generation; therefore, it becomes a vicious cycle, we squander, then we complain and bicker about racism and social injustice. We do absolutely nothing to help ourselves, only point the finger and blame the white man for our oppression we caused. Listen, I can go on and on about the problems we cause. However, I'll leave that for another writing.

Let me tell you why I became a republican. This is from an excerpt of one of my writings: Why I Became a Republican. Let's go back some years in a little classroom in 7th grade with economics being the subject. My economics teacher would be fired today because of the information shared with his students. He taught us the instability of international trade and the corruption of our government among other things. I believe this was the beginning of my journey into politics. When you are black, I believe it is an unwritten rule that you are a democrat at birth. It is what it is, so accept it. Well, I am the unique one. Let's just say I don't like politicians, democrats or republicans. I felt politicians divided America with their differences of opinions, but had one common goal, that is to benefit themselves. Therefore, at the age of 19, I changed my party affiliation from democrat to independent. I realized in a hurry that I had even less power as a voting citizen, because I couldn't vote in the primaries. So, I did my due diligence and researched for myself to find out the platform of both parties. I soon realized among the two evils, the republican party's ideals and values at least leaned towards issues I hold dear. I noticed the republicans' voting habits were conservative on a consistent basis. Almost 100% of republicans voted issues in favor of pro-life, pro-traditional family, pro-God and pro-school choice. This of course won me over; therefore, I changed my affiliation from independent to the republican party.

LETTER TO RACISM PANEL 7/10/20- DAYSTAR

Greetings,

I am a Black American, a husband of an awesome wife and father of six beautiful children (from one woman, my wife). A retired fireman of 25 years and chef desiring my own restaurant in the future. However, because of Marxist and anti-American attitudes, I want to embolden the silent majority to stand up and speak out against the tyranny that opposes our Constitution, Republic, virtues and patriotism of America.

I want to start out by saying thank you to the panel of "A Conversation with Friends: Racism and the Church" with Bishop Kenneth C. Ulmer. I commend you for at least making an effort to deal with the many issues of the Black community. However, White America is not qualified to tell about the severity of racism against blacks in America. However, as a Black American, I can tell about it. Is there racism in America? Absolutely. Is it an overwhelming amount the mainstream media is trying to portray? I say emphatically, NO! I'm sorry, but you can't make me believe that Black Americans today are worse off or equal to the times of slavery and the Civil Rights Movement in 2020.

Here is a mirror that I want to introduce into the conversation of racism. People don't want to look into a mirror concerning racism, especially Black America. Looking into this mirror means you would have to take an individual survey of your own feelings concerning another race. Take responsibility for your own actions, that's a noble thought. Black America needs to quit crying victim and blaming the white race for the woes that have plagued the Black community for decades because of self-inflicted damage. With that being said here is a News Alert! Racism comes in all colors! Just because you're black, God does not give you a pass!!

Because of the fatherlessness in the Black community, it is leading us to our demise. I explain this in an excerpt, of my original writing called, 'Cause and Effect.' It reads like this:

"I speak in respect of those single mothers who have been thrust into single parenthood involuntarily. Thank you for doing your best to raise Black boys into Black men. We expect Black mothers to be the savior of our little Black boys, molding and shaping them into Black men. Mothers are left with the responsibility to raise their sons alone, when the responsibility was really meant for fathers."

I have been saying this for a while now. This past Father's Day, I reiterated the importance of fathers in light of the death of George Floyd. Nobody should die senselessly at the hands of cops. However, the outrage, looting, assaulting, and destroying property because of a White man killing a Black man is disproportionate to the response given to Black-on-Black murder. Black-on-Black homicide is an epidemic all across America, but no outrage, no news coverage, no Al or Jessie, not a peep from the Black community or White America.

The Church is fighting a war on racism, a battle the enemy is no longer fighting. The enemy is only using it as a tool to destroy the foundation of the Church, family, and this nation. For example, how did we defeat the British? All of a sudden one day, the well-orchestrated, well-poised, well-strategized, and well-populated British army was defeated not by an army, but by common people (farmers, doctors, craftsmen, baker, etc). The Great British army went out to the open field to fight a battle like sitting ducks as they routinely line up into their formation. They were put into a derision as the British army was hit with gunfire deep from in the woods from plain ole commoners. The British army was looking for the Americans to line up in the open as they routinely did, so they could slaughter them in battle again and again. They changed up their strategy, meaning they didn't insanely keep doing the same thing expecting different results. This is a battle of Good vs Evil, not of color, not democrat vs republican, but right vs wrong.

We are getting slaughtered in 2020 for a cause the left is no longer fighting. The left and the mainstream media is only using racism and social injustice as a means to stir up the black community with anger and white America with guilt. The perfect time to do this is when there is a death by police brutality. The Black community and White America fall for it every time. It gets 24/7 coverage. If Black lives really mattered, America would be outraged about the Black-on-Black murders all across America. I can't reiterate this enough, not to mention the 15 deaths (that we know of) caused by the hands of BLM/Antifa during the riots. An 8-year-old innocent little girl was killed by protesters in Atlanta. The mother was cut off by a makeshift roadblock. As she tried to go around, the 8-year-old girl was struck by a bullet.

She was shot by thugs manning the roadblock. And Black lives matter? Where is the outrage for this young Black life?! No 24/7 news coverage for that black life because it does not fit the narrative.

Again, I was a fireman for 25 years, I rode the beat with a lot of good cops of all races whom I have a great respect for. In the cities where you live, I encourage you to ride with a cop at night into these drug-infested, gun and gang violence-ridden neighborhoods. Put yourself into their shoes. We have a lot of Monday morning quarterbacks that say I would've did it that way, or I wouldn't have done it like that. When you are given a split second to react in a life and death situation, I wonder if you would make the best split decision?

No gentlemen, my children are not afraid of the cops. They are troubled seeing teenagers on social media make a plea to Americans to ditch the red, white, and blue of the American flag on the 4th and trade those colors for the colors of the rainbow. The same teenagers made a second plea to 'F' America, all countries matter. Marcellus Wiley exposed the Black Lives Matter mission statement on a clip from ESPN. That mission includes an attack on the tradition family. The far-left liberals are using the sleight of hand by using racism as its tool to destroy traditional marriages with same-sex marriages. They also destroy Black communities by helping us lead the way in abortions. They removed prayer, the Pledge of Allegiance, crosses, and the Ten Commandments from federal buildings. Liberals have been sifting away the values and morals for decades. They believe that now in the wake of George Floyd's death they can fundamentally change the godly principles this country was founded upon. The Church is mesmerized by the sleight of hand of racial unrest, with the illusion of white oppression; while liberals work to take away the rights and values of Christians. Identity politics has separated the church with the issue of color as the plan of Marxism moves rapidly throughout our country to destroy it.

Lastly, I believe God is trying to wake up the Church and true Americans through myself and others who stand in the gap and sound the alarm. This is the reason for this letter to all of the panel participants with Bishop Kenneth C. Ulmer. Also at the end of this letter is my original poem titled, "Look to a Nation." I believe this poem gives an answer to the woes of America. Thank you all for your attention to this matter. May God Bless America!

Your Brother in Christ,
Sonny B.
Look to a Nation

LETTER TO DAYSTAR

Mr. and Mrs. Lamb
Daystar Network
3901 Highway 121
Bedford, TX 76021

Greetings Mr. & Mrs. Marcus Lamb,

1776Rewind We can be and do anything we put our minds to, not matter your race. God being the center, no man can deny you of your dreams.

My wife and I are avid watchers of Joni's Table Talk and at times we have recorded your program to educate and inform our children as well.

Secondly, I want to say, kudos for your topic of: For God and Country. It made me realize again how much I'm proud to be an American; guided by the leadership of President Trump and his Administration. In spite of some backlash, we thank you for your stand, dealing with the real issues of America with care and sincerity.

Cancer doesn't care what color you are, it kills and devastates all nationalities in every country in the world. If we continue to allow the cancer of racism to overtake the hearts of those that will allow it into their hearts, it is sure to infest, destroy and overtake our core values of this country. As it's been said unforgiveness is the poison we take hoping the other person dies. Therefore, we must ask the hard question, what can we do as black people to pardon the past, and forgive those holding on to the present bigotry?

Forgive those with malice and discontent. Isn't this what the Bible speaks of? Love your enemies, bless them that curse you, do good to them that hate you, and pray for them that persecute and despitefully use you: Matthew 5:44. However, to pray for others, we must first make sure there isn't any secret bigotry in our own hearts. Without Christ, the heart is deceitful above all things and desperately wicked. If men's hearts are not changed, the daunting task of bringing the races together would be very difficult, and I say downright impossible.

If mankind doesn't take responsibility for their own actions, we will continue to place the blame every time there is a racial encounter. This is a letter from a black man who is sickened from the racial tensions that have been perpetuated and exploited by politicians, Hollywood, sports, corporations, and especially the media.

I watched Ministry Now this morning concerning racism. I believe it was your assistant telling her story again about the bank experience. I agree that the bank representatives were wrong, and I don't deny the act of racism. However, I think we inflate the problems of racism when we have to rehash a story again and again. Manufacturing stories of racism like Smollett and Bubba Wallace proves my argument. Yes, it's sad to know there are still people in America that see the world in color, that just shows their bigotry and ignorance. However, this is not a representation of America. The real America is when a natural disaster devastates the country, all races come together. Everyone pulls together with one common goal, to help one another in the time of need. There are no Republicans, Democrats, racists, Marxist, atheist, socialist, etc. Only people, organizations, churches, fireman and the demonized cops that give their love and services to hurting people.

Another example 9/11, that dreadful day, firemen of all races went into burning towers to save lives of all races, religions, and genders. While everyone else was fleeing danger, firemen and the demonized cops were going towards it. I am a retired fireman, so that kind of qualifies me as an expert. Lol! 9/11 could've happened anywhere in this country, the outcome would've been the same, many lives of firemen and cops would've been loss trying to save people we don't even know. President Abraham Lincoln once said, "If you look for the bad in people, you are sure to find it." I choose to live in the present and not the past. Even if there was a racial encounter that would happen to me today, after one second, it's in the past. Joyce Myers says it best, "Enjoy Everyday Life." What if she held on to the past? There wouldn't be any Joyce Myers ministries. Therefore, thousands of sexually abused girls and boys wouldn't know about God's healing through her life.

As you know, this world is fallen. Therefore, evil things happen to all people. However, we have to look at this world through the eyes of God.

I only want to live in peace with my beautiful loving family. However, to see the madness mankind is capable of in light of George Floyd's death, woke up a fight in me to save the democracy of this country!

Lastly, I am not a poet, but I have enclosed with this letter a poem called "Look to a Nation," in hopes to be used to shine some light on the subject the next time Joni's Table Talk deals with the topic of racism. I want to move towards true change, and not just put a band aid on severe trauma.

I have also enclosed a donation to support the work that you are doing for the Kingdom.

Thank you for your attention to this matter.

Your Brother in Christ,
Sonny B.
Letter to Daystar

LETTER OF THANKS 2 DAYSTAR

Greetings, Daystar

I am a proud black American citizen of this great nation. I am a father of (6) six awesome children with my beautiful wife of 23 years in a few more days. I wrote you last year to tell of my displeasure of the racism panel hosted by Bishop Ulmer, and my appreciation for Daystar's stance. Well, I know my message of thanks may have gotten convoluted in my message of righteous indignation to say the least; Therefore, I am writing again to express my gratitude. I only tell of my race, because I want the world to know, everyone in the black race isn't a low information voter or ill-informed zombie of the media apocalypse.

Some say 2020 will be a year to remember because of the unstableness and chaos of our country. I would say because of 2020, I will remember 2020 as a year my eyes truly came open. As the bible mentions, the devil meant it for evil, but God meant it for good. God doesn't waste anything; He uses the good the bad and the ugly and He makes all things beautiful. Also, I would beg to differ, January 6, 2021 is a day to remember. I believe like so many Americans, I couldn't believe the cowardice act of Vice President Mike Pence. In the midst of the biggest scandal of the Century, election fraud (The Wuhan virus (Covid-19) is a close second), Pence failed to stand up to massive proof of election fraud. He failed to uphold the constitution and deliver the nail in the coffin to the political cesspool driven by the deep state. Now we know the spirit of Judas runs deep. I have never seen anything like this in my life; However, I shouldn't be surprised about this, because the bible gives a clear indication of the last days. Maybe what I'm really saying is, it's the person (Pence) we thought had the integrity and moral fortitude to stand in the midst of wicked oppositions. Such a disappointment, a huge blow and vicious assault on our Republic.

However, I will not lose faith and I will not falter in the battle of good and evil. Our country desperately needs the prayers of the righteous. The mainstream media (enemy of the people) are having their heyday along with their minions. Everything in hell is against the president and the American patriots of our nation. A prophet put our present situation in perspective, he said, we are at the red sea, we can't go forward, and we can't go back. I would add, we can't go back to the corrupt system of ole, a system of democrats and republicans equal in destroying our nation from within through governmental policies and legislations. It seems like all hope is lost, but we know how the story of the red sea ends. We walk on dry land and our enemies are drowned by waters of their wicked deeds. These enemies we see today, we will see them no more.

God is doing a purging from the church house to the White House. God is exposing every wolf hidden in sheep's clothing. The stakes are high, our country hangs in the balance, and the future of generations to come is at a standstill. Howbeit, I am confident in our God. We are in our darkest hour, the evil has been allowed to run amok, I believe so God can let everyone know who's really in charge. The world is watching America, the last country of the free world, because they know, where the United States goes, the world goes. Well, they can look on, because when it's all said and done, the world will know that our God is God.

With all that being said, thank you Daystar for your steadfastness and your stand in the midst of this war for souls' sake. I can only imagine the backlash your network got for supporting the frontline doctors, educating us on vaccinations, support for our president and being part of the solution on racism, to name a few. We are avid supporters of Daystar, and we appreciate the huge part your network plays in the kingdom of God. I realize Marcus and Joni Lamb started the vision, but I also realize a vison this big, takes support from family, friends, staffers and givers. I have given in the past, but I will be making a pledge to this great work needed in this hour. Remember the battle is not ours, it's the Lords.

May God bless America,
Your brother in Christ and Author,
Sonny B.

DAYSTAR'S RESPONSE TO MY 2ND LETTER

Dear Sonny B.

Marcus and Joni Lamb specifically want you to know how much they appreciated your letter. As you say, the backlash has been tremendous this year, but your voice has strengthened them to continue to share truth in love. They also appreciate you sharing your race, as racism has also been an issue front and center in the midst of this election. You have seen their hearts to find the solution, especially in the church body, brings tears to their eyes.

Marcus and Joni Lamb want to thank you for such encouraging comments, kind remarks and your increased support. They are passionate about the gospel of Jesus Christ being spread all across this world and believe that standing up for Biblical values will keep that avenue of freedom open. It is people like you that make that happen!

Marcus, Joni and the entire Lamb family agree with you that America is having its day of reckoning but our God is still stronger and mightier than any agenda the enemy may have, as long as His people continue in prayer and unity.

May the Lord bless you! Thank you for being a part of the Daystar family!

Many Blessings,
Senior Producer's Asst.

TO THE NEVER TRUMPERS

Greetings,

I am a proud black American citizen of the greatest country in the world, and yes, I am a huge Trump supporter. This letter is in response to recent Fox article, titled: "Ex-RNC chair Michael Steele blasts Trump supporters: Yeah, I'm with stupid." You are apparently another disgruntle, hateful and ill-informed black individual in this country. I meet those kinds of people all the time, and I am exhausted and exasperated for trying to educate narrowminded people. I love to use Jesse Lee Petersons' phrase, 'RENT A BLACK' the democratic party can always find a black person to do their wicked biddings. Going on MSNBC spreading your propaganda and non-sense says a lot about you. Anyone welcomed by fake news MSNBC and CNN are out of touch with reality. I don't understand how you can call yourself a republican, when actually you are a RINO and a person of low character. Yes please, let's vote today, sleepy Joe and Kamala 'lock a negro up' Harris don't have a chance of winning the election. I like to say, this duo isn't dynamic at all, but the duo has dynamically wreaked havoc on the black race. They don't have a slim chance of winning the election. This is why they need turn coats and never Trumpers like yourself to give them a glean of hope. The only way this duo can win, is by stealing the election with mail-in ballots, no-voter ID and ballot harvesting; In other words, CHEATING!!!

The Wuhan, China virus is real, but it is the biggest hoax of the century, and you know it. This virus is being pimped like a $.50 cent whore. The Marxist mainstream media, FDA,

CDC, and the WHO are all liars. The economy was shut down, because it was one of the many accomplishments President Trump could hang his hat on. The deep state and diabolical democratic party wanted the White House by any means necessary. Who cares if millions of American lives would be altered forever, at the hands of this evil scheme. Trump mentioned hydroxychloroquine as a cure months ago, before the scamdemic. What did the media do? Demonized this notion and discredited a drug approved by the FDA for over 65 years. People are so mesmerized under the spell of the media, they would argue me down, saying this drug wasn't made for Covid-19. I would respond, What? Who cares what it was made for, as long as it works. This is really where the term STUPID, should be used. Unlike yourself, I refrained from calling your followers stupid. Frontline Dr's, were fired after they went on social media, telling the American people their patients were all cured of the virus by HCQ; Not to mention, this video coverage was censored and taken down by the cancel culture, ex: Facebook, Twitter and YouTube, to name a few. This video was never shown to the public by fake news. What are they trying to hide?

The media condemns the overwhelming support of Trump rallies; Yet they applaud, excuse, and ignore racist BLM/Antifa thugs destroying our cities, with no social distancing. They only wear mask to conceal their identity, to create chaos and mayhem. This lawlessness is happening in democratic cities across America. We are told by the media, the protests are mostly peaceful, while buildings are burning in the background of their media coverage. One democratic mayor would put it like this, "It's a summer of love." It's been said, some people you can't tell them the truth, they have to see it for themselves. Well, people are seeing the lackluster policies and reasoning of the far left socialist. They see the unraveling of the democratic party and the lunacy of their mindless thinking.

I was reading an article on-line from one of the local columns, WRTV ABC Indianapolis, with the title: "After deadly shootings some skeptical of operation Legend's impact." For those who don't know who Legend is, he is the 4-year-old killed in Kansas City on June 29, 2020, because of foolish rioting, as a result of George Floyd. I was asked the other day, why hasn't Trump made any comments about George Floyd? I answered back with a question, do you know who Legend is? His response was, "NO." Well, President Trump does, and he spoke up for the innocent casualty of the lawlessness on the streets. Trump named the operation after Legend, in hopes to clean up the streets of violent crimes. Legend is one of nine children killed because of the riots; they're ages range from 1 to 14 years old. I don't condone police brutality, but why is a violent criminal named George Floyd heard around the world, but no one knows or even talks about the nine innocent souls killed in the name of justice for Floyd?

I digress, to my original point of the local WRTV ABC article. In that same column, black community leader Dee Ross, along with other black leaders, made the comment about operation Legend and I quote, "It's putting more law enforcement out here in the community.

It's putting more federal agents out here in the community and is directly INCREASING THE HOMICIDES." End quote. What??? The media trust to put this non-sense to print, as if it was a valid point. This recklessness is exactly why America is divided and ill-informed, because of this type of so-called journalism put out to the public. This is a ploy to discredit any accomplishment of the president, because of the disdain and hate for the Trump. However, it was refreshing to read about someone with a brain, named Josh Minkler U.S. attorney, his comment about operation Legend was, and I quote, "Operation Legend has been responsible for arresting 31 fugitives, confiscating more than 500 grams of heroin, seizing $1.39 million in drug money and removing 87 guns from the streets of Indianapolis." End quote. Mind you, at that time, the program was only operational for just a month, and we see the positive results.

Black folk are never part of the solution, we cry victimhood, we complain, we bicker, and always blame the white race for all of our woes; However, the actions are enabled and perpetuated by the media and white liberals. We feel if we point the finger in another direction, no one will notice the self-inflicted problems that has plagued the black community for decades, like: Fatherlessness, teen pregnancy, abortion, crime, black on black murder, incarceration, gang violence, illiteracy, and school dropout. Did you notice? Police brutality does not make the list. The most disheartening thing is the impoverished, high crime and uneducated black communities are mostly governed by black officials. It's no wonder why the black communities all across America never get any better.

Finally, I leave you with this, read this article and take note, an article our black leaders should take note of as well, posted by New York Post on July 4, 2020, by Gianno Cladwell, titled: "How Trump- not Biden- has helped make black lives better." The media is the cause of Trump derangement syndrome, here is a quote from Malcolm X, that explains the Marxist mainstream media to a T. I quote, "The media's the most powerful entity on earth. They have the power to make the innocent guilty and to make the guilty innocent, and that's power, because they control the minds of the masses." End quote

May God Bless America,
Sonny B.

LETTER TO MY FRIENDS

I hear it time and time again, let's not talk politics to keep our relationship as family and friends. I guess I'm a fool to think that dialogue is healthy even when we disagree. I believe we can learn from one other, even if we don't have the same opinion. We are friends, if you don't want to talk about politics, don't avoid me, just tell me to shut up, because we are supposed to be friends. I understand better since our last conversation. I promise, if you don't bring up politics, I will never mention politics again. This letter is my final reason of my passion, SO PLEASE GIVE ME THE RESPECT AS YOUR FRIEND TO READ THIS LETTER IN IT'S ENTIRETY.

The far-left socialist say they exude love, and they are the most tolerant, until you disagree with them. The far-left socialist doesn't want free speech, they want one speech, their speech. Any conservative or Christian thinking otherwise will be punished, asked to apologize, censored, and shadow banned; If your message is positively touching the lives and thinking of many Americans, then you are doxed. Do you ever wonder why the news across the nation sounds the same, or have you had the time to pay attention? That's what they're betting on, TIME, too busy working, too busy taking care of the family and too busy being entertained. There are only (6) six liberal Tech. giants that own 98% of the media Americans listen to. Repeat it enough and you can sell ice to an Eskimo. There was a meme I saw today, that explains my theory. There was a Nazi army saluting Hitler, there was a couple looking appalled at the Nazi army with Covid-19 masks on, they responded by saying, how could they all just comply? We would never do that! They must have been brainwashed!

I was awakened around 4am this morning, with words of inspiration bombarding my mind. That is a sign from God telling me to get up and write. This has been the norm since a 2020 awakening. I wasn't totally oblivious to what was going on in our country, just too busy like every other American trying to pay bills and make it through life. March of 2020 changed that for me when I was laid off my job of cooking, because of a virus the media refuses to call Wuhan. It came out of Wuhan, China so what's the problem? This same virus was hidden from the world until China was found out, even then they blamed the US military for the outbreak, to not take responsibility for it. Wow, many Americans have suffered because of an economy shut down. Wuhan, China celebrated the New Year with thousands on the streets of their downtown; Whereas, the epicenter (NY's Time Square) of our New Year's celebration was completely empty of people. Ask yourself, why are they hiding, discrediting and blocking the cures of Covid-19? Because there are several cures; Instead, Bill Gates and Dr. Fauci are pushing a vaccine with a tracker (GPS). American citizens have to know these things, to ask the questions, here again that's where the (6) six liberal Tech giants come into play I just spoke of. If you don't talk about a cure, then it doesn't exist; if you discredit it, it causes fear of usage; and if all else fails, you block the access to receive it. Ask my brother the RN, they don't give therapeutics. Hospitals are even in on the CCP takeover, a lot of federal money is given for Covid patients and a ridiculous amount for Covid deaths. This serves two purposes, payoffs and increased death toll to stoke continual fear in the American people. Believe it or not, this virus is dying out. Which is why they are already talking about a new strain of Covid.

Home without a job, just like many millions of hurting Americans, and idle for the first time in 41 years. My wife was already knowledgeable of other news outlets because she was fed up with being control by propaganda and rhetoric of the fake news media; However, I gained ground quickly as I fortified myself with knowledge. Especially, with no hope of employment in the near future. Conference calls with the employer in June, there were already talks about no reemployment until 2021. This would catapult my world and mind into learning truth, I'd been missing because of my time being occupied with essentials and entertainment.

This letter is up there with some of the most important letters I've written to date, because you both are my friends. What can cause friends to agree on issues so pertinent and so vitally important, at the same time disagree on issues so pertinent and so vitally important? The mainstream media (enemy of the people; Fake news) Yes, I realize who the real enemy is, it's satan. However, just like God uses His people to get His work done, satan uses his people with an underlining motive to get his work done. Many would disagree that the media has divided a nation with their tongues, but James 3:5-8 KJV, bears the consequences of a tongue that sow's discord. Identity politics is in the forefront of the media's daily message; How else do you get blacks and white liberals to riot? You feed them racism and make it a steady diet!!! I know God is in control, in charge, but He gives us a will to fight for truth. We can decide to stand up and fight or hide behind our salvation and criticize the Nehemiah's for building the wall to defend their country.

President Obama sat under a racist Pastor named Jeremiah Wright for over 20 years, Wright hated the white race, the Jews and America. No one can make me believe Obama didn't take on the same ideals as a member of that church. No one made a big deal about it, why? Because the media brushed it under the rug and hid it from the American people, but there is 24/7 media coverage of President Trump being a racist. I don't believe Trump is a racist but that's beside the point, the media has a way of twisting, spinning and turning a story on its head for mind control. I only mention this, to point out the bias of the media. I asked a former co-worker of mine to be honest, I asked him how much of the news do you believe is truthful of local, CNN, MSNBC, FOX, liberal news, etc …? His response was 50%. I responded by saying, if you tell 50% of a story, part of a story, a piece of the story, you leave part of a story out, or take a story out of context, what is it? IT'S A LIE!!! With that being said, why no 24/7 media coverage for Obama's racism? I'll tell you, because his policies lined up with the far-left socialist agenda. The church has to wake-up, the present fight we're in isn't about black and white, democrat and republican, it's about ridding our country of its faith, family, patriotism and freedom. Look up what the left's policies are, or should I say what are the policies that Biden and Harris support? When you do, you say to yourself, are these policies lining up with what I believe? Also, put your hate and disdain down for a moment for Trump and research his policies and see if the policies he supports line up with the word of God. Listen, we would love a saint in office, but if we can't have that, the next best thing is a politician's policies. When we do not vote or vote for someone against our core beliefs as Christians, it effects our culture as believers. I do not like politics, and I do not like republicans or democrats, but they make the policies and legislations, again that effect our lives. I know what's a stake; therefore, I fight with passion. I'm not asking everyone to fight as I do, but I do encourage everyone that name the name of Christ to know where the fight is. A Russian leader said they were going to infiltrate the U.S. to destroy it from within without ever firing a shot. I believe the CCP intercepted that call to take over a nation. Well in 2020, this was their plan on steroids. The deep state uses racism, systematic racism, social injustice and white privilege as an identity political tool to control and use offended blacks and white liberals to do their evil biddings. I believe BLM/Antifa is going to be called upon to resist the overturn of a corrupt botched election; Then you must ask yourself, what black lives? Again, I will tell you, it was never about black lives, but Marxism, traditional family breakdown, and tyranny against our country.

Lastly, there was massive voter fraud and plenty proof of it. It was a national and international collaboration to swindle this election. The media is complicit in it as well, they have ignored it and downplayed it as a nothing burger portrayed to their low information and ill-informed listeners. I don't care what side of the isle you're on, everyone should be outraged about the attack on our Republic, if it were allowed, we then become a banana republic. We may as well welcome in China and North Korea, congratulate George Soros, Bernie Sanders and AOC for ushering in socialism. There all in on the CCP hostile takeover: democrats, republicans, deep state, Big Tech, social media, mainstream media, Big Pharma, CDC, WHO, FDA, CIA, FBI, NSA, NFL, NBA, MLB, colleges, major corporations, etc, etc … I don't believe God is done with our nation, because a Biden/Harris administration would usher in the new world order. There are more souls that need salvation; Therefore, on January 6, that day will be a day to remember. What is going to take place to expose the treasonous scheme of the deep state will be biblical. The world is watching, because they realize America is the last of the free world and the world is going to know that our God is God. Malcolm X made a profound statement about the media, he said, and I quote," The media's the most powerful entity on earth. They have the power to make the innocent guilty and to make the guilty innocent, and that's power, because they control the minds of the masses." End quote

May God bless you both my friends,
Sonny B.

LETTER TO JOY REID

Greetings,

I am a proud black American citizen of this great nation. This letter is in regard to Joy Reid and the so-called journalist like her. I stopped watching MSNBC, CNN, and now FOX, and all national, local news outlets like them. This leaves a small margin of real news, but it's growing, which is how I found out about Joy Reid's non-sense. The mainstream media has been for a long time, an instigator of lies, deceit, rhetoric, and propaganda of divisive news. Now, in 2020, this proves to be catastrophic to our nation. Just take a look at the lawlessness of nincompoops destroying our cities across the country. Instead of the media condemning the unlawful disorder, they tell the American people that the protest is mostly peaceful, while total chaos is infringing behind them; it's unfortunate, low information, ill-informed citizens fall for this tactic every time. Also, a democratic mayor told us the riots were, "A summer of love." While peaceful, patriotic Trump rallies were looked down upon scornfully, as radical and racist. Again, While Marxist BLM/Antifa destructive movements were ignored and applauded. These actions from the media and democratic politicians are shameful and disgusting to say the least. The media and the democratic party have become so repudiating, a staunch democrat like Leo Terrell would denounce the democratic party on national TV. Not to mention, because of the disdain for the media and the democratic party, Brandon Straka, an openly gay citizen, would begin the hashtag walkaway from the democratic party. The party that says they are all inclusive, but I say, just disagree with them and you will feel the wrath. They really are not inclusive, but they are users.

The same real news outlets where I learned of Joys' existence are censored, shadow banned and doxed to those who pose a serious threat of exposing fake news. You know it's true, based on the massive censorship by Big Tech of conservative outlets two months before the biggest election since the emancipation of slavery.

Mrs. Joy Reid makes $1.5 million from MSNBC to have a platform to spew vicious rhetoric, deceit and propaganda; which only paints a narrative of blacks being oppressed by the white man and vilified by America. With your platform, you should express to the black community the American dream you live; instead, the golden opportunity is wasted on sheer non-sense and projected racism of a complete race of people. Your national stage given by white liberal democrats, only validate your lunacy and help perpetuate the problems in the black community. Let me say this as a disclaimer, I do not condone police brutality. Any citizen of any race handcuffed and subdued in police custody should not lose their life if they are not a threat to the officer. However, I do support forceful apprehension of a citizen that is threatening, resisting arrest and not following commands of police authority. It's unfortunate, some citizens lose their lives during alterations. In addition, I believe we forget that police are humans too, and at the end of their shift they want to go home to their families alive. Case in point, we could use Brenna Taylor, considering ALL OF THE FACTS, but we will use Walter Wallace Jr., since it is most recent. They say Mr. Wallace Jr. was bipolar, I'm calling hogwash, but I'll let it ride. If he was bipolar and an obvious threat to society, why wasn't he institutionalized after the 1 of 13 arrest that we know of? I believe far-left liberals use mental status as an excuse to justify wrongdoing. This guy was a menace to society, another product of fatherlessness. By the way, how many illegitimate children did he have? Fatherlessness is a vicious cycle that haunts the black community. Apart from his violent career criminal history, the evidence showed a clear deadly threat to cops with a deadly weapon, which would make the actions of the cops justifiable.

Back to perpetuating the problems in the black community. Here are some issues Mrs. Joy Reid should be spewing out: Fatherlessness, black on black murder, teen pregnancy, abortion, crime, drugs, gang violence, incarceration, illiteracy and school dropout. These are all self-inflicted problems that has plagued the black community for decades. The sadness of it all is, that these communities are governed mostly by black democratic officials all across America. Yet there is silence. NOTE: POLICE BRUTALITY DOES NOT MAKE THE LIST!!! Let's take black on black homicides for instance. Black on black murders account for thousands of deaths of blacks every year across the country; Yet, there is silence from: Joy Reid, mainstream media (enemy of the people), Lebron James, Oprah Winfrey, Tyler Perry, Charlamagne Tha god, Ice Cube, Snoop Dog, NBA, NFL, MLB, NHL, WNBA (does this exist?), ESPN, major corporations, colleges, Hollywood, politicians, music entertainers, Al and Jesse. Again, silence on an issue that overshadows police brutality by leaps and bounds. Black on black murder is a true epidemic, but everyone just mentioned is silent as a church mouse. All ya'll are a JOKE!!!, and you should be ashamed for the way you prostitute the notion of police brutality and social injustice as vastly pronounced in America.

I thank God for the courageous men and women who don the police uniform without the backing of democratic officials. I would rather storm the beaches of Normandy on the frontline, than to don a police uniform. Cops are leaving the force; I believe it is the ultimate goal of the far-left socialist democrats. To defund the police, run the cops out of town and bring in the brown shirts (BLM/Antifa thugs) for a hostile takeover, thus the reason why they want to eradicate the 2nd Amendment. I know my history, this is why you don't forget or destroy history under the guise of racism and confederate connections. It's been said, "Those who don't know history are destined to repeat it." I believe that is part of the plan, they no longer teach our children about the devastations of socialism and communism. This is why they are destroying history in plain view and the destruction was allowed by the media and democrats. If anyone thinks I'm a conspiracy theorist, take note of BLM/Antifa thugs yelling death to America while burning the American flag and yelling out, bring in communism. The disrespect of our national anthem started out under the Obama administration embracing the treasonous act of Colin Kaepernick. Also, this was herald by the mainstream media; As a result, along with this and so many other un-patriotic actions, in 2020 we see the devastation of gradual treachery. Malcolm X summed up the media best, I quote," The media's the most powerful entity on earth. They have the power to make the innocent guilty and to make the guilty innocent, and that's power, because they control the minds of the masses." Mrs. Joy Reid, you and the media are doing a disservice to the American people. Your actions display the diabolical gene in your DNA, and it seems as if you can't help yourself; But know this, every person shall give an account for his/her time on earth, rather it be good or evil.

May God bless America,
Sonny B.

LETTER TO MAYOR CURRY

Greetings to you Mayor,

First of all, I want to thank you for not allowing the protest in our city to end in disaster and destruction like other cities, this is a testament to your leadership.

I am a black American, law abiding, tax paying citizen. We have to admit that the lawlessness of the land is getting out of hand. I only want to live peaceably, raise a family with my wife in law and order and serenity. Although, it can be very difficult when the world around you is becoming more and more chaotic. I know sometimes when issues are flaring, makes giving an answer imminent, thrusting us into making hasty decisions. Therefore, I pray that this message doesn't come too late in making a final decision. The monuments of our city, rather seen as good or bad is a part of history in our nation. It's been said, if we forget our past, we are destined to repeat it. Here is an excerpt from a poem I wrote in hopes that you reconsider the decision on removing monuments and school names. There has to be a change of the heart before we can heal our land and removing monuments and school names won't solve the issues of the heart, but only continue to divide.

Look to a Nation (By Sonny B.) Excerpt

The civil war was a war between brothers
who bled on both sides
for a cause that should've since long died

So I say leave the monuments
for the world to see
as a reminder of what happens when we disagree
in hopes to learn not to repeat history

Blacks fought in this war
it could land them back with the master
knew if they lost the war
it would be a monumental disaster

The good book tells us
there's nothing new under the sun
everything we see today has already been done

Love your neighbor as yourself
and please don't tell a lie
we can't run from the truth
it's a word we can't deny

It's not a race issue
but an issue of the heart
can't understand this because we've grown too smart

So what is the answer to undo this MESS?
by LOOKING TO A NATION that says, GOD BLESS!!!

LETTER TO MARK KAYE

Greetings Mr. Kaye,

First of all, I want to thank you for doing your part in standing up for the true Americans. The reason for my activism is to embolden the silent majority to stand up and speak out against the tyranny that opposes our Constitution, democracy, virtues, and patriotism of America.

When I took the CLAST (College Level Academic Skills Test) at FJC (now FSCJ), I made a perfect score on the essay portion. I realized then that God gave me a talent to write and express myself. It was the plandemic, and the madness and chaos after George Floyd's death, that set me on fire. It also led me on a journey to express my displeasure for the way corrupt politicians and fake news exploited and perpetuated the mayhem. In essence, the corrupt politicians and fake news media, throw the rocks and hide their hands and blamed President Trump for all of the racial divide. Therefore, I am doing my part in exposing the hypocrisy and I will not be intimidated. I have attached my original poem, "Look to a Nation," and the letter sent to OSU on behalf of Coach Mike Gundy, while beckoning Americans to stand with me in the fight for our freedoms.

May God Bless America,
Sonny B.

WHAT IF POEM

What if Donald Trump never became President? He and his family would live a stress-free life.

He could pull up to any fast-food restaurant and order what he wants without his food being tampered with.

He could've continued to travel the world and be welcomed with a red carpet.

Eat and mingle with the Press. Continue to rub shoulders with the rich and famous.

Asked to please make a cameo appearance in my new movie.

He could fly across the nation for his favorite latte and be back home alongside his pool before sundown, chillin.

He wouldn't have the headache of trying to help people who despise him.

Would he still hang out with Ja Rule or Chris Rock?

Would he still have delightful interviews with Oprah? Would he still be chummy with Al and Jessie?

I can only imagine what he and his family had to give up and the sacrifices they had to make.

He has lost many freedoms because he wanted to drain the swamp and fix unfair trade deals.

Ask yourself this question and be honest and truthful, why would Donald Trump become president?

Some have said to get power. I say he already has power.

He had money, but you say he wanted more money, no you have him confused with Bill Gates.

So, since you're trying to avoid the question of why Donald Trump became President, I'll tell you. He loves America.

What if Trump never became President. Would law-abiding citizens lives be in jeopardy and our freedoms even more compromised?

Now that he's president, all of a sudden, he has become a racist, a bigot, a misogynist, a homophobe, xenophobe and islamophobe.

Mr. President you've lost many fair-weather, hypocritical so-called friends, but you have gained many patriotic true Americans who rally around you and support your cause to save this nation.

Thank you, Mr. President, for turning a what-if, into I am president of the United States of America.

For those of us that knows what's at stake, we are forever grateful.

A TEXT AMONG FRIENDS

Let me start out by saying, I have pretty much alienated most of my family and friends. We can no longer discuss politics in the same room together. However, anyone that will at least listen, I will use it as an opportunity to get a discussion in on politics. I hear it is the same across the nation for all Americans who have broken free from the curse of the democratic party. Yes, politics is vitally important to me, because the far-left Marxist, Anti-Americans want to destroy the Constitution, Republic, values and patriotism of America. I am a man on fire! I have a duty to my children to save what we know as the United States of America. So, liberals can call me a coon, Uncle Tom and any derogatory name they can come up with. I don't care. I will always stand up for the truth. With that being said, here is how the text went.

FRIEND: I watched the MAAFA 21 - Black genocide in the 21st century. I really enjoyed it. It showed both sides of politics.

ME: Agreed, but during those times both parties basically had the same view, but in 2020 it's different. The Democrats are out of control. They are for abortion and anti-traditional family, anti-God and anti-America and against school choice. Republicans aren't perfect, but they are pro-life, pro-family, pro-God, pro-America, and pro-school choice.

FRIEND: That's true.

ME: By the way, you know it's an election year. After November 3rd fake news, colleges, Al, Jessie, professional athletes, major corporations, democratic politicians and Hollywood won't care about social injustice and Covid-19 for another 4 years.

I still haven't gotten a response yet, but at least he listened. LOL!

LETTER TO KIM KLACIK

I am a proud black American citizen of this great nation. A father of (6) six wonderful children with my beautiful and lovely wife of 22 years. It's November 4, 2020, a very sad day for two reasons. The democratic party and their sidekick, the media (enemy of the people) are trying to steal the election. Also, a lost for Kim Klacik and a devastation for Baltimore's impoverished communities. Mrs. Klacik you are a true trooper for taking on the task of trying to help our people, especially under the republican ticket; that in itself took a leap of faith. That takes guts and tenacity to run as a republican in mostly democratic districts. I'm so glad to see you take that route because of what the democratic party represents these days. Most democratic leaders are no longer moderate to slightly left leaning, but they have gone far left off the scale. I've never seen so many radical progressives who are anti-life, anti-God, anti-family, anti-school choice and anti-America in my life. Are they pro-anything, other than becoming the party of destruction, disruption and disdain for America and its true patriots? The democratic party has no platform, this is why they have to resort to tactics of blaming racism, bigotry, systemic racism, white privilege and social injustice. This mindset, causes hate, outrage and discontent throughout the black community towards whites and America. Why? For a vote. Our people are in desperate need of a heart and mind change. I realize as I go through my journey to help the black race, mind slavery is worse than the chains of slavery. A person can be chained up but free in his/her mind; taking away the control of the true oppressor. On the other end of the spectrum, a person can be free from chains, but chained up in their mind, giving complete control of the oppressor. The black community have been told by the oppressor (liberal socialist democrats), who they are, and who they are not for so long; blacks don't even realize they are free to enjoy all of the freedoms this country affords us ALL. The combination of the media, liberal democrats and pandering of the black race, proves to be the demise of the black community. As a result, our families are torn apart by: Fatherlessness, teen pregnancy, abortion, black on black murder, crime, drugs, incarceration, gang violence, illiteracy, and school dropout. These are all self-inflicted problems that has plagued the black community for decades. NOTE: Police brutality does not make the list. The most disheartening thing is, the black community is governed by mostly black democrats; because they are black democrats, we require nothing in return for our vote. Blacks have been programmed by the democrats to think they care about the poor and minorities and the republican party are the party of white racist and the rich. When in fact, it is the total opposite. Remember, I'm black, I caught on to their diabolical scheme years ago. If the same play works, why change it? That's the mentality of the do-nothing democrats, until election time. It's an election year!!! OK, everyone ready to stir-up our base with racism and social injustice? YES, and the media is their bullhorn to get the word out to the world to divide a nation for a vote for POWER!!!

Mrs. Klacik, you exposed the complacency, hypocrisy, and corruption of the democratic party of 53 years under their rule. Real Americans saw this, and we applaud you for your courage and magnificent efforts. I truly believe, like the president, you have a heart for the nation and the people of Baltimore. It's a shame, Baltimore isn't ready for true change, even more upsetting, it is this way across the country in our communities. Which brings me to my next point. I've been on this earth for 51 years and I have been black all my life; Therefore, I know how the black race thinks. This proves once again to me, that the black race only wants something to complain about. Why do I say this? Think about it? Hypothetically speaking, if your plan worked to clean up and better the impoverished communities, that would mean the people would have to do the same; In laymen terms, they would have to clean up their act, become responsible, accountable and unreliant on the government. Could it be, the black community wants to stay in a paradigm of old habits and the familiar? Change can be terrifying, especially the drastic change you proposed. I've been on a quest to speak up for our president and America. Trying to educate black folk who are ill-informed because of the mesmerizing power of the media. I must say it is almost an impossibility. Trying to deconstruct decades of lies, deceit, rhetoric and propaganda of the Marxist mainstream media, is like me reprogramming a computer on a NASA rocket. I have been successful in some cases, but it has proved to be a daunting and sometimes hurtful task, especially when it's family and friends. I only want to have a dialogue with people I love and care about, but as a result, there is fallout and false accusations. However, I lick my wounds and keep pressing forward to save America from the socialist lunatics trying to destroy our country, because I understand what's at stake, my children's future. Malcolm X, I believe sums up the media best, I quote,"

The media's the most powerful entity on earth. They have the power to make the innocent guilty and to make the guilty innocent, and that's power, because they control the minds of the masses." End quote.

In closing, Mrs. Klacik be encouraged, they didn't reject you as a person, they rejected your policies, platform, and idea for better. They didn't give the possibilities for better a chance, and for that, I say, shame on them. It's unfortunate, the good, got to suffer with those who shunned change. Kweisi Mfume is a career politician, which is why we need term limits, because the record shows they are no good for our communities nor our country. Well let's not hold our breath, because politicians make the laws and legislations. I pray to God, that you will give it another shot, because we need more people like yourself in government. I just wanted to take a moment and write to you, to say congratulations to you and your team for the valiant effort. May God be with you and may God bless America!

WWG1WGA
Sonny B.

LETTER TO THE SPORT RUSH

Greetings,

I am a proud black American citizen of this great nation. This letter is in regard to your article published by Amulya Shekhar, titled "Michael Jordan said I was crazy: When MJ and Lakers' Magic Johnson were asked to boycott the NBA finals. Here are two quotes from your column, in response of boycotting the finals and I quote, "Michael Jordan told Hodges he was crazy, while Johnson said: "That's too extreme, man." "What's happening to our people in this country is extreme," Hodges replied, end quote. I tend to agree with Jordan and Magic. Why would you boycott the finals and take away that experience from the fans? Contrary to popular belief, NBA and professional sports in general need fans to survive. Jordan and Magic understood this, and so did the late David Stern. I now believe Adam Silver understands it as well, because he is rethinking the Black Lives Matter movement as a living organism in the NBA. Why is this? Let's see viewers (FANS) ratings!!!

Sports was a pass time, to entertain all American citizens and to get away from the 24/7 political propaganda and deceit. I and many others do not want politics shoved down our throats by overpaid, unpatriotic athletes who play a game sanctioned by ESPN and the CCP.

Let's talk about extreme issues of the black race, with the blame being the black race. Black-on- black murder is extreme, but there is silence from: sport rush, media, Craig Hodges, Adam Silver, Lebron James, Colin Kaepernick, Oprah Winfrey, Tyler Perry, Snoop Dog, Ice Cube, NBA, NFL, MLB, NHL, WNBA (Do they still exist?), politicians, Hollywood, colleges, major corporations, music entertainers, BLM, Al and Jesse. Black-on-black homicides account for thousands of deaths every year across America; Again, there is silence from all just mentioned. Let me continue on my extreme journey into the black community. Fatherlessness, teen pregnancy, abortion, crime, drugs, incarceration, gang violence, illiteracy, and school dropout. These are all self-inflicted extreme problems that has plagued the black community for decades. The disheartening thing is, these communities are mostly governed by black democratic officials, people put into office by blacks and white liberals because they think black democrats are good for the community. Kim Klacik showed the world after 53 years of democratic rule, you get complacency, deceit and corruption. Yet, we continue to put the same people into office because they are a democrat. In the words of Obama, "quit your whining and complaining, put on your walking shoes" and continue to go vote with insanity to think one day there will be change made by a democrat.

I understand that your news outlet was formulated from a team of India institute of foreign trade graduates. I love it when foreigners get involved with American affairs, when their country is in need of more help than the U.S. I noticed, your outlet is all about sports in your mission, not politics and social injustice or maybe I missed it in your statement? Again, isn't there some pressing issues in India, you all can get involved in?

I am 2 years removed from my beloved sports and ESPN because of politics. Sport Rush, why are you rehashing a topic from the 90's, to accomplish what? With the racial climate in the U.S., I can assure you it doesn't have a positive effect on our nation or sports; However, if you are trying to destroy sports altogether, I say continue on, because that's exactly what you're doing. The sentiment of my heart is resonated throughout America, plummeting ratings proves this to be true.

I played three sports growing up, starting at the age of 6. I really enjoyed playing and watching sports, it was a release from schoolwork and everyday life. In the 70's we had life coaches who taught us comradery and teamwork with all races. They taught us to give it our all and required nothing less, but to have fun in doing it. While playing together on the field or court, we didn't see color, that happened away from my teammates by adult influences; As a result, I see more and more that racism is taught by evil people of all races and pushed by the mainstream media. Racism comes in all colors, God doesn't give anyone a pass because of what has happened in the past or present, hate never brings about a solution.

There is a college university that I will keep nameless, because what I'm about to say, happens by many colleges across the country. There is a bulletin board in the common area of the college about how many and where lynching's took place in Jacksonville. Why? How can anything positive come out of that? White guilt and black victimhood never bring a people together. Why? Because if whites are going to be made to feel guilty for past sins and blacks demanding whites feel guilty, how do you ever come to a resolve? You don't; However, you do get riots with chaos, mayhem and lawlessness for months in 2020.

America is a blessed nation and all of the races that live in it. We travel to places like Jamaica, with sites of beautiful countryside's and clear beaches. Tourist accommodations are festive and plush, but travel through the city where the real citizens live, away from the glamour and prestige, and look into the eyes those living in cardboard boxes. You see hope, hopes to one day become a citizen of the United States of America. This hope is seen all over the world, immigrants of all walks of life wanting to become citizens of the United States of America. We have locked down the southern borders to keep illegals out by the masses. Why is this? PLEASE! I implore you, to turn off the Marxist mainstream media for once and think for yourself. While in your silence, ask yourself, why aren't American citizens, especially black citizens not making a mass exodus? There were 20 multi-millionaire Hollywood actors/ actresses, that said they would leave the country if Trump became president, guess what? they're still here. There are terms thrown around, that America is racist and unjust towards blacks. Let's look at it this way, black slaves risked their lives to seize every opportunity they could to flee from the southern plantations to escape to northern states and to Canada. Why? Because the conditions were ACTUALLY EXTREME, cruel, unbearable and inhumane. Black slaves didn't have to manufacture, or conjure up racism and social injustice, for EXAMPLE like: Jussie Smollett, Bubba Wallace and the Native American in the midst of the Covington Catholic students during a peaceful pro-life protest, to name a few.

Slavery is the very reason, why we don't remove, destroy, vandalize and tear down monuments, statues, buildings and street names, just because they are linked to the confederacy. There is an ole saying, "If you forget your history, we are bound to repeat it." I know my history, apparently these imbeciles out destroying cities don't. I have read about the horrors of slavery of my black ancestors, I have read and seen documentaries on the devastations of the civil rights movement. So, tell me, minus the flogging and free labor, how are the tactics used on the white race today, any different from what the black race had to endure in the past? We are all made after the image of God; Therefore, no one race should be demonized for being who God made them to be, anything outside of this notion is dead wrong. This is a quote from Malcolm X, I believe sums up the media, I quote, "The media's the most powerful entity on earth. They have the power to make the innocent guilty and to make the guilty innocent, and that's power, because they control the minds of the masses." End quote. Lastly, Sport Rush, I say to you like I've said to many others, stop pushing dirt on America, if you don't have anything positive to say, then keep it to yourself. If your words bring division and not a solution, keep them to yourself.

May God bless America,
Sonny B.

LETTER TO DOVE, NBPA, AND NBA

Greetings,

This letter is in response to Dove commit to C.A.R.E. ad, please share with the NBPA, NBA and NBA players represented on your website. I wrote many pages to express my grief, this is the result of a very very short version of my grievances, because that's how passionately disgusted I am. SO PLEASE, READ THIS LETTER IN IT'S ENTIRETY, BECAUSE I BELIEVE YOU OWE ME A MOMENT OF YOUR TIME, SINCE CORPORATIONS, SPORTS AND COLLEGES ARE IN THE BUSINESS OF MEETING DEMANDS OF THE BLACK RACE. As a Black man, the notion of this vast amount of black oppression, social injustice and systemic racism in America has become nauseating to say the least. This notion is prostituted like a $.50 cent whore and it needs to stop. Here's an idea, why don't we sign a petition for 'Operation Legend,' the innocent 4-year-old killed as a result of the rioting? Legend is one of nine (9) children killed as a result of the lawless rioting on the streets of America, the ages of the children killed ranges from 1 to 14 years old. George Floyd's name was heard around the world, no one but the grieving families, know the names of the innocent young souls that were murdered, just mentioned.

I am a proud black American citizen of this great nation, an engaged and responsible father of (6) six wonderful children with my lovely wife of 22 years. I served my community for 25 years before retiring from the fire department. I'm also a chef, aspiring to own my own restaurant; However, I put my American dream on hold because of the chaos in our country.

Therefore, presently I'm writing in hopes to become a part of a solution. I have written to the NFL, Chick-fil-a, other corporations, politicians, pastors, community leaders, city council, mayors, and sheriffs (local & nationwide), and to anyone who will listen; As a result of my writings, I was asked to become a guest writer for Eye on Jacksonville. I am living proof among many others in America, no matter your color, if you work hard and honest, you can achieve and become anything in this country. That is the American dream that this country affords us all under the Constitution of the United States of America. No one, I repeat, no one can hold you back but you; So, blacks should quit crying victimhood. Case in point, President Obama served, not one but two terms in the oval office. There are no perfect countries in this world. With that being said, does this country have racist? Absolutely. Is this country a racist country? I say emphatically, NO!!! However, here's a NEWS ALERT! Here's something I tell my black race all the time, RACISM COMES IN ALL COLORS!!! Just because you're black God does not give you a pass.

We have to agree, the BLM movement is racism and civil rights movement in reverse. Injustice for injustice never brings about a solution. I learned growing up, two wrongs don't make a right. I have a question, because maybe I'm missing something. In 2020 are there lynching's of black slaves, public flogging of blacks, black slave riddled plantations, Dogs and firehose turned onto BLM riots? Can blacks dine where they want, travel where they want, become what they want to be and live where they want to? Because I'm having a hard time finding blacks oppressed by whites and blacks who are afraid every second of their lives. However, I will say, blacks are afraid in their own communities, because of drugs, drug dealers, gang violence and black on black murders. Most black citizens are not afraid of the cops because they are law abiding citizens, the blacks who are afraid of the cops are the blacks breaking the law. It's sad to say, there are a lot of violent acts done by a few career criminals. No, I don't condone police brutality done to any race of people while handcuffed in police custody; However, I am in favor of forceful apprehension of citizens who do not comply with commands from police authority. Are there bad cops? Absolutely. Are all cops bad? Emphatically, NO. You would think so, because of the way the media demonizes, inflates and highlights the wrong doings of a few cops; as if police brutality is a vast problem across the U.S. I thank God for the courageous men and women who don the police uniform. They get no respect, I would rather storm the beaches of Normandy on the frontline, than to become a cop.

Let me revisit black on black murder. Black on Black murder accounts for thousands of deaths in America every year, but there is SILENCE FROM: The media, Colin Kaepernick, Jamil Hill, Lebron James, Oprah Winfrey, Tyler Perry, Ice Cube, Snoop Dog, Dove, NBPA, NBA, NFL, MLB, NHL, WNBA, ESPN, politicians, major corporations, colleges, Hollywood, music entertainers, Al and Jesse. Mind you, all mentioned are living the American dream. They use their influence to push false narratives, spew evil and hate towards America and the patriotic American citizens. Let's use Lebron James for example, since he is the loudest voice for the NBA and China. He went to a prestigious private school to showcase his athletic prowess on national TV. That's called school choice, something the democratic party has been fighting against for a while. Lebron went from high school to the NBA. Landed a shoe deal worth $90 million, before he played a single game in the NBA. Recently, he was questioned about the inhumane treatment of the Chinese, who work in the sweatshops that make his multi-million-dollar shoes. His response was, let's get all the facts before we come to a conclusion. I say to Lebron and the world, in the Breonna Taylor case, should we get all the facts before we come to a conclusion? That's exactly what Lebron, BLM and the world did not do, but did rush to a conclusion before getting all the facts. These types of identity politics are pushed very hard by the mainstream media (enemy of the people), but silence to the true vast epidemic: Black on Black homicides. The media has done the American people a disservice, by withholding information, telling half or part of a story, and sensationalizing headlines; As a result, we see the devastating effects of propaganda and deliberate dividing rhetoric.

I'm beginning to understand more and more as I search for the truth, outside of the mainstream media. Our media, politicians, corporations, Hollywood, colleges and sport entities are in bed with the communist China regime. China is pulling the strings, to push a socialism agenda on the American people; Needless to say, it's working.

There is a list of problems in the black community, they are: Fatherlessness, teen pregnancy, abortion, black on black murder, drugs, crime, gang violence, incarceration, illiteracy, and school dropout. Police brutality, social injustice, and systematic racism does not make the list; Because Fatherlessness etc, etc …, are all self-inflicted problems that has plagued the black community for decades. That's not the worst part of it, the worst part is, these communities are governed by mostly black democratic officials.

We are a blessed Nation and all of the races that live in it. We travel to places like Jamaica, with sites of beautiful countryside's and clear beaches. Tourist accommodations are festive and plush, but travel through the city where the real citizens live, away from the glamour and prestige, and look into the eyes those living in cardboard boxes. You see hope, hopes to one day become a citizen of the United States of America. This hope is seen all over the world, immigrants of all walks of life wanting to become citizens of The United States of America. We have locked down the southern borders to keep illegals out by the masses. Why is this? PLEASE! I adjure you, to turn off the Marxist mainstream media for once and think for yourself. While in your silence, ask yourself, why aren't American citizens, especially black citizens not making a mass exodus? There were 20 multi-millionaire Hollywood actors/ actresses, that said they would leave the country if Trump became President, guess what?

they're still here. There are terms thrown around, that America is racist and unjust towards blacks. Let's look at it this way, black slaves risked their lives to seize every opportunity they could to flee from the southern plantations to escape to northern states and to Canada. Why? Because the conditions were ACTUALLY extreme, cruel, unbearable and inhumane. Black slaves didn't have to manufacture, or conjure up racism and social injustice, for EXAMPLE like: Jussie Smollett, Bubba Wallace and the Native American in the midst of the Covington Catholic students during a peaceful pro-life protest, to name a few.

Lastly, slavery is the very reason why we don't remove, destroy, vandalize and tear down monuments, statues, buildings and street names, just because they are linked to the confederacy. There is an ole saying, "If you forget your history, we are bound to repeat it." I know my history, apparently these imbeciles out destroying cities don't. I have read about the horrors of slavery of my black ancestors, I have read and seen documentaries on the devastations of the civil rights movement. So, tell me, minus the flogging and free labor, how are the tactics used on the white race today, any different from what the black race had to endure in the past? We are all made after the image of God; Therefore, no one race should be demonized for being who God made them to be, anything outside of this notion is dead wrong. This is a quote from Malcolm X, I believe sums up the media, and why our country is in the predicament it's in, and I quote," The media's the most powerful entity on earth. They have the power to make the innocent guilty and to make the guilty innocent, and that's power, because they control the minds of the masses." End quote. I end with these words: The white race today, shouldn't have to pay restitution to the black race today, for the sins of their ancestors yesterday, and the black race today, shouldn't ask for restitution from the white race today, because we are not our ancestors of yesterday.

May God Bless America,
Silent no more!!!
Sonny B

LETTER TO THE NFL

Greetings John Elway, Joe Ellis and Roger Goodell,

I am a proud black American Father of six awesome children with my beautiful wife of 22 years. We teach our children to have honor and loyalty to God first, Family second and third to Country. I believe these are the three corner stones which has made this nation blessed under God. However, there are some people and entities set against the principles of this country to see it come to its demise. This nation has been good to all people, no matter your race. It has afforded us so many freedoms, this is why for decades immigrants have wanted to come here in droves. We can agree that still today, they're coming in droves. Why might you say? Because this is the greatest country in the world; I didn't say it was perfect, but the greatest. The president turned down an offer to throw out the first pitch at a major league baseball game. We know why he did, because of the disrespect of our Anthem on every level of all professional sports. Mind you, BLM is an organization that prides themselves and forces issues down the throats of the American people, like Marxism. Also, they want Americans to think police brutality is prevalent in the United States of America. However, I will give you one of many that has plagued the black community for decades. Black on Black homicide is a dreadful epidemic all across America in all democratic precincts, but that's not the worst of it, most of the elected officials over these precincts are black. There isn't even a whisper of this massive genocide of blacks in America. If black lives really mattered, there would've been an outcry long before the first recognized police brutality case. No, there is not one sound on this very serious issue from: Mainstream Fake News Media, Hollywood, Politicians, Al, Jesse, College/Pro-Athletes, NFL, NBA, MLB, ESPN, major corporations and BLM/Antifa Thugs. Why? Because this is not a priority; needless to say, it's not even on the agenda.

Thank you, Sam Coonrod, of the San Francisco Giants, for standing up for what you believe. This is his right under the Constitution, but Anti-Americans want to take that right away from people like Coonrod and give concessions to far left liberal Marxist that hate America. John Elway, you told NFL players, "kneel on my field and you're fired on the spot." When I heard this quote, my heart leaped as I thought to myself, there just might be hope for the NFL after all; however, when I heard this was a hoax, my hopes were quickly deflated, and my heart saddened as a proud black American of this country. Yes, kneeling on our National Anthem is an insult to present and past Veterans who gave their lives to serve this Great Nation. Veterans gave their lives so I can, you can, and all Americans can enjoy the freedoms some Americans take for granted.

Is there racism in America? Absolutely. Is it as prevalent as the mainstream media try to portray? I say as a black American, with an emphatic NO. You will never make me believe that these times for blacks in 2020 are equal to and definitely not worse than the Civil Rights Movement and Slavery. The black community has been used for decades by the left to push hate for America and to hate white people under the guise of racism and injustices. I have a News Alert for you, something Fake News won't tell the American people: RACISM COMES IN ALL COLORS, just because you're BLACK God doesn't give you a pass, and GOD doesn't like it in any race of people. I believe, I've been black all my life; therefore, being black gives me credibility; Therefore, qualifying me for what I'm about to say: Blacks can be the biggest Racist of All!

No, my children aren't afraid of the police, however, they are afraid of the ideology of three teenagers on Tik-Tok making a plea to Americans on the 4th of July: to trade the colors of red, white, and blue for colors of the rainbow, and to F America, All Countries Matter. This type of Marxism has been forged into the minds of young children: in grade schools, colleges, Hollywood, sports, and especially the media of all sorts. I'm mighty afraid if we don't have true Americans standing up for the Constitution, values and patriotism, this train is headed for a thunderous demise.

Contrary to popular belief, President Trump is fighting for this nation; However, Americans would never know it because the media force feeds a daily dose of the dividing lies spewed out of the mouths of so-called journalist. How else do you get young minds both black and white to riot? You feed them Racism and make it a steady diet.

I played baseball, basketball, and football starting at the age of 6. Sports taught me to always do your best and gave a sense of comradery with ALL races of people. This nation's pass time to be entertained by great athletes is being stripped away from America because of politics. Sports was an outlet away from the Fake News Politics. This was a chance to let it all out for your favorite team and player. How I miss those days.

It's the principle over entertainment, if a mandate doesn't go out to all players and leagues to stop kneeling to the Anthem. Also, the BLM name erased from jerseys, fields and courts; I will continue to boycott sports. Here's an honorable notion, lets wear the names of the adults and children who have been murdered as a result of the Chaotic mayhem of BLM/Antifa Thug rioters, like: LeGend Taliferro, a 4-year-old President Trump named Operation Legend in honor of this little toddler to combat the violent crime on the streets of Kansas City. Do those lives matter? Everyone knows the name of George Floyd around the world, but does anyone even know the names of those murdered by the hands of rioters? This is why I am done with sports. I refuse to watch another down, watch another quarter or watch another inning of professional sport, with ESPN being included, unless the specifics mentioned earlier in this letter are met. It's going on almost 2 years now of boycotting professional sports and ESPN. If college sports aren't careful, the disdain I have for professional sports will reach into the college sector of sports as well. Please, get this letter to others in power, because I believe, I speak the sentiments of most Americans. I don't want to see sports come to a dreadful end, because it can. History taught us that lesson through the Titanic. They thought even God couldn't sink the Titanic. I'm not saying God sank the Titanic, but it did sink. If this continues, I pray the NFL and professional sports end up in the Atlantic next to the Titanic. I am of the silent majority, but silent no more, I am a man on fire, fed up with the political cesspool on Capitol Hill, Marxist and Anti-American brainwashing of the far-left liberal media.

May God Bless America,
Sonny B.

LETTER IN RESPONSE TO BLM AND JACKSONVILLE.COM COLUMN

I am a proud black American citizen of this great nation. I say this from the offset, so that the far left socialist can save their racist accusations to try and shut me down. I have been black all my life; Therefore, credentializes me for what I'm about to say.

This article is in response to the Jacksonville.com column and Black Lives Matter movement brewing in our city. The fake news media and democratic leaders have portrayed the radical, racist, and Marxist BLM movement as mostly peaceful, a summer of love. When this notion could not be any further away from the truth. If you don't believe me, just ask the true Americans who reside in the war-torn cities governed by democratic officials. I pray that the leadership from Mayor Lenny Curry and Sheriff Mike Williams step-up and not cower to the BLM antagonizing thugs and protect our businesses, neighborhoods, and innocent law-abiding citizens of our community. I say to peaceful protesters, if you do not want to be labeled as a thug, I suggest you dissociate yourself from the BLM organization.

Case in point, if you haven't seen the attacks on Senator Rand Paul, his family and others leaving RNC convention in DC, you need to find it, watch it and put yourselves into their shoes. BLM is a mafia like organization supported by: pro- athletes, media, democratic politicians, major corporations, Hollywood, colleges, NFL, NBA, NHL, and MLB. These are all intelligent people; Therefore, they should know by now what type of organization they gave millions to. We have to see that this movement was never about a black man being murdered. They only needed a reason to project their Marxist, racist agenda, and who better to use than the always gullible black race. BLM has been declared as a domestic terrorist organization. They are diabolical, and they are out for blood, and will do anything to bring America to its demise. Therefore, we can't ignore and not take their threats seriously; Whereas Mayor Curry and Sheriff Williams needs to be vigilant in their actions to help rid our communities of these renegades. I implore to our leaders not to follow the prototype of poor democratic leadership seen all across America. No, Steve Zone, head of the Fraternal Order of Police, defunding police isn't successful in any city, especially when there is growing lawlessness across the land.

I digress in response to focus on the Jacksonville.com article, to ask this question. Why are black people always on the side of ignorance? We are the most ill-informed people on the planet, because we don't search a matter out fully, and we come to conclusions by reading headlines. We form our ideals and mentalities based on false information given by the mainstream media. I believe this ole saying holds true, "If you want to hide anything from a black person, just put it in a book."

We don't have to cut funds of JSO, a necessary entity that deals with crime and violence in our community, especially in the black community. There are federal funds that can be allotted for the purpose of building up the infrastructure of destitute neighborhoods. These are issues your black democratic representatives are supposed to do, make them finally do something for your vote. Black people are like an enigma, I'm black and I can't figure them out, so I can only imagine what the rest of the world thinks. Here are a few examples to prove my point: There are some pictures of Jaguar football players holding signs that say, "F the police, Trust God". Yes, I am confused as well, but I will say this, shouldn't the jaguars be focusing on winning a game? This is a quote directly from Jacksonville.com, the headline reads: "Saturday drive-in protest demands cuts in JSO budget to help communities in need." Here is the quote, "Called" The call for Justice," it asks the mayor to propose a 25 percent reduction of the sheriff's office's proposed budget and use more of it for communities in zip codes 32206, 32208, and 32209, where homicides are high." End quote. Where homicides are high? Are you saying, when the police budget is cut and given to the named zip codes, the high homicides will disappear immediately when the money is given? If it's that easy, I'll donate towards that cause. I don't think we realize, it takes a lot of resources and courageous police to deal with violent crime. I have a suggestion for those of you who don't have a criminal record, sign up to become a police and request to work in the zip codes you're asking JSO budget cuts for.

Here in lies the problem with the black community, we never take responsibility for things we cause. Example: Fatherlessness, teen pregnancy, abortion, black on black homicides, crime, drugs, gang violence, incarceration, illiteracy and school dropout. Did anyone notice, police brutality did not make the list? Because these are all self-inflicted problems that has plagued the black community for decades, governed mostly by black democratic leaders. Does anyone wonder why the problems of the black community never get any better? Well, it makes me wonder, as I go straight to the heart of the matter to try an reveal the answer, could we be the problem?

Lastly, again, I implore to all of the leaders linked to the funding and safety of our city: Mayor Curry, Sheriff Williams, and City Council. We see the trend of the BLM organization in cities across the United States of America. They don't bring solutions, only chaos and mayhem; Therefore, I am asking as a tax paying, law-abiding citizen of Jacksonville, FL, that you abandon any notion of cutting the budget of JSO and become more proactive with safety of all citizens antagonized by the BLM movement. Thank you for your attention to this matter.

May God bless America,
Sonny B.

KEEP THE JAGS?

Greetings Mayor Curry and city council,

I am a proud black American citizen of this great country; However, we as patriots are doing our very best to keep it that way, as long as we can keep the socialist out of power. This letter is in response to an article published by WJXT on December 1, 2020, titled," Jacksonville mayor: If lot J deal doesn't go through, NFL could drop affiliation." PLEASE GIVE ME A MOMENT WHILE I BUILD MY CASE, SINCE EVERYONE IS IN THE BUSINESS OF MEETING DEMANDS OF BLACK LIVES MATTER. I believe I'm asking a credible question, why should I care if the Jags stay or go?

Here is my case: I want to say from the offset, I do not condone police brutality done to any race of people, while handcuffed in police custody; However, I am in favor of forceful apprehension of citizens who do not comply with commands of police authority. It's unfortunate, some violent criminals die in justifiable killings in the process of resisting arrest. That's called consequences for not being a law-abiding citizen.

Unjustifiable killings because of police, should never have an effect on bringing more injustice. Injustice for injustice never brings about a solution. Will someone tell these lunatics destroying our cities, threatening and harming innocent lives. Let's be honest, if protests (riots) were about George Floyd, a black person being murdered, Black Lives Matter would set the world on fire for BLACK-ON-BLACK MURDER!!! Black on black homicides account for thousands of deaths every year across the U.S., but there is SILENCE FROM: Colin

Kaepernick, Lebron James, Oprah Winfrey, Tyler Perry, Snoop Dog, TI, Ice Cube, ESPN, mainstream media (enemy of the people), NFL, NBA, MLB, NHL, WNBA, WTA, major corporations, Hollywood, politicians, colleges, Big Tech, Al and Jesse. Again, silence from all just mentioned.

I played three sports, starting at the age of 6, as an adult I became an avid supporter of all professional sports. If I missed any games, I would catch the highlights on ESPN. Now, because of the WOKE movement, I am (2) two years removed from all professional sports and ESPN. Politics in sports has become nauseating to say the least. What am I saying? I do not want politics and social issues shoved down my throat, before, during, nor after a game. I want to leave the political cesspool behind for a moment and enjoy sport entertainment with family and friends. I have written, I know others have written and expressed their concern for bringing politics and social issues into sports. I believe it only emboldened the social justice movement, because BLM was put on jerseys, floors, pitcher's mounds and in commercials. This says to me, I don't care what you think. As a black man, I do not support the Marxist, racist BLM democratic thugs' movement and never have, even from the beginning of the chaos. This is civil rights movement in reverse, we as blacks didn't like it back then, so why are we projecting it on other races today, especially the white race? It's dead wrong, but it is tolerated as a result of white guilt and because of what their ancestors did in the past. The past is the past, if we expect to move forward together as fellow citizens in this great country, we must remember the past, so not to repeat history, but forgive and let go of the past, to be able to heal in the present.

I digress back to the subject at hand, the Jags. We penalize and fine players and coaches for disrespecting the referees but applaud players and coaches for disrespecting our Anthem and flag under the guise of social injustice. Like I said earlier in this letter, if they cared about justice, they would start by dealing with black-on-black murder, such hypocrites!!! Men and women serving our country have bled and died, so that grown, unpatriotic, selfish, and inconsiderate men and women could have the freedom to play a game. I've said it before and I'm saying it again, it's PRINCIPLE OVER ENTERTAINMENT.

Lastly, Mayor Curry you want my support as a law abiding, tax paying citizen to support a $445 million dollar Lot J deal to keep the Jags in our city. I heard that London loves the Jags, so send them there and Shahid Khan with them, or make the multi-billionaire pay for it. The NBA thought they were bigger than their fans, but after a lackluster season, Adam Silver had second thoughts for the WOKE movement; However, the damage has already been done. I compare the NFL to the Titanic, because of the worldwide popularity, the NFL thinks it can't be sunk. They said the same thing about the Titanic, they got so bold, they said even God couldn't sink the Titanic. I'm not saying

God sunk the Titanic, but it did sink. If there is not a formal apology to the patriots of this country, for the total disregard of our feelings, there can never be a mending of our relationship with professional sports. Therefore, the NFL, Jags, and all professional sports can land next to the Titanic at the bottom of the Atlantic. So, Mayor Curry, that would be a no go, on keeping the Jags.

May God bless America,
Sonny B.

LETTER TO TONY DUNGY

Greetings Coach,

I am a proud Black American husband of one wife of 22 years, and we have six (6) wonderful children together. I take my faith in Christ very seriously. It is crucially vital to my very existence, and God is the significance of my family being grounded in truth.

I want to thank you and commend you for taking a stand against the comments of Don Lemon. Mr. Lemon said, "while Jesus was on this earth, Christ was not perfect". I am reminded of a scripture in the Bible that says, "But if our gospel be hid, it is hid to them that are lost. In whom the God of this world hath blinded the minds of them which believe not, lest the light of the glorious gospel of Christ, who is the image of God should shine unto them" (2 Corinthians 4: 3-4). There are three types of people in the world: (1) A person who has read the Bible and believes they understand the truth, (2) there are people who have never read the Bible and believes they know the truth, (3) and there are people who have a personal relationship with Christ and allows Jesus to guide them in all truth (John 16:13).

We live in a fallen world, and boy is it showing. In the wake of George Floyd's death, my eyes were opened to see just how diabolical mankind can really be. I agree, no one should die in that manner while in the custody of cops no matter your race. However, are we supposed to respond with such vile and heinous acts in the name of justice? The media, professional athletes, major corporations, politicians, and Hollywood applauded and excused this lawlessness. The Bible speaks of this, "Woe unto them that call evil good, and good evil, that put darkness for light, and light for darkness, that put bitter for sweet, and sweet for bitter! (Isaiah 5:20).

Conservative voices and voices of truth are made to apologize publicly and ridiculed on social media with hideous name calling. There is an all-out attack on our values, faith, constitution, democracy and patriotism of America. I am of the silent majority, but silent no more. I am in a fight to not only save America but save the future of my children.

Lastly, I want to thank you as a respected public figure for taking a stand for righteousness; therefore, you shall be rewarded (Matthew 10:32-33). I am in the middle of finishing up with my first book. I have with this letter a poem going into my book called: Look to a Nation. It explains how America can get out of this mess. Also, a letter sent to Roger Goodell. Thank you and may God Bless America.

Your brother in Christ,
Sonny B.

LETTER TO JASON WHITLOCK

Greetings,

I am very proud black American citizen of this great nation and a huge Trump supporter. This letter is in response to a Fox news article written by Daniel Canova, titled, "Lebron James is black Trump; Outkick journalist says. "My message to journalist Jason Whitlock. I would like to start out by saying, I like you Mr. Whitlock because of your stance on the Anarchists who called themselves NBA players; However, I disagree with your opinion about President Trump; Therefore, here's my letter explaining why.

Ratings were down in the NBA this year because of the disrespect of our country. Yes, kneeling on our Anthem is a problem with patriotic Americans that have been loyal to professional sports for decades. We see it as a slap in the face of those who serve in our armed forces to protect the freedoms of all Americans, so that people like Lebron can play a game. No, the ratings were not down because of the Wuhan virus, it was because of the disdain of players disrespect and arrogance in the NBA, especially Lebron. Lebron talked about others being selfish, when he is the epitome of selfishness and hypocrisy. Case in point, he talks about social injustice in America, but got upset with the Houston Rockets GM for exposing the inhumane conditions of the sweatshops in China that makes his multi-million-dollar shoes. Telling Mr. Morey to search a matter out before coming to a conclusion; So, does he mean, BLM, and everyone else who sponsored the chaos, should search the matter out on the Breonna Taylor case before they react in uncontrollable outrage? Also, Lebron had school choice, he attended a prestigious private school to show off his athletic prowess on national TV, a choice his democratic party wants to eradicate. He was part of the last class to go straight from high school to the NBA. He landed a $90 million dollar shoe contract, before playing a single quarter in the NBA. He is living the American dream and he's still not happy. He only pushes dirt on America, and never a positive comment about the country that affords him his success. I can go on and on about the unpatriotic imbeciles.

I will digress back to my original point. Mr. Whitlock, you said Labron James is a black Trump. Please don't insult the president by using a person who is so Un-American, because our president is very American and loyal to the American people. I stated in the beginning, that I was black, so you could better understand my stance on President Donald J. Trump. I do not like politicians, republicans or democrats. This was the first thing that intrigued me about Trump, he wasn't a career politician. Excuse me for a moment as I once again digress. Why are there not term limits? We have people like Joe Biden, Nancy Pelosi, Mitt Romney, and Maxine Waters, who have been stewing in corruption for decades. Not to mention, Obama, our first black president was nice and cordial, but cordially wrecked our country, and did absolutely nothing for the black community. President Barack Obama served three terms in the Chicago, Illinois senate, the murder capital of the U.S. Still nothing has changed under the democratic rule of Mayor Lightfoot.

Back to my original point about Trump. I listened to Trump's words to form my opinion about him; instead of listening to the Marxist mainstream media tell me how to feel about him. He asked for the black vote, democrats take for granted and assume because I'm black, I'm supposed to automatically vote democrat. During Trump's inaugural speech, he told the American people, these people have failed you, as he turns towards those people sitting behind him, which was: Daddy Bush, the Clinton's, son Bush, the Obama's, the whole republican party and the one or two democrats that had the decency to attend. After he humiliates the political cesspool, he turns back to the camera and eyes the American people and says, "but I am giving the power back to the American people." I knew then that I made the right decision for president.

While in office, President Trump invited, Black: law enforcers, pastors, conservative activist, community leaders, entrepreneurs, and entertainers, to get council to better serve the black community. The NY Post gave some of his accomplishments for the black race. It was published on July 4, 2020, by Gianno Caldwell, titled, "How Trump-not Biden- has helped make black lives better. "Mr. Whitlock, you should read the column in its entirety, but here are a few highlights: Police reform executive order. The First Step Act, which released thousands of people from jail (90% of whom were black). Trump promoted "Opportunity zones" that incentivized private investment into marginalized communities (black communities). This is a quote directly from the article, "Trump increased federal funding to historically black colleges and universities by 17% - a total exceeding $100 million, more than any other president in history. Meanwhile the Obama administration infamously removed a two-year Bush administration program that annually funded $85 million directly to these prized institutions." End quote. Also, Trump's foreign policies are unmatched by any other president. He moved the U.S. embassy to Jerusalem. He negotiated peace treaty deals. Not to mention, he settled down North Korea's rocket man. His foreign trade deals are second to none, meaning we finally, have fair trading. America is no longer taken advantage of by foreign leaders and nations.

A relative of mine, asked me a question, why hasn't Trump said anything about George Floyd? I answered him with a question, do you know who Legend is? His response was no. I proceeded by saying, why is George Floyd's name known around the world? But no one knows the names of the souls killed as a result of the rioting and lawlessness? Trump knows their names, and in the honor of the little 4-year-old toddler that was killed amongst the chaos and mayhem, he created 'Operation Legend.' Legend was one of nine innocent children killed because of the barbaric activity on the streets of the U.S. The ages ranged from 1 to 14 years old. The BLM movement is such hogwash. If black lives really mattered, the world would be on fire for the thousands of blacks killed at the hands of blacks across this nation every year!!!

Some are appalled at Trump's antics, his fight and fervor to save America from the radical socialist renegades of BLM/Antifa, Capitol Hill and the deep state. Trump speaks our language, has the passion, gusto, feistiness, indignation and displeasure of the corrupt political system, just like us as TRUE AMERICANS. We have been ignored and lied to by Washington D.C. for decades and covered up by the media. Everyone who voted for Trump, loves his work, the movement is real, and the American people are on fire!!!

Mr. Whitlock, forget about how you feel about Trump. Forget about what the media is telling you how to feel about Trump. Lay down your feelings for the better good of this nation. I just lined out a number of things Trump has done for our race of people and for America; I hope that matters to you? Unfortunately, black people are known for cutting their nose off to spite their face. Some blacks are fighting against the very person fighting for us but are blinded by the deception of the media. However, this can fit any race of people, ie., Antifa and MS-13, the media is silent about these radical thugs. Here again, the media denounces the proud boys and called them white supremacists. When in fact, they are a group made up of different races, coming together because they are proud of their country; Also, to defend American rights under the constitution. The media is being the media, they spin the narrative to fit their agenda. Malcolm X said it best, and I quote, "The media's the most powerful entity on earth. They have the power to make the innocent guilty and to make the guilty innocent, and that's power, because they control the minds of the masses." End quote.

Lastly, the democratic party has done nothing for the black community but stir-up racial anger and outrage. Kim Klacik proves this by exposing the lack luster policies of the democratic party in Baltimore. If the people of Baltimore don't vote her into congress, it will be a shame on them. Again, the career politicians, the Biden/Harris duo isn't dynamic at all, but I will say, they have dynamically wreaked havoc on the black community. They don't have a chance in winning this election and the democrats knows it. Thus, the need for cheating: Ballot harvesting, phantom mail-in ballots, and no voter ID. Therefore, Mr. Whitlock, look past the rhetoric and propaganda of the fake news media and vote Trump on November 3rd; Because the other agenda is to bring America to its demise and usher in socialism, led by Bernie Sanders and AOC. You are a smart man, I don't believe you would want that for our country.

May God bless America,
Sonny B.

LETTER TO MARCELLUS WILEY

Greetings Mr. Marcellus Wiley,

Congratulations on your new job with FS1. Thank you, thank you, thank you for speaking the truth about Black Lives Matter by giving the tragic statistics because of fatherlessness.

The media for a long time has done a very poor job in journalism, instead they have fed the American people a false narrative, keeping Americans ill-informed. The media spins stories, tell and show part of the story in hopes to control the minds of the masses. We learned as a child, when you spin the truth, tell part of the story or take a story out of context it becomes a bold-faced lie.

In short, anyone straying away from the fake news media is ostracized, demonized and in most cases punished and made to apologize for speaking their beliefs. Mr. Wiley, PLEASE do not falter under pressure and never apologize for telling the TRUTH.

The purpose of this letter is to thank you for your comments, and because you're in sports, I wanted to send you a copy of the letter I sent to OSU on behalf of Coach Mike Gundy. Also, my original poem, "Look to a Nation."

God Bless America,
Sonny B.

LETTER TO CANDACE OWENS

Greeting to you Mrs. Owens,

I am a proud Black American man, married to my beautiful wife of 22 years. We have six (6) awesome children together, all from my beautiful wife. My wife is an unbelievable homemaker, which makes me the sole bread winner of our family. I am a retired fireman of Jacksonville, Florida. While employed, I went to culinary school, worked in many restaurants and catered many events to become a chef. It was my lifelong dream to own my own restaurant; however, I put my dreams on hold out of concern for my children's future. The chaos as a result of George Floyd's death, woke me up and made me realize that America is sliding down a slippery slope to its demise. So, I asked myself this question. How can I enjoy my dream when our Constitution, democracy, values, faith, capitalism, and patriotism is at stake in today's America? If all of these virtues just mentioned is at state, then my children's future is at stake. The thought of this infuriated me and made me A MAN ON FIRE!!!

Ok, now that you know a little about me. Let me talk about the appreciation that we have for you and others that have paved the way for the silent majority to be silent no more. Mrs. Owens, you are an inspiration and a trailblazer to America. You taught us to stand up to the tyranny of the far Left. Funny story: my wife was the first to read conservative news, watch and listen to conservative videos on YouTube and radio. Our whole family was inundated with real news, therefore I had to pay attention. The first time I saw you, I told my wife, "She is telling them off and she's good looking!" Lol! As a result of learning and sharing the truth, we became alienated from most of our family and friends. If I didn't know before, I certainly know now, that America has a serious problem with people that are ill-informed. This fueled my fire and set me on a journey to write a book. My book will consist of letters, writings, original poems, and sayings.

My daughter and I just recently attended a Black Voices for Trump meeting here in our city. We found out that you were coming to the World Golf Village in September. My daughter's eyes lit up before mine did when we heard the news. My daughter looked at me and asked, "Are we going?" I said emphatically, "Yes and your mother too!"

Although, I have never been to any of your events. Do you have an interaction or time for guests in the audience during the event to share a thought? If so, may I make a request to share my original poem that I wrote called "Look to a Nation"? This poem is the first of my writings that is going into my book, which I am presently working on. Also, I just ordered your new book 'Blackout,' and I can't wait for it to come in.

In conclusion, we are looking forward to seeing and hopefully meeting you in September. Enclosed with this letter, is the letter I recently sent to President Trump and letter sent to the NFL, these are sample letters going into my book. Thank you for your attention to this matter.

WWG1WGA
Sonny B.

CAUSE AND EFFECT
By Sonny B.

Define cause and effect: Cause is the producer of an effect, while an effect is produced by a cause. The cause can be a person, object, situation, or event that can result in something, while an effect is the result of the actions of the person or the outcome of some chain of events that has happened. (Webster dictionary)

I speak in respect of those single mothers who have been thrust into single parenthood involuntarily. Thank you for doing your best to raise black boys into black men and black girls into black women. We expect black mothers to be the savior of our little black boys and girls, molding and shaping them into men and women. Mothers are left with the responsibility to raise their sons and daughters alone, when the responsibility was really meant for both mother and father. I have been saying this for a while now. This past Father's Day reiterated the importance of fathers in light of the current event that has plagued the black community for decades. I sent out a text to as many fathers as I knew both black and white with this message: Fathers are a necessity and not an option (Happy Father's Day).

In the wake of George Floyd's encounter and many countless encounters with cops that land most black juveniles and black men into the system or prison. My heart goes out to the families left with the anguish of loved ones killed or imprisoned. With that being said, I understand the science of cause and effect, and as a result, it has become clearer to me, why day after day, month after month, and year after year there isn't any change. The black community moves with anger, emotions and even discontent about the effect without ever facing the cause. Asking the hard question of why (cause) this is happening? Instead, we place the blame on the effect. Why? It's easier to point the finger at another, it takes the general focus off the person pointing the finger. It takes the accountability and responsibility out of the hands of those that should try and remedy the problem and puts the problem into the hands of another. White liberals pander and enable this notion, only to perpetuate the problem that has become a long-time epidemic. Enslaving the minds of the black race without the chains, this proves to be more detrimental to black families than the slave entrenched plantations in the south. Tell a black man that racism, systemic racism, white privilege, and social injustice is his plight and watch what it yields. A 2020 explosion of his own racism and discontent for his own country. Any black person who tries to tell them different is a sellout, out of touch, Uncle Tom, coon, etc, etc … So how do we stop the effect? We must first address the cause!!!

WHAT DO BLACKS WANT?

If our ancestors lived in today's time, they would be on easy street and would have all become billionaires. In today's society, White Americans pander, pacify and provide so many opportunities to the Black community all in of the name of White guilt. What do we do with these opportunities? We squander, complain, bicker and accuse White America of not giving enough. Let me remind you it was White America who put President Obama into the White House and what did he do with the opportunity? He squandered it and only spoke about the ills of America. Not to mention he did absolutely nothing for the Black community in the 8 years … count them 8 years … that he was in office. However, he did give one thing to the Black community, a reason to resent America. While assisting the division of the United States of America. Did I mention Whites are 62% of the population? Therefore, a majority of them had to vote for Obama to get him into office. White America, as well as most of Black America, believed in hope and change. They just didn't realize until it was too late the magnitude of change would have on this nation. Remember, the kneeling of Colin Kaepernick happened on President Obama's watch. If Obama truly loved America and respected the flag and lives lost for his freedom and for our freedom, he would have told Colin there is never a time or place to disrespect our flag and national anthem. I truly believe if Obama would have nipped that in the bud, America wouldn't be in the chaos it is in, in 2020.

I can't say it enough, the mainstream media has done a disservice to the American people. The media has been deliberate and making sure the American people stay ill-formed by leaving an important part of the story out, taking a story out of context, and by giving you information they only want you to know. The media is supposed to be unbiased, share the story in a truthful manor and allow Americans to make an informed decision based on information given. Well, I know now why they spread fake news. The mainstream media has become an extended arm of the evil, diabolical democratic party. The Black community and the Black church have become engrossed with fake news, it has put them on a path like sheep led to the slaughter. The media has become so biased and agenda-oriented, even White Millennials fight against the truth. Politicians, Hollywood, pro-athletes, Al, Jessie, major corporations, colleges, and college athletes point fingers and accuse others of racism and bigotry. The same individuals and entities exemplify the very things they blame others for, and it's all well-calculated and endorsed by the media. Liberals say they are most tolerant, until you disagree with their ideologies. I have never seen such a display of hypocrisy and vast cultural suicide since Jim Jones. The fake news media has handed out for years cups of poisonous Kool-Aid, dividing and killing the very principles that unite us as Americans. Their core listeners are so mesmerized, they wouldn't know the truth if it if it slapped them in the face. The media has affected some Americans so bad; I coined the phrase media zombie apocalypse. They're following destroys everything in their path. Here's my point, when have you ever heard of a Black militia? Well, we have a group of them in 2020. They want America to carve them out a piece of land or give them Texas. Right there all of his followers should have run away cause this fool done lost his mind. These are the people the media produces because they keep up the rhetoric and propaganda. The media throws the rock and hide their hand, and report what a shame when lives are lost. Right after they make you think they care about the life lost; they pick up another rock to sow more discord. I really despise the media because they do more damage than any natural disaster. It's easier to rebuild a home or business. However, to restore the truth in the mind of a person proves to be very difficult and, in some cases, impossible.

So, what do Blacks want? I believe if they turn off the media and take a moment to search for the truth for themselves, Blacks will find out that they already have what they want in their grasp. It was right there in front of them all the time. They just couldn't see it, because they were blinded by a false narrative pushed by the mainstream media that Blacks are hated by the world, especially by Whites. So, I say to you open your eyes and allow them to see the truth, before you destroy yourself and others too.

THE POLITICAL TREND WITH ESPN

Greetings,

I am a proud black American citizen of this great nation. I have had enough of so-called Americans pushing dirt and hating on America and the patriots that reside here. This letter is in response to the Fox news article, by Joseph A. Wulfson, Titled, "ESPN's Mark Jones vows to dismiss security detail at upcoming game: I'd rather not have the officer shoot me." What? Mark Jones has been with ESPN for 30 years, are the foolish and mindless tweets made about police, a representation of your network? It is apparent, your network has the same sentiments, because he wasn't fired and sent to the unemployment line. Why? Because he's black, talk about reverse racism and discrimination. That is what we call, one sided, a double standard, and very hypocritical. Liberals and democrats are tolerant until you have a different opinion or ideal than them. However, this is typical in 2020, how does this bring a nation together, by allowing the black race to speak and do as we please. Two wrongs never make a right, every person individually should be treated with respect and kindness, no matter your race or gender. I used to watch ESPN religiously; However, this is another example of why I don't watch ESPN anymore, that's going on two years now of boycotting. Any game I missed; I would turn on ESPN to get all my highlights without the politics. Now, ESPN has become the new Capitol Hill, as if we needed another one. ESPN, you're not alone, professional sports like the NBA, MLB and NFL that disrespect our Anthem, also have been deleted from my memory; By the way, their support of the Marxist/Racist BLM movement, surely didn't help their cause, it only helped to seal their fate.

We are destroying cities for police brutality, an issue that hardly even exists, but one would think that it is an epidemic, with the massive 24/7 media coverage. With that being said, there is never a reason to repay evil for evil; Whereas I might excuse, but I won't, if blacks were outraged about black-on-black murder, a true epidemic. Thousands of blacks every year are slaughtered in the streets at the hands of blacks all across America, yet there is silence and no 24/7 media coverage.

What do black people want? Again, Mark Jones has been with ESPN for 30 years, and other networks are filled with employed blacks. The black athlete is revered by all races of people, Tiger woods changed the game of golf, Venus and Serena changed the way tennis is played today. Blacks represent the majority of athletes in two of the major sports. Opportunities the black race has thrived in and made a vast amount of money in; However, the combination of pandering white liberals and millions thrown at these athletes only enables and perpetuate the immaturity of black athletes like Allen Iverson. A person who went through $300 million like it was $300 dollars during his career. He's not alone, most black athletes end up on ESPN's documentary, 30 for 30, Titled, "Broke." Why no media coverage on that subject? Because it doesn't make for good sensationalism, can't blame the white man and can't play the racism card; Therefore, again we only get complete silence.

Lebron James, because of his athletic prowess, was catered to most of his life. He didn't attend a 'F' high school in the ghetto. He attended one of the top private schools in the country, and some of his games were televised nationally by ESPN. His class was the last class able to bypass college and go straight to the NBA. He landed a $90 million dollar shoe deal before playing a single game in the NBA. Here is guy that wanted to school us on selfishness; Yet, he ignored the inhumane treatment of the Chinese people and the sweatshops that produces his multi-million-dollar shoes, but he wants to lecture us about social injustice in America, SERIOUSLY!!! He has one of the biggest mouths about social injustice. I know his mother's rent in the ghetto was only $17 a month, I can only imagine the living conditions, but that's where his attention should be focused on, so let me educate the nation. Case in point, all impoverished, drug and crime riddled black communities across America are governed by mostly black democratic officials, the party Lebron supports. Not to mention school choice, the democratic party have been trying to take that away for years, school choice and vouchers that benefits minority families across this nation, especially black families. Let me bring it close to home, without school choice, the only choice for Lebron James would've been an 'F' school in the ghetto, not the highly regarded private school he attended. The same democratic officials get elected year in and year out, but there is never any change. That's social injustice and I would even say criminal. Again, no 24/7 media coverage, no outrage from the biggest mouths in Hollywood, sports or the nincompoops carrying out lawlessness and chaos in our cities. Not a peep, just silence.

Black athletes, entertainers and Hollywood use their influence to spew hate and discontent towards America, the president, and the white race. They whine, complain and bicker about racism, systemic racism, social injustice and white privilege. Crying victimhood and placing the blame on others, while ignoring the real issues of the black community. Let's take a look at those problems, shall we? Fatherlessness, teen pregnancy, abortion, black on black murder, crime, drugs, gang violence, illiteracy, and school dropout; These are all self- inflicted problems that has plagued the black community for decades. Notice anything? Police brutality does not make the list! Again, the disheartening thing is, these communities that harbor these aspects, are governed by mostly black democratic officials. This is why the impoverished, drug and crime infested district of Baltimore has to give KIM KLACIK a chance to clean-up the failed policies of the democratic party. The democrats have governed this district for 53 years, what makes the community of that district think, that another career politician is going to change anything. They have a golden opportunity to vote out the race-baiters and change their destiny. WHAT DO YOU HAVE TO LOSE? Democratic tyranny. DON'T ALLOW THEM TO CHEAT!!!

God bless the men and women, who have the courage to don a police uniform in these times of uncertainty and lack of appreciation. I would rather rush the beaches of Normandy on the frontline, than to wear a police uniform. Police have to deal with fools, idiots, and violent criminals of our society, while being defunded, with no support from democratic governors, mayors and politicians. Cops still have to perform their duties with courage, stability and composure, even in moments of split-second life and death situations. Constant criticism from Monday morning quarterbacks with better ideas from their comfy couches at home; Even with the demonization of the media, they still have to withstand the pressures of hate, derogatory language, assault and loss of life, and for that I am forever grateful.

I would like to ask this question, because I would sincerely like to know. What do you see when you look out at America? Apparently, my America is different from: Colin Kaepernick, Mark Jones, Lebron James, Oprah Winfrey, Tyler Perry, T.I., Snoop Dog and Ice Cube, to name a few. Mind you, all mentioned are living the American dream, they have more money than the average American will see in a lifetime. Yet, they are not happy. I love my America; I appreciate the freedoms and opportunities it affords us all. You see, it's all in how you look at America. Is our country perfect? No, but what country is? Systemic racism, white privilege, and social injustice are terms used by disgruntle blacks with hidden racism in their heart; Therefore, making a complete mockery on the many black success stories. Case in point, the George Floyd incident has sparked a lot of race relation conversations. One in particular, is a relative of mine, every time the subject of race relations is discussed, the terms: systematic racism, white privilege and social injustice is always brought up. Here is a man that is retired with two (2) pensions, every time I conversate with him, he is on the golf course playing a round of golf; Not to mention, his wife is a RN home healthcare nurse that works whenever she decides to work. He and his wife have literally traveled around the world, they go and do whatever they please. They are enjoying the American dream, sounds like a good life to me. Does systemic racism, white privilege, and social injustice exist? Absolutely, but as long as there are imperfect people on this planet, there will be some type of unfairness, corruption and partisanship. However, I believe, everyone has a story to tell of negative situations they've had to overcome. Do you know what else exists? Equality, love, fairness, benevolence, compassion, impartiality, courtesy, and kindness to name a few. Again, it's what lens you choose to look through, and what life you choose to act upon. Black people tend to look for racism around every corner and white liberals provide the racial spectrum. I love the quote from Abraham Lincoln, "If you look for the bad in mankind expecting to find it, you surely will." It's what lens you choose to look through, because life is always about choices. You can choose to be a thug dope dealer, selling your selfishness on the streets of the US. Or choose to be a law-abiding, honest hard working productive citizen of America. I do not fear for my life, I am not oppressed, and I do not fear the police. Why? Because I am a law-abiding citizen. I like to use the scientific method of cause and effect. You will have a run-in with the police 99.99% of the time if you break the law (cause). If it is a crime, you will be arrested (effect). If you resist arrest (cause), there will be consequences (effect). No, I do not condone police brutality of any race of people. However, I do support forceful apprehension to those who don't comply to authority.

The mainstream media exploits racism and social injustice like a 50-cent whore. If it is so prevalent, why do we have to manufacture and conjure up racism? Case in point: Jussie Smollett, Bubba Wallace and the Native American in the midst of the Covington Catholic students during a peaceful pro-life protest, to name a few. We are a blessed nation and all of the races that live in it. We travel to places like Jamaica, with sites of beautiful countryside's and clear beaches. Tourist accommodations are festive and plush, but travel through the city where the real citizens live, away from the glamour and prestige, and look into the eyes those living in cardboard boxes. You see hope, hopes to one day become a citizen of the United States of America. This hope is seen all over the world, immigrants of all walks of life wanting to become citizens of The United States of America. We have locked down the southern borders to keep illegals out by the masses. Why is this? PLEASE! I adjure you, to turn off the Marxist mainstream media for once and think for yourself. While in your silence, ask yourself, why aren't American citizens, especially black citizens not making a mass exodus? There were 20 multi-millionaire Hollywood actors/actresses, that said they would leave the country if Trump became President, guess what? They're still here. There are terms thrown around, that

America is racist and unjust towards blacks. Let's look at it this way, black slaves risked their lives to seize every opportunity they could to flee from the southern plantations to escape to northern states and to Canada. Why? Because the conditions were ACTUALLY extreme, cruel, unbearable and inhumane. Black slaves didn't have to manufacture, or conjure up racism and social injustice, it lasted for many centuries, and it was prevalent. Slavery is the very reason, why we don't remove, destroy, vandalize and tear down monuments, statues, building and street names, just because they are linked to the confederacy. There is an ole saying, "If you forget your history, we are bound to repeat it." I know my history, apparently the imbeciles out destroying cities don't. I have read about the horrors of slavery of my black ancestors, I have read and seen documentaries on the devastations of the civil rights movement. So, tell me minus the flogging and free labor, how are the tactics used on the white race today, any different from what the black race had to endure in the past? We are all made after the image of God; Therefore, no one race should be demonized for being who God made them to be, anything outside of this notion is dead wrong.

Lastly, if tables were turned, the other persons job would've been taken away in a New York minute. So, where is the accountability for Mark Jones reckless comments? Why isn't he in the unemployment line? Here is a little note, that I like to tell my black race: Racism comes in all colors, just because you're black, God doesn't give you a pass.

May God bless America,
Sonny B.

I JUST WANT TO SAY, I LOVE YOU

It's January 26, 2021, 4am in the morning, the day of my mother-in-law's homegoing. We're all faced with the reality that she is gone. Tears flowed from 4am until we buried her, I just could not stop crying. My mother-in-law made a lot of doctor's office visits, in her final year of life on earth. A strong woman that was used to doing everything for herself, while pastoring a church for 46 years, but needed us all to be able to maintain each day in her latter years. It became very difficult to get her in the vehicle for her appointments. She literally would have to grab hold of whoever was assisting her into the automobile; in which, most of the times it was me. It became very very difficult, ironically enough, this was the very thing I missed the most, because she had to get close to me as I assisted her into the vehicle. It was like a hug to one another, to say I love you. I would give anything to have just one more hug. This day was a day of deep hurt, pain and sadness, we just loss my wife's mother, not only did I have to cope with my feelings and emotions, but also with the pain of my wife, who just loss her mother. Let me explain, what she meant to me, in a letter I wrote and read to her on the day of her homegoing service.

I went to church, faithfully as a child, but the first time I walked through the doors of Hope Chapel, I was amazed at what I saw and experienced. I was greeted with a warm welcome and a smile. That's unusual, I thought to myself, I thought you had to look deep, sanctimonious and stoic. Then I was hit with praise and worship, with hands lifted unto God, words of hallelujah and thank you Jesus from the top of their lungs from those all around. Then it happened, in walks this preacher named Pastor Jeannette C. Holmes who was short in stature but mighty in boldness. She dissected and broke down the gospel, so that even a little child could understand the plan of salvation. I promise you; I heard every word preached out of her mouth, but at the same time, I was mesmerized in amazement during the whole service. I could not wrap my head around what I was seeing as I watched grown men crying out to God. What is this, I ask myself? Anyone who knows me, know I am very inquisitive, some people would call that being nosy. I didn't give my life to Jesus that day, because I was in shock and disbelief at what I'd seen and experienced. I asked my mother and others, what was that I just experienced? After my investigation, two Sundays later, I would give my heart to Jesus, and it would change my life forever. That day, I not only fell in love with Jesus, but I fell in love with Pastor Jeannette C. Holmes spirit, and soon would love her as a son. I would fall in love with her daughter Michelle, a perfect trifecta. Michelle would accept my hand in marriage, we would have six awesome children together and the rest is history. I told you, my life was changed forever; As a result of Pastor Holmes-Vann, her preached word would point me to salvation, oddly enough, teach me how to be a man and a father and would give me my lovely and beautiful wife. Pastor was a trailblazer of the gospel. God would give her power to tread upon serpents and scorpions and over all the power of the enemy. (Luke 10:19) However, in her latter days as her health declined, she would need assistance with normal everyday task. Everyone that helped take care of her, would obtain a greater bond of love with her, in her most difficult times. It wasn't always easy, but we did it because we loved her. No strings attached, no underlying motives, just a sincere love for her. Those who truly loved her, would capture the remnants left behind from a hard-fought warrior, that sacrificed and gave everything to the kingdom of God and to the people of Hope Chapel Ministries. There are people that think they know Pastor Holmes-Vann better than her family because they spent a day in her presence, they've been a leader in the ministry for over 30 years or they went on a retreat with her. Well, her family had 24/7 access to her, lived with her, we knew all of her idiosyncrasies and little nuances, that we all have in some way. However, we understood she was human just like every one of us, just with a call of God upon her life, but our love for her never changed. Pastor Holmes-Vann, my mother-in-law, she will be missed immensely. She was instrumental in changing the trajectory of my life forever, and I am blessed because of it. With tears flowing from my eyes as I write this last sentence, I just want to say, I LOVE YOU! Your son-in-law, Sonny (Happy Son)

GOD KNOWS WHO YOU ARE, AND SO DO I

1) The eldest- What can I say, she is a natural born leader, a bible scholar, with a warm personality that gets along with anyone. People gravitate towards her and want to be in her presence and disappointed when she leaves. She's funny and fun loving, she is the kind of person I would want to lead me.

2) The eldest son- He is intricate and very detailed in his actions, with a lot of insight. He works extremely hard to get your approval. His moves are well calculated and gives 100% in everything he does. He is patient, and cordial, with a kind spirit. He always thinks of others before himself. If he were a surgeon, I would entrust him with my care; that's how confident I am in his abilities and potential.

3) The third child- His name means God is gracious. His qualities prove his namesake. He is very gracious and forgiving, with a tender heart towards humanity and God's creatures in the animal kingdom. He is a warrior and a protector, who will take on the world because he believes he can conquer it with God's help. So, he goes routinely about his way and gets the task done at hand with a carefree spirit.

4) The second daughter- Name me anything this little lady can't do, or she won't at least try. No, you can't name one thing. Yes, she is a young 'B' Smith and Martha Stewart. She has a very strong personality (she takes after her dad) and leads by example. She gives everything she has within her and doesn't mind failing. I must say though, she has a pretty

good record of more wins to loses. However, if she does fail, she gets back up and goes to the next project or venture.

5) The third daughter- She is a proven leader, and nothing rattles her. She is a no non-sense person, eager to take on any challenge. She sets out to do every job well and with excellence with a laid-back personality. So sweet, so kind, so thoughtful and so lovable.

6) The baby- Our baby, the youngest of her siblings, but that doesn't stop her from making her presence known. She's the baby and she knows it. A renaissance child, talented on every level in the arts. She is wittingly funny, with intelligence and smarts to cap it all off.

THE RICHEST MAN IN THE WORLD

The richest man in Walnut Grove from Little House on the Prairie inspired this writing. I have to admit, my family and I still watch all of the episodes of the Little House on the Prairie. We learn so many lessons together: the value of hard honest work, treating others the way you want to be treated, and in this episode to never take your family for granted and to always appreciate your loved ones.

The plot begins when Charles Ingles is doing a job for weeks on credit for a company. He is due about 2 months of wages from this company. Well, unfortunately, when it comes time for the company to pay up, they file for bankruptcy. This of course leaves Charles in debt, owing Mrs. Olsen for goods received on credit. If you have ever seen any stories of Little House on the Prairie, dealing with Mrs. Olsen you know it went downhill from there. Lol! Needless to say, the whole family pulled together to earn enough wages to pay off the Olsen debt and had some to spare. His family did this without a single complaint and never blamed Charles for the unfortunate situation. In the end, Charles was told by Mr. Olsen that he was the richest man in Walnut Grove. Charles' response was profound. He simply said, "I know."

Being a man, I understand exactly how Charles felt going through the circumstance he and his family was ushered into. You feel less than because you are not able to pay all the bills for the month that you may have hoped. The roof leaks, the washing machine goes out. As a result, it sends your budget into a snowball effect destined for destruction. Just in general it is difficult to maintain a family of eight (8). Add a few life situations, now the journey seems practically impossible. My wife and I know the very difficult times we've had to make ends meet. We never wanted our children to know about our struggles because we never wanted them to have any thought that they were not wanted or were a problem. We would tell them, "Mommy and Daddy has to take care of some other things, but we will do our best to get what you need" and in some cases, what they wanted.

My wife is a wonderful homemaker, which of course makes me the sole breadwinner. Trying to maintain a family of eight (8) becomes very difficult at times with one income. However, I still joke today with my saying, I worked overtime, under time, and anytime to provide for my family. It would break my heart as a husband and father having to put in long hours of work away from my family, but bills have to be paid. Therefore, I have sat down with my family to convey my displeasure at working long hours and assured them that if I had a choice, I would choose being home. I remind my wife at times that we have had a rollercoaster of a life. We have had some mountain highs and some valley lows. However, I don't regret not one moment of the sometimes-wild ride. Everything we've been through together; they never blamed me and would go through it without a single complaint. At times I have been told how rich I am to have a family like mine. I respond profoundly with a simple, "I know." You see with a bank account in the negative (I've been there) or in the millions (trying to get there) regardless of my status, I realize I'm the richest man in the world.

A BLESSING ON MY CHILDREN

Lord God, we praise you that you are fully in control of all things. I pray you would protect my children, keep them healthy and help them to thrive. I thank you that you know the number of every hair on their head. Make them leaders and keepers of the faith and righteousness. You know exactly when they rise to the mountaintop and when they fall in a valley low. Whatever state they may be in, let them know you will never leave them nor forsake them, and they can come to you as the loving father that you are and find help in a time of need. Watch over our children in every area of their lives and may your angels be all about them wherever they may go. I thank you that all good gifts come from you. I thank you that we can trust you for the future of our children and family. Guide our children in every step that they take that they may know your provisions for each of their lives. Show them everyone that are good for their lives, whether it be a friend, or future wife or husband. Lord, you reveal the men that will be the husbands to my daughter's and reveal the women that will be the wives to my son's. Anyone not good for their lives, may they learn to accept it, and know when to end the relationship and pray for them. Lord there is so much in life they must learn so allow them to acknowledge you in all their ways and to lean not to their own understanding so that you can direct their path and give each of them wisdom that can only be given from above. Prepare them for the perilous times we are now in, and to dedicate their lives unto you, even unto death. For we know, to be absent in the body is to be present with the Lord. Now I anoint their heads with oil, allow their cups to runneth over and allow your blessing to follow them all the days of their lives and that they made dwell in the Lord's House forever and ever. And if Jesus should tarry, these words and blessings shall be to their seed and seed, seed. Amen.

God knows who you are, and so do I

1) The eldest- What can I say, she is a natural born leader, a bible scholar, with a warm personality that gets along with anyone. People gravitate towards her and want to be in her presence and disappointed when she leaves. She's funny and fun loving, she is the kind of person I would want to lead me.

2) The eldest son- He is intricate and very detailed in his actions, with a lot of insight. He works extremely hard to get your approval. His moves are well calculated and gives 100% in everything he does. He is patient, and cordial, with a kind spirit. He always thinks of others before himself. If he were a surgeon, I would entrust him with my care; that's how confident I am in his abilities and potential.

3) The third child- His name means God is gracious. His qualities prove his namesake. He is very gracious and forgiving, with a tender heart towards humanity and God's creatures in the animal kingdom. He is a warrior and a protector; who will take on the world because he believes he can conquer it with God's help. So, he goes routinely about his way and gets the task done at hand with a carefree spirit.

4) The second daughter- Name me anything this little lady can't do, or she won't at least try. No, you can't name one thing. Yes, she is a young 'B' Smith and Martha Stewart. She has a very strong personality (she takes after her dad) and leads by example. She gives everything she has within her and doesn't mind failing. I must say though, she has a pretty good record of more wins to loses. However, if she does fail, she gets back up and goes to the next project or venture to give it another try.

5) The third daughter- She is a proven leader, and nothing rattles her. She is a no non-sense person, eager to take on any challenge. She sets out to do every job well and with excellence with a laid-back personality. So sweet, so kind, so thoughtful and so lovable.

6) The baby- Our baby, the youngest of her siblings, but that doesn't stop her from making her presence known. She's the baby and she knows it. A renaissance child, talented on every level in the arts. She is wittingly funny, with intelligence and smarts to cap it all off.

JOE BIDEN IS ANTI-SCHOOL CHOICE

Let me count the ways of the many failed policies of the democratic party and the Biden/ Harris ticket, that hurt many Americans, the black community in general. I like to say, the Biden/Harris duo isn't dynamic at all, but they have dynamically wreaked havoc on the black community, by falsifying and withholding evidence to incarcerate blacks and a 1994 Clinton Crime Bill; With that being said, let's focus our attention on school choice.

Democrats know education is the doorway to success; Therefore, they like to place a barricade of racism and injustice in front of that door. Constantly reminding minorities every two and four years, that they can never overcome this social dilemma. However, if you vote democrat, we will give you the necessary tools to make it in life, at the same time, stripping blacks from the very right to choose. Biden/Harris will defund charter schools and take away vouchers (scholarships) that serve to fund private school students' education for low-income families, but if Biden becomes President, funding for charter schools, vouchers and school choice will be taken away.

Choice is very beneficial to minorities, especially the black race all across America. Democrats know, if they keep minorities uneducated and ill-informed, the clutches of poverty and crime will continue to undermine any possibility of escaping degradation. Keeping minorities in failing schools, democrats keep their jobs. So, what is the democratic party good for? NOTHING, but stoking flames of outrage and thoughts of racism within the black race and encouraged by the Marxist mainstream media. We see the catastrophic consequences of their diabolical scheme during many months of rioting and chaos. They love using the sleight of hand, it's called the blame game and they have become masters at it. Don't pay attention to the mayhem we have caused over here for many decades but look over there. President Trump is a racist, bigot, misogynist, homophobe, xenophobe and Islamophobe. The white race are all white supremacists. The republican party only care about the rich people. These are all examples of democrats stoking the flames; unfortunately, the gullible black community and white liberals fall for this magic trick every time. Their plan is bolstered by a plethora of influences: China, sports, colleges, Hollywood, media, social media, major corporations and easily persuaded millennials.

Let me paint a picture for you, to make things become clearer, to let everyone know what democrats really think about blacks. They don't ask for the black vote, they just assume because you're black, you are obligated to vote democrat. They believe blacks are incompetent and incapable of learning, so they lower the standards, this is why they want you uneducated, so they can make decisions for you. If you are illiterate and mindless, you wouldn't comprehend, Hillary pulling hot sauce out of her purse, should be offensive to the black race. Or trying to sound black, "I don't feel know ways tired." Hillary Clintons tremendous awe of Margaret Sanger's vision, the vision to exterminate the negro population, yes, the person instrumental in Planned Parenthood coming into existence. I know, let's entertain the negros with a Jay-Z/Beyonce concert to get their vote, they don't know any better. Let's try, "You ain't black if you don't vote for Joe Biden." Remember the famous line of Obama, or were you too mesmerized by your blackness, when he told the black race to, "Quit your complaining and go put on your walking shoes and go vote." These are all examples of soft bigotry, yet as a black republican, I hear from the black race constantly, that the republican party are the racists. WHAT?

By keeping blacks uneducated; as a result, democrats can keep the black community: impoverished, destitute, outraged, riddled with crime, and fatherless with poverty programs, as they blame the white race and the republican party. In sports, if your opponent can not stop one particular play, what do you do? You keep running the same play over and over again, until your opponent stops it. No matter how many times you run it, if it works, you keep running it. The democrat's playbook never changes, because it always works, they only have one play, only one strategy; Well actually it's four, racism, systemic racism, white privilege, and social injustice. I say one, because these terms are synonymous with one another, they work hand in hand, like cookies and milk, and peas and carrots.

Finally, blacks and citizens of America are nothing more than a vote. If you don't believe me, check out the vicious cycle, every midterm and election year. They whip up their base with racism, white privilege, systemic racism and social injustice. Democratic officials will not stop the rioting, lawlessness hurting law abiding citizens in their cities, because somehow, they believe it is hurting Trumps chances of getting back into office. It's all about a vote to get back into power. I know, I might sound monotonous, but the democrats don't have a positive platform, no vision to make America great again, only destruction to this nation. Destruction of capitalism, businesses, values, patriotism, statues, monuments, police (Authority), the nuclear family and the constitution. By voting the Biden/Harris ticket, you vote: Anti-God, Anti-life, Anti-family, Anti-America, Anti-school choice, violence and lawlessness. I rest my case!

ECHOING LLOYD BROWN
AUG. 1, 2020, COLUMN

I am writing this article to echo Lloyd Browns column on August 1, 2020, about: Politicians should show proof or stop slandering the people of Jacksonville. I am a black man, proud to be a resident of Jacksonville and a citizen of this great nation. I have been black all my life; therefore, I believe qualifies me for what I'm about to say. This is a quote from the late Herman Cain. Liberals and blacks SIN, I added blacks because in many instances liberals and blacks are synonymous. SIN is an acronym for: S: Shift the subject. I: Ignore the facts. N: resort to Name calling. Blacks who claim victimhood in America never want to face the facts, because if they did, the black community would have to take on the responsibility of changing those facts. I'm so sick and tired of hearing about racism and social injustice. These two words have become meaningless, because they have been used in every situation to shift the blame. It's easier for blacks to shift the blame to white America. If the black community and black leaders focus everyone's attention on racism and social injustice, America will be distracted from the self- inflicted problems that has plagued the black community for decades.

Did racism and injustices make the black community top of the class in: Fatherlessness, illiteracy, school dropout, gang and drug infested neighborhoods, black teenage single mothers, crime, abortion, incarceration and black on black murder? Did you notice anything unusual? Police brutality didn't even make the list. Police brutality is disproportionate compared to black-on-black homicide, where thousands of blacks are slaughtered each year by the hands of blacks across America.

Black Lives Matter is the hottest headline in America today. Demands are given and dare not speak out against the Marxist movement. The honeymoon with black lives is splendid, and black America can do no wrong. Here is a noble idea for those on the Black Lives Matter bandwagon, like: the mainstream media, NBA, WNBA, NFL, MLB, democratic politicians, Hollywood, entertainers (singers/ rappers), Al, Jesse, colleges, and major corporations. All just mentioned, gather your millions to change the face of the black community all across America. Every person within each entity just mentioned can give several millions of their own money and not even miss a dime in their bank accounts. I spoke earlier that racism and injustice is not the real problem of the black community, it is: Fatherlessness, illiteracy, school dropout, gang and drug infested neighborhoods, black teenage single mothers, crime, abortion, incarceration and black on black murder, all in precincts governed by democrats and black elected officials all across America. Again, put your money where your mouth is and stop playing the race card.

I gave a list of specifics of what's plaguing the black community. Now give us specifics of racism and injustices. Those that believe racism is rampant across America, then give us some specifics. We can then sit down and have a sincere civilized discussion to bring this city and this nation together. Otherwise, if blame is the center focus, this city and this nation will never come to an end solution and would be an impossibility for all races to unite in greatest country in the world.

May God bless America,
Sonny B.

DOES BLACK LIVES REALLY MATTER?

I believe George Floyd started it all. Or was it Rodney King? For the sake of the argument, let's just stick with the present. Actually, it was Alex Kueng, the cop that killed George Floyd that started it all. George Floyd was only used as a means to start a race war all fueled by the media. If the media really cared about Black lives being murdered, they would fuel the flames of Black-on-Black homicide. However, I'll get to that later. Looting, civil disobedience, burning down buildings, ram shacked vehicles, assaults and even death, for the illusion of social injustice? How is it that George Floyd is the only name we know? Because it has been played in our minds over and over again by the media. I really wouldn't have had a problem with that if all Black homicides got equal time. Maybe then someone would become outraged about a Black dying at the hands of another Black. Go ahead I double dare you, to tell me the name of the innocent eight-year-old killed by rioters in Atlanta without a search engine. I can't unless I use my search engine as well. Give me a minute as I search, Secoriea Turner. That's her name. This little girl shot by thugs. The same thugs the media, the mayors of democratic states and cities, politicians and athletes praised and applauded while wrecking cities. It's a "Summer of Love" one mayor put it. One article said it is 15 lives lost during the riots and most of them are Black killed by the hands of Blacks. Where is the media on this? This doesn't fit the narrative. I have been shouting Black-on-Black homicide from the mountaintop every time someone brings up a police brutality case. There are even some that are angered by it, as I'm deflating their anger fueled in the wrong direction. National Review printed an article recently showing that the death toll of Black-on-Black homicide in 2016 was

2,570. The journalist had to retract that count because he clearly understated the number of Black-on-Black murders across the country in 2016. It was many more. Does those Black lives matter? I know a Black life has to die at the hands of a white man for it to matter. If I blame the white man, I can then take all of the focus off of the Black community. Black people like to point at White racists, when Blacks can be just as racist (i.e., the Black militia). For some reason Black people think because we're Black that God excuses our racism. Sorry to burst your bubble. You don't get a pass. I've said it before and I'll say it again, racism comes in all colors!!! Blacks like to get their racism out when a White cop kills a Black person, all under the guise of outrage. No, you're not outraged, you secretly hate White people, because if it was about a life lost, you would be outraged about Blacks slaughtering Blacks across America.

LETTER TO MAYOR DANIELLA CAVA/FORBES

Greetings Mayor Daniella Cava and Forbes,

This letter is in response to Forbes article published on November 25, 2020, titled, "Florida Governor extends ban on cities imposing mask mandate penalties- critic call move a 'killing spree.' Mayor Daniella Cava is one who is critical of Governor DeSantis' decision to end the mask mandate. If Mayor Cava was following the mask mandate, because she and others say mask keeps us safe, how did she and her husband test positive for Covid-19 (Wuhan virus)? I'll tell you why, it's been clinically proven mask do not inhibit the virus.

The president, some of his family and about 27 members of his staff tested positive for Covid, everyone is healthy and back to work. The president, after his therapeutic treatments was ready to run a marathon after first day of treatment. No one died, how do I know this? Because we would still be hearing this from fake news if someone did, especially if Trump died. I spoke with an assistant to one of the city council members here in Jacksonville. She also tested positive, while wearing a mask and a shield, but mask keep us safe? Hogwash!!! She's perfectly fine and back to work.

There wasn't any reason for American citizens to die from this virus, when therapeutics were available several months ago. Therapeutics like, hydroxychloroquine coupled with zinc and vitamin C. Budesonide is another therapeutic introduced by Dr. Richard Bartlett out of Texas. Dr. Bartlett even said, this treatment works very well in saving lives in very late stages of Covid. These are just a couple of examples to help ease the fears of the American people, only if there was a desire to educate them. So, Mayor Cava, quit playing politics and crying foul on the lift of mask mandate, you're going to be ok. Here is a letter to follow this one that expressed appreciation to Governor DeSantis and Lt. Governor Nunez for mask lift and potential displeasure to Mayor Curry, and city council if they didn't uphold the mask lift.

THE BEST CHRISTMAS GIFT EVER

In Celebration of The College Graduate

Our Firstborn

My Christmas at the age of 12, I woke up after finally falling asleep because of the excitement of opening Christmas gifts. As a kid, you heard the phrase that was coined, it is better to give than to receive, just didn't apply to a child like myself at the time, so bring on the gifts, Lol. As I'm wiping the sleep from my eyes, my eyes begin to focus as I walked into the living room where the Christmas tree was standing. I saw all of the gifts around the tree as I noticed a massive gift unable to be wrapped; Therefore, my eyes became larger. It was a go kart and it had my name on it, Santa Claus had come through with his promise. That was the best Christmas gift ever. Until, Christmas of 1999, the day our firstborn daughter was birth into the world. As I held her in my arms, I understood how a parent could have so much love for a child. I said to myself, after seeing the birth of my daughter, how can anyone not know that there is a God. Or abort something so beautiful. How could a child so miraculous come from an ape? Or the big bang create such an amazing architecture of our world? All this for a baby? Yes, seeing is believing.

When I was still working as a fireman, I told the guys at the station, if my daughter is born on Christmas, I will not be to work. Their attitude was kind of nonchalant, because what are the odds of being blessed by being born on Christs' birthday. Needless to say, my officer got the call around 7am on Christmas day, with an announcement from a new father that I will not be into work today or the next shift and the shift after that.

That day, my daughter became the best Christmas gift ever; However, as I told her siblings, please do not feel slighted because I love each of you equally. I would climb the highest mountain and swim the deepest sea for my family. Which is why I always joke about working, I say it like this: I will work overtime, undertime and anytime to provide for my family.

Just before our daughter went away for college, we had a celebration or was it a mourning for the departure of our daughter, because I cried the whole day. I was excited about her accomplishments but saddened to see her off to college. Dropping her off at the Rosen College of UCF, the tears flowed from my daughter's eyes as she hugged her mother and I. This of course didn't make matters better. I told my wife, this felt like it was the beginning of the end. We are losing our babies to adulthood, it's tough to except but we must let go and move on as they leave the nest to try out their wings in life. You want to keep them close and safe from all hurt and danger. As each of them grow into adulthood, we must have confidence in the many lessons we've taught and rely on God's protection and guidance to lead the way.

Nehemiah 4:14 New International Version, says, "after I looked things over, I stood up and said to the nobles, the officials and the rest of the people, "Don't be afraid" of them. Remember the Lord, who is great and awesome, fight for your families, your sons and your daughters, your wives and your home." Fatherlessness has become a huge problem in the black community. Absentee fathers lead to: Teen pregnancy, abortion, black on black murder, crime, drugs, gang violence, incarceration, school dropout and illiteracy. These are all self-inflicted problems that has plagued the black race for decades because of fatherlessness. When I gave my heart to Christ at the age of 18, I told the Lord, I do not want to be a part of the problem; before and during should I marry and have children. Make me part of the solution by being intentionally engaging to my wife and children. When we walk away from our marriages, we become part of the problem. When we have extramarital affairs, we become part of the problem. When we walk away from our responsibility and our duty to raise our sons and daughters, we become part of the problem. Therefore, we shouldn't blame others for problems we caused as a black people.

The importance of marriage, one man and one woman in holy matrimony in the sight of God, is synonymous to a healthy society. I realize sometimes we as humans are trusted into becoming a single parent for any number of reasons; However, God never intended for it to be that way. This is why we need Christ in our lives because He makes all things beautiful. God knows we need each other, He takes two imperfect beings and makes us one, a balance of masculinity and femininity. My wife is a wonderful homemaker; Therefore, makes me the sole financial provider. Please do not underestimate the role of a homemaker, especially when there are (6) six children involved. When the children were thirteen and under, getting the kids dressed for school, it was like chaos, now that they're older, we call that controlled chaos.

To my wife I say to her, you are a vital role in our family, you make our house a home. It is impossible for us to give out congratulations and accolades to our daughter without acknowledging my wife's role in her success. It takes work as a homemaker, a lot of work, but my wife through it all, is so wise, has great insight, so gracious, so selfless and never complains. My lovely, beautiful wife, I know there are times you feel worthless, and you ask yourself the questions, am I helping? Or am I making a difference? I tell you to look into each of our children's eyes and then look into my eyes, our eyes will convince you of the truth and they will say, we love you and we certainly need you. Yes, I would be lying if I told you we didn't struggle at times and our family was desperately in need of a second income, but what would it have cost us? The children didn't understand the magnitude of our financial ruin and we didn't let on, all they knew is, mommy and daddy couldn't get this or that at the time. We never wanted them to remotely think that they were any kind of burden. We as a family made the necessary sacrifices to get through life with God's help.

Look at our blessing that far surpasses all the money in the world. There is a song by Matthew West called the beautiful things we miss, I like to use a portion of his lyrics to keep everything in perspective and I quote, "I don't wanna miss it; I don't wanna look back someday and find; Everything that really mattered was right in front of me this whole time; So open up my eyes Lord; Keep me in the moment just like this; Before the beautiful things we love; Becomes the beautiful things we miss."

Will you stand as I call my children's name, my wife, and the reason we're all here, our first born. Oprah Winfrey, Michael Jordan and Jeff Bezos, each of them is worth a billion plus. Take a look at my wealth as they stand before you, my wealth is much more, because my wealth is priceless!!!

In conclusion, in honor of the graduate our firstborn, to all our family and friends, my wife and I take no credit for this great accomplishment, it is by the grace of God our family is blessed and intact.

TO MY DAUGHTER: A college degree is a major feat, but in all your getting, get some understanding. Always stay humble and ask God for wisdom, in which He gives liberally and denies not. Remember the words of your granny, charity (LOVE) begins at home and spreads abroad and only what you do for Christ will last. Congratulations, keep God first and you will go far. Always remember, and never forget, you are my best Christmas gift ever!!! I Love you dearly, Daddy

LAND OF THE FREE

In America we are free to:
Watch fake news / Or turn it off
Vote / Not vote
Protest / In some cities you can even riot
Work / Do nothing
Laugh / Be angry
Speak / Stay silent
Honor the Flag / Kneel on the Flag
Agree / Disagree
Love / Or Hate

This list can go on and on, so many freedoms
The United States of America affords us all.
If you do not like our country, and if
America is as racist as some people say it is.
*Of all the freedoms just listed, there is only one freedom that really matters if you hate:
America

YOU HAVE THE FREEDOM TO LEAVE!!!

LETTER TO CHICK-FIL-A DAN CATHY

Greetings executive board members,

I am a black American man, proud husband of one wife with six beautiful children we have together. Dan Cathy, what you did in 2012 by taking a stand for traditional marriage resonated throughout America and the people all across the US responded with resounding support and so did I. Just recently, I couldn't understand the purpose of kneeling to a man and shinning his shoes, what were you trying to accomplish? With that act I believe you arbitrarily undermined the moral standard and trust your father built for the chick-fil-a brand. The chick-fil-a standard is a beacon of light for all Americans to see, enjoy and take part in by embracing the upstanding character of your business. Moral character and impeccable service is synonymous with the chick-fil-a way. It is what your brand is known for all over the world, they are inseparable, you can't have one without the other. I believe it is a huge let down to those that appreciate moral character and even to those who lack a moral compass. Also, if true, the decision to donate money to Black Lives Matter, an organization that wants to defund the police, an organization that has been hijacked by LBGT, Planned Parenthood and other liberals to press forward with their agendas. Again, if this is true, it is very disheartening and demoralizing to say the least. Pleading to white America to bow down and shine the shoes of a black person does nothing to change the trajectory of the black community. Pandering black people because of white guilt only enables and perpetuate the problems that has plagued the black community for decades. Pandering requires nothing from the black race in return in assisting with change. I must say again, I am outraged with the pandering and enabling of white America, politicians, Hollywood, sports, corporations and especially the media with the notion to create change. Those actions only impede growth and help sustain the problems of the black community.

I believe I speak for most Americans, for many years we see the trend for many businesses moving towards the far left, but we say, at least we have chick-fil-a always moving in the direction of the right. It gives us a sense of nostalgia, your brand says, be kind to your fellowman, and love you neighbor as yourself. Characteristics like these are becoming more and more extinct

Until the black community face and address a lot of the problems we create, we cannot expect someone on the outside looking in to cure what's ailing black America. Therefore, we can shine shoes, remove monuments, statues, school names and city names all linked to the confederacy; unless a person's heart is changed, any and all gestures only become empty acts of progress.

I pray that this letter will cause you and your board to earnestly think about future decisions that will continue to catapult your to continued success and not change the foundation and core values your company was founded on. Lastly, we can get good food anywhere, but we go to chick-fil-a for the overall experience. I end with an excerpt from my original poem,

LOOK TO A NATION (Excerpt)

Police brutality no I don't condone
but reality is I'm more likely to be murdered by my own

Police brutality so loud we can't hear the sound!
of black on black blood cryin out from the ground

Why no outrage when we kill each other?
is it because the media sees it as ok to kill your brother?
naw that just don't fit the bill
a black man taken down by a white man
yeah that's more of a thrill

Am I the only black man that can see this?
we getting sold out by judas kiss
will somebody define RACISM PLEASE!!!
media tryin to infect our minds with a sick disease
are you tellin me we're worse off in the future?
and our pain compares to Dr. Luther?

It's not a race issue
but an issue of the heart
but you can't understand this, because we've grown too smart

So what it the answer to undo this MESS?
by LOOKING TO A NATION that says GOD BLESS!

God Bless America,
Sonny B

NOT YOUR ORDINARY COMPLAINT, LETTER NOT SENT

Greetings Chick-fil-a,

Complaint:

I am a proud black American citizen of this great nation. I am a father of (6) six awesome children with my very beautiful and lovely wife of 23 years. I give you my race identity to forfeit any type of racial injustice's eluding to discrimination. There is an extreme racial climate that has been created by the mainstream media (enemy of the people) helping to destroy this nation from within. The blackness movement has been handled like a newborn baby that has no sense of itself, needing full attention for survival. It sickens me and its nauseating to say the least. The black race is the golden child these days and can do no wrong, everyone has bent over backwards to meet the demands of the black race. I'm proud to say, America just celebrated one of the greatest African American of our time, Dr. Martin Luther King Jr, I'm sure the present state of black the race is not the dream he had envisioned. SO, PLEASE GRANT ME THIS COURTESY TO HEAR OUT THE CONTENTS OF THIS LETTER. I apologize for the lengthiness of this letter, but I do not apologize for its content. I believe the contents of this letter is an observation of data my wife and I have gathered over the years from our black race and recently your black employees in question. AGAIN, PLEASE HEAR MY CASE AS I LAY IT OUT BEFORE YOU.

My wife and I teach our children to love their neighbor as themselves. Treat others the way you would like to be treated. Judge others by the content of their character, not by the color of their skin. Love God first, then family and then your country, in that order. These are biblical values taught from the bible, which is why I believe the bible is the most sought after and at the same time, most hated. We teach our children, average or mediocrity is not a household practice in our family. You do not have to be the best; However, we do require them to be the best they can be. We consistently remind them to give everything you got, no matter how small or how big the task is at hand. No one owes you anything because of your color, if you want something, get an education and put in an honest day of work to get it, don't expect handouts. Do everything as unto the Lord and good things will follow, and to always remember: RACISM COMES IN ALL COLORS, JUST BECAUSE YOU'RE BLACK, GOD DOES NOT GIVE YOU A PASS!!! We teach our children many life lessons on a daily basis, but everything just mentioned is the foundation of our family structure and should be for America.

I am writing this letter because of the lackluster and lackadaisical service my family and I have received over a period of time at the Chick-fil-a in question. I would say, began to pay attention to the type of service received after the last 6 visits. However, our last two visits were the straw that broke the camel's back. As a result, we would like to focus on our last two visits. Mind you, the infractions I'm about to mention, happened in only two visits and I emphasize only two visits to note the severity of our experience. 1) no spoon for soup 2) forgotten mac and cheese 3) spicy chicken in my chicken noodle soup 4) I had to ask for our chocolate milk 5) we received a 4 piece kids meal instead of a 6 piece kids meal we asked for 6) we were give Hi-C punch instead of lemonade 7) NO MY PLEASURE 8) I left message on voicemail for not receiving my mac and cheese, I never got a response 9) Lastly, nothing was offered as a result of their mistakes. Although we had a long eventful day, we felt it necessary to speak with a supervisor.

The supervisor's name was Ben. I want to say from the offset, this is not an indictment against Ben's character and leadership, or an attack on his livelihood or to see him reprimanded. I believe he needs the support from upper management and the right tools to carry out his job successfully. We got the impression that Ben is exactly what the Chick-fil-a corporation wants as a leader, because he was kind, cordial and apologetic. However, he looked very young, and I would even say, he looked like the same age as those he's supervising. This creates a problem in two ways. A young white male supervising a mostly all black staff, in a hostile racial climate. Let me explain, I thought I would never see the day when a white male would be the most hated in America and patriotism would be synonymous with white supremacy. Therefore, making it very difficult to deal with serious issues at hand with black employees under white leadership, because any negative feedback would be deemed racist. It's like throwing Ben into shark infested waters with a bucket of chum in his hands. We are pandering one race, while destroying another. This is racism in reverse. Is that right? Is that acceptable? All under the guise of white guilt, for reparation because of slavery? Ok, I'll have the fortitude to say it's not right, because we didn't like it, so why are we projecting racism on others? Blacks in favor of this, are no better than the slave masters that felt justified in using a race of people for gain. If excellence is not a requirement from the black employees, this would be a type of soft bigotry and very damaging to productivity. Equal rights, means equality across the board. Standards should not be lowered because of your race. If your performance is not up to par, then you should be reprimanded and if the problem continues to persist, then you should be terminated.

Listen, we were up front with Ben, we told him, it was the black employees giving subpar service. I can honestly say, this isn't a joy or a pleasure to report. As an African American, this kind of lackluster, lackadaisical and I own the place mentality feeds into the stigma placed on the black race, LIKE: We're lazy, we don't want to work, we have babies out of wedlock, we want everything given to us, etc etc etc ... Well, this is how we change things, we see something, we say something. I read on a daily basis, that major corporations are spending thousands of dollars for diversity programs to change the mentality of employees who don't have the problem. These programs are centered mainly around treatment of the black race. That's discriminatory in itself because we are focusing on one particular race, the black race, but what does it get us? A Black Lives Matter movement demanding more and more, because it's never enough for the person with the problem. You give them an inch; they'll take a mile. This is the attitude of our black men and women in the workforce, they've been told by this toxic racial climate, that America owes them something.

We pass by 3 McDonalds, 2 burger kings, 2 Popeyes, 1 churches chicken, 1 KFC, I Krystal, 2 Arby's and 1 Wendy's to go out of our way to be served by Chick-fil-a, NOTICE I SAID SERVED. As you can see, we can get food anywhere. The impeccable service Chick-fil-a is known for, we can't get at any other fast-food restaurant. There is a reason why your drive thru's stay filled to the capacity, America is fed up with spending their hard-earned money on food that sucks, served with a bad attitude. If any employee doesn't want to uphold the impeccable service standard of the Chick-fil-a brand, then tell them, the fast-food establishments just mentioned would welcome their crummy and lousy attitude with open arms.

I said this was not your ordinary complaint, so come along for the ride. Unpatriotic offended blacks and unpatriotic guilt-ridden liberal whites are destroying America with the help of corrupt politicians and the media bullhorn projecting racism 24/7. How else do you get BLM/ Antifa renegades to riot? You feed them racism and make it a steady diet. Let me be clear, I do not condone police brutality on any race of people. No one should die the way George Floyd did while handcuffed in police custody. However, I do support forceful apprehension of violent citizens breaking the law and disregarding commands of police authority; Unfortunately, violently striking back at authority sometimes ends in death. Also, injustice for injustice never yields a solution. Let's be honest, the lawlessness that transpired for almost the entire year of 2020 was not about a black life. Again, I mention this because major corporations, academia, and professional sports are spending millions for something that hardly exist, because of the CCP owned media bullhorn. My point, if the chaos in 2020 was about social injustice and a black life getting murdered, the whole world would be on fire for BLACK-ON-BLACK MURDER, IF BLACK LIVES REALLY MATTERED. Black on black homicides account for thousands of deaths in the streets of America EVERY YEAR. Yet, there is SILENCE on this EPIDEMIC. Rebels have destroyed cities while ignoring this true crisis.

The careless attitude we see on display at the Chick-fil-a in question is a direct result of FATHERLESSNESS in the home of the black community. FATHERLESSNESS LEADS TO: teen pregnancy, abortion, crime, drugs, incarceration, gang violence, illiteracy and school dropout. These self-inflicted problems have plagued the black community for decades; However, the most disheartening thing is, they are governed by mostly black democratic elected officials, perpetuated and enabled by republican politicians and the mainstream media/social giants. Yet, there is SILENCE on all of these issues from WEALTHY BLACK ENABLERS LIKE: Colin Kaepernick, Jemele Hill, Lebron James, Oprah Winfrey, Joy Reid, Don Lemon, Tyler Perry, TI, Snoop Dog, and Ice Cube, to name a few. These wealthy individuals find it easy and acceptable to use their influence to spew evil and racism out on white America from their own hearts. What? Just because they are black, are they not held to the same account as the KKK? I said it earlier and it bears repeating, RACISM COMES IN ALL COLORS!!!

Lastly, Chick-fil-a, your brand is on blast because everyone knows the company was founded on Christian values and you are hated for it because of people like the wealthy black enablers I just mentioned. You are a target like every other conservative and Christian in America. The far-left socialist despise the virtues and values we stand for. Closing your businesses on Sundays to allow that day for the entire staff attend church. Standing for tradition marriages in 2012. Backing the blue. Always remember, your business is blessed because of God and not because of a world renown Executive board and not because of the brilliance of a business plan. Your corporation is blessed because you honor the Lord, so never forget it. Political correctness and avoidance of the cancel culture is a sure path to destruction. If lackluster and lackadaisical demeanor from ANY EMPLOYEE is allowed by the Chick-fil-a brand, and straying away from godly principles, makes your corporation no better than all other fast-food establishments. I pray to God this never happens, but if it does, I can rest assure you, we will not go out of our way to get to your restaurant, the words from a very loyal customer.

May God bless America,
Sonny B.

CHICK-FIL-A DONATION LETTER

Greetings Chick-fil-a,

I believe we can acknowledge that most Americans have supported Chick-fil-a for the food and certainly because of the impeccable service. I can say as a proud black republican father and husband, my family and I have supported Chick-fil-a for the reasons just mentioned; As a result, your corporation has prospered financially because of the consumer.

The GOP/ Black voices for Trump are exposing the Black Lives Matter movement, among other issues. BLM denounces the western nuclear family. In other words, rid western society of the traditional family (The marriage of one man and one woman in holy matrimony).

In 2012, Mr. Dan Cathy stood up for traditional marriage, America stood up with you, and so did I. Even though I believe that it was a noble act to shine a black man's shoes, I don't believe it would serve the purpose of changing a race of people. I think we can agree on the ole saying, "If you give a man a fish, he will eat for a day, but if you teach a man how to fish, he will eat for a lifetime." The GOP/ Black voices for Trump are teaming up to better the lives of the black community for a lifetime; By educating and assisting them in making an informed decision of political party affiliation. I don't believe I have to convince you that elections can have grave consequences. Meaning, democratic states and cities want to defund the police and also have allowed destruction and lawlessness to continue for months. While law abiding citizens were threatened jail time by democrats for wanting to go back to work to provide for their families. This is just a few examples of what our organization is working towards to prevent, by voting the best candidate(s) in upcoming elections. The vote is powerful; Therefore, we must exercise our right to vote candidates into office(s) with the same ideals, values, and beliefs. It is imperative we make the right decision, because the wrong decision can have long term negative effects on a nation. This is why we are hitting the streets to try and gain the black vote.

Therefore, we are asking for a donation of 1000 (one thousand) Chick-fil-a gift cards in the amount of $10 each. Your donation will help sponsor our survey; which in turn, will give the black community an opportunity of a lifetime. A chance to choose a political party that will direct and change their lives forever. We believe, this will not only impact their lives individually, but have a huge positive influence on society as a whole.

As we know, this coming election is just around the corner; Therefore, getting voters registered is crucial and time is of the essence. If Chick-fil-a was to donate and invest in our cause, our organization would need your donation as soon as possible to meet electoral deadlines. Thank you for your attention to this matter, we look forward to hearing from you soon.

LETTER TO SAN ANTONIO EXPRESS NEWS/CITY COUNCIL

Greetings,

I am a resident of Florida; However, I am a concerned conservative Christian citizen of this great Nation. I am concerned because conservatives, Christians and Trump supporters are attacked, ridiculed and punished for our beliefs all over the country; thus the reason for this letter.

I am a proud black American father of six (6), and husband to my beautiful wife of 22 years; Therefore, makes the nuclear family (one man and one woman in marriage) vitally important to me. I would like to say from the offset, just because I disagree with LBGTQ community, doesn't mean I hate gay and lesbians as a person. No, I do not hate, I only disagree with their lifestyle.

I read the article posted by the San Antonio Express News, about: Texas appeals court rejects, save Chick-fil-a lawsuit, hands San Antonio a victory. When I read this article, I said to myself, how is this a victory? A company like Chick-fil-a that has the same belief as I do, concerning the nuclear family. If we go back to 2012, when the restaurant chain was attacked for standing up for traditional marriage; Remember the majority of America stood with this corporation and so did I. Chick-fil-a have a reputation for impeccable service and standards serving and hiring all people. This is why I believe the Chick-fil-a brand has been prosperous for so many years. Again, this company treats everyone with respect and dignity, unlike the lackluster service and quality of food from other fast-food chains. That is why this is mind boggling to me, and it makes me mortified at the treatment of such an admirable company.

In this present world of censorship, shadow banning, and doxing; It has become blatantly obvious the people this is aimed towards, they are: Christians, conservatives, and Trump supporters, so please don't insult my intelligence. I wasn't born yesterday. We are the only group of people who are bullied, harassed, assaulted, and in some cases murdered, it's just excused, tolerated, and treated as if nothing ever happened. I like the saying: "Liberals say they believe in tolerance until you have a different opinion than them."

Yes, Ladies and Gentlemen, I am infuriated, I am fed up and tired of Christians and conservatives being pushed around like second class citizens because of our beliefs. The article said a city council member did not want to support the restaurant chain on grounds of supporting organizations against LBGTQ. What do you mean, when you say against? My interpretation of against, sounds like you are accusing Chick-fil-a of hate. Chick-fil-a supported organizations in the past that did not agree with the gay and lesbian lifestyle, again that is not the same thing as hate. This indictment against their company is exactly why Chick-fil-a doesn't donate to conservative organizations and that is a violation of the first amendment of the constitution. It's not a law or a crime against humanity because we have a difference of opinion; However, if we listen to the mainstream media, you will think we just committed the unpardonable sin if we disagree with the left's ideology.

It sounds to me the city of San Antonio is singling out a corporation for its Christian values. Is the city council tracking other businesses record of support to organizations they donate to? Case in point, are you going to ban businesses that supported Black Lives Matter? Because I can assure you the majority of America doesn't support the racist, Marxist organization and I don't either. This sounds like a discrimination case to me. The judges that ruled against Chick-fil-a, obviously went against the rule of law. Therefore, this case should be appealed, retried and reversed by the Texas Supreme Court. Also, Judges and city officials sworn to protect the constitution, should have to pay restitution when there is obvious negligence of the law. Money talks, I believe if governmental officials begin to pay for their bias acts, this will curtail many wrong doings.

No, Attorney Andy Segovia, Religion is not a political agenda, being bias is, and can be unconstitutional and in this case it is. Tell me, how is this different from the Civil rights movement? Certain people, organizations and businesses are ostracized, alienated, banned and punished for having a different belief and opinion. It was because of race in the past, but now it's a difference of ideology. I've had enough of the cancel culture. We have allowed this to go on, much too long. We are long overdue for justice; Therefore, I am fighting back. There is an ole saying, "If you see a good fight, get in it." Well, I'm getting in it! I am of the silent majority, but silent no more, I am a man on FIRE. WWG1WGA

May God Bless America,
Sonny B.

NOT YOUR ORDINARY COMPLAINT

Greetings Chick-fil-a,
Complaint: Store
FL.

I am a proud black American citizen of this great nation. I am a father of (6) six awesome children with my very beautiful and lovely wife of 23 years. I give you my race identity to forfeit any type of racial injustice's eluding to discrimination. There is an extreme racial climate that has been created by the mainstream media (enemy of the people) helping to destroy this nation from within. The blackness movement has been handled like a newborn baby that has no sense of itself, needing full attention for survival. It sickens me and its nauseating to say the least. The black race is the golden child these days and can do no wrong, everyone has bent over backwards to meet the demands of the black race. I'm proud to say, America just celebrated one of the greatest black American of our time, Dr. Martin Luther King Jr, I'm sure the present state of the black race is not the dream he had envisioned. SO, PLEASE GRANT ME THIS COURTESY TO HEAR OUT THE CONTENTS OF THIS LETTER. I apologize for the lengthiness of this letter, but I do not apologize for its content. The contents of this letter are an observation of data my wife and I have gathered over the years from our black race and recently your black employees in question. AGAIN, PLEASE HEAR MY CASE AS I LAY IT OUT BEFORE YOU.

I am writing this letter because of the lackluster and lackadaisical service my family and

I have received over a period of time at the Chick-fil-a in question. I would say, we began to pay attention to the type of service received after the last 6 visits. However, our last two visits were the straw that broke the camel's back. As a result, we would like to focus on our last two visits. Mind you, the infractions I'm about to mention, happened in only two visits and I emphasize only two visits to note the severity of our experience. 1) no spoon for soup 2) forgotten mac and cheese 3) spicy chicken in my chicken noodle soup 4) we had to ask for our chocolate milk 5) we received a 4 piece kids meal instead of the 6 piece kids meal we purchased 6) we were given Hi-C punch instead of lemonade 7) NO MY PLEASURE 8) I left message on voicemail for not receiving my mac and cheese, I never got a response 9) Lastly, nothing was offered as a result of their mistakes. Although we had a long eventful day, we felt it necessary to speak with a supervisor.

The supervisor's name was Ben. I want to say from the offset, this is not an indictment against Ben's character and leadership, or an attack on his livelihood or to see him reprimanded. I believe he needs the support from upper management and the right tools to carry out his job successfully. We got the impression that Ben is exactly what the Chick-fil-a corporation wants as a leader, because he was kind, empathetic, cordial and apologetic. However, he looked very young, and I would even say, he looked like the same age as those he's supervising. This creates a problem in two ways. A young white male supervising a mostly all black staff, in a presently hostile racial climate in the U.S. Let me explain, I thought I would never see the day when a white male would be the most hated in America and patriotism would be synonymous with white supremacy. Therefore, making it very difficult to deal with serious issues at hand with black employees under white leadership, because any negative feedback would be deemed racist. If excellence is not a requirement from the black employees, this would be a type of soft bigotry and very damaging to productivity. Equal rights, means equality across the board. Standards should not be lowered because of your race. If your performance is not up to par, then you should be reprimanded and if the problem continues to persist, then you should be terminated, no matter the ethnicity. Please, do not misunderstand me, I'm not saying the employees in question are bad people; However, I am saying, they may not be right for the Chick-fil-a brand. This is an issue that needs attention by a thoroughly seasoned mature individual or team, because Ben did note to us about other complaints similar to ours. So, apparently this issue has been ongoing. I can't reiterate it enough; your service is what brings me back time and time again.

My wife and I teach our children to love their neighbor as themselves. Treat others the way you would like to be treated. Judge others by the content of their character, not by the color of their skin. Love God first, then family and then your country, in that order. These are biblical values taught from the bible, which is why I believe the bible is the most sought after and at the same time, the most hated. We teach our children, average or mediocrity is not a household practice in our family. You do not have to be the best; However, we do require them to be the best they can be. We consistently remind them to give everything you got, no matter how small or how big the task is at hand. No one owes you anything because of your color, if you want something, get an education and put in an honest day of work to get it, don't expect handouts. Do everything as unto the Lord and good things will follow, and to always remember: RACISM COMES IN ALL COLORS, JUST BECAUSE YOU'RE BLACK, GOD DOES NOT GIVE YOU A PASS!!! We teach our children many life lessons on a daily basis, but everything just mentioned is the foundation of our family structure and should be for America.

Listen, we were up front with Ben, we told him, it was the black employees giving subpar service. I can honestly say, I take no pride or delight in reporting this issue, nor do I think it's minuscule or petty. I have more important situations to tend to, as I consider your time as valuable as mine. However, I do not want to miss the opportunity to convey the urgency of addressing an issue of grave importance to my wife and I. As an African American, this kind of lackluster, lackadaisical and I own the place mentality, feeds into the stigma placed on the black race, LIKE: We're lazy, we don't want to work, we want everything given to us, etc etc etc … Well, this is how we change things, we see something, we say something. I don't care if you have mostly black, mostly white, or mostly Hispanic staff, the service should never decline because of race. I read on a daily basis, that major corporations are spending thousands of dollars on diversity programs to change the mentality of employees, who I believe don't have the problem. These programs are centered mainly around the treatment of the black race. That's discriminatory in itself because we are focusing on one particular race, the black race, but what does it get us? A Black Lives Matter movement demanding more and more, because it's never enough for the person with the problem. You give them an inch, they'll take a mile. This is the attitude of our black men and women in the workforce, they've been told by this toxic racial climate, that America owes them something.

We pass by 3 McDonalds, 2 burger kings, 2 Popeyes, 1 Churches chicken, 1 KFC, I Krystal, 2 Arby's and 1 Wendy's to go out of our way to be served by Chick-fil-a, NOTICE I SAID SERVED. As you can see, we can get food from anywhere. The impeccable service Chick-fil-a is known for, we can't get at any other fast-food restaurant. There is a reason why your drive thru's stay filled to the capacity, America is fed up with spending their hard-earned money on food that sucks, served with a bad attitude. If any employee doesn't want to uphold the impeccable service and standard of the Chick-fil-a brand, then tell them the fast-food establishments just mentioned would welcome their crummy and lousy attitude with open arms.

Lastly, Chick-fil-a, your brand is on blast because everyone knows the company was founded on Christian values and you are hated for it by the far-left liberal socialist. You are a target like every other conservative and Christian in America. The far-left socialist despise the virtues and values we stand for. Closing your businesses on Sundays to allow that day for the entire company to attend church, makes the enemy furious. Standing for tradition marriages in 2012and backing the blue. The gainsayers look on with deceit and envy to try and destroy what God has blessed. Always remember, your business is blessed because of God and not because of a world renown Executive board and not because of the brilliance of a business plan. Your corporation is blessed because you honor the Lord, so never forget it. Political correctness and avoidance of the cancel culture is a sure path to destruction. Please do not allow a lackluster and lackadaisical demeanor from ANY EMPLOYEE to damage the Chick-fil-a brand. Embracing political correctness, and straying away from godly principles, can lead into a fallen state of latency that would make your corporation just like others, mediocre and average at best. I pray to God this never happens, because this nation needs the character, integrity and work ethics your company provides to us all as a beacon of hope. So, stay true to what got you here. I can rest assure you, if you hold to your standard and never falter away from the truth, we will continue to go out of our way to get to your restaurant. These are the words from a very loyal customer.

May God Bless America,
Sonny B.

NOT YOUR ORDINARY COMPLAINT REWIND

Greetings Chick-fil-a,
Complaint Part II: Store
FL.

On February 16, 2021, I wrote an extensive letter of a complaint and a plea concerning the store in question. I want to start out by saying, I do not take delight in making complaints, nor do I have the time to address them; However, I do sacrifice the time for issues I deeply care about. Hopefully, it will become apparent how much I care after reading this letter.

Please, feel free to refer back to my original letter sent several months ago, because nothing has changed, as a matter of fact, it has become worse. I've come to realize this location has become a paradigm, a breeding ground for sub-par employees who lack the qualities and high standards of the Chick-fil-a way. The very notion of rehabilitating the situation seems to have become an impossibility. What do I mean and how I believe it can be resolved? Fire, and hire men and women with attributes of integrity, work ethics and vibrant enthusiasm to conform to the Chick-fil-a excellence we've all come to know and love about your corporation. I know for a fact there are people like this, because they are at every location except the regency location.

Just last night, I went about 3.5 miles out of my way to purchase dinner at another location. That location was the Chick-fil-a on Southside Blvd at Tinseltown, store #01198. My bill was $78.57, which is typical and sometimes even more for a family of (8) eight. I refuse to spend my hard-earned money on lackluster service. My experience at the Tinseltown location was outstanding and representative of what a Chick-fil-a establishment is supposed to be.

I asked one of the attendants, if he knew about the horrible reputation and poor quality of service at the Regency location. He reluctantly responded in shame with a yes. It's apparent, this location has been a black eye to the Chick-fil-a brand for a while now. The Regency location does an astronomical amount of business, in return brings in good fortune to the owner; That's awesome, that is the American dream. However, with issues of this magnitude without resolution, says to me as a faithful customer, I don't care about the service you are receiving, as long as the money keep rolling in. The owner may say he cares, but the proof is in the pudding, the uninspired service is on exhibition for those who frequent his establishment.

Lastly, I've said if before in my last letter, I can purchase food anywhere, but in the fast-food world, there's only one place impeccable service is given and appreciated, that is Chick-fil-a. Minus the service, Chick-fil-a would be like all others, food served with an attitude. I don't know the future of the Regency location, but I do know, if the issues are not resolved, I will not be back in the future. As mentioned, that new journey began last night at another location. I pray this issue will be solved promptly, thank you for your attention to this matter.

May God Bless America,
Sonny B.

CHICK-FIL-A TRILOGY

This is just a little side note, a back-up to the last two letters of concerned. Well, I finally had a personal conversation with the franchise owner, and as a result, we have become friends. After hearing firsthand about why this particular location were having the issues it has. Now I have a clear explanation; as a result, I felt awful criticizing him harshly the way I did.

I found out, he is a proud American taking advantage of the American dream. He and his family work long hours together to keep their investment afloat. With the effects of Covid-19 (Wuhan virus), they have found it very difficult keeping staff in the midst of exaggerated stimulus money from a fraud Biden administration. It's been a revolving door of employment, with constant training of the Chick-fil-a way. Not to mention, trying to remind millennials of the importance of showing up for work. This of course, is in a time, where work ethics have become a distant memory in the old school way of living. Therefore, he gets a pass, I wish you well my friend.

NEVER GONNA BE A PERFECT WORLD

It's never going to be a perfect world, so why do we live our lives as if there isn't a problem? Since the fall of man, mankind and the earth has been dying. The most brilliant minds in the world can convene with a plan to genetically engineer human DNA to live forever, I guess to try an avoid judgment? Here is a scripture right out of the bible I believe should clear things up for you. "And as it is appointed unto men once to die, but after this the judgment:" (Hebrews 9:27). This means you will die, and you will give an account for your existence on this planet, rather good or evil. Furthermore, the globalist can continue to resurrect the notion of a green new deal before each election cycle to sell us on saving the planet, but it's never going to stop the earth from eroding. Can our lives and the caring of the earth be better? Absolutely!!! We should always strive towards progress to become better. However, I'm saying, we should be more concerned about where you will spend eternity. How you can make the world a better place by starting with you. Don't look away from the mirror to find faults in others before you deal with you first. Which brings me to my next point. Statements I've made before in my letters and writings, I believe bears repeating.

I never thought I would see the day when the white male would be the most hated in our country and patriotism would become synonymous to white supremacy. BLM would become the new Karen, and California school districts would encourage hexing towards the opposition, if you said ALL LIVES MATTER. Michael Savage made a valid point, he said, "Liberalism is a mental disorder." I say, liberal Marxism is the lunacy killing our nation, and the demonic mainstream media has played an intricate part by using identity politics.

Which race do they exploit the most? You guessed it, the black race. "Rent a black" (Jesse Lee Peterson). Peterson says, you can always rent a black to do evil. Why? When you have offence in your heart towards another race of people, you can be manipulated to do anything. All you have to do is sprinkle racism on any subject, like Candace Owens would say, and they'll jump on it like a dog in heat.

The media paints the narrative that America is a racist country and tell the black race you're the major recipient of that racism. They found the perfect potion, 24/7 coverage of police brutality. Side note: I like to say, police justification, because the majority of the incidents are justifiable. I explain this in detail in my 'Cause and Effect' writing. Police brutality was the doorway to ignite terms like: systematic racism, white privilege, white supremacy, oppression, discrimination, bigotry, and racist. Is there racism in America? Absolutely!!! I coined this statement to bring recognition to a global problem with no color discrimination, especially to my black race, "Racism comes in all colors, just because you're black, God does not give you a pass." But no one in this world, cannot convince me that the black race isn't extremely better off today than during the civil rights movement and slavery. If you say we're not better off than both of the historical atrocities just mentioned; I will tell you to prove it before I suggest the insane asylum for the rest of your life on earth to be carried out.

I don't believe the black race understand the magnitude and damage caused because of their offended hearts; As a result, we become unknowingly willing participants in the scheme of Marxism and the demise of the United States of America. The more the black race baiter, whin and complain, it helps to destroy the very fiber of our country, which is, life, liberty and the pursuit of happiness for all people under the constitution of America. What do I mean? Take note because this is a vitally important point. Blacks can drink at any water fountain, eat at any restaurant, get and education, learn to read, travel where we want and live where we want to; I believe you get the point. We can do and be anything we set our minds to do. It's not about race, or black vs white, or gender equality, or conservative's vs liberals, vaxed vs unvaxed, and LBGTQ vs church. It's about globalism, the great reset, destroying the constitution so that NO ONE WILL HAVE THE FREEDOM TO DO WHAT WE WANT!!! They use Covid-19 (Wuhan China virus) to accomplish multiple things to fulfill their sinister agenda. The elites want everyone to take this deadly experimental vaccine to depopulate the world or lose all your freedoms. Just because you're in favor of the jab, should I be forced to take it? This has never happened in the history of our nation. What is the fetish or fixation on making everyone take a jab for a curable virus? It's about governmental control, not about We the People. Allow me to tear you away from the mesmerizing spell of the media and listen for a moment. Look around you and see what a rogue tyrannical Biden administration is doing. First it was $600 spent to use IRS to look in on your personal accounts, under the guise to catch wealthy tax evasion. However, after the outrage from the dog and pony show on Capitol Hill, they increased it to $10K. If passed, this will be the beginning to confiscate your accounts, so that you won't be able to buy or sell unless you become vaccinated. Where is the media, you depend on for giving you information?

The church is just as ignorant and ill-informed about what's going on in our nation. Or they are part of the deep state system. I say most just don't have a clue, when you have a white pastor washing the feet of a black church member, while apologizing for the past and massive oppression blacks have to overcome because of the white race. This kind of ridiculousness is what's killing America and they think they are doing a just service to the kingdom of God. The liberal global Marxist hate the God you serve and want to shut down the church. Look at what they did to churches in places like California during the 'PLANDEMIC' SHUTDOWN. While people like Nancy Pelosi got her hair done and bragged on social media about eating ice cream instead signing off on the stimulus bill. Or Governor Gavin Newsom, broke his own strict lockdown rules to have dinner party at the very exquisite French Laundry with no mask or social distancing. Where is the media, you depend on for giving you information? These people are lying to you, because they are in on the diabolical plan to destroy America, by using identity politics. Because we haven't realized it's never gonna be a perfect world. 1776 REWIND!!! Let's Go Brandon!!! Masks are about as useless as Joe Biden!!! May God Bless America!!!

REGULATIONS, SCAMDEMIC, AND DEMS OH MY!

This column was inspired by an article I read from the Chicago Tribune. The headline reads: "Chicago closes 4 more restaurants and bars for Covid-19 guideline violations." This type of non-sense is happening all across this Nation. Has anyone stopped to think, why restaurants may violate Covid-19 regulations? Or does anyone even care? This type of reckless rationale is happening all over this Nation.

I am a retired firefighter and a chef. I have worked in many kitchens and did a lot of catering since 1997. I don't own my own restaurant and dare not to with the regulation Nazi's on your back. I've seen and know what it takes to operate a full service restaurant; Whereas, your main bread and butter are from patrons dining in. Of course, if you're a fast-food establishment, they can survive the ordinance madness, because 75-85 percent of their business relies on drive thru. Therefore, going to a 100 percent drive-thru service is as simple as putting a sign on the door. Again, for a full-service restaurant to stay afloat, Humpty Dumpty has to sit on a wall and the cow has to jump over the moon, this sounds ridiculous, but this is the enormous effort it takes to survive in a shutdown economy because of the virus.

We've seen a vast majority of restaurants take a nosedive during this economy shutdown. Any businesses hanging on, are hanging on because of President Trump's relief funds given to hurting businesses. In which, large chains, colleges, mega churches and large businesses applied for a loan meant for small businesses; Therefore, left a lot less money if any for small businesses the funds were meant for.

What do we want these business owners to do? They are hanging on for dear life, they need just a little bit of empathy from local government; Not to mention, the citizens they employ, they have bills to pay and families to feed as well. These regulations are pushed by democratic local government to do their dirty deeds, that is to keep the economy locked down. This is simply a ploy to destroy a thriving economy under President Trump. To add insult to injury and talking about pouring salt in the wounds of law-abiding hard-working citizens; There are democratic governors and mayors like Lori Lightfoot of Chicago allowing BLM/Antifa thugs to destroy their cities, while businesses are closing their doors permanently.

Let's take a blue city like Chicago for example. This city is riddled with crime and violence on a daily basis and increased significantly during the shutdown because of protests turned riot and shutting down restaurants is their top priority. In Chicago alone, this past weekend of August 28th – 30th 2020, there were at least 54 shootings and 10 killed, but Mayor Lightfoot is more concerned about social distancing, wearing mask and the amount of people that are in a restaurant, this type of thinking from the democrats is inconceivable. Shouldn't we be focusing on the violent criminals, instead antagonizing hard working Americans? There is only one clear answer, the democratic party's lack of action indicates no concern for their citizens they took an oath to protect and serve. The criminals have been allowed to run amok for months and never condemned. The chaos and mayhem is applauded, condoned and celebrated from fake news as mostly peaceful, as one mayor would put it "it's a summer of love." All the while, we see in the background of reporters: looting, assaulting, destroying property, burning down buildings and provoking the cops. These war-torn cities like Chicago are ruled by BLM/Antifa thugs. There is no social distancing, and they only wear mask to hide their identity, and nothing is said while they are wreaking havoc on their cities. The disdain and hate for Trump is so massive, they would rather see their cities burn to the ground. This type of gross injustice and negligence of the constitution is exactly why President Trump got into office.

The democrats want to try and steal the election by voting by mail and no voter ID, because that is the only possible chance to get sleepy Joe in office. I say to that, if you can riot, you can go vote. I'm fighting with our president on behalf of the true Americans, because if we sit back, do nothing and say nothing, the America as we know it will be gone forever. We have to wake up from the lies told to us from the mainstream media and bond together as Americans. Go in person and vote on November 3rd for President Donald J Trump, so we can give him another four years to finish draining the swamp. Also, continue to work for us, the American people. Contrary to popular belief, he is the only person standing in the way of a corrupt government, a political cesspool.

May God bless America,
Sonny B.

SCHOOL CHOICE

Education in America has become a battle ground for the possession of young impressionable minds, easily persuaded by every whim thrown their way. During this hostile political climate, we see the effects of the media, grade school, and college indoctrination. Unfortunately, public schools have become a breeding ground for early radical progressive thinking. This is why having school choice is so significant.

Just before I get into the benefits of having school choice, I would like to tell you a little bit about myself and a young lady who became the face of school choice.

I am a proud black American father of six (6) wonderful children and husband to my beautiful wife of 22 years. My wife is an awesome homemaker, which makes me the breadwinner of our family. Even though it can be difficult at times to maintain a family of eight (8) on one income; However, the one income with my wife at home fortunately affords us the opportunity to direct the path of our children without public school influences. We decided on two choices for our children; That is: a private Christian school or home schooling. Public school was never an option for our family. We wanted our children to be educated in a wholesome environment with Christian values. The kind of education our kids receives is vitally important to us. Having the ability to choose benefits a majority of black students here in Florida and students of all races across the country.

I mentioned earlier about a young lady who became the face of school choice. Denisha Merriweather is someone my wife and I mentored as a young teenager. She was recognized during President Trump's first, State of the Union speech. Therefore, we know first-hand the positive results from having a choice. Denisha was a failing student in public school but became an honor roll student instantaneously while attending a Christian private school. She persevered from a failing student, to an honor roll student and into a young lady working very closely with Secretary of Education Betsy DeVos. If that isn't a success story for school choice, I don't know what is.

By choosing radical progressive incumbent Tracie Davis, you side with the teacher's union, which is totally against school choice.

School choice gives students a better chance to excel in life; Therefore, becoming productive and successful men and women in society. This is why it is crucial we vote candidates in office who are in favor of school choice, because elections can serve to have lasting negative consequences.

Lastly, District 13 House of Representative ballot is a universal primary election, which makes it unique; Therefore, both republicans and democrats will be able to vote on this ticket. With all of the information given, electing Dr. Cynthia Smith as the District 13 House of Representative on August 18, 2020, is the ONLY CHOICE, because Dr. Cynthia Smith understands the importance of SCHOOL CHOICE.

May God bless America,
Sonny B.

LETTER IN RESPONSE TO FSR PUBLICATION OF FIRST WATCH ARTICLE

Greetings,

I am a proud black father of six (6) with my lovely wife of 22 years in the greatest country in the world. This letter is in response to comments made by, CEO Chris Tomasso in a publication from FSR on-line magazine. I apologize for the lengthiness of my letter; However, I do not apologize for its content, because the subject of race relations, I believe is blown way out of proportion and should've been dealt with a long time ago.

I never thought I would see the day, when being white in America would make you the most hated race in this Nation, especially the white male. If you are rich or wealthy, they say you only think about yourselves and never about the poor people. Again, I'm black; Therefore, I hear this all the time, but it's ok if you're black and wealthy, there are no grips, no complaints and no judgment, only silence from the same people that accused the white race for not having empathy, so please hear me out. I'm sorry, I have had enough, I wrote many pages to express my grief, this is the result of a very very short version of my grievances, because that's how passionately disgusted I am. SO PLEASE, READ THIS LETTER IN IT'S ENTIRETY, BECAUSE I BELIEVE YOU OWE ME A MOMENT OF YOUR TIME, SINCE CORPORATIONS, SPORTS AND COLLEGES ARE IN THE BUSINESS OF MEETING DEMANDS OF THE BLACK RACE. I continue, if whites love their country, they are considered white supremacist. If Caucasians, speak up against wrong doings of blacks, they are deemed a racist and a bigot. Blacks are not ignorant, thus the reason for the name BLACK Lives Matter, they know, with anything black in the phrase, becomes the white race KRYPTONITE. Whites can't say anything about the Marxist BLM movement, because it has black in the name, and any blacks not on board, get labeled as out of touch, Coons, Uncle Tom's, and a sell-out; Therefore, giving this MAFIA like organization the freedom to orchestrate total chaos and mayhem, I gotta give it to them, the plan is brilliant, and I would even say it's GENIUS. Also, dare not say America first, that makes you not only a racist, but a Nationalist as well. This type of non-sense is shoved down our throats by the media, Hollywood, and the likes of Oprah Winfrey, Lebron James, Tyler Perry, TI, Snoop Dog, Ice Cube, NBA, NFL, MLB and other sport entities to the point I can't even stomach watching one second of sports, especially ESPN. Sports used to be America's pass time, now sports have become the symbol of the political correctness we ALL used to be able to get away from. Now, social media and major corporations have become a part of this propaganda, mind you, all mentioned are living the American dream, that this country affords us all with hard work and determination, yet they use their influence to divide a Nation. Totally disbarring the freedoms from men and women who bled and died on the battlefields, so that ALL Americans could take advantage of the many opportunities, while living in peace with our fellow countrymen. Yet we trample, disrespect and burn the very flag that is supposed to unites us. What we are seeing today in America, is what we used to see from Muslim extremists, now in 2020 it has become common ground to kneel on our Anthem and burn the American flag, they say, for social injustice? They make millions of dollars by playing a game, but has never seen a battlefield, except from the comfort of their multi-million-dollar mansions. They are traitors, and those who condone it, and I say to those who applaud this gesture, you are as Un-American and just as guilty as those taking part of this unpatriotic act.

Systemic racism, white privilege, and social injustice are terms used by disgruntle blacks with hidden racism in their heart; Therefore, making a complete mockery on the many black success stories. Case in point, the George Floyd incident has sparked a lot of race relation conversations. One in particular, is a relative of mine, every time the subject of race relations is discussed, the terms: systematic racism, white privilege and social injustice is always brought up. Here is a man that is retired with two (2) pensions, every time I conversate with him, he is on the golf course playing a round of golf; Not to mention, his wife is a RN home healthcare nurse that works whenever she decides to work. He and his wife have literally traveled around the world, they go and do whatever they please. They are enjoying the American dream, sounds like a good life to me. Does systemic racism, white privilege, and social injustice exist? Absolutely, but as long as there are imperfect people on this planet, there will be some type of unfairness, corruption and partisanship. However, I believe, everyone has a story to tell of negative situations they've had to overcome. Do you know what else exists? Equality, love, fairness, benevolence, compassion, impartiality, courtesy, and kindness to name a few. You see, it's what lens you choose to look out of, to see the world; Are you the person that looks out at the world and people in a positive or negative way? Life is, and always will be about choices. We can choose to be an honest hard worker, or a thug dope dealer, poisoning the streets with your selfishness. It's the choices we make, that makes us honorable men and women in society. I would like to borrow the words from a song writer, it goes like this: "I don't wanna miss it, I don't wanna look back someday and find, everything that really mattered, was right in front of me this whole time, open up my eyes Lord, keep me in the moment just like this, Before the things we love, becomes the beautiful things we miss."

Mr. Chris Tomasso, you mentioned in the article about how your black employees are treated and disrespected. One instance, you said one of your black employees was on his lawn at 5:30am about to head to work, when he was approached by a cop to ask what he was doing. Your employee took offense to being approached, maybe there was an all-out alert to be on the lookout for a suspect that might have fit the description of your employee. Also, your black GM's saying they feel disrespected because they feel like customers don't respect their authority. I say investigate the situation first before we pre-judge, give the benefit of the doubt because there are always two sides to one story. Also, preconceived ideas about another race, can sometimes obscure your reasoning to make a logical informed decision because of hate in your heart. I have been black for 51 years and I know how my race can be, we can a lot of times look for racism around every corner. I love the expression of President Abraham Lincoln, "If you look for the bad in people expecting to find it, you surely will." Let's say for the sake of the argument, that it's true they are being disrespected, be big enough to ignore ignorance. You are a General Manager, a leader that should have the attributes of a leader, like: Humility, Confidence, Authenticity, Calm in Chaos, Fairness and Forgiveness. They are leaders, tell them to quit whining, complaining and toughen up. Tell your black GM's and employees to take note of the way police are being disrespected during the riots. They still have to serve the public in the midst of chaos and mayhem, they are assaulted, called derogatory names, provoked, severely injured and some have lost their lives. They serve each day, in-spite of those wanting cop defunding. I take offense to the horrific and shameful treatment of the cops with no regard. Just because you have one bad cop, that doesn't mean all cops are bad. We have bad people in all professions, that doesn't mean all people are bad in those other professions. As a firefighter for 25 years, I rode the beat with many cops of all races, were there bad cops? Absolutely, however, the majority of cops were dog gone good cops and good people with families. 9/11 happened, where the bulk of the police and fireman died serving the citizens of New York city. While everyone else was leaving the burning building and running away from danger, firemen and police were running towards it. 9/11 could've happened in any city and the outcome would've been the same. Brave and courageous men and women serving the public would've lost their lives trying saving someone they never even met. So yes, this lunacy infuriates me, and yes, I do take it personal, when I see the attacks on brothers and sisters, I served alongside for 25 years. With that being said, your GMs are not being threatened with their life, COPS ARE, and without a thanks from those who need them the most.

The media is pushing a narrative, an agenda to divide a country once united. The notion that black people are oppressed and should fear their lives when they walk the streets, especially when they come in contact with a cop, is Ludacris. This notion is disgusting, a disgrace and is criminal to put it lightly and they should be ashamed to call themselves journalist. Listen, black law-abiding citizens don't have to fear the police, blacks should be concerned about the violent criminals in their own neighborhoods. I dare you to take some time out of your schedule and check the criminal background of each of the victims BLM base their case on as police brutality. One of my writings explains this nonsense to a T. It's titled, "Cause and Effect." 99.99% of the time, if you have a run in with a cop, you did something unlawful. You do something illegal (Cause); the cop makes an arrest (Effect). If you didn't do the cause, there would be no effect. Why are we not talking about the cause? Listen to this: Fatherlessness, teen pregnancy, abortion, black on black murder, crime, gang violence, incarceration, illiteracy and school dropout. These are all self- inflicted problems that has plagued the black community for decades, the most disheartening thing about this is, these communities are governed by mostly black democratic officials. (Cause)

We are a blessed nation and all of the races that live in it. We travel to places like Jamaica, with sites of beautiful countryside's and clear beaches. Tourist accommodations are festive and plush, but travel through the city where the real citizens live, away from the glamour and prestige, and look into the eyes those living in cardboard boxes. You see hope, hopes to one day become a citizen of the United States of America. This hope is seen all over the world, immigrants of all walks of life wanting to become citizens of the United States of America. We have locked down the southern borders to keep illegals out by the masses. Why is this? PLEASE! I implore you, to turn off the Marxist mainstream media for once and think for yourself. While in your silence, ask yourself, why aren't American citizens, especially black citizens not making a mass exodus? There were 20 multi-millionaire Hollywood actors/ actresses, that said they would leave the country if Trump became President, guess what? they're still here. There are terms thrown around, that America is racist and unjust towards blacks. Let's look at it this way, black slaves risked their lives to seize every opportunity they could to flee from the southern plantations to escape to northern states and to Canada. Why? Because the conditions were ACTUALLY extreme, cruel, unbearable and inhumane. Black slaves didn't have to manufacture, or conjure up racism and social injustice, for EXAMPLE like: Jussie Smollett, Bubba Wallace and the Native American in the midst of the Covington Catholic students during a peaceful pro-life protest, to name a few.

Slavery is the very reason, why we don't remove, destroy, vandalize and tear down monuments, statues, buildings and street names, just because they are linked to the confederacy. There is an ole saying, "If you forget your history, we are bound to repeat it." I know my history, apparently these imbeciles out destroying cities don't. I have read about the horrors of slavery of my black ancestors, I have read and seen documentaries on the devastations of the civil rights movement. So, tell me, minus the flogging and free labor, how are the tactics used on the white race today any different from what the black race had to endure in the past? We are all made after the image of God; Therefore, no one race should be demonized for being who God made them to be, anything outside of this notion is dead wrong. This is a quote from Malcolm X, I believe sums up the media, I quote, "The media's the most powerful entity on earth. They have the power to make the innocent guilty and to make the guilty innocent, and that's power, because they control the minds of the masses."

Black juveniles and young adults are always going to have confrontation with the police, why? Let's be honest, black juveniles/young adults can cut the fool, why? Because they have no respect for authority, why? Because of FATHERLESSNESS. Fathers bring authority to a little black boy and girl in the home. How do I know this? Because I am an engaging black father in my home of six (6) children with my one wife; Therefore, I am exposing and standing up to the lie of this notion that blacks are being severely oppressed and should fear their lives every single moment in America. I'm not falling for reverse psychology 101, or reverse racism. The BLM movement is the civil rights movement in reverse. Don't just take my word for it, you assess the characteristics of the WOKE movement. It's unfortunate, the white race falls for this scheme every time; Although, I believe most whites mean well, bowing down to this recklessness proves to be catastrophic to the black community, and to America as a whole. What your corporation and many other corporations and colleges, vowed to do for the black race is all well and good, but make sure it's for the right reasons. Not because of white guilt and because you think the black race is abused and mistreated in America.

Lastly, as dreadful as slavery was to OUR ANCESTORS, as a black man I end with these words: The white race today, shouldn't have to pay restitution to the black race today, for the sins of their ancestors yesterday, and the black race today, shouldn't ask for restitution from the white race today, because we are not our ancestors of yesterday. I tell blacks this, when we are discussing race relations. Check your heart, and just in case you didn't realize: RACISM COMES IN ALL COLORS, JUST BECAUSE YOU'RE BLACK, GOD DOESN'T GIVE YOU A PASS. I, the defense, rest my case against the false allegations of my beloved country that I appreciate and love so dear. Now will the prosecutors of these false allegations against America, please present your case with a response back to me.

Thank you, & May God bless America,
Sonny B.

THE RESPONSE FROM FIRST WATCH

Whenever I write a letter because of an issue of concern, I never really think there would be a response. Although, I would love a response, but it is not necessary for me to keep writing and standing up for what I believe. I always thought to myself, if nothing else, it will be used for my book for the world to see, to hopefully effect change. Well, I wrote a letter to First Watch restaurants Inc. about a new program on diversity concerning blacks, I felt was unnecessary. Why? Even as a black man, I was fed up with the pandering of liberal whites, major corporations, colleges, NFL, NBA, MLB, etc. ... of BLM and Blacks crying victimhood. I sent my letter by email that morning and received a response very late in the evening on the same day. Needless to say, I was surprised to get a response and even more surprised from the words of the response. The next paragraph is First Watch response, and the next two are my emails in regard to their response.

First watch: "I just finished reading your email below (for the second time). Thank you for taking the time out of your schedule to send such a thought-provoking and poignant response to the FSR article about our diversity and inclusion efforts. I appreciate your perspective and insights and I will take them into further consideration as part of a larger discussion. As you read in the aforementioned article, we established a Race Inclusion and Support Exchange (R.I.S.E.) Advisory Council as part of our #beabetterhuman initiative. I plan to share your email with the group for a productive discussion around different viewpoints and how we can best embrace them."

Me: Good morning, I want to apologize for this very early email, I'm up throughout the wee hours of the morning, because I'm just about to finished with my book dealing with race relations in America from a proud black American republican perspective. I have been writing local and nationwide letters to politicians, corporations, NFL, etc. I have to be honest, I am thrilled with excitement, because I hardly ever get a response back, especially in the magnitude of your response. I love people, that means all races of people. It sounds like you didn't take it as an attack, because it definitely wasn't and never is my purpose. I just feel white America and this country is getting a raw deal and it's unfair and it's not right to try and take advantage of anyone, while using social injustice and racism as a means to project the hate in your heart. Again, I am elated and honored, that you would even consider my letter as a prototype to educate those representing your program. I really honestly believe corporations like yourself are really sincere in your endeavors to help and assists the black community and I want to say thank you. Lastly, my wife and I love eating at First Watch sometimes twice a week here in Jacksonville after our workout. My real name is H.B. but I do all of my writings in my nickname Sonny B. because it's to sort of hide my identity to shield my family from attacks, I can tell you it is not popular breaking away from the democratic party as a black person; However, I feel comfortable telling you my true identity. Thank you, and May God bless America 🙏US🙏 Sonny B.

Me: Good morning again, I apologize for the early morning email, I could not sleep with excitement because of your response. I don't believe you truly understand the meaning of your response to me. I have to reiterate my statement of the difficulty of a black person leaving the democratic party. I get my greatest attacks from my own race of people, especially family and friends, but they want to talk about racism and injustices, when you treat those who have a different opinion or ideology with disdain. I'm a husband and a father, which make issues like pro-life, pro-God, pro- family, pro- school choice and pro-America vitally important to me, all the valuable things the republican party are in favor of, I didn't say they were perfect, I said they support my ideals. I know it's not popular with the black race, but I will stand up for what I believe, and they may do the same because it is our 1st amendment, that's what makes America the greatest country in the world, because we have a choice, and we should respect everyone's choice. Well, when my book finally hit the shelves, America will hear the sound of people like: Thomas Sowell, Candace Owens, Larry Elder, Brandon Tatum, etc., voices trying to save America from the tyranny of socialism and the cry of victimhood from the black race. Thank you again for your response, and words are priceless to a man that hates Chaos, especially ill-informed Chaos pushed by the mainstream media. Best wishes and an even greater success with your corporation. Thanks again, Sonny B. May God bless America 🙏USUS

LETTER IN RESPONSE TO FSR PUBLICATION OF FIRST WATCH ARTICLE

Letter never sent

Greetings,

Introduction: I am black, but I never thought I would see the day, when being white in America would make you the most hated race in this nation, especially the white male. If you are rich or wealthy, they say you only think about yourselves and never about the poor people. Furthermore, republicans are the biggest racist. Again, I'm black; Therefore, I hear this all the time, but it's ok if you're black and wealthy, there are no grips, no complaints and no judgment, only silence from the same people that accused the white race for not having empathy, so please hear me out. I'm sorry, I have had enough, I wrote many pages to express my grief, this is the result of a very very short version of my grievances, because that's how passionately disgusted I am. SO PLEASE, READ THIS LETTER IN IT'S ENTIRETY, BECAUSE I BELIEVE YOU OWE ME A MOMENT OF YOUR TIME, SINCE CORPORATIONS, SPORTS AND COLLEGES ARE IN THE BUSINESS OF MEETING DEMANDS OF THE BLACK RACE. If whites love their country, they are considered white supremacist. If Caucasians, speak up against wrong doings of blacks, they are deemed a racist and a bigot. Blacks are not ignorant, thus the reason for the name Black Lives Matter, they know, with anything black in the phrase, becomes the white race KRYPTONITE. Whites can't say

147

anything about the Marxist BLM movement, because it has black in the name; Therefore, giving this MAFIA like organization the freedom to orchestrate total chaos and mayhem, I gotta give it to them, this is GENIUS. Dare not say America first, that makes you not only a racist, but also the scum of the earth. This type of non-sense is shoved down our throats by the media, Hollywood, and the likes of Oprah Winfrey, Lebron James, Tyler Perry, TI, Snoop Dog, Ice Cube, NBA, NFL, MLB and other sport entities to the point I can't even stomach watching one second of sports, especially ESPN. Sports used to be America's pass time, now sports have become the symbol of the political correctness we ALL used to be able to get away from. Now, social media and major corporations have become a part of this propaganda. Mind you, all mentioned are living the American dream, that this country affords us all with hard work and determination, yet they use their influence to divide a nation. Totally disbarring the freedoms from men and women who bled and died on the battlefields, so that ALL Americans could take advantage of the many opportunities, while living in peace with our fellow countrymen. Yet we trample, disrespect and burn the very flag that is supposed to unites us, what we are seeing today in America is what we used to see from Muslim extremists, now in 2020 it has become common ground to kneel on our Anthem, for what, social injustice? They make millions of dollars by playing a game, they have never seen a battlefield except from the comfort of your multi-million-dollar mansions. They are traitors, and those who condone it, and I say to those who applaud this gesture, you are as Un-American and just as guilty as people who take part in this unpatriotic act.

I have read about the horrors of slavery of my black ancestors, read and seen documentaries on the devastations of the civil rights movement. So, tell me, minus the flogging and free labor, how are the tactics used on the white race today, any different from what the black race had to endure in the past? We are all made after the image of God; Therefore, no one race should be demonized for being who God made them to be, anything outside of this notion is dead wrong. This is a quote from Malcolm X, I believe sums up my introduction. I quote," The media's the most powerful entity on earth. They have the power to make the innocent guilty and to make the guilty innocent, and that's power, because they control the minds of the masses." End quote.

Again, I apologize for the lengthiness of my letter; However, I do not apologize for its content, because the subject of race relations, I believe is blown way out of proportion and should've been dealt with a long time ago. This letter is in response to a publication from FSR on-line magazine. Before I get into my response, I would like to say, my wife and I love to dine at First Watch restaurants here in Florida. Just a little side note.

I am a proud black American of six (6) children with my lovely wife of 22 years. My wife is a homemaker, which makes me the sole bread winner of our family. Trying to feed a family of eight on one salary can be quite challenging to say the least but rewarding. I am now, a retired firefighter and chef desiring to own my own restaurant at some point after the ridiculous Covid-19 regulations. However, before the pandemic and uprising of lawlessness, I was set, with my ultimate dream of owning my own restaurant in view. After retirement, I was going to cook for about a year at the Marriott Sawgrass, then set my dream into action. Unfortunately, the plan didn't go as desired, I was placed on furlough after the Covid madness.

While employed as a firefighter, I worked overtime, undertime, and anytime to provide for my family. I even had part-time jobs cooking as well; Needless to say, it would break my heart being away from my family for long periods at a time. I would at times sit down with my family and remind them of the dread being away but was necessary to put food on the table and keep a roof over our heads. You see, I know about hard honest work as a law-abiding citizen of this great country. My mother would always say, no one owes you anything but to love you. Thus, the reason, I never look for handouts, just an opportunity to be the best worker I could be. My wife and I teach our children the same, among other goodly qualities of being a productive citizen in society.

Well, being laid off landed me home, doing absolutely nothing for a couple of months. I was doing family things, but that doesn't count, that's not work at all, just pleasure and a joy. For the first time in my life as an adult, I had time to ponder and think about how precious but fragile life is.

Then George Floyd happened and all hell, literally broke loose. I have seen many riots in my day, but this one was off the chain. In the case of, George Floyd, I would like to say, no one of any RACE should die in that manner while handcuffed in police custody. However, injustice for injustice will not bring a solution and the people destroying cities and wreaking havoc, makes you no better than the original perpetrator. Any person, college, corporations or sport entity like: NBA, NFL, WNBA, MLB, and NHL etc. etc … who are pandering, and funding demands of a racist/Marxist organization are just as guilty as well. Mind you BLM (Black Lives Matter) has been labeled as a domestic terrorist organization, yet we are ignoring their behavior and rewarding their unlawful acts. Just this past weekend, video footage of BLM in Rochester, NY, captured them turning over tables at a restaurant and demanding white diners to leave. Just a day ago, BLM in a McDonalds in Pittsburgh with bull horns towards black employees trying to make a living, demanding what? Everyone is silent on this matter. Why? Because it's not about a black life, it's about changing the face of America, I explain my hypothesis throughout this letter.

In 2020, blacks can do no wrong, as we see in my two previous examples, the black race is the golden child. I'm a black man and I can truly say, watching the suck up and pandering has become nauseating, to say the least. Blacks are met with demands on every side, which only enables and perpetuate the problems in the black community. I feel my race of people are taking advantage of a golden opportunity to seize the moment, or punking the system as racial injustice is pushed hard by the mainstream media and far left socialist. Case in point, George Floyd is a name heard around the world, but who knows the names of the nine (9) black children victims who lost their lives to the violence of the rioting? Or the names of dozens of adults and cops who were murdered as a result of protests turned riot? Silence, no one to speak up for those lives' loss, we call that type of action, hypocrisy. Especially, when black-on- black murder is an epidemic, thousand for black lives are loss at the hands of blacks every year, but there is still, silence. Again, we defined that as hypocritical. This is why I say, this movement isn't about a black man being murdered, because based on the numbers of black-on-black murders, if anyone cared, the world would be on fire.

We are blessed in this nation. We travel to places like Jamaica, with sites of beautiful countryside's and clear beaches. Tourist accommodations are festive and plush, but travel through the city where the real citizens live, away from the glamour and prestige, and look into the eyes those living in cardboard boxes. You see hope, hopes to one day become a citizen of the United States of America. I pay close attention, I'm very observant of how precious life is; Therefore, leaves me little or no time for criticizing America and the people in it. This is why I'm outraged and sickened by the media's false accusations that blacks live in constant fear in this country and shame on those blacks living the American dream crying victimhood. Corporations like First watch, I believe have good intensions and mean well in your endeavors to somehow save the black race from the onslaught of slave traders by having diversity programs.

Mr. Chris Tomasso, you mentioned in the article about, about how your black employees are treated and disrespected. One instance, you said one of your black employees was on his lawn at 5:30am about to head to work, when he was approached by a cop to ask what he was doing. Your employee took offense to being approached, maybe there was an all-out alert to be on the lookout for a suspect that might have fit the description of your employee. Or your black GM's saying they feel disrespected because they feel like customers don't respect their authority. I say investigate the situation first before we pre-judge, give the benefit of the doubt because there are always two sides to one story. Also, preconceived ideas about another race, can sometimes obscure your reasoning to make a logical informed decision because of hate in your heart. I have been black for 51 years and I know how my race can be, we can a lot of times look for racism around every corner. I love the expression of President Abraham Lincoln, "If you look for the bad in people expecting to find it, you surely will." Let's say for the sake of the argument, that it's true they are being disrespected, be big enough to ignore ignorance. You are a General Manager, a leader that should have the attributes of a leader, like: Humility, Confidence, Authenticity, Calm in Chaos, Fairness and Forgiveness. They are leaders, tell them to quit whining, complaining and toughen up. Tell your black GM's and employees to take note of the way police are being disrespected during the riots. They still have to serve the public in the midst of chaos and mayhem, they are assaulted, called derogatory names, provoked, severely injured and some have lost their lives. They serve each day, in-spite of those wanting cop defunding. I take offense to the horrific and shameful treatment of the cops with no regard. Just because you have one bad cop, that doesn't mean all cops are bad. We have bad people in all professions, that doesn't mean all people are bad in those other professions. As a firefighter for 25 years, I rode the beat with many cops of all races, were there bad cops? Absolutely. However, the majority of cops were dog gone good cops and good people with families. 9/11 happened, where the bulk of the police and fireman died serving the citizens of New York city. While everyone else was leaving the burning building and running away from danger, firemen and police was running towards it. 9/11 could've happened in any city and the outcome would've been the same. Brave and courageous men and women serving the public would've loss their lives saving someone they never even met. So yes, this lunacy infuriates me, and yes, I do take it personal, when I see the attacks on brothers and sisters, I served alongside for 25 years. With that being said, your GMs are not being threatened with their life, but cops are among other things and not even a thanks from those who need them the most.

I saw where your corporation wanted to give to black colleges and money towards scholarships for minorities. I think that's great, but amazing to me how the president is labeled everything under the sun, especially a bigot and a racist by the media. Among the many things this president has done for the American people, especially the black community, his accomplishments are totally ignored by the Marxist mainstream media. The American people, if they want to find news that's real and not chopped up, taken out of context and telling half of a story, they have to do serious detective work, because the search engines like Google don't make it easy. This is purposely done to demonize a sitting president to divide the nation. Like many Americans, they do not search, they read a headline because they trust the media. Therefore, they take the media's word for it, which proves to be catastrophic, when we glance out at our nation and see the turmoil. To prove my point, here is an article about President Trump in the NY Post, I bet you didn't know about. Straight out of the NY Post. I quote, "His (Trump) recent police reform executive order, The First Step Act, released thousands of people from jail (90 percent of whom were black). He has promoted "opportunity zones" that incentivized private investment into marginalized communities and also increased federal funding to historically black colleges and universities by 17 percent- a total exceeding $100 million, more than any President in history. Meanwhile, the Obama administration infamously removed a two-year Bush administration program that annually funded $85 million directly to these prized institutions. As I mentioned in my book (by Gianno Caldwell) "Taken for Granted," during the 2016 election Trump did something few republicans had the courage to do, he targeted the black vote and spoke directly to the

African American issues." End quote. But Trump is a racist and a bigot? Who are the people withholding information, so the citizens of this great nation can believe that this man is evil? Ladies and Gentlemen, I say to you, what else is the media hiding, what are they lying about? The notion that blacks are oppressed, and should fear their lives when they walk the streets, especially when they come in contact with a cop. This notion is disgusting, a disgrace and is criminal to put it lightly and they should be ashamed to call themselves journalist. Listen, black law-abiding citizens don't have to fear the police, blacks should be concerned about the violent criminals in their own neighborhoods. I dare you to take some time out of your schedule and check the criminal background of each of the victims BLM base their case on as police brutality. One of my writings explains this nonsense to a T. It's titled, "Cause and Effect." 99.99% of the time, if you have a run in with a cop, you did something wrong. Let me take you back to school, you do something illegal (Cause), the cop makes an arrest (Effect). If you didn't do the cause, there would be no effect. Why are we not talking about the cause? I have to end here, because I can go on and on about the problems of the black community, which is: Fatherlessness, teen pregnancy, abortion, black on black murder, crime, gang violence, incarceration, illiteracy and school dropout. These are all problems that has plagued the black community for decades, the most disheartening thing about this is, these communities are governed by black democratic officials. Again, I say stop the pandering, the programs, they only perpetuate the problems we as a black race so desperately need to face. Thank you for your attention to this matter.

May God bless America,
Sonny B.

ATTORNEY AT LAW (CHEESECAKE)

The Lord began to speak to me this morning concerning your accomplishment, so I began to write, and this is what He gave me. You have just committed an amazing feat. WOW, WOW, WOW!!! You passed the bar exam to become an Attorney at Law, but first, there would be hard work, commitment, dedication and long hours of studying on every level of: Grade school, college, and grad school; However, your life in Jesus Christ would prove to be the most important commitment you ever made. You accomplished something, some people only dream about, and few people set out to finish, no matter the race, nationality, ethnicity or creed. I know, it sounds like a Dr. King speech, Lol. I believe you realize this great achievement didn't just happen on your own. You've had a supporting cast, like: Family, friends and most of all, God and two awesome parents in your life to top it all off.

I believe fatherlessness has become the leading cause of the black community's undoing's. Six young black men were just arrested in Nassau County on a drug sting, I wonder if they had engaging fathers in their lives, would they have taken a different path? If I were a betting man, I would set all of my cards on the table and say, they didn't have fathers in their lives. Fathers are vitally important in a family and especially to a child's life and I must say, you have an excellent father to be proud of. He is a wonderful provider, protector, and a godly example of what a husband and a father should be. He's my friend; Therefore, I know first-hand. I call the latter, a one two punch, and an unbelievable combination to have in your corner. With that combination, how can a daughter, now a beautiful and intelligent young lady like yourself fail? Yes, you may have had some major obstacles, but you prevailed, why? Because nothing can stop or defeat a righteous man or woman, even if he or she falls seven times, God's people always get back up.

My wife and I, keep ever before our children, that only what you do for Christ will last, and everything else will fade away, like the future becomes the past. We continue on by saying, you can do and become anything you set your mind to be. No one owes you anything, whatever you want, go and work for it, without complaining and whining. Cheesecake, you just proved that no amount of oppression from: Systematic racism, white privilege or white supremacy can hold you down. We remind our children, never to allow anyone to tell you that you are a victim, but rather you are a victor. Be a productive product of our society and don't be a menace to society. We understand our sons and daughters are well aware of current events running rampant in our nation; Therefore, we educate them on the components of being a godly person and an example to the world.

We debunk the notion that America is a racist nation, and that all white people are inherently hateful bigots, and blacks are weak and pathetic. Letting them know that 'Racism comes in all colors, just because you're black, God does not give you a pass.' By showing them real facts and statistics like: In 2019 there were 7,484 black murders in the U.S. In 2020 there were at least 8,600 black murders in the U.S. It's disheartening to say, over 90% of those said murders and prior to, were black on black, where is BLM on that issue? Police brutality only accounts for .02% of police altercations ending in death and they are not all black. Which destroys the myth and the narrative that cops are slaughtering the black race by the thousands. We can see with those startling numbers just mentioned, we do exponentially more harm to one another than any other race combined.

Moreover, we teach our children, how many unborn black babies are murdered in the womb by legal genocide of planned parenthood. Around 400,000 black abortions occur each year: Where is the mainstream media, LeBron James, Oprah Winfrey, Colin Kaepernick, Don Lemon, Joy Reid, and Tyler Perry to name a few? Yes, we want our children to succeed in life, what caring parent wouldn't? But most of all, we want our children to have a biblical world view. To Love God with all their hearts. To do unto others, as you would want them to do unto you, and to love your neighbor as yourself. If everyone individually was accountable for those 3 things, as the lyrics of a popular Louis Armstrong song would say, 'What a wonderful world it would be.'

Lastly, Cheesecake, we now have another beacon of light, and another story we can point our children to, because your achievement is extremely commendable. Your success as a young black woman, says to little black boys and girls and young black adults, that all things are possible with the Lord on your side. Attorney at Law sounds so refreshing and so encouraging, in a time of racial tension in our world, especially our nation. We are saying once again, my family and I are so proud of your success and the respectable young lady you have become. I pray that your husband realizes the rare catch and a priceless ruby to be cherished in his newly wife, because godly, successful women are a rare find. I managed to do well myself, when my wife took my hand in marriage. I must say, as the bible, he that findeth a wife, findeth a good thing and obtaineth favor of the Lord. (Proverbs 18:22) Cheesecake, YOUR BEST IS YET TO COME, as long as you keep your sights on Jesus.

May God bless America
We love you,
Bro. Bread pudding and family

WHAT IF A WHITE MAN DID IT?

I like to start out with my writings revealing what my ethnicity is, so not to be labeled as a racist, you may call me an Uncle Tom, but not a racist. In this hostile racial climate, one can never be too careful. I am a proud black American law-abiding citizen of this great nation. I am not oppressed, and I thank God for the opportunities and freedoms the United States of America affords me as a native, husband and a father. I love all people and ALL LIVES DO MATTER. I tell it like it is and that doesn't make me popular amongst my race of people, but I like the ole saying, "The truth hurts." Occasionally, I use a passage out of one of the most celebrated and most hated books in the world, the Holy Bible. It always shines the light on you as an individual. How you should treat others as yourself. How we should love our neighbor as ourselves. You know, those goodly characteristics every person should strive for. So, let me set the tone for where I'm heading. (NIV) Matthew 7:15 "You hypocrite first take the plank out of your own eye, and then you will see clearly to remove the speck from your brother's eye." In other words, you're pointing out a very tiny problem of another person, when your problem is enormous.

This is a response to the Lit Chat online author talk with Frederick Joseph, titled "The black friend: On being a better white person. This conversation will be shown live on zoom, Wednesday, March 31, 2021 at 7pm with the support of our local library. A 17-year-old named Taylor Richardson was instrumental in bringing popularity and attention to Frederick Joseph's book all over the world. This column isn't to throw shade on the young lady, because she is obviously a brilliant and motivated student at the Bolles School; In which, the administration should be proud to have her as an asset in their school. However, this article is written to expose the hypocritical lie and the bill of goods that's been sold to the black race to keep us angry, bitter and ignorant to the truth.

The division between blacks and whites is spread out all throughout our nation by way of the: media, academia, Hollywood, sports, music, major corporations and now our very own libraries here in our wonderful city. The book by Frederick Joseph is one of the few books recommended for reading, highlighting the notion, to show white people how to become a better white person. Do we think that this would be offensive to white people? Or do we even care because of the hostile racial climate favoring the black race? I have a question, **what if a white man did it?** I mean, wrote a book on how black people can become a better black person and made it live on zoom in our public library. If we were honest, we know there would be hell to pay. I would even say that the library would deny it on the basis of racism. We would see the double standard in rare form as it has become the norm all over America. Blacks and the far- left liberals can say anything they want, but the conservative voice is told to sit down and shut-up. In other words, if you do not agree with leftist ideals, you do not have a voice under the first amendment of the U.S. Constitution. The left lump everything under hate speech, rather it fits the description or not. The Canadian rapper Tom MacDonald said it best in his Fake Woke lyrics, "There's a difference between hate speech and speech that you hate."

The left say they are tolerant, until you disagree with them. If your ideology doesn't line up with theirs: then they resort to name calling; if that doesn't work, then they censor you; threaten your livelihood; for anyone that is a major threat of exposing their propaganda, then they dox you; and finally use physical violence to shut you up; A very brutal, and violent attack against conservative journalist Andy Ngo is a prime example of the lefts tolerant level. We saw this all during 2020 with the protest (RIOTS) as mostly peaceful and as one mayor would put it, "It's a summer of love." A year of chaos, yet the media celebrated it and ignored the lawlessness, destruction and violence. Dr. Martin Luther King Jr. always led a true peaceful protest, because I believe he realized that injustice plus injustice never equals a solution. I tend to wonder what he would think about the Black Lives Matter movement (BLM) today.

Meanwhile, for some odd reason, we as blacks think we have a corner on the market about who's racist. I call us the racism Nazi, we see racism in everybody else, except us. We look for racism around every corner to have something to complain about. Here is a quote from Abraham Lincoln to give everyone something to think about, "If you look for the bad in mankind, expecting to find it, you surely will." I like to add to that by saying, Racism comes in all colors, just because you're black, God does not give you a pass!!! I'm fed up with the blackness movement and how the black race uses victimhood to get demands. White progressives are perpetuating this non-sense by giving way to the divisive platform. Let's just be honest, the George Floyd death was about a white man killing a black man.

If we really cared about black lives, we would be lamenting in the street's day and night because of BLACK-ON-BLACK MURDER, that take the lives of thousands of blacks every year in America; Yet we want to tell white people how to be better? The elites want it to be about race, this is why police brutality gets 24/7 coverage. This is called identity politics and it is destroying our country from within. This is an excerpt from my 'Look to a Nation' poem: "How else do you get blacks and whites to riot, you feed them racism and you make it a steady diet."

Police brutality, systematic racism, social injustice and white privilege is a diversion tactic to direct your attention away from the real issues in the black community. What do I mean? Let me explain. I was reading and article from Fox 45 News out of Baltimore, by Chris Papst, posted on March 1, 2021, titled "City student passes 3 classes in four years, ranks near top half of class with 0.13 GPA." This is a black student by the way. He ranks 62 out of his class of 120. That means 58 students in his class has a 0.13 GPA or lower. This was appalling as I shook my head in disbelief. I asked myself, how could this even be possible? The student in question, is the son of a black single mother of (3) three, with (3) three jobs to make ends meet and to provide for her children. **WHERE IS THE FATHER?** Needless to say, my heart aches for black single mothers in the same predicament all across America. Yet, there is silence from wealthy black enablers like: Lebron James, Colin Kaepernick, Oprah Winfrey, Tyler perry, Jemele Hill, Don Lemon, Joy Reid and Snoop Dogg to name a few. These are some of the loudest mouths on issues like racism, police brutality, and social injustice. They only spew racial hate and disdain for our country, but ignore the fact of: Fatherlessness, teen pregnancy, black abortion (Legal Genocide, that's depleting the black population), crime, black on black murder, incarceration, gang violence, illiteracy and school dropout in the black community.

I have been screaming from the mountain top about these self-inflicted issues of the black community to my black race, only to be scorned and reminded about police brutality, something that hardly exist; However, with 24/7 coverage by the mainstream media, you would think police brutality is an epidemic. The black race can be gullible and emotional, this is why we accept this narrative, because the harsh reality is, it's very difficult to take responsibility for our own undoing's. Unfortunately, all across America, black ghettos are in ruins. The disheartening thing is, they are mostly governed by black democratic officials sworn to serve these communities. While republicans are complicit in this sham of humanity, as they hide behind conservative values and Christian principles. 2020 taught me a lot, but November 3, 2020, told me that there is no difference between a wolf and a wolf in sheep's clothing. We have a one-party system! Think on this question for a while, why if your party affiliation is independent, you don't have the same voting privileges equal to a democrat or republican?

I never thought I would see the day when the white male would be the most hated and scrutinized in America. Or that, patriotism would become synonymous with white supremacy. Or that, I would see so called Americans yelling death to America and bring in Communism while burning the American flag. Or Coca-Cola, a major corporation in the United States of America telling their white employees to be less white. What? Am I the only one dumbfounded? I don't have any words for this lunacy; except, when virtue leaves the room, it's replaced by chaos.

Lastly, as I digress back to my original point. **Let's be realistic, if a white man wrote a book on how black people can become a better black person, BLM, black community leaders and black pastors would be on fire. The bias media bullhorn would be more than happy to stoke the flames with 24/7 coverage.** How does a foreign entity destroy the USA without ever firing a shot? Without using brutal and bloody traditional war tactics? You use identity politics, a plan directly from The Art of War: white vs black; women vs men; left vs right; democrats vs republicans; homosexuals vs heterosexuals and poor vs wealthy. Or just write a book telling white people how to become a better white person and display it for all to see on zoom.

May God bless America,
Sonny B.

THE CASE FOR DR. BEN CARSON

"Detroit school board votes to remove Ben Carson's name from High School"
Published by Essence Magazine on November 19, 2018, by Breanna Edwards
This was my response to DSB and Essence!!!

Greetings,

I am a black man, who recently found out, the Detroit school board voted 6-1 to rename Benjamin Carson High School of Science and Medicine.

I am not a resident of Detroit; However, I am a Proud American citizen of this great nation. I was outraged at the very thought and suggestion to rename the school. I was astonished, my jaw dropped, my heart was very heavy, and my soul sickened. I sit here in tears as I write about this travesty, mockery, shameful and contemptuous act. Rather you are a democrat or republican, we should be proud as Americans for the monumental accomplishments of a world-renowned surgeon that is a citizen of the United States. One would think, if no one else gave gratitude and accolades to Dr. Ben Carson's great feat to overcome all obstacles, the black community would.

Dr. Ben Carson at the age of 33 became the youngest chief of pediatric neurosurgery in the US. He performed the only successful separation of conjoined twins, joined at the back of the head. He performed the first successful neurosurgical procedure on a fetus inside the womb. He performed the first completely successful separation of type-2 vertical craniopagus twins. Also, Dr. Carson developed new methods to treat brain stem tumors, and revitalizing hemispherectomy techniques for controlling seizures. He wrote over 100 neurosurgical publications. He was given numerous honors for his achievements throughout his career. They would make a movie called "Gifted Hands" to portray his life story. Why are these accomplishments not breathtaking to the Detroit school board? Because Dr. Carson associates himself with President Donald J. Trump, how trivial. I don't believe we can fathom what this man had to do to accomplish what he did with all of the odds stacked against him; he should be celebrated not condemned. Every black child should learn of his success story all across America, in the inner cities, especially right here in your hometown of Detroit. That is how we uplift a community, not tear it down by destroying the reputation of a black man who came out of the inner-city. I know this isn't popular, what I am saying, but it is long overdue; Therefore, I am risking backlash by telling the God honest truth. Someone needs to call on the carpet, small thinkers like those on the Detroit school board and staff members of Essence that allowed Mrs. Breanna Edwards to write about such nonsense. We as black people could be so much further along if we use the resources and freedoms this nation has already afforded us with. Not to mention the black billionaires, multimillionaires, millionaires, and even those making six figures or less, we can all play a part in saving the black community. We only serve to help tear down when we work against one another, especially against a president that has done more for the black community than any other president, that includes President Obama. We should act like civilized adults and put down our differences and hate for the greater good, for our black race of people. I can only imagine if influential people like: The Obama's, Oprah Winfrey, LeBron James, and other black professional athletes, and rappers like TI, Snoop Dogg and Ice Cube, who are living the American dream, what effect it would have on a little black boy and girl with no direction and seemingly no way out of the ghetto. If we spend more time using what we already have and less time spewing hate, bitterness and discontent. Which are all negative attributes that would bring down any people our nation, especially the black race. So, call me Uncle Tom and, coon to distinguish the difference of blacks like me from the rest of the black race, go ahead, you're no better than the black African clans who helped sell blacks into slavery. We use the white race as a scapegoat, when black people are our worse enemy. I'm fed up, sick and tired of the lies thrust out at the black race by our own people, mainstream media, professional athletes, major corporations, colleges, Hollywood, politicians, music entertainers, rap artist and those never lived as a black person in America. I will not be silent anymore; I am a man on fire! Because I realize my children and all children's future all across this great nation is at stake. If we allow these Marxist, socialist and Anti-Americans to overtake our country, this country will be doomed to fall to socialism and all freedoms lost. It's been proven time and time again that freedom, capitalism, and our Republic work, but socialism is a destroyer of any people.

Let's take a turn as I digress to talk about the many things President Trump has done for all Americans, but I want to highlight five major factors he has done for the black race. 1) He asked for the black vote, unlike the democratic party, he didn't assume we were going to vote for him because we're black. 2) He sat down with black lawmakers, black leaders, black Pastors, black entrepreneurs, black entertainers and black activist to receive council on how better serve the black community. Before I get to number 3-5, I want to bring you to the attention of the Biden/Harris duo. This duo isn't dynamic; However, they both dynamically wreaked havoc on the black race with incarceration and withheld evidence to indict blacks. Here is part of a column written by Gianno Caldwell of the New York Post, posted on July 4, 2020. Here is number 3-5 the trump administration has done for the black race, straight from the New York Post, and I quote, "His (Trump) recent police reform executive order, The First Step Act, released thousands of people from jail (90 percent of whom were black). He has promoted "opportunity zones" that incentivized private investment into marginalized communities and also increased federal funding to historically black colleges and universities by 17 percent- a total exceeding $100 million, more than any president in history. Meanwhile, the Obama administration infamously removed a two-year Bush administration program that annually funded $85 million directly to these prized institutions. As I mentioned in my book (by Gianno Caldwell) "Taken for Granted," during the 2016 election Trump did something few republicans had the courage to do, he targeted the black vote and spoke directly to the African American issues." End quote. These kinds of accomplishments are overlooked and ignored by the mainstream media and so are the riots and total chaos from BLM/Antifa thugs. Listen, I don't know what President Trump has done in the past and I won't judge him for it; However, I do know what he's done presently for this country, especially for the black community. No one is perfect, I'm sure if we opened your closet, we probably would find a skeleton or two in your closet. The question is, what are we doing today to make the world a better place?

Based on your opinions and disdain for Trump, you can risk the future of America by voting for the Biden/Harris ticket. Two progressive radicals who want to fundamentally change America. They are Anti-God, Anti-Traditional family, Anti-life, Anti-school choice and Anti-America; Therefore, as a father and a family man, make these things vitally important to me. Not to mention Biden/Harris supports a racist Marxist Black Lives Matter organization that wants to burn down this nation to get their point across. These are real concerns that I have, and true Americans have. Issues that would bring America to its demise. Why aren't we focusing on these matters? Matters that are detrimental to America.

I ask, why do we name buildings and schools after a person? We want to commemorate individual merits that honor. Well Dr. Carson was top of his class and top of his profession based on accomplishments previously mentioned. Dr. Ben Carson's name on the school can speak volumes to a black child and say to them, you don't have to be top of the class in:

Fatherlessness, teen pregnancy, abortions, black on black murder, crime, drugs, gang violence, incarceration, illiteracy and school dropout. Did anyone notice? Police brutality did not make the list. These are all self- inflicted problems that has plagued the black community for decades, governed mainly by black democratic leaders. Democratic leaders, black athletes, media and Hollywood, accuse, blame, complain, bicker, and point fingers at the white race, while white radical progressive liberals pander and enables black America to continue the denial, which only perpetuates the problems in the black community. If we shift the blame, this way we don't have to take responsibility for the woes of the black community. It's no wonder why poverty-stricken areas never get any better.

So, when I read that a black school board member named LaMar Lemmons lead the way of this vicious assault on Dr. Carson's Character, I was deeply saddened. To add insult to injury, Essence a historical black news outlet had the audacity to publish this outlandish notion and did it with arrogance as if they were making a valid point. How can any decent, levelheaded black person concur with such lunacy to renounce the name of an honorable man like Dr. Ben Carson? One would have to come to only one conclusion, hate for President Donald Trump. The bible speaks about envy being as cruel as the grave, I believe hate is a close second. I want to give a shout to the world, especially to black America: Racism comes in all colors, just because you're black, God doesn't give you a pass. I would also like to interject here, hate is of the heart and not in some monument, statue, school or building name. Radical thugs can tear them down and lawmakers can legislate names off, but if hate is still in the heart, we've done nothing to effect change.

I say to you, this is America when 9/11 happened: We joined together as countrymen of all races and mourned with our brothers and sisters across this great nation. We all were angry with the enemy from without, as there were no enemies from within who called themselves an American. There were no blue states or red states, no democrats, no republicans and no independents. No man or woman was left alone to fend for themselves, but we joined together as one Nation under God as our flags of patriotism waved in the sky. There was no kneeling to our Anthem, only standing at attention with our hands on our hearts and our heads held high as true American citizens do. We knew somehow as horrific of a tragedy it was, we all knew deep in the depths of our pain, we would get through this with God's help. That's America! 9/11 could've happened anywhere in the United States. Before retirement as a fireman, I rode the beat with a lot of cops of all races. Were there bad cops? Absolutely, but what profession doesn't have bad people? However, we shouldn't allow a few bad apples to spoil the bunch. We as firefighters and police have high energy stressful jobs, while serving the public with professionalism and composure, with sometimes split decision life and death situations. When everyone else is fleeing danger, firefighters and cops are running towards it; Therefore, I take it personal when I see these Anti-Americans and the media wanting to defund and demonize the police.

This is a little off the subject, but it explains why America is in the predicament it's in.

Someone might ask, where did the love for your neighbor and love for country go? Well, I have an answer for you. The mainstream media divided this country slowly through the years by keeping the American people ill-informed, by keeping the truth of current events away from the American people. We saw the incredible surge of lies when President Trump got into office. Never a nation been so divided since the civil war. Brothers killing Brothers, for what? Hate, hate is a powerful word of the heart, it has, it can, and it will destroy a nations common bond, the bleeding of red, white and blue. While others were mesmerized, I paid close attention, this disdain for our country came under the watchful eye of President Obama's administration. Remember, Obama allowed a multi-millionaire named Colin Kaepernick who wore a T-shirt in honor of Fidel Castro to disrespect millions of Americans who respect and love our country. Men and women died while serving our country, so that Mr. Colin could have the freedom to play a game of football. Mr. Obama should have told the young man: (kneeling on our Anthem is never the time nor the place. Your President believes in peaceful protest and standing up for what you believe but do it in a respectful way. Protesting against our country is not the way.) Instead, openly, President Obama used his influence on black America and white liberals, by condoning, welcoming and applauding Kaepernick's actions. This would begin the insurrection of the United States of America. Obama's actions and the media combined would prove to be catastrophic. In 2020, we see the results of renegades swimming in hate, discontent and disgust for this country and for anyone that doesn't have the same ideology.

Dr. Martin Luther King Jr., in the midst of AUTHENIC RACISM and INJUSTICE, wanted equality with peace, unity, and togetherness for all people. If he were alive and looked out upon our nation today, what would he say?

Lastly, Dr. Ben Carson represents black law-abiding citizens across the country. I make only one apology to the families who have lost loved ones to police brutality, no one of any race should die at the hands of cops while bound in handcuffs in police custody; However, George Floyd and others like him do not represent black America and should not be revered as an honorable martyr. Everyone wanting to rename the school has made their case, none of which justifies stripping Dr. Carson's legacy of a well deserve flagship. Can we jointly say this unjustly act is erroneous to say the least? Therefore, I say to the Detroit school board, Judge, Jury, or anyone who would bring charges to the forefront to eradicate the Benjamin Carson High School of Science and Medicine be put to rest, from the past, present and in the future. Those involved in this heinous injustice should beg for forgiveness of one of the greatest neurosurgeons of all time. Do the honest thing and make it right, apologize to him publicly because he was embarrassed publicly.

May God bless America,
Sonny B.

DUVAL COUNTY SCHOOL BOARD

Greetings Superintendent Dr. Greene, DCSB, and Leadership Team,

I am a proud black American citizen of this great country. Married to my lovely wife for over 23 years, with (6) six wonderful children together. Our children's future and the future of our nation is the reason for this little introductory. How did having the freedom to choose, become unconstitutional? In this case, another mask mandate. Governor DeSantis policy says, the parent has the right to choose rather their child wears a mask or not. Pardon me if I'm wrong, but if you want your child to wear a mask or 10 masks, put them on, that's your prerogative. If I don't want my child wearing a mask, that's my prerogative. Prayerfully out of the 26 of you receiving this message and the letter to follow, will somehow ponder the sentiments of my bleeding heart, and have a once of integrity to stand-up for the American people. The letter to follow explains my anger towards government, politicians, and the mainstream media concerning Covid-19, titled, 'Enemy of the People.'

BUSINESS INSIDER INTRODUCTORY

I am a proud black American citizen of this great country, I believe Capitol Hill and the mainstream media is instrumental in bringing to its demise, but at the moment let's consider the media. Your news outlet published an article on September 4, 2021, by Yelena Dzhanova, titled, "Florida official wants Gov. Ron DeSantis to make the controversial and unproven Covid-19 treatment ivermectin more widely available." I believe your editorial should be more responsible and to research a matter out for all of the facts before publishing a column. God forbid, but if I ever have a love one die of Covid because of false information given in the news; I'm going to make it my life's mission to sue every news outlet in America that put out misinformation concerning Covid-19. Therefore, I urge and encourage each of you, especially the editor in chief Nicholas Carlson, because the propaganda and lies are happening under your watch. Please read my letter entitled, 'Enemy of the People,' to follow this Intro. It explains it all!!!

BARTOW, FL GOV. OFFICIALS INTRODUCTORY

Greetings,

I am a proud black American law-abiding citizen of this great country. I tell you of my ethnicity to inform you that all blacks are not spellbound by the media zombie apocalypse. There was an article wrote by Yelena Dzhanova of Business Insider published on September 4, 2021, titled, "Florida official wants Gov. Ron DeSantis to make the controversial and unproven Covid-19 treatment ivermectin more widely available." This kind of headline is not only disturbing and disingenuous to me, but it pisses me off. First, it was hydroxychloroquine in the headlines for months being demonized by the mainstream media, now its ivermectin. What's disturbing to me is, these so-called journalists, either know these prescriptions work and are covering it up; Or, they haven't done any research and just repeating what national news outlets are saying. Either way, this is diabolical and reckless during a "PANDEMIC" where many lives have been lost and livelihoods wrecked forever. Following this introductory is my letter entitled, 'Enemy of the People.' This letter will explain exactly why I'm so pissed off. Just a little note, I recently sent this letter to about 26 governmental officials here in Florida, including Gov. Ron DeSantis, the FDA, CDC and NBC news who wrote an article that started me on this journey to seek answers for the action of this recklessness.

I apologize for the lengthiness of my letters, but I do not apologize for the content, so please, if you care about America and its citizens, you will read both intro. and letter in its entirety. JUST A LITTLE NOTE: THERE WAS A DUVAL COUNTY PUBLIC SCHOOL TEACHER, RECENTLY AWARDED 350K BY THE DUVAL COUNTY SCHOOL BOARD FOR DEFENDING A MARXIST, AND RACIST BLACK LIVES MATTER FLAG ABOVE HER CLASSROOM DOOR. THEREFORE, I BELIEVE, I SHOULD BE DUE A MOMENT OF YOUR TIME, FOR THIS PERTINENT MOMENT IN THE HISTORY OF OUR NATION!!! So, without further ado, I present to you, 'ENEMY OF THE PEOPLE.'

CIRCUIT JUDGE TALLAHASSEE

Greetings Judge John C. Cooper,

I am a proud black American citizen of this great nation. I want government out of my life, because it has proven over the years, how irresponsible, incapable and incompetent they are with making proper judgement on behalf of our country. We the people under the United States of America's Constitution, have a right to make our own decisions on behalf of our families, and in this case, our children. Governor Ron DeSantis' new policy prohibits mask mandates, giving each parent(s) the right to choose. In other words, if you want to wear a mask, you are at liberty to do so, and if I don't, it's my prerogative, so what's the issue here? The freedom to choose, what's unconstitutional about that? Your ruling takes away my constitutional right to choose on behalf of my child, we call that 'TOTALITARIANISM.' I have a letter to follow, that expresses my anger towards government, politicians, and the mainstream media, concerning Covid-19, titled, 'Enemy of the People.'

ENEMY OF THE PEOPLE

To: FDA, NBC and CDC,

I am a proud black American citizen of this great country, that I believe the mainstream media is trying to ruin. I tell you of my ethnicity, because I want to inform you that all blacks are not captivated, mesmerized, brainwashed and controlled by the media zombie apocalypse. This is a response to the article titled, "Stop it: FDA warns people not to take veterinary drugs to treat Covid-19." Published on August 21, 2021, by NBC's Nicole Acevedo.

I want to say from the offset as a disclaimer, I know the coronavirus is real, because it was created in the Wuhan institute of virology in China and funded by corrupt Fauci the fraud's 'Gain of Function.' However, this virus has been prostituted like a $10 dollar whore. This has become one of the greatest cover-ups since 9/11 and the media is complicit in the diabolical scheme to usher in the Great Reset. I am inflamed with great anger and fortitude to continue my fight against the propaganda and lies of the enemy of the people (media). I was saddened the other day when I heard that a long-time friend of mine succumbed to the pressures of taking the Covid vaccine. Deadly vaccines without research for short or long-term affects to the human body. However, what we can confirm about the vaccines that they are fatal to lab specimens. So fatal, those who made the vaccines refuses to get the jab; Yet, the FDA, and the CDC want all Americans to get vaxxed with the experimental vaccines, but exempt themselves, while we obey the elites. Unfortunately, many Americans have already became lab rats, and tyrannical governments all over the world are pushing hard for the rest of humanity to become an experimental project. I forewarned my friend of the dangers of the vaccines, and educated him on the therapeutics like (Ivermectin, budesonide, and hydroxychloroquine, to name a few) to treat the Wuhan virus (Covid-19). In addition to, Gov. DeSantis introduced the monoclonal clinics here in Florida as a means of prevention for the exploited Covid virus. I guess friendship and family is meaningless when you're up against love one's who are entrenched in the beguiling trance of the media. I recently contracted Covid, Ivermectin was one of the prescriptions I took to cure me of my Covid case. I am alive and well today because of it; Whereas, if I was admitted to the hospital, I would've been intubated and placed on a vent like so many thousands of Covid patients and left alone to die without being treated with the proper medications needed. So, MEDIA, you tell the FDA to STOP IT!!! And hold them accountable for the propaganda killing Americans.

Governor Ron DeSantis defied the powers that be, by making the statement, that Florida will no longer participate in lockdowns because they don't work; Also, he continued on by saying, lockdowns do hurt the citizens of America. Not to mention, lifting the God-awful mask mandate that doesn't work, it's just a control mechanism to takeaway a right to choose. Fauci the fraud, changed his story on the subject several times, one day the masks work, one day they don't. Now we come to understand that Fauci is responsible for 'gain of function'. Yet, these types of individuals the media holds in high regard. True Americans, like myself, thank God for governmental officials like Ron DeSantis who want to do the right thing for the citizens under their jurisdiction. These are the kind of patriots the media demonizes and attack character to make them unpopular with citizens of our country. It's blatantly obvious, the media bias, of how they loathe those that don't go along with their narrative and agenda to change the face of America; Whereas, they protect corrupt renegades like Andrew Cuomo posing as Americans. The fake news media are the biggest gangsters of manipulating the truth. Yes, our nation and our world would be much better off without these HYPOCRITES!!!

Isn't journalism supposed to be about checks and balances, searching a matter out to get down to the truth about a story? Let's take for instance one of the corrupt three letter agencies like the FDA, since this is the agency in question. Real news would ask the first question, how many Americans are using Ivermectin? If there is a massive amount, then why? Does it actually cure Covid? If it does, isn't that a good thing for a deadly "pandemic" (SCAMDEMIC) that has interrupted and devastated our lives for over a year? If through your research, you found that Ivermectin cured Covid. Then the final question to the FDA would be, why is the FDA strongly encouraging Americans to stop using an approved prescription for humans in the right dosage amounts that is known to kill Covid dead? But of course, how can the media hold the FDA accountable, when they are just as guilty. Here is a quote from NBC's Yahoo's article, "The agency clarified that the FDA approved ivermectin tablets meant to treat people with certain conditions caused by parasitic worms as well as topical formulations used for head lice and skin conditions like rosacea are different from the drugs used on animals. Ivermectin tablets and topical formulations for humans have "very specific doses" that are significantly smaller than the doses meant for animals." Let's use the phrase, 'VERY SPECIFIC DOSES' for example. Do you think doctors are prescribing humans with the same dosage they would prescribe for a horse? And I don't believe Americans are getting there ivermectin from a veterinarian, when your primary doctor can prescribe the medication to you, as long as he/she isn't trolled and threatened by the deep state controlled federal government. Also, the only reason anyone would call the FDA to ask a question concerning ivermectin, would be that, apparently, they are completely oblivious of the corruption of our government. In other words, why would anyone trust them with actually giving you the truth.

I had lunch with a friend; In which, we had a strong disagreement because of the enemy of the people. Hydroxychloroquine was the prescription in question. He said he wouldn't use a 60-year-old FDA approved drug because it wasn't meant for Covid. I in turn asked him, if Tylenol was known to cure cancer, you wouldn't take it because it was originally meant for relieving pain and fever? The jury is still out on his answer, typical avid CNN and MSNBC watcher, once the talking points have come to a dead end, they SIN (S: Shift the subject; I: Ignore the facts; N: Name call). I told him that this is absurd, ludicrous and you need to stop watching fake news immediately, because it has syphoned out all of your brain cells of critical thinking, logic and simple common sense.

This is exactly why I am far removed from watching fake news, even the sounds of their voices are eerily sickening because I know every other word coming out of their mouths is a lie. I can only read articles, this is the only way I can stomach it and to remind me that the mainstream media are such fabricators of the truth. News personalities have no integrity, they've lost all morals, values and virtue to be able to be truthful. I've never in my life seen so much betrayal and beguiling of the truth. It has become almost laughable, except nothing is the least bit funny. To fraud the citizens of this nation is intentionally done to deceive with a cause, with no thought of the severe repercussions it has caused. There is no hesitation to tell a bold face lie, with no sense of ethics. It's a deliberate focus to be disingenuous to the American people.

While the Communist News Network (CNN), MS(DNC) and FOX in the hen house News are allowed to speak freely, Frontline Doctors in D.C. were censored of their rights of free speech under the first amendment of the constitution. This type of strong-arm bullying is happening all across America, to whom ever opposes the communist agenda. Frontline Doctors are putting their lives, safety, careers, and livelihoods on the line to serve the American people they were sworn to treat medically to the best of their ability. The least thing I can do as a citizen of the United States of America; Is to voice my displeasure and vehement hatred for the media and the deep state system. The rhetoric and propaganda have divided our nation with purposeful identity politics, this in itself has proven to be lethal to our Republic, democracy, constitution, values, and freedoms of our nation. Well, I'm here to defy and expose the sorcery thrusted upon the common man. To fight against the tyranny with my life if necessary, because if we lose our country to communism, then we are already dead!!! 1776 REWIND!!! I cannot understand how a person can sellout their own country, for what? Money, fame, or loyalty to the CCP? There can't possibly be any love for God, country, or mankind, when your career is to create dissension with your tongue as you keep a straight face. I leave each of you with this, "It's appointed unto man once to die, and then there is judgement." (Hebrews 9:27). Yes, this means everyone will die, no exemptions, and must give an account for what he/she did on this earth. So, on your next broadcast, announcement, or article published, choose your words wisely.

May God bless America,
Sonny B.

PART II ENEMY OF THE PEOPLE

Greetings The Intercept, Washington Post and Impact Dr's,

This letter is in response to a recent article posted by The Intercept titled, "America's frontline doctors plans to open clinics as California medical board investigates founder." Subtitle, "The disinformation doctors are expanding, even as congress and state medical boards scrutinize the operation and the group founder, Simone Gold." Written by Micha Lee and published on December 20, 2021. Also, article used as a reference in The Intercept posted by Washington Post titled, "Opinion: State medical boards should punish doctors who spread false information about covid and vaccines." Written by Nick Sawyer, Eve Bloomgarden, Max Cooper, Taylor Nichols and Chris Hickie posted on September 21, 2021.

    I like to start out by revealing my ethnicity so not to be prejudged and dismissed as a racist. I am a proud black American law-abiding citizen of the greatest country in the world. I am not mesmerized by the witchcraft propaganda by news outlets like: The Intercept, Washington Post (Compost), CNN (Communist News Network), MSNBC (MS(DNC)), and FOX in the hen house news network. Local and national news outlets across the country use 'Operation Mockingbird' a tactic to deceive, program and brainwash a nation of people. We see the disingenuous, divisive, and blatantly obvious partisan trickery benefiting the liberal Marxist democratic party. Don't think for a moment that I would give the republican party a pass. The republican party is a party of wolves in sheep's clothing, using the conservative and Christian values as a prop for their platform; Nevertheless, corrupt just the same.

2020, I believe taught us all a good lesson, if you were paying attention. It schooled me on a one-party system working towards the same goal. That is to destroy America and to usher in globalism, the great reset. Using the mainstream media (Enemy of the People) as a bullhorn to divide our country through identity politics. The media conveyed to the world, that a year of 2020 riots, turmoil, havoc, mayhem, chaos, destruction, assaults, lives lost, livelihoods torn apart, and lawlessness as 'MOSTLY PEACEFUL'. One mayor would put it, "IT IS A SUMMER OF LOVE". Yet, January 6 was somehow an insurrection and attack on our democracy. Almost a year later, the media is still talking about it. The Washington Compost has a moto; "Democracy dies in darkness." That is a very true statement, but one of the most hypocritical statements I've ever seen in my life. Why? How can you make this claim, when your news outlet work so hard to keep the American people ill-informed and in the dark? Only well-trained liars can deceive a person into thinking they're getting the truth.

It's amazing to me how fake news media want to crucify Dr. Simone Gold for helping American people get through this 'PLANDEMIC'. While Fauci the fraud responsible for 'Gain of Function' is allowed to run amok continuing his sinister plan backed by the political cesspool on Capitol Hill and all of the corrupt three letter agencies like: FDA, CDC, WHO, FBI, CIA, DOJ to name a few.

I have a letter following this one that I wrote to the FDA, CDC and NBC fake news entitled 'Enemy of the People.' Giving my testimony among other revelations of how I was treated with ivermectin prescribed by a frontline doctor like Simone Gold and cured from Covid-19 (Wuhan China virus) and so was: Joe Rogan, my brother, sister-in-law, (2) brother-in laws, (3) aunts, (2) cousins and many thousands you say are being robbed out of millions of dollars. On the other hand, the experimental vaccines are useless, just ask the 97% fully vaccinated NBA players and Commissioner Adam Silver. The NFL is 95% fully vaxxed, but will no longer test for Covid-19 unless symptoms arise, I wonder why? That's a rhetorical question by the way. Not to mention, theses deadly experimental jabs have cause thousands of adverse effects to the vaccinated even death. Even with the 1% of cases being reported to VAERS are staggering enough and in another time and era, logically thinking people would've stopped this madness.

A 60-year-old cousin of my wife that was in good health passed away suddenly 2 months after being fully vaccinated. Healthy strong fully vaccinated athletes around the U.S. and world are dropping dead. If I know this, I know you generation of vipers know this, but there is not one investigation from so-called journalist and news anchors. It's stunning to me, how our country can have so many traitors among the media causing enormous discord in academia, government, sports, corporate America, Hollywood, neighbor relationships, family, friends and society in general with no accountability or repercussions because everyone is in the same bed together with the CCP. I cannot understand how a person can sellout their own country, for what? Money, fame, or loyalty to the CCP? There can't possibly be any love for God, country, or mankind, when your career is to create dissension with your tongue as you keep a straight face. I leave each of you with this, "It's appointed unto man once to die, and then there is judgement." (Hebrews 9:27). Yes, this means everyone will die, no exemptions, and must give an account for what he/she did on this earth. So, on your next broadcast, announcement, or article published, choose your words wisely, and take into account for the lives you could be destroying.

May God Bless America,
Sonny B.

DCSB SUPERINTENDENT RESPONSE TO MY EOTP

Sonny B.,

Thank you for your email to School Board regarding Duval County Public Schools' Emergency Rule on facial covering requirements for students. We have received a high volume of inquiries regarding the Emergency Rule. Please be assured that the school system gave tremendous thought and consideration into the development and implementation of this rule, including consultation with both medical experts and legal counsel. The basis for the Emergency Rule, including the medical and legal foundations, are found in the attached Emergency Rule. With respect to student requirements for facial coverings, those requirements, including consequences, will be governed by the Code of Student Conduct. The Code of Student Conduct can be found at this link https://dcps.duvalschools.org/Page/9868.

Thank you for your interest in Duval County Public Schools.

Dr. Diana Greene
Superintendent
Duval County Public Schools

MY RESPONSE TO DCSB
SUPERINTENDENT RESPONSE

Good evening, thank you for your response, usually I get dismissed as a conspiracy theorist and they don't return a response, so thank you again for having some sense of integrity. With that being said, did you read my letter titled, Enemy of the People in its entirety? If so, are you even the least bit curious about the therapeutics (cure) for the Wuhan virus (Covid-19), that the fake news media, FDA, CDC, WHO, Capitol Hill, Hospitals, Big Tech, social giants, Fauci the Fraud, Big pharma, Teachers union and Doctors are censoring, to keep this vital information from the American people? Because you did not address the cure at all. We're talking about a cure here, shouldn't that be good news, in the midst of a "PANDEMIC". No excitement, no curiosity to find the truth? If the truth was let out to the American people, this SCAMDEMIC is over. No, the elites, don't want it over, they want to continue to push the experimental vaccines, that are killing thousands of people and giving adverse effects to hundreds of thousands. Lastly, the only reason why you wouldn't take note and ponder what I'm saying, would be you're in on the cover-up to usher in the global reset. I believe you were placed in the position as superintendent for a reason, to truly care and protect the interest of our children. If you need information from credible Frontline Doctors all over the country treating patients with the cure mentioned in my first letter to you, I can send it to you. If our conversation ends here, with no investigation on your part, then maybe you weren't the right person for the job, and again, you're complicit in the cover-up; However, I will continue to move on elsewhere in my fight to save America, because I realize this is another dead end. May God bless America 🙌USA🙌 Sonny B.

LEADERSHIP TEAM FDOE

Florida Dept. of Education

Greetings,

I am a proud BLACK AMERICAN CITIZEN of this great country. I have been married to my lovely wife for over 23 years, we have six (6) wonderful children together. I realize our children's future it at stake, which is why I'm fighting so hard to save the freedoms of America. PLEASE EXCUSE THE LENGTHINESS OF BOTH LETTERS, BUT THERE IS PERTINENT INFORMATION NEEDING RESOLUTION!!! SO, PLEASE GIVE ME A MOMENT OF YOU TIME TO READ BOTH LETTERS IN IT'S ENTIRETY!!! A DUVAL COUNTY TEACHER WAS JUST AWARDED WITH 300K BY THE SCHOOL BOARD FOR DEFENDING A MARXIST AND RACIST BLACK LIVES MATTER FLAG ABOVE HER CLASSROOM DOOR; THEREFORE, I BELIEVE, THAT IN ITSELF SHOULD EARN ME A MOMENT OF YOUR TIME FOR A VERY SERIOUS AND CONCERNING MATTER!!! I sent a message to Governor DeSantis and Lt. Governor Nunez to express my thanks and appreciation for a job well done. I also sent them a letter, I'm sending you today, a letter I sent to the FDA, CDC, and NBC news for an article they published that pissed me off greatly.

I've read several articles concerning the ridiculous mask mandates; However, this is the straw that broke the camel's back. Published by news channel 8's Mike Vasilinda, posted on 8/26/21 titled, "We're not joking: Florida education commissioner defends mask policy." Instead of the media staying neutral and unbiased, the media stoked the flames to generate more fear with Covid false positive numbers, let me explain.

I recently contracted Covid as well as my brother-in-law. We both were cured of Covid with the therapeutics I mentioned in the letter to the FDA, CDC and NBC news. My brother-in-law felt 100% in his body, but went to get a post-covid test anyway, it came back POSITIVE. I told him to take another test at a different location and just as I knew it would, it came back NEGATIVE.

My brother is a RN working on a Covid floor. He said the difference in cases of post-vaccines is a significant increase of children Covid patients who received the vaccine. Pre-vaccines, the adult cases were mainly mature adults with pre-existing illnesses, now it's mature and young adults who have taken the vaccines. Is this a coincidence? Are the vaccines causing these 'Delta Variant' cases? Not to mention, in a recent article here in Jacksonville, the Impact Church had 7 deaths from Covid, all under the age of 35. The article continues on to read that the pastor pushed the vaccines to his members in early March of this year; In which, over 800 of his members were vaccinated. Were the 7 deceased vaccinated? This is the type of questions the media should be asking, but they can't because they're compromised and complicit in the whole scandal to change the face of America. So, it takes a normal Joe like me, to ask the hard questions no one wants to ask, because of negative publicity and backlash. Like every other American I was working hard to provide for my family and live in relative peace and harmony. I was living the American dream this country affords us all, no matter your color. While minding my own business, the 2020 chaos, mayhem and devastation of our economy hit. This would be a wake-up call to begin my research to see what is actually going on in our country. Well, in my journey, I have found some very disturbing issues, needing to be addressed; As a result, this would make me a man on fire!!!, destined to cause change.

A committee of one needs to look into the Covid deaths and false positive Covid tests that fabricates the Covid cases to induce fear mongering. As a law-abiding tax paying citizen, I would like some answers with results to solve the issues mentioned in my letters. Our country is going to pot under a deep state controlled and compromised Biden administration. Maricopa County will start the domino effect to prove that his presidency is a fraud, but of course the media will do their normal evil deeds to try and discredit the unprecedented proof of election fraud. This is the only way we can fix our election process before 2022 midterms and win back our country from these renegades posing as Americans. There is a connection with the virus, mostly peaceful protest (RIOTS), mask mandates, out of control border and Afghanistan to name a very few. Biden is out of control because this farce is allowed to run amok with no one holding him accountable. By the way, Duval County school board just issued a 90-day mask mandate for students. Like Broward, Alachua and other counties, will Duval be punished as well for violating Governor DeSantis mask policy? Stand with the governor and fight for the American citizens of this country and in this case, the people of Florida!!! So, without further ado, here is my letter: 'Enemy of the People.'

WILL YOU STAND WITH AMERICANS?

Letter to Plano, TX. Police Dept.

Greetings,

ATTENTION: I AM BLACK; Therefore, I cannot be categorized, and dismissed as a racist against my on people by telling the truth. However, this letter is in response to the racist, Marxist Black Lives Matter (BLM) movement allowed to inhibit traffic flow. I call the BLM movement racism in reverse. How is this right? BLM is doing the very things done to the black race for decades since the emancipation of slavery. We didn't like it, but it's ok to project hate towards the white race, because somehow, we believe it's ok because we're black or because they feel justified. As if the black race deserves some type of reparations for past sins. Let's be honest, if we all had to pay for our past sins, we all would be in trouble. I know, forgiveness can be a tough pill to swallow, but we must forgive, for our own healing. This is a quote that bears repeating, "Unforgiveness is like you ingesting poison, hoping the other person will die." By the way, injustice plus injustice, never brings about a resolve, it only equals to more injustice and total chaos. We saw the effects all throughout 2020, with no signs of slowing down; Which is why, I'm on a mission, a journey to save America from the tyranny of so- called Americans. Therefore, I put my pen to paper, and I write, this is an authentic peaceful protest through letters. This is just one example of peaceful protest expressed under the first amendment of the constitution. In other words; I do not: Block traffic, Loot, Assault police authority, Assault far-left socialist lunatics (regardless of their ignorance), cause deadly assaults, Assault fake news media (regardless of their propaganda and division), Destroy my fellow citizens businesses, Destroy/Burn down federal property, buildings, statues, monuments or vehicles, Beating unconsciously innocent by-standers defending the communistic view or murdering the lives of men, women and children by recklessly and intentionally shooting American citizens. Why? Because I am a proud black American law-abiding citizen of this great country. I am an engaging father of (6) six wonderful children with my lovely wife of 23 years, no illegitimate children here. They were all birth out of love in marriage. I am concerned about the future of this nation; Therefore, makes me very concerned for my children's future. My children are the reason why I fight, so excuse me if this letter doesn't come across to you as nice and cordial. However, if you listen with your heart, you will hear an undeniable truth, that will help put this nation back on course as the United States of America, a symbol of freedom. There is a lady, standing tall in the New York harbor as a reminder of what our country means to the world.

NO, America is not a racist country, imperfect, but not racist; When one of you race baiters and identity politic villains find a perfect country, you let me know. The only racist in this country is those pushing racism through identity politics, like: Mainstream media, Capitol Hill, Academia, Social media giants, Major corporations, Professional sports, ESPN, Hollywood and Wealthy black enablers, like: (LeBron James, Colin Kaepernick, Oprah Winfrey, Snoop Dogg, Jemele Hill, Don Lemon, and Joy Reid, to name a few). I am not oppressed by systemic racism, neither by white privilege nor social injustice. I am not afraid of police authority and never have I been. However, the black race should be afraid of the black race. Why do I say this? Let me explain, in 2019 there were 7,484 black murders, in 2020 there were at least 8,600 black murders, over 90% of those said murders in 2019 and 2020 were black on black homicides. Let's not forget, this happens every single year, a monstrosity of black-on-black killings. Numbers don't lie. You ask yourself, how is this even possible? How do you keep staggering numbers like this away from the public? Of course, you use the greatest diversion tactic in the world, YOU BRING IN THE CLOWNS!!! This lets us know how detrimental mind control can be, when there's 24/7 news coverage of racism, social injustice, and police brutality across every network. This creates chaos and division on one hand and blindness to reality on the other. I've had enough of 21st century slave masters and mind enslavement house negroes telling me how much racism is in America but ignore the real problems of the black community. Also, I love it when white liberals try and lecture me on racism in America, this is laughable to say the least. Let me be clear, there isn't any white person in this world who can educate me on being black. I sound like a broken record, because

I have to repeat myself on so many occasions; As a result, I'm beginning to feel like the 90's Chicago Bulls.

That is my introductory rant, but a much needed one, as I digress to the point of this letter. I have stood up for the men and women in blue as they endure: Slander, defunding, derogatory explicit language, no support from their police department administrations, compromised governors, mayors, and elected political officials, 24/7 trashing from the mainstream media, and assaults, even killings from BLM/Antifa thugs. I'm not foolish or ignorant to understand that cops can be puppets, controlled by the elites, but there comes a time when you have to cut the strings. Again, I have and so many others have stood with the men and women in blue; Now, will you stand with Americans? Stand with the true, hard-working and patriotic citizens abiding by the laws of the land.

What happened in Plano, TX a few days ago, happened all throughout 2020 with no repercussion as BLM/Antifa destroyed cities and created chaos all across the United States. Cops stood by and watched renegades defy the laws of the land as they blocked traffic of hard- working Americans heading to work and other destinations. Citizens should not have to exit their vehicle to deal with an angry mob, especially in the presence of cops. You have an unbelievable governor in Greg Abbott as we do in Florida under Ron DeSantis backing their police departments and citizens of their state. It's unfortunate the backlash they receive from the fake news media, socialist journalism funded by the Chinese Communist Party (CCP); Whereas they allow these governors to run amok and give a pass to this political cesspool line-up: Governor Gavin Newsom, Brian Kemp, Gretchen Whitmer and Andrew Cuomo, to name a few.

There is a system, a deep state system, a CCP system that has infiltrated and taken control of every facet in the U.S. Wreaking havoc on the first amendment by cancel culture to only let out one side of a story, their story as they spin it to their liking. They are indoctrinating generations through academia, teaching children to hate their country and have contempt for authority. This isn't freedom, land of the free, home of the brave, this is generational suicide as we watch the death of a nation.

Lastly, there is a difference between fear of the unknown and too coward to stand against a barbaric mob because of political correctness. We can't rescue this country without the men and women in blue. Police are the first line of defense against a domestic invasion; Which is why they want to defund and rid communities of police altogether. The second line of defense is our second amendment, ridding citizens of their weapons, this is a project the far-left has been working on for decades. If you rid the United States of these two major cornerstones, they can successfully bring in the brown shirts and take over the country with a Nazi-like swiftness. I will not allow this nation to go down without a fight. I leave you with a quote from Aung San Suu Kyi, "The only real prison is fear, and the only real freedom is freedom from fear." In other words, if you fear losing your job, if you fear backlash and repercussions, if you fear for your life, if you fear for your livelihood, and if you fear expressing your opinions and ideals; THEN YOU ARE NOT FREE!!! So, men and women in blue, Will you stand with Americans before it's too late?

May God bless America,
Sonny B.

THE CASE FOR OFFICER NATE SILVESTER

Greetings: Mayor Ned Burns; Idaho PD and City Council,

This letter is in response to the suspension of Officer Nate Silvester. I am a proud black American law-abiding citizen of this great country. I am an engaging father of six (6) wonderful children with my lovely wife of 23 years. I want to say from the offset, America is not a racist country, imperfect, but what country isn't? I am not oppressed by systemic racism, neither by white privilege nor social injustice. I am thankful for the freedoms this nation affords us all under the Constitution of the United States of America. I am not afraid of police authority and never have been. Yes, I've had run-in's in the past with rude nasty cops, but you don't judge all cops by a few bad apples. Everyone should take a lesson from Dr. Martin Luther King Jr., don't judge a person by the color of their skin, but by the content of their character. Now, with that being said, I tell you of my race identity to serve notice that all blacks are not gullible low information voters, ill-informed, nor mesmerized by the zombie media apocalypse. Also, since everyone is in the business of meeting demands of Black Lives Matter (BLM), rather it's beneficial to society as a whole or not, for the sake of political correctness, and not because it's the right thing to do, so will you meet my plea? Being that I am a sensible logical thinking black man and a gentleman, I cordially ask that you take a moment out of your busy schedule and read my case presented on behalf of Officer Silvester. I read in one of the articles that there was a complaint from one of the social justice warriors because of the dislike of Officer Silvester's TikTok video. Well, this is a rebuttal to that complaint, in which the contents of this letter will reveal a more disturbing problem lurking in our nation that we should be focusing on; Other than punishing a cop for something every police department across the country should be outraged about. This is one letter of many that I have written to help save America, because my children's future, and the future of America is at stake.

I've heard it said that this country would be much better off without the media. Here is a quote from Malcolm X concerning the media, "The media's the most powerful entity on earth. They have the power to make the innocent guilty and to make the guilty innocent, and that's power, because they control the minds of the masses." 35 years ago I would've disagreed with that statement. This only reveals how intelligent he was and how ignorant and naïve I was. It's amazing how father time has a way of exposing mind control, indoctrination and ignorance, if you only give way to his wisdom.

LeBron James hate and disdain for cops, caused him to act irrationally, foolishly and irresponsibly once again because he did not get the full understanding of the story. The action of LeBron is unacceptable and reckless to say the least, but I guess the Fake Woke NBA doesn't think so, because they do nothing to those who think like they do. Would you agree that the hate for cops by Lebron and many others are a direct result of 24/7 demonization of cops by the mainstream media? Officer Silvester made light of LeBron's idiotic actions in a hilarious parody video to expose LeBron's lack of accountability. Here's the irony of it all, the double standard and hypocrisy. Officer Silvester gets suspended, for what? LeBron on the other hand, puts a target on a cop by posting his picture on social media for the world to see, threatening the cop with vigilante intentions to see a cops life ended for doing his job. Silence from the NBA, Commissioner Adam Silver is a joke. A message of ZERO TOLERANCE should've been sent to LeBron and the rest of the Fake Woke professional athletes by suspending him indefinitely. Instead, we only hear the sounds of crickets. This is exactly why I am 3 years removed from all professional sports and ESPN.

Because of the propaganda, rhetoric and obvious bias news coverage by the media; We get Officer Anastasios Tsakos being tragically ran over by a lunatic named Jessica Beauvais. Mind you, Ms. Beauvais is an anti-police activist and podcast host, who told her Facebook audience to 'F' the police just hours before she struck and killed Officer Tsakos. COINCIDENCE??? This is the type of consequences we get with reckless fabricated journalism. Blacks should be afraid to walk the streets because of the police. Are you kidding me? This is the false narrative and non-sense the media is brainwashing half of America with. That white police officers have a personal vendetta against the black race.

Now, let's take a moment and examine a true and proven reality, one we don't have to manufacture, like: (Bubba Wallace, Jussie Smollett and The Covington Catholic students with a provoking native American). It's so much racism they have to conjure it up. That's called sarcasm by the way. Now, back to my original point. This is what everyone is silent on concerning the black communities and should be focusing on: FATHERLESSNESS- is the catalyst for all other self-inflicted problems in the black communities. Let me give you some: TEEN PREGNANCY, ABORTION (Legal genocide eradicating the black population, sponsored by PLANNED PARENTHOOD; Margaret Sanger's legacy lives on), BLACK ON BLACK MURDER, DRUGS, INCARCERATION, CRIME, GANG VIOLENCE, ILLITERACY, and SCHOOL DROPOUT. This reality has been going on for decades in the black communities all across America; However, the most disheartening thing is, these communities are represented by mostly black democratic elected officials.

Yet, the silence is so deafening from the Fake Woke Mob, like: LeBron James, Colin Kaepernick, Oprah Winfrey, Tyler perry, Snoop Dogg, Mainstream media, Social Giants (Facebook, Twitter, and YouTube), Academia, Major corporations, NBA, NFL, MLB, NHL, WNBA, ESPN, and BLM. However, they are quick to spread the false narrative that police brutality towards blacks is an epidemic or incredibly massive compared to any other issue. Let's talk black on black homicides, because NUMBERS DON'T LIE!!! So, here's some numbers for all you race baiters and identity politic hustlers: In 2019 there were 7,484 black murders; In 2020 there were at least 8,600 black murders. The two years mentioned, plus prior years not mentioned, over 90% of all black homicides are BLACK ON BLACK!!! Excuse my southern accent, but the slaughtering of blacks by blacks happens like this every year y'all!!! That is astounding and startling, but not one wealthy black enabler ever talks about that issue. No, they only spew hate on white America and disdain for a country that made them wealthy. Ladies and gentlemen, money does not make you happy; This is true, because I have never seen so many sour pusses and unhappy wealthy blacks in my life.

Those destroying the Republic of America, count on blacks' ignorance and emotions; As a result, they can manipulate and exploit the innocence of honest law-abiding blacks who want real change. They use the mainstream media to cover 24/7 social injustice to create a recipe for disaster; A year of violent protest by BLM and Antifa proved to us the detrimental influence of the media. The media and corrupt politicians tried to make us believe that the riots were mostly peaceful. One mayor would put, "It's a Summer of Love." Here's an excerpt from my original poem called, 'Look to a Nation,' "How else do you get whites and blacks to riot? You feed them racism and you make it a steady diet."

BLM co-founder Patrisse Khan-Cullors used millions of dollars on houses and land contributed by people, academia, corporations and businesses who thought BLM was a worthy cause. After she received backlash on social media, the social giants silenced those asking for accountability. REALLY??? This is what we call a double standard. Not to mention, all of the fund me organizations allowed monies to be funneled to this Marxist, racist, and barbaric BLM organization that destroyed cities across the country all throughout 2020. Yet, they cut off monies given to conservative causes or causes they don't support.

SUCH HYPOCRITES!!! I'm sitting here shaking my head in disbelief of what has become of our America. Whoever would've thought that patriotism would be synonymous to white supremacy. Or so-called America citizens would stomp on and burn the American flag while shouting "death to America, bring in Communism." The storyline is always a battle between good and evil. This is evil personified; they want to silence every voice that doesn't line up with their socialist ideology and let the renegades run amok. So, will someone get the courage to stand-up for Officer Silvester?

Lastly, but certainly not least. I thank God for the brave men and women who have the courage to don the police uniform in this hostile racial climate. Policing is a thankless career, serving and saving the lives of people, mostly of which, they don't even know. They have to stay under control in extreme conditions and make life or death decisions in split second situations. They have to deal with violent felons and career criminals under the scrutiny of attorneys, their own administration and elected officials. So, who wants to be a cop? I'll answer it for you, NO ONE, but everybody wants to criticize, and play Monday morning quarterback. Cops are unique individuals who want to keep the peace so that every citizen can feel safe. I am a retired fireman of Florida, I served along- side many passionate officers of all colors who put their lives in danger every day. Needless to say, with the hate, disrespect, ill-will, hostility, disgust and contempt towards cops; I would rather storm the beaches of Normandy on D-Day than to become a cop for an ungrateful society. MJ is the G.O.A.T. I rest my case.

May God bless America,
Sonny B.

MR. JOHNSON THANK YOU FOR YOUR RESPONSE

First of all, I would like to thank you for responding to me expeditiously, even responding at all, because most of the time I just get ignored without a response. Also, thank you for acknowledging my service to the community, I really appreciate that. Secondly, yes, I agree we shouldn't judge a person by one video. This is not to justify any wrong doings of Officer Silvester, but this is how the mainstream media channels the thinking of American citizens every day, consistently, repetitiously by telling part of a story, a piece of a story, half of a story, omitting words and sentences, and taking meaning out of context to make a person innocent or guilty. This is unethical, distasteful, diabolical, and disgusting to say the least. This is why I despise the media and the reason why our nation is so divided.

With that being said, I am disappointed to hear of Officer Silvester's history. I am a firm believer, if you do the crime, you should do the time, if you're wrong, you should suffer the consequences accordingly considering the severity of the circumstance. I hear you on professionalism and I would even add accountability, but you have to agree, accountability should be equal across the board. Instead of taking a situation at face value, we tend to judge a person by status, gender, political affiliation and religious preference. This is a prototype of how free speech is suppressed (Cancel Culture) and punishment is handed out. Case in point; Lebron James threatened the life of a cop, but nothing was done. What do you have to say about that?

However, some things pale in comparison and it's worth conceding. What do I mean by this? The black race is only about 12-13% of the U.S. population; Yet we are among the highest in violent crime. Case in point, there was a mass shooting in Morrell Park of Baltimore this past weekend, where five people were killed and two injured. Where is the national news on this? Communist News Network (CNN), MSNBC, and FOX. Why isn't this a huge story? Because it doesn't fit the narrative, (White cop killing a black man) does. Contrary to popular belief, police brutality is not a real issue and should not be a headline; However, the story just mentioned happens across the nation every day, THIS MY FRIEND, SHOULD BE IN THE HEADLINES 24/7. We should be inundated with this type of news if BLACK LIVES REALLY MATTERED??? Sir, I don't mean to belittle Officer Silvester's situation, but we have to accept the truth; Admit the monumental disparities of epic proportions and know when to bow out and concede to the real problem in the black community. Thanks again for your time.

May God bless America,
Sonny B.

REBUTTAL TO BYRON HEATH'S FACEBOOK POST 7/27/21

Omar Denmark Jones posted back to Byron Heath in response to his post on Simone Biles, and I quote. "Quitters never win. There is a difference between pushing through discomfort and foolishly risking injury. Fear and insecurity are not mental illness. Claiming mental illnesses, the moment something is uncomfortable is quitting and weakness. A person like that needs to strengthen their mind. Arriving to the Olympics not mentally prepared is no different than arriving physically unprepared. Ultimately Biles got control of her mind and was able to go back and win a bronze. She grew from not quitting. Hearing all of the bleeding hearts praising Biles for quitting was worse than Biles herself quitting. This country is getting weak."

Mr. Jones said it in a nutshell, but a writer always has more to say on a subject, and boy do I. Under any other circumstance, I could say bravo to Heath's post, to be fair, as I understood his intent. Let me say from the offset, I don't have an issue with mental illness, legitimate injury, or getting a medal or not getting a medal; As long as an athlete gave his/her best, I can applaud that individual. It's the unpatriotism I'm having a difficult time swallowing. I believe I can speak for most patriotic Americans, since we have the media apocalypse speaking on behalf of the fake woke. I think it was brilliant, the way Heath used the 1998 Olympics to bring about empathy to make a point. This is identical to fake news; they create an illusion to divert your attention from the real issue. They mesmerize by purposeful misinformation to draw their audience in by hypnotizing with subtle savvy, this sounds similar to a certain snake in the Garden of Eden. I've been on this earth long enough not to fall for the lights and glamour, and I hate a dog and pony show. Like the one going on presently in our country under Biden the fraud.

I'm paraphrasing Byron Heath's FB post on 7/27/21 defending Simone Biles by using the 1998 performance of Kerri Strug from a totally different era; to justify her poor performance and why Biles dropped out of the competition. He uses an era, when Americans loved their country and considered it an honor and a privilege to represent the United States of America. Here is my rebuttal to Mr. Heath's post.

There is a climate of ungratefulness, unthankfulness, and unpatriotic privilege black Americans on this fake woke journey; As a result, I can hardly stomach a post like this, or even appreciate what Heath was trying to convey. I've never seen so many, so-called Americans who take for granted the freedoms and opportunities this country affords us ALL. It's a massive amount of bellyaching, whining, bickering and complaining; While white liberals condone, coddle, enable, and pander the black offended. This only perpetuates and justifies their erroneous feelings towards this nation. I think this quote says it best, "The feeling of being used ... I guess it's better than being forgotten." (Joan L. Trejo) So, maybe it helps their insecurity, because it definitely doesn't inhibit the fact that: Fatherlessness, teen pregnancy, abortion, black on black murder, domestic abuse, drugs, gang violence, incarceration, illiteracy, and school dropout are all ignored undoing's of the black community. I'm going to scream it from the mountain top until the mainstream media and fake woke listen. All just mentioned, are self-inflicted problems that has plagued the black community for decades. Problems we can't blame on police brutality, white supremacy, white privilege, and systematic racism. I've said it before in some of my letters, no white person in the world can lecture me about being black in America. Also, no wealthy black enabler can project poverty, marginalization, oppression, fear of cops, and social injustice into my everyday life as an American of this great country. Especially when they are enjoying the highlife but are trying to convince low information blacks and whites because they are controlled by the CCP. So, stop it, for I will not become a brainwashed zombie of the ill-informed apocalypse, and I will warn everyone against you.

My pastor used to say, y'all blackness is y'all's God, in the midst of a church full of black people. In other words, when anything dealing with race is presented, essentially black and white, godly principals and Christian values go out the door. Christ teachings are no longer relevant in a conversation about police brutality (In most cases, justified police action), or voting for the candidate with a platform closest to what you say you believe in. Let's take Barrack Obama for example. Black Christians didn't care what he stood for and white liberals with guilt didn't either, as long as we got our first black president. I'll be the first to say, I longed for the day of our first black president; However, I'm sorry, but I make no apologies when I say, I did not want a black president by any means necessary. By totally disregarding my conservative ideals and religious beliefs. Some blacks are blinded by color!!! As a result, right and wrong takes backseat and skin color, preferably black, takes center stage. Everything mentioned in this letter brings me to this moment, a rebuttal of a white man's Facebook post in defense of Simone Biles quitting her Olympic events.

Byron Heath's Facebook post on 7/27/21 was sent to me, I guess to show me how I should feel about Simone Biles quitting on America and her teammates. Heath took a proud moment in history from another era and mocked it. Needless to say, Heath's post did not convince me of a sincere reason to drop out of competition; However, it does fortify my earlier statement about blacks being ungrateful. I believe Biles was too focused on social injustice matters, instead of focusing on her craft. This would lead to a poor performance for a gymnast that was picked to win gold; As a result, she was mentally embarrassed by her subpar performance and immaturity superseded her will to think rationally because of the distraction. Gwen Berry would have a similar story as she would place 2nd to last place, a horrendous showing. Not only is Berry Un-American, excuse my French, but she ain't even good.

Here is a proud moment I can get behind and celebrate. Tamyra Mensah should be a household name everyone should know and remember. She should be the face of United States Olympics. Mensah is the second women in U.S. history to win an Olympic gold medal since the inception of women's wrestling. After winning her gold medal, during an interview, she was draped and adorned with the American flag, how patriotic. It brought tears to my eyes, because it's been a while since we've seen a black American proud to represent their country. It doesn't matter what color you are, because I celebrate and support Americans, but did I mention, Mrs. Mensah is black? Again, such a proud moment in history, it's unfortunate I didn't see it in real time. Why? The unpatriotic, enough said!!! I removed myself from viewing the Olympics for the first time in my life. The Olympics was once gratifying, but now it is a disgrace, well, at least for true Americans. Also, did I mention, I am about 4 years removed from all professional sports and ESPN for the same reason? I'm so sick of the fake woke renegades posing as Americans, and the enablers who don't hold them accountable. It's principle over entertainment and I'm not buying mental illness.

LETTER TO OSU ADMINISTRATION & ALUMNI

Greeting Oklahoma State University Administration and Alumni,

I am a Black American man of the silent majority. I have had it with Marxist Anti-American attitudes. The far-left socialist not only strut their opinions, but they also shove them down your throat and do it with arrogance, daring you to challenge them. My eyes were already open to the corruption of the mainstream media and the political cesspool of Republicans and Democrats alike. News Alert: This is how President Trump got into office just in case you didn't know or refuse to acknowledge it, because the American people are tired of the political circus. In the wake of George Floyd's death, and seeing the protest turn into complete chaos with no consequences, infuriated me. These criminals were told if they went to jail that their bonds would be paid. The whole deep state system is corrupt. I agree that police brutality is wrong, and no one should die in that manner. However, Black on Black homicide is an epidemic, and we should be outraged about that as well. Of course, black on black murder doesn't the narrative to cause racial tension.

I digress to the reason for this letter, it's about Coach Mike Gundy, and a message of free speech. Due to pressure that he received from Black players, media and your administration, Coach Gundy had to apologized for wearing an OAN T-shirt. If his shirt had CNN or MSNBC as the logo, would there have been a need for an apology? This is the double standard the left is so good at, they say they are most tolerant, until you disagree with their ideology. Despite his apology, he still gets punished. Coach Mike Gundy or any coach or any citizen of America should not have to apologize because of an opinion, especially when it is the truth. There's an old saying: the truth hurts. Especially when the truth hits you square between the eyes and makes you take notice of decades of self-inflicted issues in the Black community. I'm harping on the black race since your black players were the ones who initiated this conversation, and I want your pandering white players to take note as well in hopes to lay aside the white guilt.

I will give you one example, for the sake of the many issues that plague the Black community. However, the one I'm about to mention creates a snowball effect: fatherlessness. This is an excerpt from my original writing, "Cause and Effect."

I speak in respect of those single mothers who have been thrust into single parenthood involuntarily. Thank you for doing your best to raise Black boys into Black men. We expect Black mothers to be the savior of our little Black boys, molding and shaping them into Black men. Mothers are left with the responsibility to raise their sons alone, when the responsibility was really meant for fathers. I have been saying this for a while now. This past Father's Day reiterated the importance of fathers in light of the current event that has plagued the Black community for decades. I sent out a text to as many fathers I knew both Black and White with this message: Fathers are a necessity and not an option (Happy Father's Day). Look around the Black community with your eyes and let them convince you of the truth. There's an old saying, "Numbers don't lie." Well, statistics don't either.

Beginning at the age of 6, I played three sports: basketball, baseball and football. I learned about having fun, hard work and most of all being a part of a team no matter your color. Sports was the one thing that brought races together, a nation together even the world together. This racial climate has brought destruction to sports, especially to the NFL and NBA. Sports was the only thing we had to get away from corrupt politics, fake news media and racial divide. I can't even tell you the last time I've watched the NFL, NBA and ESPN, I know at least a year and a half. What do I mean by destruction of sports? I believe I speak the sentiment of most Americans that supported sports. With the racial climate and politics in sports I can honestly say, I can care less if the NFL and NBA play another game … ever! Because of professional sports, this attitude has trickled down to the high school and collegiate levels and if you're not careful high school and college sports will succumb to the same destiny.

Lastly, I hope that this letter is a message to Coach Mike Gundy, OSU and all of America that the left and the mainstream media not only wants to silence you, but they want you to know that they own you by punishing you if you dare speak against their ideology. It's people like Coach Gundy, Drew Brees and corporations like Chick-Fil-A that they want to censor and keep silent. They make a spectacle of those that have a different opinion and they do it openly to warn others with a different view and opinion. They tell you to shut up or this is what's going to happen to you. I see the handwriting on the wall, it's them today but it's you and I tomorrow. Well, I won't be silent anymore and I'm speaking out against this tyranny. Final note, what is fame, position, title, money, when your name has been stripped of honor and dignity publicly for all the world to see? Especially when you did nothing wrong.

Thank for your attention to this matter,
Sonny B.

Below is my original poem, "Look to a Nation," which expresses how I feel about the current woes facing our nation.

LETTER TO NAOMI OSAKA

Greetings,

I am a very proud Black American citizen of this great nation. I didn't say it was perfect, but the greatest. However, name a country that is perfect? Naomi Osaka made some comments, like many black athletes do, without any regard for the full truth. They listen to a piece of a story the media only wants us to hear; In hopes to get a response of outrage from black athletes and the black race in general. I honestly believe they know; black people are the most gullible, ill-informed people on the planet. Here is what the media and the democratic party knows about the black race. Bait them with racism and we got them, hook, line and sinker. This agenda does three things, it divides a nation, it causes black victimhood and white guilt. Now that's power to control the masses. Well, I will not be mesmerized under the spell of the Marxist mainstream media. Therefore, I'm writing this letter in response to an article published in the National Review on August 30, 2020, by Dave Seminara, titled, "Tennis pauses to protest. "I must say, the ignorance caused by the fake news media, gives me unlimited material to write about. I literally can't keep up with the endless non-sense. In my research of TRUE BRUTALITY (Black on Black MURDER) I found that police brutality isn't the real issue, it's blacks killing blacks. I stumbled upon another ridiculous story about police brutality in the U.S.; Not to mention, from a tennis player who earned $37.4 million in 2019, with dual citizenship of Japan and the U.S. It's ironic, Naomi Osaka has connections with (3) three countries; Japan, U.S., and Haiti; but she only has citizenship with Japan and the U.S. I ask myself, why not with Haiti? Haiti is in desperate need of help. Why not, have a citizenship with Haiti? Assist that country with your millions and help relieve the Haitian people of inhumanity and social injustice, instead of pushing dirt on America. Case in point, this is a quote from sakala-haiti.org on-line site, and I quote: "Haiti is one of the poorest nations on earth, and this program takes place in Cite Soleil, which is the poorest neighborhood in Port Au Prince, Haiti. The children we work with are sometimes homeless and parentless. They face extreme hunger, gang violence, and high risk of AIDS/HIV. Some children lack access to school, education and safe places to play sports. Youth in Cite Soleil rarely have the opportunity to just be children." End quote.

If we are speaking in terms of disproportionate inhumanity between two countries; Yes, tennis would take a pause for America, but stop altogether for Haiti. No, police brutality I don't condone, against any race of people, not just against blacks; However, thousands of blacks are murdered at the hands of blacks every year across America. Yet, there is silence from: Naomi Osaka, Colin Kaepernick, Lebron James, Oprah Winfrey, NBA, NFL, MLB, BLM, media, politicians, major corporations, colleges, Al and Jesse to name a few. There is no outrage, civil unrest or city destroying. Black Lives Matter is just a slogan for blacks and liberal whites to have a reason to impose chaos and mayhem on hard working businesses of law-abiding citizens. Also, an opportunity to express the hate in their hearts, under the guise of wanting justice. Evil for Evil never produces a solution. After months of lawlessness, what has been accomplished? Nothing but turning away patriotic Americans like myself, from professional sports altogether.

Ms. Osaka compared police brutality to genocide. What? That is the way people think or don't think, when they don't have all the facts and they go strictly on emotions and anger. You take a term like genocide and use it loosely for every occasion. Please, let's define Genocide: the deliberate killing of a large group of people, especially those of a particular ethnic group or nation. Let's look at some examples of Genocide, shall we: The holocaust, Cambodia, Rwanda and black abortions; I know the media and Ms. Osaka would like to make the American people think that police brutality is prevalent in the U.S. to fit the narrative; BUT POLICE BRUTALITY DOES NOT MAKE THE LIST FOR GENOCIDE!!!

Lastly, enough about America, Haiti has it's on set of problems, like civil unrest, or do you care, or do you even know Ms. Osaka? This is an article from AP news, published on October 6, 2020, by Edith M. Lederer, I quote from the column, "Haiti has been roiled by street protests and economic stagnation for much of President Jovenal Moise's time in office since February 2017 as opposition leaders demand his departure. They say he has mismanaged the economy and failed to prosecute years of unbridled corruption that siphoned billions in international aid into bank accounts overseas." End quote. Police brutality is not an epidemic, but black on black murder is. I have been black in America longer than you've been alive and I can honestly say, I do not fear the police, I do not fear for my life, I am not oppressed, and America is not a racist country. Here is a News Alert, the fake news won't tell you: RACISM COMES IN ALL COLORS! JUST BECAUSE YOU'RE BLACK, GOD DOES NOT GIVE YOU A PASS! Yes, I do have a grave concern for my children's future, because of unpatriotic people that want to see my country turn into socialism, that is my fear. Reckless, mindless thinking from people like yourself living the American dream frightens me. I'm saying to myself, if their mentality is like this with millions, what is the ordinary American thinking that don't have the millions? Therefore, we can understand why the media can manipulate everyday citizens with their propaganda and rhetoric. Again, I will not be controlled by the media, I think for myself. Which is why I can say, I love America, the freedoms and opportunities this country affords us all with hard honest work and determination. Therefore, I will fight for our democracy, the constitution, values, patriotism and sovereignty of our nation. With that being said, Ms. Osaka, there is plenty for you to do in your father's homeland of Haiti, so get to work and stop hating on America!

May God bless America,
Sonny B.

LETTER TO OREGONLIVE

This letter is in response to a resent post on December 19, 2020, by OregonLive, titled "The New abnormal: Steve Duin Column. I am a proud black American citizen of this great nation. A father of (6) six awesome children with my beautiful and lovely wife of 22 years. My residence is in Florida, but I am a concerned citizen of all the states who went rogue in the 2020 nightmare under the guise to seek social justice. I want to start out by saying, where was Mr. Steve Duin's voice (8) months ago when the lawlessness began? Did he not know, if you return evil for evil, you get more evil? Maybe if more people read the bible, they would know this, also they would understand everything that is going on in our world today; For then they can become a part of the solution and not the problem. Just like the Big Bang Theory of an explosion cannot bring order; Moreover, chaos and mayhem cannot bring peace. Why is anyone surprised about what is going on in Oregon and states across the country? Savages destroying cities and lives for something that hardly even exist (police brutality and social injustice). Where are the voices for BLACK-ON-BLACK MURDER? Where are the voices for the One Thousand black babies murdered everyday through abortion? Where are the voices for FATHERLESSNESS in the black community? Because FATHERLESSNESS leads to: teen pregnancy, abortion (in which we surpass massively all other races), black on black murder, crime, gang violence, drugs, incarceration, illiteracy, and school dropout. These are all self- inflicted problems that has gone on for decades in the black community. The sad part of it all, these communities are governed by mostly black democratic politicians. But there is silence from: Lebron James, Oprah Winfrey, Tyler Perry, Snoop Dog, Ice Cube, TI, NFL,

NBA, MLB, mainstream media, etc, etc, etc, you get the point. SILIENCE FROM ALL!!!
WE CALL THAT HYPOCRISY.

To the journalists being assaulted, oh cry me a river, do you want some wine with that
cheese? So called journalist has wrecked lives all across America with their divisive propaganda.
I should be celebrating the treatment from BLM/Antifa thugs towards so called journalist, but
I won't because I still have some humanity and decency in my heart for mankind, despite the
evil divisiveness of the media. I don't wish evil on no man; However, I am a firm believer, we
do reap what we sow. There is only one thing BLM/Antifa thugs and I can agree upon, the
mainstream media is the enemy of the people!!!

Although, I tend to disagree with Steve Duin's notion of President Trump being a
malignant. He has the malignant cancers, confused with corrupt democrats and RINO's in
sheep's clothing. Let me explain, I found myself accusing democratic run states and cities for
the downfall of our country. However, as I gain more and more knowledge of the greatest
election fraud in US history, I realize democrats are not singly to blame. Also, it's republican
wolves in sheep's clothing. The media is complicit in this scandal as well, because there is
massive proof of election fraud, but the media downplays it as a nothing burger. I don't care
what side of the isle you're on, if we allow the reckless corruption of our voting process because
of a disdain for President Trump, our republic is finished, and America is done. We may as
well welcome in the CCP and North Korea. Congratulate George Soros, Bernie Sanders and
AOC for ushering in socialism or maybe that's what you want? I have to ask these things,
because I've seen stranger things these days; As a result of low information and ill-informed
people because of the media's rhetoric and propaganda.

What do liberals think? Why can't they understand? When virtue leaves the room, it's
replaced with chaos. Why do you think conservatives scream this from the mountain tops,
but we are despised by the far left for it? Do you seriously want to give Mayor Ted Wheeler
kudos for a vain attempt to finally denounce autonomous zones? When for many months,
he allowed and celebrated the radical civil disobedience and awarded the thugs with police
defunding. What? As if less cops and resources will make a brighter future. Not to mention,
the cops foolish enough to don the police uniform without the backing from their mayor were
told to stand down and allow the foolery. The police were stripped from all authority and
duty to act upon what they were sworn to uphold, to serve and protect. Now all of a sudden
no one can understand why the criminals are emboldened and your once beautiful city is
in shambles. Yet, the media and liberals blame the president for the chaos, when Trump has
pleaded with the governors and mayors to deal with the lawlessness. God forbid, if he would've
sent in the National Guard without the permission from politicians sworn to serve and protect
the citizens of their cities. The media would've been the first to call President Trump a racist

and a dictator, if he sent in the National Guard without permission; Even though, it would be his prerogative as the president to do so, especially when a person isn't doing his/her job.

Here is an article from spectrum news staff-Wisconsin dated on August 26, 2020, titled, "President Trump says he's sending federal law enforcement, additional National Guard to Wisconsin." Here is a quote from that article, "Trump said he spoke with Gov. Tony Evers and is sending federal law enforcement and the National Guard to Kenosha. He said he wants to restore "Law and order." The governor welcomed the help from the president to restore law and order. Once the National Guard hit the ground, it took less than an hour to restore order. That's what happens when you love your country and the citizens who live here, you protect the law-abiding citizens, their neighborhoods and their businesses from criminal gangsters.

In conclusion, the problem with liberals, they want their cake, and they want to eat it too. You can't support injustice for injustice and expect a good outcome, or to think it will bring a resolve. What do we expect from a city with a Persian poet named Anis Mojgani born in New Orleans and describes himself as a "Black Iranian southern boy." Yes, I'm confused as well. The liberals in Oregan, is like trying to decipher the difference between right and wrong, that's almost an impossibility.

May God bless America,
Sonny B.

LETTER TO NJ. COM/KEVIN MANAHAN/PGA

Greetings,

This letter is in response to recent column of NJ.com, titled, "UPDATE: PGA has stripped Trump Bedminster of 2022 PGA championship-Trump responds," posted by Kevin Manahan on January 10, 2021.

    I am a proud black American citizen of this great nation. A father of (6) six wonderful children with my lovely wife of 23 years. I only tell you of my race to let you know, every black person isn't a low information voter and ill-informed zombie of the media apocalypse. You see, every black person cannot be bamboozled by the George Floyd identity politics of police brutality pushed by the mainstream media 24/7 for something that hardly exist; Whereas, black on black murder is an epidemic across the nation, yet there is SILENCE!!! Around one thousand black babies are aborted everyday (murdered in the womb); As a result of abortion, the black race is no longer the minority majority, we only account for about 12% of the population and Hispanic origin about 16%. Abortion is a choice supported by the democratic party through Planned Parenthood to extinguish the black race founded by Margaret Sanger. Black on black homicides and black abortions, why no outrage and destroying cities and livelihoods for those black lives? BLACK LIVES MATTER, RIGHT? BLM is the biggest Marxist and racist organization on the planet. What? You do realize the KKK isn't the only racist organization because their white? I like to say this to my black race, RACISM COMES IN ALL COLORS, JUST BECAUSE YOU'RE BLACK, GOD DOESN'T GIVE YOU A PASS.

What has been the fault of our country's unpatriotic citizens and racial climate? The indoctrination of our children in public schools and colleges. They are not told of the dangers of socialism/communism as in the past. They show millennials on paper how inclusive socialism would be for all, especially the poor, and bury the past atrocities of a Fidel Castro's reign. How else do you get young liberal whites and offended blacks to riot? You FEED them: social injustice, systemic racism and white privilege, and make it a STEADY DIET.

It's amazing to me, after all the years I've lived in the United States, and a year of total chaos in 2020, it didn't click until several weeks ago. I always knew there was corruption lurking in the waters, but I didn't understand how deep until after hearing messages from Joshua Philipp and Mike Pompeo on the CCP takeover, which is the reason for censorship of conservative voices. Keep the American people dumb and in the dark. The identity politics played all throughout America by the media explains how the China regime will try and takeover America without firing a shot. If you divide a whole nation, you can conquer it. However, President Trump was the juggernaut not accounted for and the huge following of millions of fed-up American patriots. How do you try to oust a sitting president that could hang his hat on a thriving economy? You introduce the Wuhan virus (Covid-19), created by the Wuhan institution of virology and funded by the US during the Obama's administration. Killing the economy didn't work, it only increased the support for President Trump and anger against our corrupt politicians. Let's see, let's do a recap, demonizing the president 24/7 didn't work, unleashing the virus didn't work. Let's go for the trifecta, let's go for the greatest scandal of the century, massive election fraud. This was a domestic and international collaboration to steal a landslide victory from President Trump, while the media ignores it and treat it as a nothing burger. Mr. Manahan, we saw the election on November 3, 2020, President Trump was ahead by hundreds of thousands of votes in the battle ground states in question with 85-95% of the precincts in. Then it happened, something that has never happened in the history of an election, they were told to stop counting. This was appalling, but what was even more appalling, Biden was up the next morning. Like myself, 80 plus millions of Americans said, somebody got some explaining to do.

There are at least 50 thousand sworn affidavits from both democrats and republicans witnessing fraud; Not to mention, all of the fraud caught on camera. Mr. Manahan, you have it all wrong, the resounding electoral defeat was with the Biden/Harris duo, who couldn't draw flies even if they had dung smeared completely over their entire bodies. Trump on the other hand had record crowds at all of his rallies, BUT BIDEN GOT MORE VOTES THAN PRESIDENT OBAMA? By the way, did you know, NY Post published an article about Trump vs Biden? It was titled, "How Trump- not Biden- has helped make black lives better," by Gianno Caldwell, posted on July 4, 2020. You should look it up and read it.

Among the many things President Trump has done for this country, there are some great accomplishments done for the black race coming from a racist (we call that sarcasm).

How did Trump incite the riot or as the article put it fueled the riot in the Nation's Capitol? Let me give you a couple of democrats fueling violence. "If you see a Trump cabinet member in public, let them know they're not welcome here," a quote from Maxine Waters. "When they go low, we kick them. That's what this new democratic party is about," quote from former Attorney General Eric Holder. Those are both real examples of fueling violence. The media takes a story and just runs with it, they don't care if it's the truth or not as long as it stokes division. I remind you; it doesn't take much for the deceitful media to run with a narrative, just ask the Covington Catholic student, Nick Sandmann. Trump Tweeted out to the everyone, with a message of understanding of our hurt and pain from the election scandal, but said, violence is not the way we do things, go home in peace. Why did Twitter take down a message of peace? I'll tell you why, we call that suppression of free speech and hiding the real truth to push propaganda and rhetoric of Trump fueling violence.

Let's talk about violence, what happened on January 6, 2020, was vastly disproportionate to the violence and chaos that went on for about 8 months with BLM/Antifa. The lawlessness, murders, assaults, destruction, and mayhem across the country by BLM/Antifa, again for at least 8 months was applauded and celebrated as mostly peaceful from the media. A democratic mayor would call the riots, "A summer of love." Yet, the same media and people who did nothing to eradicate the violence, are the same one's crying bloody murder for a moment of disorder, such HYPOCRISY!!! It's been over 4 years of non-stop bashing of the president; However, he is popular among the common man because we despised democrats, republicans and the media, but LOVE OUR COUNTRY. We understand now more than ever in 2021, they are the enemy of the people (common man). People hate the president because the media told them to, and they've never even met the man. There is a grotesque political lackluster, lackadaisical attitude towards the American people; In other words, politicians (democrats and republicans) don't give a crap about the common citizens of our country. Let's take the 2nd stimulus bill for example, we have millions of hurting Americans, every penny should be going to the American people; Instead, a large majority is going to foreign countries and other non-related items. President Trump redlined all of the pork approved by the congress and the senate and suggested more money for the American people. Needless to say, that part of the bill is still on the desks of the POLITICAL HIJACKERS!!! Convincing media zombies of Trump's many successes are practically an impossibility. So, when I read articles like NJ. Com, with the PGA, NFL, NBA, and people like Kevin Manahan, you embolden the Capitol Hill political gangsters. I can't help but shake my head at the infantile mentality of some of the people in this nation.

Lastly, it is shameful, disheartening and disgraceful to say the least, to see how the PGA and the political cesspool has turned their backs on the president. I say to that, finally we have a president not part of the deep states Great Reset (New World Order). I believe I speak for many millions of Americans when I say, I will fight next to President Trump in a fox hole to war against the enemies of America, domestic and foreign at any given time. I don't care if you are democrat, republican, independent, humanitarian or libertarian, you should be furious about the CCP assault on our nation, unless you are complicit in it. If we were to allow the attack on our election process to just pass as if nothing ever happened, we may as well welcome in North Korea and Communist China. Then congratulate George Soros, Bernie Sanders and AOC for ushering in socialism. However, why do I get the feeling half of the country has no clue what socialism/communism is all about. When you have BLM/Antifa thugs yelling death to America, and bring in communism, while burning the American flag. This treasonous and unpatriotic act at one time was only done by radical Islamic terrorist. Now it's done routinely by so called American citizens. It was said, America would be better off without the media or at least if they just told the truth. It's blatantly obvious the media is on the side of the far-left socialist. Malcolm X made a profound statement concerning the media, and I quote," The media's the most powerful entity on earth. They have the power to make the innocent guilty and to make the guilty innocent, and that's power, because they control the minds of the masses."

May God bless America,
Sonny B.

AN UNLIKELY RELATIONSHIP

I'm writing this based on an article in Mashed.com, titled "The untold truth of Martha and Snoop" written by Joel Stice on August 8, 2018, and updated on November 30, 2021. Yes, I am behind time on this story, simply because I dismissed this relationship or should I say TV show as utterly ridiculous. The show I'm speaking of is 'Martha and Snoop's potluck dinner party'. Anyone that know me, know I love everything food. However, after conjuring up the sanity to watch the show, I could only watch about 30 seconds. I guess I fell into the typical stereotype blackhole I believe we can all fall into when we prejudge.

I read quite a bit, and this is how I get my newsworthy fix because I cannot stomach even 1 second of listening to the Marxist mainstream media. I came across this article on December 28, 2021, and I'm glad I did, because this proves, validates, legitimize and authenticates all of my letters and writings. If America is a racist nation, and the white race is inherently evil and racist, while the black race is pathetic and weak, how do you get a loving relationship like this? Two polar opposites in color and culture but coming together with care and respect. I acknowledge there is racism, but any racist you find is ignorant and should be avoided like the plague. Furthermore, racism isn't just a one race commodity, as if the white race has somehow cornered the market on the subject according to BLM and BLM supporters. Here is a statement, BLM and every BLM sympathizer should take note of, 'Racism comes in all colors, just because you're black, God does not give you a pass.'

Who would've thought that their show would survive one season, not to mention two? I know I didn't and if you were honest, you either. The column speaks about their real, sincere care for one another. A west coast gansta rapper, and a domestic goddess would hook-up. Yes, I agree, it does sound far-fetched and absurd as the journalist would put it, but that's the beautifulness of humanity. The problem arises when we allow the media to dictate and form our thinking on race relations and holding on to the past with a death grip. We have positive results, when we respect, love and care for each other, no matter the color, race, gender, creed or nationality background. Whenever you are gaslighted by the media, just take a moment to settle down and think before you act irrationally (RIOT). For example, ask yourself, why does the media have such a fixation on a white cop killing a black person, when there are so many thousands of other cases: Like, black on black homicides?

Again, their relationship is proof all white people aren't inherently evil and racist and black people can subdue their disdain for the white race. Let's be frank, racism is learned. It's learned by intentional lessons, cultural stereotypes passed down from generation to generation, academia indoctrination, Communist foes and 24/7 subliminal messaging by the Marxist media (Enemy of the people). Where there is one story of racism, rather made up (Jussie Smollett) or real, there is a hundred like Martha and Snoop. I will not be controlled by the media; they will not convince me to be a pessimist. I choose with my own mind to be an optimist and see the good in humanity. I leave you with a quote that should make anyone ponder and rethink on the notion of racism by President Abraham Lincoln, "Those who look for the bad in people will surely find it." In other words, if you always look for racism around every corner, you will find it every time, and it very well maybe your own. Life is short, why waste it on the stupidity of someone else's hate.

CRITICAL RACE THEORY

What is critical race theory (CRT) in a nutshell? Do you want the truth? Or do you want to hear the misinformation and rhetoric the progressives try to drive deep into our psyche? Okay, I'll give it to you straight, because I don't like to filibuster around, something Capitol Hill has become experts at. CRT says white people are inherently evil and black people are weak and pathetic. Another method to put us back centuries and to destroy true progression to see a better world; Whereas, in this case, a better America. It is more legal indoctrination of our youth in academia from K-12th. Unfortunately, CRT is already taught and has infiltrated the collegiate level; which is why mostly peaceful protest (RIOTS) are a prerequisite for getting a college degree. What ever happened to learning your craft or skill to become the best at your job, or simply providing life lessons on having good work ethics? Work ethics, that says, if you're scheduled to work, you have an obligation to your employer and co-workers to at least show up. May I add, showing up is the first hurdle employers must face across the country; The second, is doing an honorable and commendable days' work everyone can be proud of. I guess this would be too much to ask, from millennials needing a safe space.

I guess you can hear my sarcasm, frustration and indignation in my writing; Yes, I'm inflamed, exasperated and infuriated to say the least. I've heard it said, we can't get weary in well doing, but I tell you, sometimes it can be exhausting protecting virtue from those who want to destroy value through outlandish wiles. It seems like every other day, there is some new tactic thrown into society to change the face of America. Therefore, we must be vigilant in this fight, stand up for what we believe is right, or else our nation will be overtaken by renegades posing as Americans.

American communist has mastered the art of identity politics, taking two subjects that would normally get along with one another and cause them to oppose one another, even despise their country. Please!!! Can someone tell me, if you hate your country, why do you want to represent the United States of America in the Olympics? That is why blacks take center stage on identity politics whenever racism or social injustice is mentioned. We are so busy living in the civil rights and slavery days, there's no time for living in the present and exploring the American dream this country affords us all. We allow race baiters like: CNN, MSNBC, Al, Jesse, Colin Kaepernick, LeBron James, Oprah Winfrey and Tyler Perry to name a very few, to tell us we're downtrodden with no hope of leaving their pre-conceived modern-day plantation. It's amazing to see, just how many blacks say that the republican party is racist but are hard-core democrats. Blacks vote religiously for the democratic party that wanted to keep us enslaved. Their tactics are different, but yield the same results, enslavement, now it's of the mind. Blacks haven't learned yet, the elites see us as a lab rat project for their disposal to be prostituted for their socialist agenda and Great Reset. If blacks' undoing's didn't benefit their political movement and order of business, the black race would be useless to the democratic party. Democrats want to expand, which is why they want open borders for more votes. It's all about power, and they don't care how they accomplish it.

National Geographic put out a study saying, fireworks are racist because smoke disproportionately harms black people, this kind of thinking is insane. Yet, during the fireworks in question, in Chicago this past fourth of July, 80 blacks were shot and 14 killed, so you tell me what's more hazardous to the black race? Not to mention, 41 percent of Baltimore high school students have a 1.0 GPA or less (I WONDER HOW MANY ARE BLACK?), shouldn't the teachers unions be focusing on this, instead of CRT? CRT is just another scheme to divert the attention from the real crisis in the black community, like: Fatherlessness, teen pregnancy, abortion, black on black murder, drug addiction, gang violence, domestic abuse, incarceration, school drop-out and illiteracy. These are all self-inflicted problems that has plagued the black community for decades. CRT, social injustice, systemic racism, white privilege, police brutality and oppression, does not make the list of problems in the black community. Sadly enough, these same communities are represented by mostly black democratic elected officials. So, BLM/Antifa thugs can assault and threaten conservatives and Big Tech can try to censor our voices by taking away free speech; However, it will not change the fact or the reality of the cultural problems within the black race.

Why are we not talking about Michaela DePrince? Because she doesn't fit the narrative. Here was a little black girl, called the devil's child, was rescued from a war-torn South African town by a **WHITE AMERICAN COUPLE**. This would change the trajectory of her life forever. Once unwanted, now she's a loved, beautiful, amazing and a talented ballet dancer hidden from the black race. Why doesn't this story get 24/7 coverage by the fake news media? Because they want to keep the country divided, they want blacks to believe they are victims, oppressed and should be terrified of police authority every second of our lives. **This is such HOGWASH!!!**

Lastly, there are so many stories like Michaela's heart-felt, heart-warming and life changing encounter; However, the only stories that deserves publicity in the eyes of communist, are career criminals evading and disrespecting cops to keep up the image of black inferiority and white supremacy. It's no wonder why black brilliant minds are suppressed, never to blossom into the God given talent we were created for. I say to you, this is intentionally done to keep young black minds in the gutter and enslaved in the mind with no hope in sight. The black race is fed propaganda consistently through the mainstream media, social media, academia, sports, major corporations and funded by the Chinese Communist Party. This is why so many success stories never come to fruition, because blacks are told on a regular basis that the American dream is unattainable through subliminal messages given throughout a child's lifespan. By the time they become an adult, they think: All cops are racist, whites are bigots, they hate their country, they see racism in everyone else except themselves, the American dream is unachievable, and they vehemently proclaim victimhood, it's a recipe for disaster. So, you tell me, who are the real racist? I give you the answer, those pushing identity politics and CRT to try an immobilize and control a whole race of people of color. May God Bless America, Sonny B.

PLEASE!!! END MASK MANDATE

Greetings Mayor Lenny Curry and City Council,

I am a proud black American citizen of this great country. I am a father of (6) six wonderful children with my lovely and beautiful wife of 22 years. This letter is to Mayor Lenny Curry and the whole city council, in regard to the mask mandate. Governor Ron DeSantis proposed a mask mandate lift on November 30, 2020, for the state of Florida. I am pleading with the mayor and city council to stand up for the citizens and businesses of Jacksonville. As a free man of the United States of America and citizen of our great city, please comply with the mask lift, by using the media to reverse this madness they've help cause. I don't want to be told from government how to live my life. Especially, while democratic politicians like Governor Gavin Newsom and other elected officials attend a dinner party at the exquisite French Laundry without social distancing or mask. The false narrative of mask protection is pushed by the democratic mainstream media (enemy of the people), to project fear into the American people. This is why I despise the media because they are liars, deceitful, diabolical, and dividers of our nation. With their propaganda and rhetoric, we see the catastrophic devastation of very high racial tensions going on presently in our country. The media has become very cunning in throwing the rock and hiding their hand. Malcolm X, I believed summed up the media best, I quote, "The media's the most powerful entity on earth. They have the power to make the innocent guilty and to make the guilty innocent, and that's power, because they control the minds of the masses."

It has been proven scientifically, that mask does not protect you from the Wuhan, China virus (Covid-19), but the government wants us to believe otherwise. They also told us casinos and abortion clinics were essential, REALLY? We go into a restaurant with mask on, but we take them off the whole time while we're eating, does the virus not attack while we're eating? That's a rhetorical question by the way. Hypothetically speaking, if the mask does protect as the government and media says it does, then those wanting to continue to wear the mask, then let them wear them. However, I do not want to wear a mask, and do not want to be told to, it's my life, right? Laws tell women, it's their body and their right to have an abortion (murder unborn babies), but I don't have a choice to wear an irritating, oxygen depriving mask. The NFL gives penalties and fines for disrespecting the referees, but it's ok to disrespect the National Anthem and flag. This is a good example of calling wrong, right and calling right, wrong, the lawmakers and officials really have their priorities in order; That's called sarcasm by the way.

Listen, I'm not saying the virus isn't real, but I am saying that this virus has been propagandized and prostituted like a .50 cent whore and you know it. Why do I say this? One of the many successes of President Trump was, he could hang his hat on a flourishing economy. The democratic socialist, republican establishment, foreign foes, and mainstream media were enraged with this success, because it didn't come by the chosen one (Barack Obama). Millions of Americans have and are suffering because of a disdain for President Trump. What? Do you think we're blind and can't see the obvious contempt for the president? All Americans are not ill-informed and foolish because we ditched the fake news media a long time ago, Fox included; As a result of REAL NEWS we've come to the realization of the political games played by both political party affiliations, which is why we need a new political party for the patriots. For instance, we know about the different therapeutics to treat patients with the coronavirus. Unfortunately, the therapeutics are blocked by: FDA, CDC, WHO, politicians, big pharma, hospitals, hospital ER's, pharmacies and told by the media that therapeutics are more harmful than the virus itself. Not to mention, Big Tech: Twitter, YouTube, Facebook and Instagram censor the very information given to help and inform the American people. Because of this grotesque willful negligence, people are allowed to die, to promote fear and destroy the economy. Why? Again, for a hatred for the president and lack of concern for the citizens of America. The media is complicit in the success of this well thought out wicked scheme.

FEAR, FEAR, FEAR!!! Program the American people to correlate Covid-19 cases with death. Speak fear 24/7, so when the virus becomes ineffective of actually taking lives, the brainwashing will be complete, Covid cases and deaths are now synonymous. Let me give you an example of the mass mind control: People I know have shunned the idea of therapeutics because they say it wasn't made for Covid-19. I'm literally arguing the fact by saying, if extra strength Tylenol cures Covid-19, who cares if it was made for fever, aches and pain, if it cures Covid-19, bring on the Tylenol. No changing their minds from the mesmerizing spell of the media. What lunacy!!! Again, if the virus was so deadly, why aren't the homeless dropping like flies? Their immune system, I would image would be compromised due to lack of a proper nutritional diet and doctor's visits. I pass by them all the time going through downtown, there is no social distancing or mask, since the pandemic (scamdemic) started. I'm quite sure, if there were massive homeless deaths, the lying media would've told us by now. So why do citizens with balanced nutritional eating habits and regular doctor's visits, need to social distance and wear a mask? Again, not to mention, shut down the whole economy!!! I was born, but I wasn't born yesterday. Here we are in December, and some states like California want another round of economy shut down, I'm calling shenanigans. Ladies and gentlemen, we've been duped, and bamboozled.

The media predicted another surge of virus cases several months ago. How do they know? Sweden was ridiculed for not shutting down their economy. Why didn't Japan get scorned for not shutting down their economy? I'll answer if for you, because the media and the world know that Japan doesn't care what they think. Sweden, a country of 10.2 million people only had 6,681 deaths because of the virus. Please understand, I am not belittling the loss of life by any means, I believe every life is precious even though BLM/Antifa doesn't think so. This is a quote from worldlifeexpectancy.com, "According to the latest WHO data published in 2018 influenza and pneumonia deaths in Sweden reached 2,701 or 3.57% of total deaths. "This is pretty close to half of the covid deaths in Sweden. Let's talk about influenza and pneumonia in the U.S., there are between 60-80 thousand deaths every year, but there isn't 24/7 coverage of those deaths and fear mongering. This says to me there were other underlying causes of deaths in other situations, other than Covid-19. Again, the media trying to finagle information to hide the truth. For example, hospitals using Covid-19 as the actual cause of death to receive more money from the state and to pad the death toll to increase fear. Call me a conspiracy theorist, but I believe everyone was in on one of the greatest scandals of our time. What? Was I the only one who paid attention to the eagerness of the media to increase the death toll? Now, they are reporting cases, with no death toll, why? Because they don't have to, again cases and deaths are synonymous, mission accomplished.

Lastly, before the proof of massive voter fraud of the general/presidential election, I thought the virus was the biggest hoax of the century. I thought to myself, how can the assault on the presidency of Donald Trump get any worse? By an assault on the Republic and freedoms of the United States of America. BLM/Antifa democratic thugs yelling death to America and saying bring in communism, while burning the American flag. This act was once only seen by radical Islamic terrorist, now the unpatriotic act is done by so called Americans (enemies from within courtesy of the media and foreign foes). With that being said, PLEASE, PLEASE, PLEASE!!! DO NOT COWER AND FALTER UNDER THE PRESSURE OF PROPAGANDA, RHETORIC AND DECEIT OF THE LYING MAINSTREAM MEDIA OR TO THE PEOPLE UNDER THEIR SPELL OF WITCHCRAFT. END THE MASK MANDATE AND PUSH A THERAPEUTIC MANDATE FOR OUR CITY!!! Meaning, make it mandatory for the media and healthcare officials to educate the American people on therapeutic options. This would end fear, give a relief and a real cure for the hard-working, law-abiding citizens of Jacksonville. Thank you for your attention to this urgent matter.

May God bless America,
Sonny B.

THANK YOU FOR OPENING OUR CITY AND STATE

Greetings Governor DeSantis and Mayor Curry,

I am a proud black American, law-abiding citizen of this great country and appreciative of the freedoms this nation affords us all. I like to reveal my ethnicity to let you know all black people are not mesmerized by the mind control of the media. We are not all low information voters, nor are we all ignorant, ill-informed and oblivious to what's going on in our nation. No, I am not oppressed by systemic racism, social injustice and white privilege. I am not petrified of cops and never have I been.

Now, with that off my chest, let me proceed to the purpose of this letter. I am quick to write, when there is an issue that needs addressing; Therefore, I should be just as vigilant to take note of virtuous efforts and address them accordingly as well. I'm quite sure you both are inundated with a plethora of problems and complaints in need of immediate attention. I, on the other hand with this letter, want to say thank you Governor Ron DeSantis and Mayor Lenny Curry for your valiant efforts given to serve the citizens under your leadership. This can be a daunting task given the civil unrest, the racial tension and political correctness overshadowing our constitution.

I never purchased a real mask and never intended to, because I was never going to accept the new normal. I realize God made us fearfully and wonderfully, with an immune system to ward off sickness, diseases, and viruses. God never intended for us to have a permanent mask plastered to our face and social distancing from all human contact, bonding and connection with other human beings. This is an example of fear mongering, brainwashing, propaganda, rhetoric and disservice the mainstream media provides to the American people, which is why I no longer tune in to their lies. I thought the definition of journalism was, finding, creating, editing, and publishing the truth, without spinning the story for political biases or political advantage. It has become blatantly obvious to those who are truly awake, which side the fake news media has chosen to be on and it's not the conservative rational side. Which is how you get mostly peaceful and a summer of love, out of chaos and mayhem all throughout 2020. The media fed us travesty to distort the reality of what we were really seeing, as if we were imbecile's or infants in need of constant nurturing to survive.

2020, and now 2021 has proved to us the importance of local and state level government. Those elected officials who are closest to us can make our lives miserable or pleasant. Especially, when we have to rely on a presidential election that has no integrity and no transparency. What happened on November 3, 2020, was a monumental failure of our election process and an assault on our Republic. The 2020 election was stolen by: international interference, compromised dominion machines, corrupt democrats and RINO's, kangaroo courts across the country, Captain kangaroo (The United States Supreme court), fake mail-in ballots, after hours ballot counting, election workers and officials, deep state, social giants and complicity of the mainstream media. Anyone, doubting this notion, ask yourself this question, why would the fake news media be screaming bloody murder and the democratic party instrumental in sending 73 attorneys to Maricopa County to stop the forensic auditing of the 2020 presidential election, if there wasn't anything to hide? Again, this was a collaboration of domestic and foreign interference, and it must be fixed before we can move on to 2022 and 2024.

Covid-19 (Wuhan virus) was spread to the world by the Chinese Communist Party (CCP), with intent of a global reset by well calculated international heads scheming together to overthrow a global beacon of freedom, the United States of America. There are many facets and people of our country willing to sellout our Republic for a price. The love of money truly is the root of all evil and this is evil personified. I've been out of work for the first time in 41 years because of the Wuhan virus. So, I guess you can say that the virus made me, angered me and woke me up to the reality of our country's desperate need for being rescued from its demise. As we experience covid and identity politics, coupled with the 24/7 media bullhorn as the engine pushing for socialism, we cannot waiver in our faith in God to turn our nation around. We need real politicians standing in the gap with true patriots fighting for America. Again, thank you for opening our state and city, defying the scrutiny and pressures of the media (Enemy of the people).

May God bless America,
Sonny B.

THANK YOU, MR. GOVERNOR

Greetings Gov. Ron DeSantis,

I'm sending you this letter by way of mail because I want you to have a hardcopy to touch and feel, and to share with your staff as a constant reminder that there are still patriotic citizens in America that love their country. In addition, we have a vehement hatred for RINO's and socialist Dem's, that I just distinguished, but really, they are the same. One is a wolf and the other a wolf in sheep's clothing, both renegades posing as Americans. Our country is on life support, 'We the People,' and the few uncompromised governmental officials with God's intervention are here to revive our beloved nation. I believe there are millions of Americans like myself who are tired of the old establishment ruining our country by catering to lobbyist and the deep state for their own personal gain. Playing politics, democrats pointing the finger at republicans and republicans pointing the finger at democrats, divide the citizens with the media circus, while politicians on Capitol Hill conquer. People are waking up and that is what the elites are afraid of. The movement President Trump started only increased when the country saw the 2020 election stolen in plain sight, along with a rogue administration wreaking havoc presently on our nation. There was a domestic and international collaboration to shred our Republic. As the media ignores and denies the atrocity with arrogance. They feel they're untouchable, because they have been allowed to run amok for so long, but this bible scripture comes to mind, "When the sentence for a crime is not quickly carried out, people's hearts are filled with schemes to do wrong." (Ecclesiastes 8:11 NIV). In time, everyone will be judged and punished that had a hand in this treasonous act. They should spend the rest of their lives in GITMO or be hung. Anything less than this, would be an insult to the citizens who once had confidence in our election process. If this grotesque injustice isn't fixed, American freedom is finished.

I digress, who am I? A proud black American law-abiding citizen with six wonderful children with my lovely wife of 24 years in the greatest country in the world, the rogue totalitarian Biden regime is deliberately trying to destroy, and hand over to the CCP. Elections has consequences, but stolen elections have severe consequences. We are in a fight for the soul of this nation, for the future of our children and generations to come. Therefore, as a husband and a father, I fight with vigor and passion, willing to die for what I believe. I tell you of my ethnicity to assure you, all blacks are not ignorant and ill-informed. Governor, you don't need any convincing based on the excellent selection of our recent surgeon general, which speaks volumes about your character.

The disingenuous news coverage of the local and national media has divided our nation, is an understatement to say the least. I have my own mind and couldn't be influenced by the media's non-stop 24/7 support of a Marxist and racist BLM organization in 2020. Furthermore, even though the fake news media won't say it, I will, Antifa are the real terrorist and insurrectionist, not the patriotic citizens on January 6. Gov. DeSantis, you said January 6 is the democrats Christmas, which was well said, and I say in addition to that statement, a year of civil disobedience, lawlessness, destruction, chaos, violent and deadly assaults in 2020 of mostly peaceful riots is the crucifixion; that's how enormously disproportionately ridiculous the two instances are miles apart. Anyone saying any different is insane and should be sentenced to a mental asylum for life.

Becoming a political official can be a thankless job, especially when you actually work on behalf of the people. The lame-stream media makes sure the life of an honest politician becomes hell on earth, while years of deep state political corruption is held in high regard; Like: Biden, the Clintons, Pelosi, Fauci and Maxine Waters, to name a very few. I've led people and students as an athletic director. I always strived to lead with my heart for the benefit of the athletic program as a whole. I can tell you, when you get accused falsely while trying to do a job honestly, with good intent, it doesn't feel good, and it hurts. Therefore, I can only imagine the weight of the world on your shoulders dealing with millions of people depending on your leadership and guidance. Therefore, my family and I want to give you a sincere thanks for your genuine efforts to retain law and order, restore election integrity, freedom and patriotism in our country, especially our state. Yes, Florida is the freest state, and for that, we are so very grateful.

Governor, you remind me of the real President, Donald J. Trump, just more subtle in your choice of words. Needless to say, I don't have a problem with either temperament as long as I know you're fighting on behalf of 'We the People.' I realize the PLANDEMIC has destroyed many lives and purposely sabotaged a thriving economy under President Trump. However, governor, you have weathered the storm and opened our state despite the continual backlash from the fake news media. I've written to you several times; Needless to say, the one entitled 'Enemy of the People' explains in great detail of my understanding of the Wuhan virus and disdain for how this virus has been prostituted. Therefore, I won't belabor the point.

In conclusion, I realize it takes an amazing staff alongside you to wade through the political cesspool and zombie media apocalypse to successfully run an entire state. In addition, it takes a great leader in yourself to make it all come together and support from your family. I appreciate your sacrifice and allegiance to our country and for that I am eternally grateful. Our country is infiltrated with Marxist who hate America and wants to destroy and totally disregard our constitution. We hear and see your daily fight against tyranny. Again, thank you Mr. Governor for standing up for 'We the People.' Please send our regards to your wife, we're praying for her speedy recovery. The masks are as useless as Joe Biden!!! Let's Go Brandon!!! 1776 Rewind!!! And may God bless America and may God bless you, your staff and your family Mr. Governor.

WWG1WGA,
Sonny B.

ENSHRINE J.R. SMITH'S WORDS

J.R. Smith could flick it, that's shoot the basketball in old school terms. The only problem with J.R. was playing for the Cleveland Cav's alongside LeBron, a player I do not like for his fake wokeness. He is one of the main reasons I do not watch the NBA. The other reasons are explained within my book of why I am about 5 years removed from all professional sports and ESPN.

Let's move on because this writing has nothing to do with the fake woke; well, actually it has everything to do with the fake woke and how they influence society inside the black culture. J.R. Smith said some things on an episode of 'I am Athlete' about the black race I believe should be very noteworthy. His words should be held in high regard and encapsulated inside a shrine to remind the black race of our ancestors' mindset.

In 2021 the Marxist mainstream media highlighted the 100-year anniversary of Black Wallstreet or should I say highlighted the atrocity of the Tuskegee massacre. Need I say, this was intentionally done to stir-up more racial tensions to an already volatile society on the verge of 'Civil War.' I'm not saying forget what happened, because we should never forget lest we repeat it. Which is why I'm set against name changing and tearing down monuments tied to the confederate. I've said it before and I'll say it again, racism and hate are of the heart. We can spend millions on name changing and tearing down history, but until there's a heart change, there will be no change. Since these senseless legislations to erase history is in the interest of the black race, I'll say, there will be no change in the black race until there's a heart change. Here's a little note or should I say a huge note? 'Racism comes in all colors, just because you're black, God does not give you a pass.' So, why not let the main focus be on highlighting the brilliance of the black race and what we've accomplished despite racism. In other words, let's stop focusing on the color of evil to push an agenda and recognize that evil is just evil, no matter who does it.

Let's just be honest, this isn't about democrat vs republican, right vs left, black vs white, or vaxxed vs unvaxxed, this is about a deep state system wanting to control all Americans through identity politics for the purpose of a Global agenda or should I say the Great Reset, New World Order. Don't believe me, just look at the way the Wuhan China virus has been handled and used to control and mandate unconstitutional extremes, or should I say Ukraine virus? What? You thought it was about keeping grandma safe? If that was the case those corrupt governors wouldn't have thrown known covid granny cases back into the nursing homes to kill off the rest of the grannies. There were about 50 thousand nursing homes residents who lost their lives as a result of their sinister actions, yet the Marxist media is silent. With stories like Black Wallstreet, they want the black race to see America as a racist nation and to hate all white people. In addition, they want to see the white race pander after the black race as they drown in their white guilt. As a black person, if you secretly desire to see the white race suffer, to become inferior or bow down to the blackness, I ask this question, how are you any different than the KKK? A black person under the mask to hide your identity and shame of catastrophic hate.

Before we move on to J.R's words, I would like to clarify some things and the way I feel about Eurocentric and Afrocentric thinking. I am not a fan of either, because I believe they both focus on a preeminent mentality that one is above another. However, in the terms of having your race best interest at heart is a necessary attribute in order for your race to progress as a whole. An attribute in desperate need inside the black race as J.R. alludes to this in his conversation. Some might criticize J.R. and say, he did what he wanted to do most of his career, but now all of a sudden, he wants to become the savior. Let's look at it in a positive aspect, he got it, but most black professional athletes never get it, and he now wants to right his wrongs. I digress to the purpose of this writing.

The question was asked of J.R. Smith in a conversation on a 'I am Athlete' episode, what is your next move in life? Here is the long version of that answer in his own words. Note: These are not grammatical errors, but a message in his own words.

"My next move is to change is to change as many minds who look like us, back to the Afrocentric mindset. Everything we're just talkin bout right now, after he jumps on that grenade, who's gonna follow him? We are so trained and embedded to have that Eurocentric mindset, worry about myself, worry about me, worry about mines. I'm not gonna help no one else who looks like me build up. When everybody else does it, but us. When you made over a 100 million dollars in your career right, is 105 gone change? Is 110 gonna change your lifestyle? Realistically, you know how many people who you can change lifestyles with 10 million dollars in our hood? In our communities?"

"We were in the bubble, and George Floyd happens, we stopped playin, what we gone ask the owners for? What we gonna ask the owners for?!!! Stop asking them for s##t! What are we asking them for? I went down the line, no bulls##t, you can ask these dudes or not, I got Paul George sitting right here, I got DeMar DeRozan sittin right here, I got Russell Westbrook sittin right here. I'm literally sitting next to all these dudes who are LA guys. I'm like bro, I'm not counting your chips, but everybody else is, you make 200, you make 200, you make 175, you make 150, and you make 180 (My side note: That's million). Why y'all don't have your own gym? Why we gotta go to UCLA in LA to work out every time? Y'all all come from the exact same community, you wanna inspire kids that look like you. All it takes is 5 of us 5, 250, 250, 250, 250 (That's thousand), what bank gonna turn us down? We bout to build this s##t out for our whole community, we gone build gyms, rec centers, start leagues, and all the s##t. And who's gone stop us?"

"We got the money, but we don't have the mindset. Our mindset, we'll rather throw 60K in the f#cking club, in the strip club, go throw 60K in a strip club than go feed 2500 people in the hood. Think about, I've done it, I can't sit here and say y'all a hypocrite. I've done it myself; I've thrown money in the club, I've literally thrown money blindlessly, aimlessly, drunk, I had a ball. Now I sit back and say, I'm a stupid a## nigg#. I could've fed my whole community 10 times over, but I was wrapped into me. I had that Eurocentric mindset, I need this designer jacket, I need these jeans, I need this bookbag, I need to be looking like this cause the vets got this, I want this car, why? Who am I impressing? I'm not even fulfilled with me."

Brandon Marshall asked J.R., when did that click for you? "It clicked for me probably a year after we won the chip (Championship). A year after we won the chip, I felt like I had everything, but I still wasn't whole with me, because I knew there was still something missing. For a long time, I went through bad depression because I couldn't figure out what it was. I've always had the mission because my parents instilled in me, help people who look like me, it was always about the kids. When I was growing up with my pops, it was always about the kids. I always wanted to do something like that. I was tired of putting my name on it and not being on the forefront. Know what I'm sayin? I was tired of talking about it and not being a person walkin it. I can't tell you to help out with this, this and that if I'm not doing it." You can see the rest on, 'I am Athlete' Season 3: Episode 19.

What is the moral of the story? We are all going to experience tragedy in some manner, shape or form, but what you do with it, is up to you. You can complain, riot, hate and look for someone else to change the situation or you can step up and be that change. So, what's stopping us? We have more black millionaires and billionaires today than our ancestors could have ever dreamed of. The difference of the past to the present, our ancestors didn't have the opportunities the black race squanders today, but our ancestors kept a positive mindset to achieve what looked to be impossible under the circumstances, but they overcame. We are reaping the benefits on the backs of our ancestors, but a lot of us can't enjoy it because we have allowed the media to manipulate and control the way the black race think. In addition, most of those who have made it, only think of themselves. Therefore, the vicious cycle progresses as we continue to live in a paradigm of victimhood and blaming the white race for our undoing's.

COMMENTS TO U.S. SUPREME COURT OSHA LETTER

Greetings PIO and U.S. Supreme Court Justices,

Please accuse my rant as I express my grievances over a totalitarian ridiculous and unconstitutional deadly experimental vaccine mandate before I digress to the reason for my comments. I am a proud black American law-abiding citizen of the greatest country in the world the rogue Biden regime is deliberately trying to destroy. Also, I resent how my black race is exploited for a political agenda. I never thought I would see the day when Marxism would run rampant all throughout our beautiful nation. I believe this is the reason our forefathers left us with the constitution to combat such sinister acts. Here's the problem, when you have a lawless society that arrogantly ignore and defy the law because lawlessness is allowed to run amok, you get a year of 2020 chaos, violent assaults, civil disobedience, and destruction the media called mostly peaceful. The constitution was always meant for 'We the People', not for the president, the political cesspool on Capitol Hill, governmental agencies (ex, OSHA, FDA, CDC), the court system, major corporations, academia, professional sports, music industry, Hollywood, Big Tech, Big PHARMA, insurance companies, nor foreign entities to dictate control of the United States of America. While the media bullhorn (Enemy of the People) orchestrates the Chinese Communist Party (CCP) hostile takeover by using a curable virus and identity politics. A very curable and treatable virus if treatment isn't delayed or blocked. LET ME EXPLAIN!!!

We learned that Fauci the fraud was instrumental in 'Gain of Function' and funded by our corrupt government and supported by the CCP. We who understand completely what's going on, call it the Wuhan China virus, better known by fake news as Covid-19 or is it the Delta variant, or is it the omicron, or the omicron BA.2, or maybe the flurona, no it has to be the Deltacrom. Do you see how absurd this has become? This is literally a clown show, a three-ring circus. The most disheartening thing is, we have all of the FAKE WOKE watching this in real time, while enjoying the circus destroying our freedoms because of the mesmerizing witchcraft spell of the Marxist media.

PROOF, PROOF AND MORE PROOF!!! Like Joe Rogan, I too had Covid-19 and many others in my family. We were all treated by and cured by ivermectin. Yes, ivermectin a 40yo FDA approved prescription that has been: blocked, vilified, censored, and demonized as a horse dewormer with lethal ramifications if used by humans. In addition, this wonder drug was given a Nobel prize in 2015 for its amazing multi-healing attributes. Now we've learned, NFL star Aaron Rodgers took the advice of Joe Rogan to take ivermectin for covid, AS WELL AS THE NFL SECRETLY!!! BUT AARON RODGERS EXPOSED THEM!!! On the other hand, the experimental vaccines are useless, just ask the 97% fully vaccinated NBA players and Commissioner Adam Silver. The NFL is 95% fully vaxxed, but will no longer test for Covid-19 unless symptoms arise, I wonder why? That's a rhetorical question by the way. Furthermore, over 80 million asymptomatic American workers have to test weekly if they deny the foreign substance into their bodies, the ingredients the diabolical pharmaceutical companies won't reveal for many decades from now. SERIOUSLY???

Here is a headline for you to ponder, "Fully vaccinated Mississippi Sheriff found dead in his home after positive Covid-19 test". This article was published by Black Enterprise and written by Charlene Rhinehart posted on August 7, 2021. I was shocked when I found this column because the media is hiding the thousands of deaths and adverse effects from the experimental vaccines. The late Colin Powell was fully vaccinated and died of covid, so why is the government demanding the jab for the entire country except for a select few? Like Capitol Hill.

Lastly, if this is the greatest "Pandemic" the world has ever seen; then why are they blocking, censoring, hiding and vilifying the cures, while hiding staggering numbers of vaccine deaths and adverse effects? Think about it, if they were really concerned for human lives, shouldn't they want to exhaust every possibility known to mankind to get rid of this deadly virus killing millions of people worldwide? There is going to be hell to pay when the rest of the nation finally wakes up from the zombie media apocalypse and realize there never should've been a "Pandemic". Prayerfully GITMO will await everyone that had a hand in this PLANDEMIC!!! I'm asking OSHA administrators to stop the lunacy of vaccine mandates, masks that don't work but harm those who wear them and covid test altogether for asymptomatic workers. If you care anything about the livelihood and humanity of the American people and the constitution, STOP THE DICTATORSHIP THAT HAS NOTHING TO DO WITH SCIENCE. "If science can't be questioned, it's not science anymore, it's propaganda and that's the truth." -Aaron Rodgers. 1776REWIND!!! Masks are as useless as Joe Biden!!! Let's Go Brandon!!! And may God bless America because we sure do need him now!!! Thank you for your attention to this matter.

Sonny B.

COVID, THE REAL TRUTH

Greetings TCB Staff,

This letter is in regard to the truth about Covid-19 (Wuhan-virus). My apologies for the lengthiness of this letter, but there is vital information about the Covid-19 scandal, I believe you need to hear and share with your members as well. If you already know this information, then it is conformation, if not, then I believe God wants you to be intellectually informed. So, please allow me a moment of your time as I lay out my case. I am a proud black American citizen of this great nation. Husband to my lovely wife for over 23 years and an engaged father to our (6) six wonderful children together; Whom three presently attend and three graduated from TCA.

I'm in the process of completing my book, to help save America from the tyrannical renegades who call themselves Americans. I understand the urgency and the responsibility, we as Christians must carry to preserve the future of our children. This country affords us many freedoms under the constitution, no matter your race. Corrupt politicians on Capitol Hill are trying to dismantle our republic under the pretense of protecting blacks from: Social injustice, and police brutality, while pushing Critical Race Theory, race baiting and the likes, and instituting what we call identity politics. These tactics have served to divide our nation and it is intentionally done through the liberal fake news media. Well, I'm fed up with the diabolical scheme to change the face of America. I see the socialist agenda being push by the progressive far left as their voice is allowed to be heard, as they censor the free speech of the conservatives/Christians. Through my book, I'm giving a wake-up call as a black American tired of my race being used as a modern-day slave, by those posing as our allies.

A Christian friend made a cowardly observation by saying to me, that the content of my book would get me attacked and assaulted, because of my strong conservative views and Christian values. I responded, "If our country is that far gone, where I have to fear conveying moral free speech, then I am dead already, and my children's future is in jeopardy of becoming endangered." Looking back at the chaos of 2020 up until now, I say to you, yes, this nation has gotten that far. I've even heard the excuse, that Jesus is soon to return, this is true, but Jesus said to occupy until I come. In other words, get off the couch, get off the church pew and get busy doing My will until I return. However, I will say as Nehemiah did as he built the wall in the midst of his enemies, "I am doing a great work and I cannot come down." (Nehemiah 6:3).

Identity politics has plagued our nation for decades funded by the CCP (Chinese Communist Party). If this is foreign intel to you, then you are nowhere near the fight. The far-left have been legislating policies to undermine our constitution, republic and freedoms of our country; While the church was asleep, or should I say, too busy with programs, concerts, conferences and meetings. It would take one dedicated, committed atheist, Madalyn O'Hair to single handedly destroy the very foundation of our nation by getting prayer out of schools, as Christians entertained one another in churches. As we say, the rest is history.

Socialist, would reach the pinnacle of unpatriotism, defied authority in the form of Black Lives Matter (BLM) and Antifa mobs would destroy cities and livelihoods across the nation under the guise of caring for black lives. Yes, George Floyd would become the face of a radical, Marxist and racist movement called BLM. Just in case you doubt me and dismiss me as an Uncle Tom, let me provide some statistics. In 2019, there were 7,484 black murders. In 2020, there were at least 8,600 black murders. Including these two years and prior to, over 90% of those said murders were BLACK- ON- BLACK. Somehow through 24/7 media coverage, they have convinced the church that police brutality is the problem in the black community. Police brutality does not even make the list of problems in black neighborhoods. Let me tell you what does: Fatherlessness, black- on- black homicides, teen pregnancy, abortion, domestic abuse, drugs, gang violence, incarceration, school dropout, and illiteracy. These are all self-inflicted problems that has plagued the black community for decades. The most disheartening thing is, these neighborhoods all over the country are represented by mostly black democratic elected officials, while republicans watch, as they become equally at fault.

Not to mention, the silence is deafening from: Mainstream media, Colin Kaepernick,

LeBron James, Oprah Winfrey, Tyler Perry, Ice Cube, Snoop Dogg, TI, Don Lemon, Joy Reid, Gwen Berry, Naomi Osaka, Simone Biles, NBA, NFL, MLB, major corporations, academia, and the church. We've been sold a bill of goods, to think that the black race is oppressed, slaughtered in the streets by white cops and should fear every moment of our lives in America. If truth be told, corrupt politicians, white liberals, offended blacks, fake news media, and the CCP are dismantling the U.S.

I digress, to the general point of this letter. I believe fear and over exaggeration brings the Covid-19 virus to your doorstep; However, my case is an exception, I believe the Lord allowed me to contract the virus so that I could have my own testimony of therapeutic treatment for Covid-19. Ladies and gentlemen, THERE IS A CURE!!! But corrupt politicians, Fauci, FDA, CDC, WHO, Big Tech, Big Pharma, doctors, hospitals and mainstream media have managed to keep it away from most of the American people by censoring and threatening those like the frontline Doctors. This was the new headline on Sunday 8/1/21, "Florida sets a record with 21,683 cases reported Saturday, the CDC says." Bring on another round of fearmongering. They are furious with governors like Ron DeSantis who opened up their states and told the corrupt politicians, we are no longer shutting down our economy, because it doesn't work, but does hurt the citizens of our country. If you rely on the fake news headlines without doing your own research, you will be manipulated into brainwashing mind control and attacking those trying to educate you on the truth. Yes, the virus is real, because it was manufactured in the Wuhan institute of virology in China and funded by immoral politicians in DC. Also, I'm saying, that this virus has been prostituted like a $10 whore to shut down churches, kill the economy, and control the American citizens for a political agenda. They want to seize the opportunity of a global reset, to try an push the green new deal and usher in the new world order. Ask yourself the question, why are they pushing an FDA unapproved experimental vaccine? Because it's not a true vaccine. There have been thousands of deaths from this covid shot that we know of and thousands having adverse effects from the shot. I have a relative of mine that just passed away mysteriously at the age of 60 after taking the vaccine two months ago, the same length of time Hank Aaron lived before dying, after taking the vaccine. All I have to say is, Bill Gates spoke about depopulation of the human race, because he felt like there were too many people on earth. Gates was one of the biggest investors of the vaccine, I'm calling foul on my relative's death and maybe even Hank Aaron's.

Something else to think about. Politicians used the media to fabricate the covid numbers to paint the narrative that the world was in a pandemic. The fact of the matter was, those that were truly diagnosed with covid were neglected. Hospitals neglected proper treatment to increase the death toll. If you still have faith in a deep state-controlled Capitol Hill, then I have some Enron stock that I want to sell you. This is how wicked their scheme is, regardless of rather hospitals gives proper treatment or not; FEMA pays hospitals a hefty sum of over $13,000, just for receiving covid patients, and receive over $40,000 for placing covid patients on the vent. I know first-hand, after the hospital received my aunt, doctors immediately wanted to place her on the vent, which is a death wish. We went to combat with the doctors to keep my aunt off the vent, thanks be to God, she is alive today because of our intervention to keep her from being intubated.

I believe sincere churches like Trinity Baptist are stuck in the middle of the politically correct world-wind. Which is why, I'm writing you this message. To remind you, that we as Christians, the remnant must stand up and fight back against this assault on the freedom of our nation and our faith. Acts 17:30 says, "And the times of this ignorance God winked at; but now commandeth all men everywhere to repent." In other words, God let it slide because we didn't know better, but now that you know, He wants you to do something about it. He doesn't want you to be ignorant and ill-informed of the truth. Now that you know; God requires obedience and a response with righteous indignation.

We play right into the hands of the enemy, when we shut our churches down. Satan wants, fellowship, hugs, handshakes and human touch to disappear. This goes totally against the word of God, which states, "Not forsaking the assembling of ourselves together, as the manner of some is; but exhorting one another: and so much more, as ye see the day approaching." (Hebrews 10:25). Jesus is soon to return and, satan knows his end is near; Therefore, he uses the media and anyone that will allow him to shut down churches with propaganda and lies. Satan knows we have the only real answer for the world, sometimes I believe we don't know it. We draw strength from one another as we assemble together. The live stream has its place, but true anointing and strength comes when we come together. If the church continues to take the opposite approach of Shadrach, Meshach and Abednego, how will we defeat satan's kingdom if we bow down to the system of this world. I remind you, we are in this world, but not a part of it; Therefore, the government does not have a right to coerce, encourage, nor dictate when the people of God can attend church. Walmart was essential, Casinos were essential, planned parenthood was essential, but the church isn't? I have one better for you, if this virus was as deadly as they say it is, wouldn't there be massive deaths of the homeless; Their immune systems are compromised. I'm quite sure, most, if not all don't have a primary doctor. They don't social distance and they don't wear a mask. Every time I go through downtown, the homeless are gathered together, but no deaths, they have totally disregarded this SCAMDEMIC!!! Not to mention, the secret hair appointments and dinner parties by dishonest politicians during the "pandemic" while churches were on locked down along with the economy crashing to a screeching halt. These same politicians are saying to the American people, Do as I say, not as I do!!! SUCH HYPOCRISY!!!

Lastly, I leave with a quote from Aung San Suu Kyi, to sum up this message, "The only real prison is fear, and the only real freedom is freedom from fear." In other words, if you fear opening your church, if you fear losing your members, if you fear the government, if you fear the media, backlash and repercussions, if you fear for your life, if you fear losing your livelihood, if you fear expressing your opinions and ideals, and if you fear expressing your faith in Jesus Christ; THEN YOU ARE NOT FREE!!! May God bless America.

Respectfully submitted,
Sonny B

FIGHTING FOR HUMANITY
To the Brotherhood

Greetings,

I want to start out by saying, you have done an amazing job with the brotherhood and I'm proud to be a part. I realize you have a team of people who have been instrumental in making it go, but it never had the success it has today until you became president. I would like to say thank you for your hard work and dedication to a thankless job. With that being said.

I learned of McArthur's sudden death on Tuesday, I normally sleep like a baby that has been well fed with a dry pamper and tucked in for the night, but I haven't been able to sleep since the news. I am writing this letter at 2:39 in the morning. I assure you this isn't a political stunt, because I hate politicians, democrats and republicans, they equally along with the disingenuous mainstream media (locally and nationally) have done the American people a disservice to say the least.

I write for eyeonjacksonville.com as a guest writer, everything I've written is going into my book and has a purpose, meaning: I've written to mayors, governors, city council, political representatives, school boards, media, sheriff offices, etc, etc, locally and across the country to save the soul of our nation, because our nation is on life support. However, 'We the People' like myself is fighting with everything within me to revive it. I'm willing to die for what I believe in, which is, God, family and country, because if we lose the freedom of life, liberty and the pursuit of happiness, then we are dead already. I don't have to spell it out for you, you see the Great Reset in progress, not just in the U.S., but all over the world, courtesy of the Wuhan China virus AKA Covid-19 (or is it the Delta-variant, omicron, omicron BA.2, flurona, deltacron, stealth omicron and now an HIV-variant) they're not going to let it go. We're going into the third year of this virus, WHERE HAS THE FLU GONE? I've heard it said, the virus is the new world order. I see the handwriting on the wall, but I will not roll over and let it happen. Even though, lawlessness is allowed to run amok, the wicked are calling right wrong and calling wrong right, I will stand for the truth. I believe everything dealing with the virus is in connection with Klaus Schwab's depopulation plan to usher in Globalism and bring down the constitution of the United States.

There is another recent death, the sudden death of Michael Freeland of an aneurysm as the article would explain, is alarming and puzzling to me; However, the sudden death of a good friend (McArthur) would put my curiosity into motion, especially because of what I already know about the experimental vaccines. Furthermore, my wife had a cousin that died suddenly of a heart attack, and my yard guy's 24-year-old assistant would die suddenly of a heart attack as well. The common denominator of the 4 deaths of healthy individuals is that they were all fully vaccinated. I'm contacting you because I know you are in favor of the vaccines, but let me be clear, this letter isn't accusatory in anyway, or to bring fear nor to say you did anything wrong. I know it's a lot to digest. This letter is to only ask you to have an open mind, step back, examine and put aside everything you've been told for a minute and look at the way the virus has been handled from a different perspective. There is a New York union leader who is having some reservations about the vaccines after 3 recent deaths on their fire department that could have ties to the vaccines. He is having the cases investigated. (The article will be in the reference section below).

I'm not saying you're going to feel this way, but everyone I speak to who has been vaccinated, makes this comment. They all say I'm doing fine after my vaccinations, but I say that's awesome, and I pray nothing ever happens. However, just because you haven't had any effects or witnessed any effects or don't even realize the possibility of injury from the vaccine, doesn't mean injury or death doesn't exist. We can't see gravity, but it doesn't care if you don't know it exist, gravity is lethal to anyone jumping from a 150-story building, and it doesn't discriminate. I continue on by saying, if you had a talk with the family members who have experienced death and life changing adverse reactions to the vaccines, I believe would bring a greater understanding, but is that possible? Which is why I'm an advocate for the therapeutics like ivermectin, the media, government, Big Tech and Big PHARMA is hiding, blocking, vilifying, censoring, and demonizing as harmful to humans with severe or lethal implications. Like Joe Rogan, Aaron Rogers, the NFL secretly, congress and congresses family members secretly, my 81-year-old mother with pre-existing conditions, and about 7 other family members, thousands of others worldwide, I TOO had Covid-19, was prescribed, treated and cured by ivermectin.

The last time I checked, VAERS recorded about 12,304 deaths from the vaccines and God only knows the real number of adverse effects from the vaccines. Medical professionals say only about 1% of covid vaccine deaths and injuries get reported, because people don't suspect the vaccines. Why? Because they have been told over and over that the covid vaccines are safe. Nevertheless, even if the numbers were at 100%, this should be very concerning for vaccines they deem as safe. Which is why I believe in my heart of hearts that there are 4 deaths I personally know of mentioned in this letter wasn't or will not be recorded to VAERS. There is a commercial I believe is appropriate for this part of the conversation. The commercial starts out by saying to a gentleman that over a 100 thousand bicycle deaths occur as a result of vehicle accidents. The question is given to him, do you think that's too many? If so, how many bicycle accident deaths do you think is acceptable? The gentleman, says about 50, by this time 50 members of his family comes out, and the last question is asked. Now is 50 acceptable? He answers, no zero. In other words, if the deaths are going to involve any of my family members, then zero is the only acceptable number.

Many people all over the world, not just in the U.S. are sharing their horror stories of covid vaccine injuries on social media, but Big Tech is snatching them down as fast as they get put up. Why is this? What are they trying to hide? That's a question we all must ask when we're hit with the truth. You can dismiss me as a conspiracy theorist and that would be ok, but I ask that you at least do a deeper investigation into everything I've said, if you choose to dismiss any of my beliefs spoken in this letter. It's been said, 'Truth is like a Lion, let it loose and it will defend itself.' Well, I'm freeing the Lion every time I believe God is inspiring me to do so. I don't want any blood on my hands when I could've at least helped someone see the truth.

Lastly, I have so much more to say, but I will end this letter here, because I'm putting 2 more letters in attachments for you to read that will explain in detail what's been going on while American citizens were asleep and why I'm fighting with every fiber in my being. The first is why I became an 'Information warrior,' written for eye on Jacksonville. The second is 'Enemy of the People' written to the corrupt CDC, FDA and dishonest NBC news for true disinformation. Please, I ask you to take the time to read both in its entirety, I write under my nickname Sonny B. I'm putting doctors to research, articles to read and websites that uncover the nefarious acts of our government complementary of the deep state and the CCP in the reference section below as well for you to dig into. I'm highlighting one of the doctors, Dr. Robert Malone the inventor of the mRNA, who went on Joe Rogan's podcast with skepticism for the covid vaccines and was banned from all of his platforms for medical misinformation. Why? Because they do not want any of us to make an informed decision, but they would rather make the decisions for us through the deep state/CCP controlled media to push their narrative. 1776REWIND!!! May God bless America, Sonny B.

Here are some references of just a few frontline doctors, articles and websites of proof mentioned in this letter:

I. Frontline doctors (Advocating for therapeutics like: ivermectin, budesonide and hydroxychloroquine)

   A) Dr. Richard Bartlett
   B) Dr. Simone Gold
   C) Dr. Robert Malone

II. Articles

   A) Ivermectin: a multifaceted drug of Nobel prize-honored distinction with indicated efficacy against a new global scourge, Covid-19. Published by Sciencedirect.com in September 2021.
   B) Researchers call for access to ivermectin for young children. Published by wwarn.org on March 18, 2021.
   C) FDNY union head seeks investigation into recent Dept. deaths and covid jabs. Published by redvoicemedia.com on February 22, 2022, by Gregory Hoyt
   D) Baby of fully vaccinated mom dies after born bleeding from mouth, nose: VAERS report. Published by lifesitenews.com on December 10, 2021, with 8 more reports in same article.
   E) NBA player got blood clots from covid vaccine that ends his season- NBA told him to keep it quiet. Published by thegatewaypundit.com on October 14, 2021, by Jim Hoft.
   F) Fully vaccinated man dies from Covid-19 after month in hospital. Published by whsv. com on October 12, 2021, by WPBF staff.

III. Websites

   A) americasfrontlinedoctors.org
   B) vaxxchoice.com
   C) budesonideworks.com
   D) banners4freedom.com

LETTER TO DENVER POLICE DEPT ...

Greetings Denver Police Department, Mark R. Levin, Michelle Malkin, Mayor Hancock, Governor Polis,

I am a proud Black American patriot of the United States of America. I first of all want to thank Mr. Mark Levin for his continuous stand to save America. Mark Levin called out Nancy Pelosi in reference to her silence on an attack from BLM/Antifa thugs. I don't blame Pelosi for her silence, because we've come to expect evil things from this corrupt politician. However, for police to stand around and do nothing to help Mrs. Michelle Malkin as she is being assaulted at an event that is pro-police is mind blowing. There are true Americans all across the nation that support cops, to see this travesty happen to a true fellow American was a major disappointment. Although I wasn't in attendance to the pro-police event. However, as a true American, the evil act was as if it happened to me. Mrs. Michelle Malkin like others were there in Denver in support of the police department and this is the thanks she gets, a bunch of gutless cops standing around while Macklin is being brutally assaulted. If this is the heartless attitude of the Denver Police Department should be defunded and dismantled; I understand Police departments in democratic states and cities are told to stand down. I say to the Denver Police Department, what do you have to lose? Democratic states and cities want you defunded and eradicated anyway. It's amazing to me how conservative voices are moved away quickly from similar situations of non-violence, but BLM, Antifa gangsters all allowed to have free reign wherever they desire. I am of the silent majority, but silent no more. I am a man on fire, to protect our Constitution, democracy, values, and patriotism of America.

I have joined arms with countless Americans seeking justice for the Conservative voice. Fake news mainstream media has done a good job keeping the American people ill-informed; thereby, dividing America. Fake news, leave part of a story out, cut a valuable sentence out and show you only what they want you see and hear. How can you call police brutality an epidemic when it's only a handful of incidences? Because the media told you so. If Black lives really matter, why doesn't the media report the onslaught of Black-on-Black homicide? Because the media doesn't want the American people to know that this is the real issue. Journalist Andrew C. McCarthy of National Review wrote an article on June 25, 2020, about Black-on-Black murders. He stated that the 2.570 Black on Black murders in 2015 was a complete understatement. The number that year were much higher.

No anger, no outrage, not a peep from Fake News, politicians, pro-athletes, college athletes, colleges, Al, Jessie, Hollywood, major corporations and especially the Black community. Why? Because Black lives really don't matter. Police brutality, a white police officer killing a Black man, is only a tool to push the corrupt democratic agenda to dismantle America. Well, I am not letting the ship go down without a fight. Lastly, this is a grotesque injustice. I pray Michelle Malkin hires an attorney and sue the city of Denver for so much money, they will name the city after her.

May God Bless America.
Truly we need Him.
Sonny B.

THE CASE FOR 'RIGHT TO TRY'

Greetings,

The case for 'Right to Try' off label brands like: hydroxychloroquine, ivermectin and budesonide for Covid-19. This letter may come across like I'm ranting or rambling, but the lunacy of a totalitarian rogue Biden administration is conjoined chaos leading to a communist agenda, set out to destroy our freedoms under the constitution. Examples are: Blocking, demonizing, censoring, and hiding proven treatments of Covid-19 (Wuhan virus), mask mandates, mandatory covid vaccines, open borders, retraction of foreign trade policies, foreign oil dependency once again, against voter ID, against school choice, CRT curriculum mandate, monoclonal clinic Biden takeover (I believe to sabotage an already successful and safe program), and a Afghanistan debacle; these are just some of the acts of tyranny, and just a few acts of plain stupidity against the sovereignty of our nation and the list goes on for an incompetent administration compromised by Ukraine and China. I know some may disagree, but you can't say our country is better under Biden and keep a straight face. YES, I AM PISSED OFF!!! I believe the plethora of issues mentioned in this letter will all make sense in the end. So, please follow me as I make my case for 'Right to Try'. MY APOLOGIES FOR THE LENGTHINESS OF THIS LETTER BUT I DO NOT APOLOGIZE FOR ITS CONTENT, AND AS A LAW-ABIDING TAX PAYING CITIZEN, I BELIEVE EACH OF YOU OWE ME THE COURTESY OF READING AND ADDRESSING MY LETTER.

I want to say from the off-set, I really do appreciate governmental officials like: Gov. Ron DeSantis, Rep. Majorie Taylor Greene, Rep. Vernon Jones and Gov. Kristi Noem that don't cower from the deep state pressure and media backlash. It takes courage and integrity to stand in the midst of false ridicule and accusations attacking your character. I applaud you all for your tenacity and steadfastness to represent 'We the People'. Sadly, I cannot say the same for the RINO's and most of the democratic party on Capitol Hill. Despite the cancel culture of Big Tech, we still get real news from alternative independent outlets. We know all of the corrupt politicians that fill up the political cesspool and as soon as we fix our broken election process, they all will be voted out, including the Resident in Chief. (No, Resident is not a typo). Maricopa County forensic audit is the beginning domino effect to fix this mess. OUR COUNTRY CAN'T MOVE ON UNTIL 2020 ELECTIONS IS FIXED!!!

I continue on to say, I commend Gov. DeSantis for making an excellent choice in Florida's new black Surgeon General Dr. Joseph Lapado. Already the fake news media and more than 100 physicians controlled by the Chinese Communist Party (CCP) are trying to discredit Gov. DeSantis new hire. I get it, if it's not a black like George Floyd stirring up racial tension, then the disingenuous media shuns the law abiding and intelligent black who can think for themselves, and to them they are irrelevant and should be scorned. SUCH HYPOCRITES!!! Needless to say, identity politics like this is destroying America from within, along with offended unpatriotic blacks and white socialist liberals. It's been said liberals hate freedom, they enjoy chaos, and they destroy everything they touch, I tend to agree whole heartedly with this notion.

Before I get dismissed as a racist and a bigot. I would like to say, I am a proud black American citizen of the greatest country in the world. Anyone disagreeing, you are welcome to leave, and may I suggest leaving by way of the southern border, since the Biden administration has it open for the whole world to migrate to the U.S; However, it's just as easy to exit the country, so if you despise our country then pack your bags, it's still a free country for now. With a toxic racial climate, I tell of my ethnicity because I have been known to say some controversial things about my black race of people. Therefore, I want you to hear my words and not consider them racially motivated or racist and dismiss me as a white supremacist. Also, maybe my letter and strong suggestions can be put to the front of the line because I'm black. What? Everyone made concessions for Black Lives Matter (BLM), a Marxist and racist movement orchestrated under the guise of black lives mattering. Yes, corporations donated millions to BLM, did it serve to help black people? Yes, it most certainly did, it made co-founder Patrisse Cullors a very wealthy woman, so wealthy she resigned. The black community didn't see a dime; However, the DNC did, but the black race continue to be loyal to the modern-day slave master. So, let's take a look at how black lives really matter.

In 2019, there were 7,484 black murders. In 2020, there were at least 8,600 black murders all across the U.S. Over 90% of those said two years and prior to, were BLACK ON BLACK HOMICIDES!!! YOU DO THE MATH, NUMBERS DON'T LIE. Where is BLM and all of the wealthy black enabling race hustlers, like: Colin Kaepernick, Al and Jesse, Oprah Winfrey, LeBron James, Don Lemon, Joy Reid and Tyler Perry, to name a few? THERE IS TOTAL SILENCE, while the media is a 24/7 bullhorn for police brutality, as if blacks are being slaughtered by the thousands in the streets by white cops. This narrative couldn't be more false. Blacks are so gullible, we haven't learned yet, we are being used like a ten dolla whore. All the left has to do is sprinkle racism on any subject, and there we go like a dog in heat. Just say social injustice and we became outraged, while destroying cities by mostly peaceful protest (RIOTS). Not to mention, Antifa went along side BLM to wreak havoc on our nation for almost a year. Yet, no one speaks out about the legal genocide of over 350 thousand black babies being aborted each year. How else do you get young minds, both black and white to riot? You feed them racism and you make it a steady diet, while real issues go ignored. BLM/Antifa burned the American flag during their mostly peaceful protest, while yelling out "Death to America, Bring in Communism." This is a serious problem Y'all!!! EXCUSE MY FRENCH. Our elected officials are failing the American people, as they see the madness transpire right before their eyes with their hands in their pockets. Please continue to take this journey with me, because the hostile takeover of our republic and constitution is all connected to the 'Right to Try'. Meaning, our freedom to choose is fading away, and being replaced with liberal progressive ideals, that are killing America.

I was enjoying the American dream that our country affords us all, no matter your race. On March 23, 2020, my job came to an end because of Fauci the fraud's 'Gain of function', known as Covid-19 (Wuhan virus), so excuse me as I make no apologies, YES, I'M PISSED OFF!!! Why is Fauci still walking the streets? This kind of person has been allowed to get away with murder, literally speaking, with no consequences, and all politicians have done is question people like Fauci before congress, which is a dog and pony show, with a finger up their butt. This academy award ceremony is supposed to make us think that they care, as if they are going to get down to the bottom of the criminal activity. Well, I'm fed up with the shenanigans. You want to know who else is fed up? Many Americans being targeted by one of the corrupt three letter agencies called the FBI for standing up against the public schools pushing curriculum that has nothing to do with learning. Let's see, law abiding patriots are being arrested for being outraged in school board meetings, while BLM/Antifa thugs destroyed cities, livelihoods, assaulted and even caused death for almost a year and not a single thing was done. They were never demonized, criticized, ostracized, nor immobilized for their violent and destructive behavior. All we heard on fake news 24/7, that the riots were mostly peaceful, and as one mayor would put it, "It's a summer of love." Yes, we are inflamed with rage because we see the handwriting on the wall. We see exactly where our country is heading, into totalitarianism just like the newly inducted Australians into communism. Now, it all makes sense, why they have been working overtime to take away our second amendment rights; so, we wouldn't be able to defend ourselves from a tyrannical dictatorship. I believe our forefathers could see that this day was coming; Therefore, they put into the constitution, the right to bear arms. We the people got to step up to the challenge, because our lackadaisical, lethargic, and egocentric politicians are doing absolutely nothing to save our country, neither for the future generations to come. My children's future is at stake; Therefore, I FIGHT!!! I believe there are some that don't mind where we're headed, and some are truly oblivious to where we're headed, and some are in on the CCP takeover. I can tell you; the patriots are on fire, and we're not going to let that happen. We realize, if we lose our freedoms, there would be no reason to live. 1776 REWIND!!!

I digress to the real point of this letter; Although, everything in this letter is vitally important to me. I contracted Covid-19; I was very ill for about 5 days before I found out I had the virus. Thankfully, because I am so far removed from fake news, we already had the therapeutics on hand and they were: ivermectin, budesonide and doxycycline (antibiotic) that was prescribed by a frontline doctor, who honors her oath to treat patients with care to the best of her ability. It's sad to say, I can't say the same for so many doctors, hospital institutions, hospital administrators, and pharmaceuticals all across America. They all should be charged with crimes against humanity as should Fauci the fraud.

THERE IS A CURE!!! I am alive and well today because of a drug the media classifies as a horse dewormer that will kill humans. I have several stories like mine, people who we have been able to convince that there is a cure. There is absolutely no reason anyone has to suffer and definitely not die from this virus, as long as there is quick, precise and proper care given as mentioned in my case; IN OTHER WORDS, 'RIGHT TO TRY'. On the other hand, I have devastating stories of those we were not able to reach or just didn't believe, and death was the end result. I believe because of disingenuous coverage, misinformation, propaganda and lies by networks like: CNN, MSNBC, and FOX in the hen house news, and the trickling down effect to the local news networks throughout the country has kept half of the nation in the dark and divided. As a result, a lot of unnecessary lives have been loss because of these corrupt CCP owned networks, and they should be indicted for crimes against humanity as well.

Can you see the importance of 'Right to Try'? Or at least let the citizens know what treatments are available, and give the option to choose what's best for their life, this is America, RIGHT? Which makes all other points made in this letter vitally important, because if we keep at the rate we're going, there won't be an America, we will be the new North Korea. I remind you; we are in the greatest "PANDEMIC" (SCAMDEMIC) the world has ever seen. So, why are we blocking, hiding, censoring, demonizing cures and saying they are ineffective with deadly side-effects? And why are we mandating experimental vaccines that we have no idea of the ramifications of short- or long-term effects? Maybe I can shine some light on the subject.

Here is a headline for you to ponder, "Fully vaccinated Mississippi Sheriff found dead in his home after positive Covid-19 test". This article was published by Black Enterprise and written by Charlene Rhinehart posted on August 7, 2021. I was shocked when I found this column because the media is hiding the thousands of deaths and adverse effects from the experimental vaccines. They label these deaths, covid deaths, but any logical thinking person would question the cause of death. Asking, why did this person die of covid after being fully vaccinated? This is a likely story of so many Americans with the same story, because Big Tech is censoring to keep this knowledge away from the American people. Why is this? This is an open book test, so I'll give you the answer, so citizens won't fear the jab and keep believing they're safe. And you wonder why there is a huge pushback from well-informed patriotic citizens not mesmerized under the spell of the fake news media.

Here is what I think and it's just my opinion. I believe the covid vaccine is the 'Delta Variant,' because I am hearing of too many cases that are similar to this sheriff. Case in point, my wife had a 60-year-old cousin in good health that suddenly passed away two months after being fully vaccinated. Hospitals are filling up with fully vaccinated patients, young and old; when before the vaccine craze there were mainly older covid patients with pre-existing conditions. Not to mention, hospitals giving a prescription known for causing renal failure in covid patients called remdesivir, instead of treating them with known cures as mentioned earlier in this letter. Kill the kidneys, intubate them and collect over 40K from FEMA. Is this a coincidence? Then why is there such a fetish and fixation on getting everyone vaccinated? Is this the depopulation plan Bill Gates alluded to? Of course, the fake news media fact checked this notion all over the CCP owned news outlets, but I find it very difficult to discredit actual officially recorded transcripts.

Lastly, I am reaching out to about 17 governmental officials to get a bill legislated for a 'Right to Try' for prescriptions, and medical methods concerning our individual health; without doctors, hospitals administrators, pharmaceuticals and politicians having the final say on our lives. Also, I'm adding to that bill, 'A right to Know'; making it illegal and a crime for Big Tech to censor legitimate information and resources. By the way, there was a bill presented to congress concerning the cancel culture practices of Big Tech that was never acted upon. Which proves my earlier point about congress; a whistleblower from Facebook recently sat before congress; BLAH, BLAH, BLAH!!! How many times does Facebook have to go before congress, before something is done? What a waste of taxpayers' money. It took less than a year to make the deadly vaccines and coerce the other corrupt three letter agency called the FDA into approving the jab for emergency use. That could be the reason why two top senior FDA officials resigned. So, how soon can we get a bill passed and into law? I do understand with the present House and Senate it would almost be an impossibility, which is why we have to fix our internationally and domestically compromised elections; to have fair elections and vote every one of those crooks out, including Biden. We have American citizens suffering and dying for no other reason than corruption, and if we're not careful, we will be responsible for allowing the unpatriotic liberals to dismantle America and ruin the lives of so many citizens of this country. Ladies and gentlemen, I am not going away!!! I call for a response.

Drain the Swamp
1776 REWIND!!!
May God bless America,
Sonny B.

MADE IN CHINA

Anyone still tuning in to the radicalized CCP owned NBA, you are either oblivious to what's going on, or you just don't care. With an attitude, that I want my entertainment by any means necessary, who cares about the citizens human rights of China. Not realizing you are unknowingly willing participants of the greatest takeover and demise of our country. If the subject isn't about race, meaning black and white, I don't want to hear about it, until fake news exposes the atrocities. Well, I say don't hold your breath, because the mainstream media is owned in some way by the CCP as well. Talk about the epitome of selfishness and tunnel vision with concerns of only one race, the black race. Evil is evil, I don't care what color it's wrapped in. It's unfortunate the white liberal Marxist have bought into this ridiculousness, so I say shame on you both, especially when there's no outcry for BLACK-ON-BLACK MURDER!!! However, this is a lesson straight out of the book, 'The Art of War.' Turn the citizens on one another by causing a race war. I'm quite sure China is proud of the progress they've made over several decades. Infiltrate the country from within by first buying up everything in our economy and controlling sell-outs with money. I can understand even more why the bible says, "The love of money is the root of all evil." (1 Timothy 6:10).

Ok, I'll take it even further, if you are watching any type of professional sports, you are being entertained by the clowns sent to distract you from reality. Just about everything is made in China, or at least has China's carbon footprint on it. I was even made in China. What? How is that even possible when I've never stepped into the country? Do you really want to know, or do you want to ignore and avoid the question altogether?

I was enjoying the American dream this country affords us all, no matter your race, gender, creed or nationality background. So, don't believe the non-sense from wealthy black race hustlers. Should I repeat my list of wealthy black race baiters? Yes, I will because I enjoy exposing the fake woke like: Colin Kaepernick (NBC's Michele Tafoya was reassigned, and not by choice, for speaking truth on The View about this renegade posing as an American). Furthermore, Colin is the imbecile who wore a Fidel Castro T-shirt on national TV in support of his regime, this was totally ignored by fake news, ESPN, LeChina James, Oprah Winfrey, Tyler Perry, Snoop Dogg, TI, Don Lemon, Joy Reid, Jemele Hill, Al and Jesse, to name a few. SUCH HYPOCRITES!!!)

Where was I? Oh yeah, I was living the American dream until March 23, 2020, hit, the day I was laid off my job because of the coronavirus, Covid-19, or was it the delta variant, omicron, omicron BA.2, Wuhan virus or China virus. You can't make this lunacy up. By the way, March 23, 2020, was the same day ivermectin was introduced to the world and was told to disappear like a black man with a newborn. The 2015 Nobel prize winning drug would hit an all-time record of fact checking when you search this miracle drug. These Marxist have been emboldened by the tyrannical Biden regime, when Facebook can admit to the world that fact checking is just an opinion, not based on any facts. Will that change the minds of the brainwashed zombie media apocalypse fake news avid watchers? Like my aunt would say it, H to the no.

I know personally ivermectin kills covid dead. I too, like Joe Rogan had the China virus and was cured by this very safe (corrupt FDA) approved drug. So can we say Plandemic/ Scamdemic, I like to say Scamdemic, because this was the greatest hoax and crime of the century, with the 2020 election fraud (Treason) coming in a close second. Is the virus real? Absolutely!!! I just told you I was cured from it. In addition, it was made in the China's Wuhan Institute of Virology. However, like I've said before, this virus was and is being prostituted like a $10 dolla ho. The media has stoked fear into the American people. Some people are so frightened, they totally look pass the idea of a cure and was willing to allow a deadly experimental gab to be induced into their bodies.

I was made by China. Without the quote unquote "Pandemic", no one would've heard about Sonny B., an ordinary Joe minding his own business. I was enjoying the life God gives us all, enjoying my family and enjoying the American dream. So, don't get angry at me, get angry at Fauci the fraud's 'Gain of Function', the Wuhan China virus. I like the ole saying, "You're barking up the wrong tree" FOOL. Fool is my addition to that saying. I'm sitting here typing, and shaking my head in disbelief, because we have been had, bamboozled, hoodwinked and swindled.

The liberal Marxist have been trying to change the face of America for several decades. They finally came up with the perfect storm, a well calculated formula of social injustice, create a pandemic, and massive election fraud to unseat a sitting President not part of their globalism, great reset or new world order plan. I must admit, this plan was brilliant, but they would need enormous help from two major entities, 1) indoctrination thru academia, 2) witchcraft and sorcery of the mainstream media (Local and National) collaboration. A diabolical scheme transpired with satan himself from the deep depths of hell.

This is how bad our country has become, it's gone to pot, to say the least. Right is called wrong and wrong is called right. The sinister villains are allowed to run amok, while patriots in this country are demonized as insurrectionist. The disparities between conservatism/patriotism and Marxism are startling and mind-blowing. In addition, any punishment given is greatly disproportionate, this is an understatement. For example, Proud Boy leader Enrique Tarrio was sentenced to five months in jail for burning a BLM flag, a banner symbolizing racism and Marxism. On the contrary, BLM/Antifa can stomp on and burn the American flag while yelling 'Death to America and bring in Communism.' Furthermore, they were allowed to destroy cities across the country for a year, costing taxpayers millions, upon millions of dollars. While this transpired right before our eyes, we were told the RIOTS were 'Mostly Peaceful' as one mayor would put it, 'It's a summer of love'. Not to mention, if these renegades were arrested, the George Soros owned DAs would release them right away to return and commence with destruction of our nation. There was a meme showing The Statue of Liberty about to be totally submerged into the Hudson River, symbolizing freedom coming to an end if we don't stand up and fight. I would like to add to that meme to highlight Lady Justice, because justice is not blind and certainly not balanced. I go in-depth about the way I feel about the justice in our country with the letter I wrote to the U.S. Supreme Court. Go ahead, search Proud Boys, you will see a barrage of negative stories. Now search BLM, you'll see Big Tech categorized them as a sanctimonious organization that can do no harm or that has done no harm. The mainstream media and Big Tech are so bias and disingenuous. If it wasn't for the citizens who are still brainwashed by the witchcraft of fake news, they would no longer have a platform. Here's an excerpt from a Malcolm X quote, the media can make the innocent guilty and the guilty innocent. However, Trump's new truth social media site, I believe will end Big Tech, which is why they are scrambling to discredit and demonize a site before it comes into fruition.

I digress to the CCP owned NBA, with a story of double standards that has become all too familiar. NBA player Enes Freedom is calling out the hypocrisy of the NBA and players benefiting from China, like LeBron James for the inhumane treatment of the Chinese people. I'm quite sure the NFL, MLB, NHL, ATP, Nascar, Hollywood, The View, The Breakfast Club, and others were listening in on this. So, where are all of the BLM sympathizers concerned about social injustice, police brutality, black oppression, white privilege and systematic racism? The NBA of course denied that the two gentlemen that begged Freedom to not wear his social justice for China basketball shoes during NBA games, but my question would be, who else would have that authority to confront Enes except NBA personnel? These people think we're all ignorant because they think we're all mesmerized by the fake news media. Or they're just that arrogant and don't care if you know they are lying because who's going to hold them accountable when they're all in the same bed with China?

Would you say, Enes continuing to wear his shoes upset the CCP? Is Boston Celtics games cancelled that were scheduled in China a punishment for defying the powers that be? Or Freedom losing substantial amount of playing minutes be a form of punishment? How did China come to gain so much power? President Jimmy Carter, Ronald Regan (My honorable mention, I loved Regan but he was still owned in some degree, Daddy Bush, Clinton, Son Bush, Obama, the political cesspool on Capitol Hill (republicans and democrats), Big Tech, FEMA, all of the corrupt three letter agencies like: FDA, CDC, NSA, FBI, CIA, and DOJ, Hillary Clinton's emails, Big PHARMA, academia, Mega churches, professional sports, ESPN, Hollywood and we cannot forget the fake news mainstream media (Enemy of the People).

The media bullhorn, the propaganda machine that pushes rhetoric and lies, while hiding, demonizing, vilifying and covering up the cow manure load of corruption. The government helped create the social giants and would shield them with section 230 of any repercussions from the 'Cancel Culture' to censor everyone not in-line with the Marxist agenda. Identity politics would be spawned from the culture of cancellation. Dividing a nation by pushing the narrative that America is a racist country and President Trump is the very definition of racism. Go look in your dictionary, under the word's fascist, misogynist, xenophobe, racist, bigot, homophobe, islamophobe, and white nationalist and you will find Trump's name because that is what the media told you to see him as. Identity politics is killing America, it's a distraction to cover up the real agenda of these trained Marxist; A hostile CCP takeover. President Trump said it best, he said, "They can't get to you, because I'm in the way." Well, they removed him out of office with a stolen election in plain sight. What's standing in the way now? Those pesky evangelicals and patriotic citizens with the 1st and 2nd amendment rights. However, the second amendment being the most important of the two. How do I know this? Just look at Australia, they gave their weapons up willingly to their government and it came back to bite them in the butt. The tyrannical government is trying to subdue and strong arm a whole nation. This is a story the media doesn't want to get out. So, you don't think about all of the many times the Marxist liberals have been trying to take away our second amendment. I believe with the help of God, 'We the People' and the military will have to turn this mess around, because we can't depend on a rogue Biden regime, because they are the problem. Certainly not the political cesspool on Capitol Hill, they've proved to us time and time again that they are just as corrupt and worthless. "Let's Go Brandon"!!! 1776 Rewind!!! And may God bless America!!!

DON'T GET MAD AT ME

We've heard it said, "Absolute power, corrupts absolutely." This is the case all over the world, tyrannical, corrupt governments that is. The citizens are never really the problem, except those who are indoctrinated and manipulated by academia and the deep state-controlled media. Those same people would get angry at the president for calling Haiti a crap hole. Well do you deny the truth that it is a crap hole? I believe the president was calling out the lackadaisical, non-caring Haiti government that does nothing for the infrastructure, lack of food and safety of the country. That statement was not directed at the people of Haiti. Let's see if I can bring some clarity to the situation. If you were told to leave the United States, and you were given a choice to pick any country in the world for your permanent residence, would Haiti be your first choice? Better yet, would it be in your top 100 choices? I'll answer it for you, because you probably won't be honest, NOT!!!

I'm so fed up with these self-righteous hypocrites. All I ask, is to be fair and honest across the board, equally; Rather it's a democrat or republican. Case in point, there were BLM/Antifa riots and chaos for a whole year. Now, compare the media coverage and treatment of the citizens on January 6th. I was told from a friend, "But this was an attack on the Capitol, an insurrection." I told him first of all, "You need to quit watching fake news, because that's a talking point from CNN and MSNBC." So, are you telling me that politicians are more important than the American citizens that loss their lives, businesses and properties destroyed because of the mostly peaceful protest? The jury is still out on his answer. Here's an excerpt from one of the greatest movies ever made to solidify my argument, or if nothing else, some great entertainment, and say it in your Scottish voice.

(Braveheart 1995) Robert the Bruce: I respect what you said but remember that these men have lands and castles. It's much to risk.

William Wallace: And the common man, who bleeds on the battlefield, does he risk less?

Robert the Bruce: I'm not a coward, I want what you want, but we need the nobles (Politicians)

William Wallace: We need them?

Robert the Bruce: Aye

William Wallace: Nobles (Politicians)

[Laughs a little]

William Wallace: Now tell me, what does that mean to be noble? Your title gives you claim to the throne of our country, but men don't follow titles, they follow courage. Now our people know you, noble and common, they respect you. And if you would just lead them to freedom, they'd follow you, and so would I.

Lastly, when I call Covid-19 the Wuhan virus, it's not an attack on the character of the Chinese people, so DON'T GET MAD AT ME. Get furious at the tyrannical Chinese government that manufactured the virus with the assistance and funding of Fauci the fraud's 'Gain of Function.' So, all ill-informed, brainwashed, self-righteous hypocrites, go and take a hike!!!

CREATE THE ILLUSION

Las Vegas, Nevada Chef/Owner Natalie Young of EAT. Restaurant recovery- Design intervention S1 Ep7 with host/owner Todd Graves of Raising Cane's chicken fingers restaurant. Restaurant recovery is the name of the program to help restaurant owners get back on their feet from the Scamdemic.

I fell asleep very early, which is very unusual; However, when that happens, I can wake up early in the morning. That time was around 1am in the morning. I was kinda awake, so I cut the TV to one of my favorite networks, the Cooking Channel. As mentioned, this program helps struggling family-owned businesses because of the Wuhan virus (Covid-19). This episode brought tears to my eyes, because I understand how the elites have exploited this virus for a political agenda.

Natalie Young is a gay chef. I would like to clear up the lies of identity politics the left pushes to divide a nation. I do not agree with the gay lifestyle, and **I DO NOT HATE THEM!!!** I tell you of her sexual preference to make my point. It doesn't matter that she is gay, because she is an American, and we don't have to agree to get along with one another. This virus came to destroy the livelihood of all Americans, especially the privately owned businesses. Everyone felt the devastation of an economy lockdown. Here is the problem for me, the whole economy was shutdown, except business giants like Walmart, Target, Casino's, Bars, Planned Parenthood, secret hair appointment (Nancy Pelosi), exclusive dinner parties (Gavin Newsom). These were all essential, except churches and small businesses.

Please excuse my two-letter acronym, but the virus is a bunch of B.S. and yes, I'm pissed off. Why? Because I know about the therapeutics (Budesonide, Ivermectin, and an Antibiotics), this is one of the regimens for the cure of covid. No one has to suffer or even die, sadly enough, they knew about this before the illusion of the pandemic. Ladies and gentlemen, contrary to popular belief, Covid-19 is curable. I am a living witness, because I contracted the virus. I medicated myself with the therapeutics just mentioned and as a result, I am alive and well today. It's unfortunate, because of fake news, it takes an act of congress to convince the people you love and care about, that there is a cure. They would rather believe some news anchor they don't even know and never met. People cannot believe, when I say, they wanted people to die for a political agenda, they think I'm insane. They just cannot believe anyone could be so wicked and evil to allow a human being to die, when there is a cure. I tell them to look at a few hours of the I.D. channel, and I guarantee it will change your mind. Did you know, hospitals received over 13K for receiving covid patients? And they also receive over 40K when a covid patient goes on a vent? No wonder why, the hospital wanted to put my aunt on the vent, immediately receiving her in a hypoxic state because of covid. Long story, short, she is alive today, because my mother threatened to sue the hospital and everyone in it, if they put her on the vent. My aunt is alive today because of our combined efforts to hold the hospital staff accountable for the type of treatment for my aunt, so many thousands weren't so fortunate. Here is a reference just in case you want to go down the rabbit hole of corruption, titled, "Biden's bounty on your life: Hospitals' incentive payments for Covid-19, published on November 17, 2021, by Association of American Physicians and Surgeons and written by Elizabeth Lee Vliet, MD and Ali Shultz, JD.

I am a retired fireman and an inspiring chef to one day own my own restaurant; Not to mention, I was approved just before the virus outbreak, to sell my desserts at a very prominent local market. Yes, I too was affected by bioterrorism released by the Wuhan Institute of Virology, funded by Fauci the fraud's 'Gain of Function.' Needless to say, I want peace, I don't want any trouble, I just wanted to be left alone to live the American dream this country affords us all. I worked hard to provide for my family, and to establish myself as a productive citizen in society by reputable and honest employment. In other words, I was minding my own business, but the tyrannical Chinese and American government made me who I am today, an author, writing to save this nation. They have awakened my suspicion and a hornet's nest of anger towards the political cesspool on Capitol Hill, the one-party system.

I was enjoying cooking at a major hotel, when the Wuhan virus hit. We all were told; we would only be shut down for about 2-3 weeks and everything should be back to normal. Weeks turned into months, and over a year later, the elites want a new normal. Now it's a new variant. A nurse doing covid testing was asked, "How do you test for the Delta variant? Nurse responded, "With the same PCR test for Covid-19." The second question was asked, "How do you tell the difference?" Nurse responded, "We can't." They are not going to let this thing go!!! Fauci the fraud is pushing the delta strain, now that states like Florida are opening up and defying the powers that be. So, they have to come up with more fear mongering to control the American people. There are huge spikes, the covid cases are at an all-time high, but they fail to tell you, that most of the cases are from those that have gotten the vaccine. Ask yourself the question, why are there just as many children cases as adults? Because of the vaccines, the covid vaccine make you more susceptible to the virus. We are fearfully and wonderfully made by God. The problem is, we want to play God and try and make the immune system better; Instead, we screw it up.

If you don't know by now, I have put my American dream on hold. Did you hear me? I said, I put it on hold. No, it wasn't systemic racism, white privilege, white supremacy, police brutality, oppression, marginalization, or fear for my black life, that put my dreams on hold. It was the concern for my children's future and love for my country. Normal human beings, call that storge and patriotism, something pedophile's and the unpatriotic despise, because they have no love. Liberalism, pushes away virtue and allows chaos to reign and somehow think this will make a better America, just take note of the mostly peaceful protest all throughout 2020. I believe Michael Savage coined the phrase best, "Liberalism is a mental disorder."

Lastly, here is what gets my goat, all of these fake woke organizations, networks, corporations, individuals, etc, etc, etc. For example, the same networks, i.e. (Cooking Channel) that helped implode businesses and jobs through social injustice ads. Ads to dictate to Americans to stay home during the scamdemic, are the same networks today, patting restaurant owners on the back and telling them it's ok through an episode of Restaurant Recovery. When they actually promoted an economy sabotage the whole time, by deep state, CCP controlled politicians, while Americans suffered across the country. Then threw the American citizens the scraps and leftovers from the pork filled stimulus package to payback foreign countries for being complicit in domestic corruption to destroy America. The government has created an illusion to divert the attention from the real problem, sinister politicians. Sadly, offended blacks and white liberals can't see through the smokescreen, instead they fight against American citizens who can see through all of the baloney. If you can divide, you can conquer. Well, I'm on the battlefield to help open the eyes of those manipulated and brainwashed by the mainstream media (Enemy of the people). This is a quote from Malcolm X, I believe sums up the media, I quote, "The media's the most powerful entity on earth. They have the power to make the innocent guilty and to make the guilty innocent, and that's power, because they control the minds of the masses." I rest my case.

UNTIL THERE'S PUBLIC OUTCRY

Greetings Publix Executive Team,

PLEASE, BEFORE I DIGRESS TO THE POINT OF THIS LETTER, GIVE ME A MINUTE TO EXPRESS MY FEELINGS AS I SEGUE INTO THE LUNACY HAPPENING IN REAL TIME RIGHT BEFORE OUR VERY EYES. I am a proud black American citizen of the greatest country in the world. No matter how many times the Marxist media and Black Lives Matter (BLM) says that America is a racist nation, I vehemently resent this notion. I am not oppressed by white privilege, white supremacy, or systematic racism. I tell you of my ethnicity to inform you that all blacks are not ignorant and ill-informed because of the disingenuous 24/7 propaganda of the Communist media bullhorn. I am sitting here typing with a heavy heart and so many emotions going through my mind, asking myself the question, what has happened to my beloved United States of America? I never thought I would see the day where the Caucasian man would be the most hated in America and BLM would become the new Karen. While white supremacy would become synonymous to patriotism; Or even the possibility of a totalitarian Biden regime giving illegals 450K and illegal families up to 1 million dollars. What does the black race get, "You ain't black if you don't vote for Joe." "Quit your whining, put on your walking shoes and go vote," (Obama). Or a bottle of hot sauce in the purse, (Hillary Clinton). I can tell you what the black race gets, being burnt up by the gas lighting. Instead of the mainstream media being an instrument of truth, facts and of 'Checks and Balances', Americans have gotten rhetoric and obviously bias Marxist news, that would prove to be detrimental to the freedom of our nation. While we were busy working to provide for our families, attending church and being entertained by Hollywood and sports, academia has been indoctrinating our children from kindergarten to college. Is there a wonder why our nation is divided by patriotism and socialistic ideals? Now we have to fight for the right to obtain medications prescribed by our doctors for illnesses that could become fatal. I'm shaking my head in disbelief and bewilderment, wondering when will I awake from this nightmare of a country becoming unrecognizable.

I digress to the point of this letter. I have two other vitally important letters I'm sending the Publix Executive Team: Randall Todd Jones; Kevin Murphy; David Phillips; Charles Roskovich; David Bornmann; and Laurie Douglas. Publix is known for its impeccable service by anyone who shops at your grocery stores, I can attest to that statement because of countless hours of shopping and spending my hard-earned money in your store, which can seem like endless shopping when providing food for a family of (8) eight. "Where shopping is a pleasure" is your slogan, I believe is being tested by the politically driven Covid-19 insanity. Unfortunately, this situation isn't just isolated to Publix pharmacies, but has become worldwide crimes against humanity. A left leaning liberal of all people made this comment, "This pandemic has become a political bureaucracy, and I'm done, I'm not doing it anymore." Even liberals are waking up and I could not agree more with her statement.

HERE'S THE COMPLAINT: My aunt had an unsavory personal encounter with Mr. Kendall in your Publix pharmacy location: 4854 Sun City Center Blvd, Sun City Center, Florida 33573 concerning her niece's prescription on January 25, 2022. The prescription in question, the infamous 'IVERMECTIN' a 40-year-old FDA approved drug, winning the Nobel Prize as the wonder drug in 2015 for curing just about anything it comes in contact with SAFELY including Covid-19 in 2020. My aunt told me of her encounter with Mr. Kendall was appallingly rude and my conversation with him was equally astounding. I listened to his groundless reasons of why he would not fulfill the ivermectin order, but he refused to listen to my reason why it should be fulfilled. He talked over me and when he became irritated with our conversation, he put me on hold without acknowledging he was putting me on hold and never returned; In other words, he politely hung up in my face without actually hanging up. I had to call back to continue our conversation, so you be the judge of this act of blatant disrespect. One of his reasons for not fulfilling the prescription of ivermectin was, "There was not enough public outcry," the audacity and then wanted to patronize me by offering to transfer the prescription to another pharmacy (In other words, lets kick this can down the road for someone else to deal with this issue). Here is the problem with this notion, if we give in and allow Publix to transfer the prescriptions to another pharmacy, what's stopping the next pharmacy from doing the same thing? As a result, we could eventually run out of pharmacies to obtain a lifesaving drug because of pharmacies with the same mindset as Publix to withhold a doctor prescribed proven drug that cures the: Wuhan China virus or is it Covid-19, Delta-variant, omicron, omicron BA.2, Flurona or is it the Deltacron. Sometimes I believe they just close their eyes, open a medical dictionary and point to the next virus to cause never ending fear, this has become a three-ring circus.

It's happening all over the country, citizens see the ridiculousness; As a result, they are shunning the deadly experimental vaccines and opting for the safer options like: hydroxychloroquine, ivermectin, budesonide, and monoclonal clinics (The FDA just put a halt to, WHY? That's a rhetorical question by the way). Then again, we've had issues getting ivermectin from other pharmacies, but I thought Publix was more ethical with integrity in that regard. I guess I was wrong, you're no different than the political cesspool on Capitol Hill. I'm not foolish, I know the government want you to push the vaccines, but do you do this at the expense of the right to choose? Or denying fellow citizens the right to receive medical treatment and to live? Is this America or is this North Korea? Lately I can't tell the difference!!!

Furthermore, like Joe Rogan, Aaron Rodgers, the NFL secretly, the politicians on Capitol Hill secretly, myself and countless others were treated and cure by using ivermectin. This is not a fallacy Mr. Kendall, I don't care how much Fauci the fraud, FDA, CDC, WHO, NIH or any corrupt three letter agency tell you ivermectin isn't proven to cure covid; It does, I don't care how much smoke you blow up my butt. Frontline doctors and American citizens across the country are screaming from the mountain top that ivermectin is a cure for covid, with decades of documented safe usage all over the world; Needless to say, it's being blocked, vilified, demonized, canceled, censored, and ignored as a cure. So, Mr. Kendall there is massive proof, you and Publix Super Markets Inc. choose to ignore it. In addition, Publix and others participating in this baseless assault on our constitutional right to use ivermectin will not be exempt from the fiery consequences once justice is declared. I pray that everyone that had a hand in this grotesque injustice spend the rest of their lives in GITMO or be hung, because a lot of innocent lives have been lost prematurely and livelihoods taken because of the sinister scheme to usher in the Great Reset. This isn't about democrat vs republican, left vs right, liberals vs conservatives, this is a war of Good vs Evil, Publix which side are you on? Will you cower under the pressure of a tyrannical government and the fake woke, or will you stand with patriotic citizens and our illustrious governor fighting on behalf of 'We the People'? If you are on the side of good, then stop this non-sense.

Lastly, in addition, ivermectin is being prescribed by the doctors for their patients, despite the ridicule, threat to life, threat of fines and threat of losing their practice for upholding the oath to save human life. My next two letters will explain in great details why Mr. Kendall feels emboldened to arrogantly refuse fulfilling the medication requested. The two letters are entitled: 1) The Right to Try, I sent to Governor DeSantis and other governmental officials. 2) The Enemy of the People, I sent to the FDA, CDC and NBC news for an article published by NBC because of pure propaganda. Again, these two letters explain in great detail of my acknowledgment of what's happening in our nation. Mr. Kendall said there was not enough public outcry, well it's coming and I'm just the beginning. Hopefully my letters will generate sound and sane judgement with integrity made on behalf of ivermectin being distributed at all Publix locations, so we can move past this potential atrocity. There was no problem a few months ago, getting ivermectin from Publix pharmacies, is this the political bureaucracy I spoke of earlier in this letter? I WANT ANSWERS, BECAUSE MR. KENDALL'S LAME EXCUSE IS UNEXCEPTABLE, AND SHOULD BE FROWNED UPON AND REJECTED BY YOUR EXECUTIVE TEAM!!! Thank you for your attention to this matter, and may God bless America, Sonny B.

Addendum NOTE: There were many attempts made by phone conversations and emails of why the Publix pharmacy location mentioned in this letter refused to fill ivermectin prescriptions. This can was kicked down the road and eventually the case was given to the Florida Pharmacy Association with no answer. **Does this give off any red flags?** They literally want the American people to accept the B.S. the Marxist media is telling us and shut up!!! The only conclusion I can come up with as I shake my head in disbelief of what's going on in our country is, **THIS IS A MELTING POT OF CORRUPTION!!!**

II UNTIL THERE'S PUBLIC OUTCRY

Greetings Mrs. Maria Brous and Mr. Augie Alvarado,

I would like to start out by saying, my conversation with Mr. Alvarado was pleasant and professional. Unlike, Mr. Kendall, he made me feel like a valued customer, worthy of hearing all my concerns. He was attentive, cordial and relatable to my unsettling pessimistic outlook on where our country is headed presently. However, this is no disrespect or attack on Mr. Alvarado's character, but our conversation felt like a listening conclave with a therapist in hopes that I would just go away, because deep down I felt like nothing would be done. From my first letter to this letter and all conversations that has transpired this far, I want to assure a credible stake in this claim. Furthermore, I do not want to come across as a meager or vague attempt to restore the freedom for a right to choose. If somehow, you don't think that there's an all-out assault on freedom, maybe you should have a conversation with the citizens who have lost their jobs or the freedom to dine or shop where they want, because of vaccine mandates and passports. Or covid patients who were denied treatment of ivermectin and budesonide, but instead was given Dr. Fauci's protocol of remdesivir and midazolam, placed on a vent and left to die alone without family. I'm fighting for life, liberty, and the pursuit of happiness, something the tyrannical Biden regime is feverishly attempting to strip away. America is heading down a dark path of Communism, but I'm fighting to shine the light on the subject in hopes to awake those who are still asleep before it becomes too late. It's been said, 'The truth is like a lion, let it loose and it will defend itself,' well I'm letting loose the Lion!!!

I spoke with Mr. Alvarado on February 8, 2022, with no response; In which he assured me someone would be getting right back to me to address my concerns. We are almost at a month, since the incident with Pharmacist Kendall; As a result, precious time has elapsed for possible customers wanting Mr. Kendall to fill their life saving prescription of ivermectin. Unlike, other pharmacies like: Walmart, CVS and Walgreens, I felt like I could have a dialogue with the Publix company who I've come to trust as family oriented, 'Where shopping is a pleasure.' I felt like your company couldn't be a part of Big PHARMA's corruption being supported by: mainstream media, Big Tech, CDC, FDA, NIH, WHO, DARPA, doctors, hospitals, kangaroo court system and the political cesspool on Capitol Hill. With that being said, I'm starting to think differently. I'm beginning to feel like I'm on trial, as if I'm in front of an interrogation panel to prove to your company of something that's already been proven. Pleading my case to the prosecutor (Pharmacist) without the prosecutor (Pharmacist) having to show any factual evidence of why they are refusing to fill ivermectin orders. Let me explain.

Mr. Alvarado made the comment to me, "You wouldn't want the pharmacist to be mandated to fill ivermectin prescriptions, would you?" I in turn said, "Of course not." No one should be mandated, forced, coerced or blackmailed into doing anything against their will, because this is America. However, their decision not to fill the order takes away my choice as a patient to receive ivermectin prescribed by **MY DOCTOR!** Not to mention, we're talking about a medication that won a Nobel Prize in 2015 for killing just about every disease it comes in contact with, and now the Wuhan China virus, AKA: Covid-19, Delta-variant, omicron, omicron BA.2, flurona, deltacron, and the stealth omicron. Now the media is pushing 'HIV variant' narrative as cover story for vaccine-induced immune system collapse. Educate me on why anyone would be fearful or hesitant about using or filling the prescription in question, especially to a well-trained and knowledgeable pharmacist. His/her major duty is to know and understand the purposes of medications; However, there are other duties a pharmacist must acquire, like: How to consult with prescribers (DOCTORS) if there are any discrepancies, or concerns as highlighted in this article by, thebalancecareers.com, titled, "Top 9 pharmacist duties and responsibilities," written by Edward Lamb and published on February 6, 2019. Here is number 2 on the responsibility list in this article and I quote, 2. COMMUNICATE WITH PRESCRIBERS. "Any time a prescription order is unclear or potentially harmful for a patient, you need to confirm the dosage and formulation (e.g., liquid or tablet), as well as whether brand name product is required or if you can substitute a generic equivalent." Part of this responsibility means, inquire before denying a prescription (IVERMECTIN). I believe doctors will be more than happy to discuss the purpose and success of the prescription in question. **DEFINITELY MY DOCTOR WHO TREATS OVER 800 COVID CASES A DAY, SUCCESSFULLY!!!** I was prescribed, treated and cured of covid by ivermectin and again so was: My 81-year-old mother with pre-existing conditions, 1 sister-in-law, 2 brother-in-law's, 2 cousins, 3 aunts, Joe Rogan, Aaron Rodgers, the NFL SECRETLY, congress and congresses family members SECRETLY!!! Is the Publix corporation concerned about the wellbeing of the patient, or the political scandal surrounding the therapeutics like ivermectin? If it's the latter, I question the integrity of your company. Again, if this is the greatest pandemic the world has ever seen, shouldn't you want to throw everything imaginable at this virus to bring fear and death to a halt?

Ivermectin has been on the market for over 40 years with only about 5 deaths worldwide and half of those are overdoses; However, on the other hand, the experimental vaccines only started 14 months ago (December 11, 2020) to today (February 18, 2022) and has at least 12,304 deaths according to VAERS. God only knows the real number of vaccine injuries from the covid vaccines because: (Most citizens don't know to report it; naive, innocent and trusting family members are oblivious to the possibility of the vaccine being the cause for the death of their loved ones because of the faith in the government; doctors, pharmacies and hospitals are not reporting all the cases; citizens are told by the mainstream media that the vaccines are safe; citizens are told their injury wasn't from the vaccine or just being ignored altogether as a possibility). I know of 4 deaths personally of young healthy adults who died suddenly soon after being fully vaccinated that wasn't reported to VAERS. Why? Because they were oblivious to the possibility of the cause being the vaccine. Yet, there is no hesitation for all Publix pharmacies giving out vaccine shots like candy but somehow pharmacist is afraid and skeptical to fill ivermectin orders proven to be extraordinarily safer? Medical professionals say that only about 1 percent of deaths and injuries from the covid vaccines get reported to VAERS, but even if it was a 100 percent, the numbers are staggering for a vaccine said to be safe. It's troubling to me, that some pharmacists are leery of ivermectin but embraces the vaccines. I'm crying foul, political bureaucracy, money or maybe even punishment to the unvaccinated by blocking and denying the use of a lifesaving drug.

I had lunch with a friend; In which, we had a strong disagreement because of the enemy of the people (Mainstream media, local and national news). Hydroxychloroquine was the prescription in question. He said he wouldn't use a 60-year-old FDA approved drug because it wasn't meant for Covid. I in turn asked him, if Tylenol was known to cure cancer, you wouldn't take it because it was originally meant for relieving pain and fever? The jury is still out on his answer, typical avid CNN and MSNBC watcher, once the talking points have come to a dead end, they SIN (S: Shift the subject; I: Ignore the facts; N: Name call). I told him that this is absurd, ludicrous and you need to stop watching fake news immediately, because it has syphoned out all of your brain cells of critical thinking, logic and simple common sense. I tell you this, because the non-sense and lunacy has been said about ivermectin.

Lastly, as if the tyrannical, corrupt and incompetent Biden administration could go any lower in character and in polls. They still astonish those of us who think for themselves and can't be controlled by the propaganda of the media. Even when we think it's not possible, the Biden administration rolls out an insane program. Here is another example of the lunacy, titled, "GOP outraged at $30m Biden plan to fund 'crack pipe distribution' in effort to reduce drug harm." Written by Josh Marcus and published by Independent.co.uk on February 10, 2022. Biden sabotaged the monoclonal clinics but can roll out this ridiculous plan. These types of things are happening in real time right before our very eyes, but there's an issue getting ivermectin? Pharmacist like Mr. Kendall are well educated, so show us proof and facts of why they are indignant on not filling ivermectin prescriptions, because going on the basis of feelings and saying they don't feel comfortable is unacceptable to the customers and to the public they are hired to serve. There is a considerable amount of information on ivermectin and thousands of frontline doctors who have treated and cured their patients of covid with ivermectin, again I'm one of them. Furthermore, this shouldn't be common practice of Publix pharmacy employee's and should be unacceptable to the corporate administrator's as well. They are blocking and interfering with doctor to patient treatment of a curable virus and can be held liable for the deaths of citizens who were unable to obtain their ivermectin prescription by Publix Super Market Inc. I pray that this second letter will cause your corporate team to look deep within their hearts to make an educated decision to allow the filling of ivermectin prescriptions in every Publix pharmacy. NOTE: Mr. Lloyd Brown editor-in-chief of Eye on Jacksonville is receiving this letter as well.

Here are some references of just a few frontline doctors, articles and websites of proof:

I. Frontline doctors (Advocates for therapeutics like: ivermectin, budesonide and hydroxychloroquine)

   A) Dr. Richard Bartlett
   B) Dr. Simone Gold
   C) Dr. Robert Malone

II. Articles

   A) Ivermectin: a multifaceted drug of Nobel prize-honored distinction with indicated efficacy against a new global scourge, Covid-19. Published by Sciencedirect.com in September 2021.
   B) Researchers call for access to ivermectin for young children. Published by Wwarn.org on March 18, 2021.

III. Websites

    A) americasfrontlinedoctors.org

    B) vaxxchoice.com

    C) budesonideworks.com

May God bless America,

Sonny B.

LETTER TO TEESPRING

Greetings,

I am a proud black American citizen of this great nation. A father of (6) six awesome children with my lovely wife of 23 years. I tell you the identity of my race simply because Black Lives Matter (BLM) is met with demands, so take a moment of your time to read about the concern for MY AMERICA. Unlike BLM, I will be polite and respectful as I give you my sincere apologies for the lengthiness of this letter; However, I do not apologize for its contents.

This letter is a complaint in regard to the cancellation of LT's (And We Know) product line. When LT told his audience about his apparel being cancelled by TeeSpring, I was moved and inspired to write a rebuttal to what I believe to be groundless evidence against his company. I know, I maybe the only one writing you in contempt of this baseless accusation; Nevertheless, in light of the massive amounts of cancel culture across America towards conservatives, patriots and Christians, I love to use the story of the starfish. With miles of beach and hundreds of starfish to be saved as a little boy gently place one starfish back into the water at a time, a gentleman passing by thought it was ridiculous and an impossible task. How can you possibly make a difference the man replied? "After listening politely, the boy bent down, picked up another starfish and put it back into the surf. Then smiling at the man, He said … "I made a difference for that one." With hundreds of stories similar to LT's (And We Know) all across America, I'm trying to make a difference one story at a time. Just a little side note: My wife and I are avid listeners of (And We Know), LT's message has never caused us to induce violence into or onto society, so where is your proof of glorifying hate and violence? Would you want someone to see the pics of your staff with no blacks represented and call you a racist company? Well, that is the ridiculousness that is happening in our country today, if it's a message or a person you don't like, you accuse them of being a racist, homophobe, islamophobe, xenophobe, misogynist or a white supremacist. These terms are used so loosely today, they've lost the meaning.

Please, allow me to present my case and explain why I am fed up with the corruption and political cesspool, I believe is in connection with my complaint of why companies like TeeSpring are canceling conservative messages: A one party system (republicans and democrats), Fake news, Big Tech, The Elites, corrupt three letter agencies (FBI, CIA, DOJ, NSI, IRS, CDC, FDA, WHO) and Hollywood. I was laid off my job in March of 2020 because of the Covid-19 virus, a virus the media and politicians refuse to call the Wuhan, China virus. Needless to say, it's February 2021, almost a year later, and my position is still closed. Therefore, if my writing comes across to you as a little perturbed, infuriating, and enraged to say the least, don't get angry with me, blame it on the China virus because it made me a man on fire.

The BLM/blackness movement has become nauseating, and I'm sickened by the enablers that have allowed this racist/ Marxist organization to run rampant across the nation. BLM, along with Antifa, have been allowed to destroy cities, lives and livelihoods for almost a year in the name of social injustice. I've been on this earth for almost 52 years, and I have never seen anything positive come out of serving up violence to bring about justice. I like the lyrics of Tom MacDonald in Fake Woke, "We use violence to get peace and wonder why it isn't working, that's like sleeping with a football team to try and be a virgin." Americans across the land watched in real time as the chaos unfolded, but we were told by the mainstream media (enemy of the people) that the riots were a protest, and it was mostly peaceful. One mayor would say, "It's a summer of love," as we watched looting, violent and deadly assaults on police authority and law- abiding citizens, burning buildings and vehicles, destruction of federal properties, monuments and statues, even deaths of innocent little children like 4-year-old LeGend Taliferro. Mind you, LeGend was one of nine children ranging from 1 to 14 years of age who lost their lives as a result of a mostly peaceful protest. I say to you TeeSpring, where was your voice on this? Or maybe you just didn't know because fake news didn't cover it? If you didn't know, this is the reason why you should support outlets like And We Know, instead of canceling them. The media has sold us a bill of goods to deceive half of America. The sad part of it all is, because of the media, the BLM/Antifa lunacy was funded by Big Tech, major corporations, academia, NFL, NBA, MLB, and Hollywood to name a few. Yet, companies like TeeSpring wants to cancel a former military man like LT, and ignore his sacrifice and service to our country, which affords us all the freedoms to own an apparel company or any business for that matter. Here is a quote from the most sought after and the most hated book on earth, the bible: "Woe to those who call evil good and good evil, who put darkness for light and light for darkness." (Isaiah 5:20)

There is a difference in hate speech and speech that you hate. I have some examples of people spewing hate speech and inciting violence that the mainstream media/social giants choose to ignore, here is a lineup of just a few: Maxine Waters, Eric Holder, Kamala Harris, IIhan Omar, Cory Booker, Nancy Pelosi, Joy Reid, Don Lemon and Chris Cuomo. There is proof of these low life's inciting violence all over the internet and social media. They are allowed to spew their hate; Yet TeeSpring, organizations, businesses, and wealthy black enablers (ex. Lebron James, Oprah Winfrey, Colin Kaepernick, Tyler Perry) GO SILENT. WE CALL THAT HYPOCRISY!!!

I never thought I would see the day, when a white male would be the most hated and scrutinized person in America, or patriotism would be synonymous to white supremacy. Even so call American citizens yelling "death to America, bring in communism," while burning the American flag. Many of us see the handwriting on the wall, there are many still asleep and fail to realize the Chinese Communist Party (CCP) has infiltrated our country from within, through: mainstream media/Big Tech, academia, Professional sports, Hollywood, corporations, trade and social issues. There is only one difference between Nazism and communism, that is, the death toll is significantly higher in communism. Pay attention to the signs: Riot by using identity politics, defund the police, destroy history, academia indoctrination, make citizens hate their country, remove God, take away the second amendment, and dictating and taking away first amendment rights to certain businesses and people the Elites disagree with; Consequently, canceling, censoring and punishing American patriots standing up for America. The media is the bullhorn to spread the propaganda throughout our nation. I've noticed that corporations are afraid to identify with patriots fighting for the constitution and freedoms of America because of getting backlash themselves. Well, let me put it like this, communism doesn't discriminate. If the CCP is allowed to take over, eventually everyone will succumb to the strong hand of dictatorship. Everyone means Everyone, that would include TeeSpring and all of your employees.

Lastly, we saw a major assault on our republic on November 4, 2020. America saw President Trump ahead by hundreds of thousands of votes in battleground states in question with 94% of precincts already in. Governors did something in those said states that has never happened before in election history, they told everyone to stop counting. We woke up to a Biden candidate in the lead, a person that couldn't draw flies even with dung smeared all over his body, but he got more votes than former President Obama? Something stinks corruption, and the stench was ignored like the burning bodies of Jews during the holocaust. You know something was deafly wrong, but you refuse to acknowledge it because of a vehement disdain for Donald Trump. There was massive proof of election fraud, with over 50,000 sworn affidavits from democrats and republicans who witnessed it. It was a domestic and foreign collaboration to steal an election, while the media ignored the grotesque injustice to our election process. All of the kangaroo courts didn't want to even look at the evidence, including Captain Kangaroo (U.S. Supreme Court). I don't care if you love or despise Donald Trump, if you're a democrat, republican, independent, humanitarian or libertarian, you should be outraged. If this is allowed, all candidates from here on out will be pre-chosen, with no reason for anyone to ever vote again. Therefore, welcoming in China and North Korea, and to congratulate George Soros, Bernie Sanders, and AOC for ushering in socialism. Our republic will become a banana republic, and our constitution would become obsolete. I understand TeeSpring, your company think it's doing the right thing when you cancel an American citizen out of fear, because of the cunning, obvious bias opinions and deceptive influence of the media. Here is a profound quote from Malcolm X, that explains the division of our nation, and I quote," The media's the most powerful entity on earth. They have the power to make the innocent guilty and to make the guilty innocent, and that's power, because they control the minds of the masses."

May God bless America,
Sonny B.

LETTER TO BISHOP T.D. JAKES

Greetings,

I am a proud American law-abiding citizen of this great nation. Also, a father of (6) six wonderful children with my beautiful and lovely wife of 22 years. It is a shame to say, that this letter can be given to most mega churches and churches across the country. However, in this letter, I focus on one man, Bishop T.D. Jakes and my disappointment of what I've seen over the years. A very influential man of God, afraid to take a stance on biblically founded issues, in desperate need of addressing in the public eye.

Where do I begin? I have to start with the church in general, to bring home my point. When there is mention of the church, there are so many directions we can take. I'll start with what I believe is the most important component destroying the unity and common bond of America. The cry of victimhood from the black church, and the white church who pander this notion. Secondly, why does the church have a color separation, is beyond me. I can assure you, God didn't have color in mind when He established the church. Thank God heaven isn't based on color and more importantly my opinion or your opinion but based on the truth of God's word. We as humans don't get to decide, rather child sacrifice (abortion) is right or wrong, or if same sex marriage should be herald in the same fashion as one man and one woman in holy matrimony, or if little white lies are as innocent as a newborn baby. Extramarital affairs cannot be justified by public opinion because of unhappiness with a spouse. These are examples of sin, laid out plainly in God's word; Which is why so many

268

people want to discredit Christianity as just a religion some people choose to follow. This notion only bolsters the continued journey of wrong and evil doings. In other words, if God doesn't exist, accountability doesn't exist either; Therefore, I can do as I please and not have to answer to anyone after this life on earth.

The church is in a conundrum, which is why the world is in trouble. The church has no sense of itself, because the church doesn't hear the voice of God, but rather listen to and befriend the likes of: Oprah Winfrey, Tyler Perry, Charlamagne tha god, The view, politicians and the mainstream media (enemy of the people). Pastors like yourself, stand before thousands in mega churches, while influencing millions of lost souls across the TV air waves with a message of: another level, name it and claim it, give and have everything you desire and get your breakthrough. Conference after conference after conference, with nothing to show for it, other than very wealthy mega pastors and congregations without a biblical world view or sound biblical doctrine concerning the wages of sin. While the devastation, chaos and corruption looms over America in 2020, the church is too busy fighting against flesh and blood and aligning themselves with a racist, Marxist Black Lives Matter movement under the guise of black lives mattering. If black lives really mattered, the world would be on fire for black-on-black murder, but that's another story.

There was a preacher that put everything in perspective for me about homosexuality. A statement I wish, I'd heard years ago, because I fought with the conception of homosexual's time and time again. Are homosexual's born that way? To the point, I would avoid this conversation altogether. The preacher's statement was, we are all born homosexuals. What? Was my reply, but as I continued to listen, it became clear to me. As the preacher continued with his message, he said, we are born adulterers, fornicators, pedophiles, liars, murderers, and serial killers; Because mankind is born into sin, we are all these things unmanifested. Which is why we need to be born again, before these sins do manifest in our lives. So, now when a homosexual says to me, I was born this way, I agree but tell them they can be born again.

Bishop T.D. Jakes, you've received backlash in the past from Christians about your stance on same sex marriage and your recent support of Kamala Harris, rightfully so. Let's say from the offset, the mainstream media cannot call an election; Therefore, Harris is not Vice-President elect. There is proof of massive voter fraud in the presidential election and it's under investigation, but one wouldn't know this by listening to the democratic mainstream media. Bishop Jakes, everything you are supposed to stand for, she and the democratic party is against, they are: Anti-life, Anti-God, Anti-traditional marriage (Harris was proud to marry the first gay couple in California, when it became legal in the eyes of man), she and Biden supported the 1994 Clinton crime bill by incarcerating as many blacks as they could, even if it meant withholding evidence to indict a negro. Anti- America (Pro-Socialism), and Anti-school choice and vouchers.

Bishop Jakes, you are well versed in the gospel and dissecting the word in the pulpit but lack the integrity of the God's word in the public eye. It's as if you're not at all knowledgeable about social culture or don't seem to care. Why do I say this? You used a silhouette of Ruby Bridges, I guess to symbolize where we as minorities have come from and to congratulate Harris's future ahead? I remind you, Ruby Bridges was the first black child to destroy the segregation law in Louisiana; that's called school choice in today's time. Again, school choice is something Harris and the democrats have tried to eradicate for years, and vouchers (scholarships provided to low-income families for private school choices), which benefits minorities, especially the black race in the state of Florida.

The black community, pastors, leaders, and activists believe the republican party are racist because the media tells us they are. When this allegation is far from the truth, when in fact history tells us who the real racist is. This is why the racist, Marxist BLM/Antifa democratic thugs are trying to annihilate history by destroying names, monuments, and statues linked to the confederacy. President Trump debunked the racist lie in a grand way, by proving it in his policies and actions. To realize this, you must use your own brain, do your own research and not rely on the lying, deceitful, diabolical and divisive media to inform you. In my own research, I stumbled upon an article while searching for information on black-on-black homicide, that's how far buried this article was. It was an article about President Trump's contributions to the black community, written in the NY Post. It was published on July 4, 2020, by Gianno Caldwell, titled, "How Trump-not Biden- has helped make black lives better." Bishop Jakes, you should read the column in its entirety, but here are a few highlights: Police reform executive order. The First Step Act, which released thousands of people from jail (90% of whom were black). Trump promoted "Opportunity zones" that incentivized private investment into marginalized communities (black communities especially). This is a quote directly from the article, "Trump increased federal funding to historically black colleges and universities by 17% - a total exceeding $100 million, more than any other president in history. Meanwhile the Obama administration infamously removed a two-year Bush administration program that annually funded $85 million directly to these prized institutions." End quote. Also, Trump's foreign policies are unmatched by any other president. He moved the U.S. embassy to Jerusalem. He negotiated peace treaty deals. Not to mention, he settled down North Korea's rocket man. His foreign trade deals are second to none, meaning we finally, have fair trading. America is no longer taken advantage of by foreign leaders and nations. Also, he asked for the black vote, unlike the democratic party, he didn't assume because I'm black I should vote for him; That's called respect from a sitting President and disrespect from a lackluster and sinister democratic party.

A relative of mine, asked me a question, why hasn't Trump said anything about George Floyd? I answered him with a question, do you know who Legend is? His response was no.

I proceeded by saying, why is George Floyd's name known around the world? But no one knows the names of the souls killed as a result of the rioting and lawlessness because of Floyd? Trump knows their names, and in the honor of the little 4-year-old toddler that was killed amongst the chaos and mayhem, he created 'Operation Legend.' Legend was one of nine innocent children killed because of the barbaric activity on the streets of the U.S. The ages ranged from 1 to 14 years old. The BLM movement is such hogwash. Again, if black lives really mattered, the world would be on fire for the thousands of blacks killed at the hands of blacks across this nation every year!!!

Some are appalled at Trump's antics, his fight and fervor to save America from the radical socialist renegades of BLM/Antifa, Capitol Hill and the deep state. Trump speaks our language, has the passion, gusto, feistiness, indignation and displeasure of the corrupt political system, just like us as TRUE AMERICANS. We have been ignored and lied to by Washington D.C. for decades and covered up by the media. Everyone who voted for Trump, loves his work, the movement is real, and the American people are on fire!!!

Lastly, Jesse Lee Peterson said it best, RENT A BLACK, you can always find a black to do evil. I used to wonder why black folk seem to always be on the side of wrong and why white guilt excuse this notion, while pandering the perpetual self-inflicted problems of the black community. Also, why is the church combat ineffective? I came across this quote from Malcolm X that explains our societal downfall in a very clear way. I quote," The media's the most powerful entity on earth. They have the power to make the innocent guilty and to make the guilty innocent, and that's power, because they control the minds of the masses." Therein lies our problem in a nutshell, the Marxist media.

May God bless America,
Sonny B.

LETTER TO NATIONAL GOVERNORS ASSOCIATION

Greetings,

I am a proud black American citizen of this great nation. I am a father of (6) six wonderful children with my lovely wife of 22 years. I am writing to you because my children's future is at stake and our country as we know it, is at stake. In question, is the presidential election under Governor Brian Kemp's state of Georgia. Why isn't he in the public eye in the midst of one of the greatest scandals in American history? Does the NGA hold governors accountable for not doing their job? Is there any politician out there with any ounce of integrity? Your Governor Brian Kemp sees the fraud going on in his state but has yet to come out and denounce the fraudulent recount of the ballots. I don't care what side of the isle you're on, our civil liberty as voting citizens is at stake; especially with current massive voter fraud across the country, namely in your state of Georgia. Elected officials, are sworn to uphold the constitution and to serve the American people, also to step up and contest this grotesque corruption of our voting system. If this is allowed our Republic is DEAD, and America as we know it, is DONE!!! Again, if this major voter fraud is allowed, we may as well welcome in China and North Korea, congratulate George Soros, Bernie Sanders and AOC for successfully ushering in socialism.

About (Doctrine): National Governors Association

"We're the bipartisan organization of the nation's governors. Founded in 1908, the National Governors Association is the voice of the leaders of 55 states, territories, and commonwealths. Our nation's governors are dedicated to leading bipartisan solutions that improve citizens' lives through state government. Through NGA, governors identify priority issues and deal with matters of public policy and governance at the state, nation and global levels."

I quoted you your organizations' doctrine to remind and bring to the forefront the issue at hand. If this is the real purpose of NGA, there should be a phone call made and MY EMAIL FOWARDED TO Governor Brian Kemp, telling him to come out of the dungeon and fight for his state. It is very difficult to get a full letter in detail to any elected official concerning an issue. Therefore, I'm relying on NGA to convey my concerns to Governor Kemp, his wife and staff.

Our voting process under the constitution of the United States of America, should be done fairly without prejudice. Well, unless you've been under a rock or in a dungeon or listening to the mainstream media (enemy of the people), one wouldn't know about the all-out assault on our Republic. I don't care if you love or hate President Trump, we all have a responsibility to protect our voting process. The audacity to attempt to overthrow an election should make everyone not involved in the scandal, outraged. There is massive proof of voter fraud, but the media is projecting it as a conspiracy theory; Just like they told us the protest throughout 2020 were mostly peaceful, while buildings were burning down behind them, such evil liars.

As citizens of the United States of America, we have an obligation to protect our freedoms in this country. NGA, I am depending on you to relay my letter to the proper channels asked in this letter because you have the capability of obtaining information, I'm unable to obtain. Lastly, I told a relative of mine, I don't care if you are democrat, republican, independent, or libertarian if we allow the socialist in our country to usher in socialism, WE ALL LOSE!!! This is where we are in our country, at a crossroad of freedom or socialism. BLM/Antifa and radical progressives are trying to bring down our country to its demise with the help of mainstream media. We not only have to combat our foreign enemy foes, but now we have to contend with the enemies from within America, "yelling death to America, bring in communism." While they stomped on and burned the American flag. No, this was not from radical Islamic terrorist, this was from, so called Americans. God help us!

May God Bless America,
Sonny B.

LETTER TO STATE SECRETARY OF GEORGIA/NR

Greetings Mr. Raffensperger and National Review,

This letter is in response to the article written by Secretary of State of Georgia Brad Raffensperger, published on November 26, 2021, titled: "One year ago, Trump called me an 'Enemy of the People'. Rising costs and inflation are the real enemy". Also, I believe this article is a conflict of interest, when National Review news outlet would allow a governmental official to write about government issues Mr. Raffensperger is very much a part of.

I like to start out my letters by stating who I am, so not to be mistaken as a racist or white supremacist. Extreme leftist love to use the word racist to their advantage and to shut-up non-blacks who call out their lunacy. Well, I am a proud black American law-abiding, patriotic citizen of the greatest country in the world. However, I'm doing my best to prohibit Marxist liberals from destroying it. Also, I tell you of my ethnicity to let you know all black people are not enamored nor influenced by the media's craftiness to deceive. The media have become experts in the art of deception and illusion, Houdini would be proud. Our corrupt government, mainstream media and Big Tech. collaborated the scheme of 'Cancel Culture'. Killing free speech, to make it one speech, the speech that only lines up with Marxism. Anyone talking out of line, is canceled, and deemed as promoting hate speech and a domestic terrorist. This serves as three purposes: to encourage you not to speak out and to create fear, and to keep as many American citizens ill-informed and in the dark about the truth. We can learn a lesson from Sun Tzu's 'The Art of War,' you can cause much more damage and division by posing an Information War, it's less bloody that way. However, I believe we are on the verge of Civil War 2.0, which will be bloody, but the 'The Art of War' says that's ok as long as the citizens are fighting each other.

I digress to Mr. Brad Raffensperger, the Secretary of State to Georgia. I believe you are compromised, which explains your opinions in the article and your eagerness to shift the blame. Like I said earlier in my letter, this is exactly why you are given the freedom to express your propaganda in the National Review, because you have the same goal to demolish the Constitution of the United States of America. Yes, I agree wholeheartedly with President Trump, Raffensperger you are 'The Enemy of the People', but don't worry, you are not alone. The mainstream media, Big Tech, Big PHARMA, the political cesspool on Capitol Hill and academia is 'The Enemy of the People' as well. However, I hold fake news (National Review) and the many others like them more highly accountable. News should procure checks and balances of current events by telling the story as is, not making it up as you go, not taking words out of context, not splicing, splitting or cutting out vital information of a story, not spinning the story with propaganda and rhetoric to paint a narrative, and journalism never should be partisan or bias. Needless to say, it has become blatantly obvious, that the mainstream media is an extension of the democratic party and their agenda to change America. Without the lying media, our country and our world would be much better off. Here is a quote from Malcolm X, I believe explains to us who the media really is, he said, "The media's the most powerful entity on earth. They have the power to make the innocent guilty and to make the guilty innocent, and that's power, because they control the minds of the masses."

Here is a quote from the article by Raffensperger, "Conservatives need to do more to push back, as these policies do very real damage to the American families that are struggling to get by." My response to this is, conservatives did, democrats did, and independent voters did by voting to give President Trump a second term, but the election was STOLEN!!! Let me explain!!! President Trump had record numbers of people to attend his rallies. The Biden/Harris ticket could not attract flies even if they had cow manure smeared all over their bodies, BUT BIDEN GOT MORE VOTES THAN PRESIDENT OBAMA? I continue, something happened on election night, something that has never happened before in election history, 'THEY STOPPED COUNTING'!!! President Trump was on his way to a second term. We would go to bed with an insurmountable Trump lead and wake up to a Biden lead. This was the greatest scandal of the century to destroy our republic, and to desecrate a legal and supposedly honest process for the American people to determine the outcome of an election. National Review, CNN (Communist News Network), MSNBC (MSDNC), FOX in the hen house news and Newsmax (NewsLax), ignored, vilified and covered up the massive election fraud all over the country. Especially, in the states in question, yes, Mr. Secretary

Raffensperger, that would include your state of Georgia as well. The treason in your state happened under your watch. This act was tremendous in nature and extremely treasonous to say the least; I pray that everyone who had a hand in this grotesque injustice finds themselves in the newly renovated Gitmo prison. We can't move on until this mess is fixed.

A close second to the greatest scandal of the century was the "Pandemic" (Scamdemic; Plandemic). The 'Gain of function' Wuhan virus, China virus, Fauci virus (Covid-19), was used to destroy a thriving economy under President Trump, control the citizens and manipulate the election to usher in the New World Order (Great Reset, Globalism). There was domestic and international collaboration with the use Dominion machines, fake mail-in ballots, deceased voting and discarded Trump ballots to create massive election fraud (TREASON). The mainstream media (Enemy of the People) was complicit in the diabolical plan. However, Maricopa County was the first to do a forensic auditing with huge evidence that the 2020 Presidential election was manipulated, with more forensic auditing to come in other states. We are still waiting to see if Arizona will be the first to de-certify their electoral, THE CORRUPTION RUNS DEEP!!!

When I say SCAMDEMIC, I'm not saying the virus isn't real. I'm saying the virus was prostituted like a 'Ten Dolla Whore'. Like Joe Rogan, I too was cured from covid by the use of ivermectin. An FDA approved drug that has been demonized by the media (Enemy of the People) as a horse dewormer with fatal implications if used by humans. While mandating with strong coercion to push deadly experimental vaccines with lethal consequences. I ask a question, if this is the deadliest pandemic the world has ever seen, killing millions worldwide; shouldn't we want to exhaust every means known to mankind to rid the world of this virus? So why are therapeutics known to treat and cure Covid-19 being: blocked, demonized, censored, vilified and discouraged, if we are in the greatest "Pandemic" the world has ever seen? That's a rhetorical question by the way.

This is the type of disingenuous news coverage the mainstream media is known for, which is why anyone with a brain to think logically, sensibly, critically and with common sense, don't tune into fake news. American people that dared to tune into fake news were told that Kyle Rittenhouse was enroute to kill Black Lives Matter (BLM) protesters (RIOTERS), and three white by-standers were trying to stop him. The three assailant's color was not mentioned initially to stir up more racial tension. In addition, the media failed to mention the character of these three individuals, that all three were career criminals and one of them was a disgusting pedophile and another a felon with a pistol, but quick to label Rittenhouse as a murderer and white supremacist. I continue, those that dared to tune into fake news were told that a red SUV accidentally crashed through a Christmas parade in Waukesha, Wisconsin. What should've been said was, there was a black lunatic, and BLM sympathizer, who drove savagely with intent to kill innocent adults and children. These are endless examples of disingenuous news coverage; However, I believe this is the best example of all times. An NBC reporter turning the phrase 'F' Joe Biden into "Let's Go Brandon" to cover-up the incompetent, rogue and totalitarian Biden regime. We who are not mesmerized by the media zombie apocalypse can never forget the media storm of January 6. How the media portrayed that day as a day of insurrection and an assault to our democracy, but a YEAR of chaos and lawlessness by BLM/Antifa was MOSTLY PEACEFUL, AND A SUMMER OF LOVE, SUCH HYPOCRISY!!! Prime examples that the media is filled with propaganda, rhetoric and divisive lies to dismantle the sovereignty of our nation. They divide, we fight one another, and they conquer with more totalitarianism throughout America.

Lastly, the media plays the racial game with my black race, but some of us haven't learned yet. We can be the most gullible people on the planet and the media knows it; which is why they exploit race relations between blacks and whites, especially during election cycles. It's very sad, these Communist can just throw out trigger words to the black race, like: racism, white privilege, systematic racism, oppression, social injustice and police brutality, and we jump on it like a dog in heat. On the other hand, mention Fatherlessness in the black home, and we go silent, no outrage on this subject. Oh, I have more we go silent on, like: Black on black murder, teen pregnancy, abortion (Legal genocide), domestic abuse, drug abuse, crime, gang violence, incarceration, illiteracy, and school drop-out in the black community. These are all self-inflicted problems that has plagued the black community for decades. The most disheartening thing is, these neighborhoods across the U.S. are represented by mostly black democratic governmental officials, while the republicans standby idlily watching these atrocities with their finger up their butt. Furthermore, wealthy black race hustlers use their influence to stoke the racism flame, like: Colin Kaepernick, LeBron James, Oprah Winfrey, Tyler Perry, Snoop Dogg, Jemele Hill, Joy Reid, Don Lemon, Al and Jesse, to name a very few. All they do is hate on our country and stir-up offended blacks that won't let go of the past, I sound like a broken record, but I'm going to shout it from the mountain top until somebody listens. Their wealth and influence are missed opportunities to encourage little black boys and girls to know that they can be anything they want to be in this country of freedom; Just look at me, should be their mantra. There are some people in the black race who don't realize they are unknowingly willing participants in a Chinese Communist Party (CCP) controlled U.S. government takeover. I'm going to continue to expose the lie, I don't care if you like it or not. I will die standing for the truth, because if we lose our freedom, then we are dead already. 'We The People' are here to take back our country from renegades like Raffensperger, posing as Americans. 1776 Rewind!!! Let's Go Brandon!!!

May God Bless America,
Sonny B.

LETTER TO REP. MARJORIE TAYLOR GREENE

Greetings,

I write this letter with tears in my eyes as I think about the atrocities of our beloved nation. So, excuse the lengthiness of this letter, but not its content, because I have something to say. I want to start out by giving my apologies for using a random home for sale in your district to get an audience with you. I actually live in Florida with an unbelievably awesome governor in Ron DeSantis. However, there are literally only a handful of politicians who are working for the American people. Politicians that will not bow down to the pressures of the CCP owned fake news networks, deep state system nor to the fake woke mob. I wrote a letter to President Trump back in early 2020, I told him, I would join him in a fox hole to do battle with him any given day of the week, because he fights with unwavering passion without ever retreating, even after all of the vicious attacks he's had to endure. I come from a line of strong and bold fighters; I too will not retreat in the heat of battle. I understand, this is not a fight of democrat VS republican (A ONE-PARTY SYSTEM), conservatives VS liberals, or right VS left but good VS evil, and we cannot allow evil to prevail. The freedom in our nation hangs in the balance. I believe our children and generations to come are depending on us to protect the colors of the red, white and blue, a banner representing freedom.

Again, I reside in Florida, but all of America is my home; Therefore, I believe I must defend it by any means necessary. Drastic times calls for drastic measures; Therefore, we have to take desperate measures to take back our country from Communist renegades posing as

Americans. This country affords us all the freedom to pick and choose what you want to be in life, no matter your race, gender, creed or nationality background. No, I am not oppressed by social injustice, systematic racism, white privilege or police brutality, nothing can hold me down, but me. However, after 2020, I realized there was something that could hold me down and it's called the deep state system of Globalism, driven by Marxists'.

My wife and I have six (6) children together. I am a retired fireman in Florida and chef, to one day own my own breakfast/lunch restaurant. I used my hard-earned money to attend culinary school; As a result, I have been able to work in some of the best kitchens in Jacksonville and surrounding areas as a part-time line/prep cook to hon my culinary skills. After retirement, I told my wife I was going to take a short sabbatical before going back to cook. Four (4) months after retirement, I began working for an exclusive hotel in Ponte Vedra Sawgrass. My plans were to work there for about a year and open my first restaurant. Furthermore, I was approved to sell my desserts at a very prominent outside market on weekends. Well, the world would be hit with the coronavirus and the world would come to a complete halt.

I was minding my own business like every other American. I went to work to provide for my family and would wind down and relax with entertainment from Hollywood, dining out, vacationing, theme parks, sports and ESPN. The PLANDEMIC came to shatter all dreams and aspirations of taking advantage of the privileges of the greatest country in the world. So yes, the corrupt deep state system can hold you down, and yes, I'm pissed!!! To say the least. All I want to do is cook, I want peace, I don't take pleasure in fighting, I just want to be left alone by the deep state, CCP controlled government; However, as a patriot I cannot stand idly by and watch our country go to pot. Just about everything in America is made by China, so I guess you can say I was made by China, Covid-19 the Wuhan China virus. Without the virus, we wouldn't be having this conversation, so I call it a blessing in disguise, because my eyes came open to the evilness in our nation.

The wicked and corrupt are shielded by the fake news media and allowed to run amok with little or no consequences. While homes of innocent patriotic citizens from January 6 were raided and taken into custody, where they are still presently incarcerated for no reason. When BLM/Antifa was allowed to destroy cities across the nation for about a year with no repercussion. Instead, the lawlessness was called 'MOSTLY PEACEFUL' and a 'SUMMER OF LOVE.' While 98% of democrats and republicans sat, watched and did nothing, but point fingers at one another. They bring sinister people to congress for questioning (WHICH IS A DOG AND PONY SHOW) as if they are trying to get to the bottom of the crime committed. There is concrete evidence against Fauci the fraud, he committed crimes against humanity with 'GAIN OF FUNCTION', but he is still allowed to run the streets while continuing his diabolical deeds. Fauci went before congress, so my point should be well taken. WHAT A JOKE!!! Sorry to inform you Ringling Bros.-Barnum and Bailey Circus, the political cesspool on Capitol Hill has The Greatest Show on Earth.

2020 taught me a good lesson, it showed the future of America going down the drain, which is why I'm fighting with every fiber in my being. Therefore, I put my dream on hold to fight for my children's future and generations to come. I battle to save America with my writings. I have over 100 actual letters like the one I sent to you a few weeks ago. Letters sent out to President Trump, politicians (local, state and federal), U.S. Supreme Court, corporations, academia, NFL, NBA, MLB, you name them, and I've written to them. I am presently attending all school board meetings and addressing them as well. I am taking all of my letters and compiling them into a book, a memoir. It will be a very unique book with no chapters, entitled, 'Cloudy; With the Chance of Communism.' It's already finished, the last phase is to get it published and promoted. I'm putting together this book in hopes of motivating, encouraging and inspiring ordinary patriots like myself across the country to stand up against tyranny, because 'We the People' have to take control of our destiny and where America is headed. Now that you know a little about who I am, I digress to the vitally important reason for my second letter to you.

Governor Ron DeSantis is doing everything he can to restore our Republic and faith in our elections. You know, I know, and everybody knows, the 2020 Presidential election was stolen with massive election fraud (Treason), domestic and international collaboration with the mainstream media complicit in the greatest scandal of the century. Gov. DeSantis implemented the National Guard to assists law enforcement on election day in 2020, to prayerfully curtail the criminal activity and violence for the 2020 election. I believe the proactiveness can be very beneficial for all upcoming elections across the nation, if the Nation Guard and law enforcement are vetted and educated on how honest elections should be run. Here is the title of the article I received the information from, "Gov. DeSantis activates National Guard to assist law enforcement on Election Day" Published by Florida Politics and written by Renzo Downey on November 3, 2020. Here is a quote from that article to give an explanation why DeSantis implemented the National Guard, "Across the country, Governors have activated their state National Guard to potentially play law enforcement roles if there is election-related violence. Some have filled in as un-uniformed poll workers or to provide cybersecurity expertise in monitoring potential intrusions into election systems."

Lastly, Rep. Greene, you know if we do not fix our election process, America is finished. Our elections need something like what was just mentioned in the prior paragraph or something similar, along with voter ID, and ridding our elections of mail-in-ballots except for military and homebound handicap. I'm asking that you speak with your constituents in D.C. to divulge a plan, if you haven't already. I've heard many say, if this isn't fixed, there would be no need to vote, and I tend to agree wholeheartedly. I will go as far as to say, I will not vote. My continued prayer is, something will be done, because I do not want to lose America as we know it. If our elections aren't fixed, we will become the new Australia. If the Marxist continue to have a clear path for stealing elections, the totalitarian Biden regime will continue to destroy our freedom, right from up under the Constitution. There is a letter following this letter that I sent to your Secretary of State, Brad Raffensperger and his administration and National Review news outlet called (Enemy of the People).

May God Bless America,
Sonny B.

LETTER TO GEORGIA CONGRESS REPS

Greetings,

In short, is there any politician out there with any ounce of integrity? Your Governor Brian Kemp, saw the fraud that went on in his state, but has yet to come out and denounce the fraudulent recount of the ballots. I don't care what side of the isle you're on, our civil liberty as voting citizens is at stake; especially with the current massive voter fraud across the country, namely in your state of Georgia. I'm asking you as an elected official, sworn to uphold the constitution and to serve the American people, to step up to contest this grotesque corruption of our voting system. If this is allowed our democracy is DEAD, and America as we know it, is DONE!!! Again, if this major voter fraud is allowed, we may as well welcome in China and North Korea, congratulate George Soros, Bernie Sanders and AOC for successfully ushering in socialism.

LETTER TO LAW.COM, NATIONAL BAR ASSOCIATION AND GA. BAR ASSOC

Greetings,

I am a proud black American citizen of this great nation. I am a father of (6) six awesome children with my lovely wife of 23 years. I only tell of my race identity to let you know I am a black man well aware of what's going on in our country and that all blacks are not ill-informed, low information voters. Also, I am no longer swayed by the bias opinions of the mainstream media (enemy of the people) to divide our nation with propaganda and rhetoric. The black race has become the golden child, presently speaking, in our country. Professional sports, major corporations, academia, Hollywood, social giants, big tech, republican and democratic politicians have bent over backwards to cater to the black race. Therefore, give me a moment of your undivided attention to express my concerns and to plead my case of a double standard, hypocrisy, and unbalance justice in our justice system.

This letter is in response to Law.com's daily report titled, "Refusing plea for bond, judge says lawyer at capitol riots was corrupted." Published on January 21, 2021, by Jonathan Ringel. I was able to read only a portion of the article due to subscribing regulations. However, I am intelligent enough to read between the lines, because articles like these with attacks towards Trump supporters come a dime a dozen.

My wife and I teach our children to love their neighbors as themselves, no matter who they are. Also, to treat others the way they would want to be treated. Be color blind and see everyone individually and not as a whole; in other words, don't paint a race of people with a broad brush just because you've had several bad experiences. If we all took this advice, what a wonderful world it would be. We also remind our children, Racism Comes in All Colors, just because you're black, God does not give you a pass!!! These are all biblical values, which is why I believe the bible is the most sought after and the most hated by those who want to judge by their own prejudice standard.

Lady Justice is in federal court houses, law offices and legal institutions all over America as a reminder to all that enter, that justice is unbiased, fair and transparent. Lady Justice is symbolic of what our justice system should uphold; Unfortunately, this country has swayed far away from impartiality, honor, and integrity. The meaning behind Lady Justice was taken from Heather and Little blog; The symbols of justice: BALANCE SCALES- "These represent impartiality and obligation of the law (through its representation) to weigh the evidence presented to the court. Each side of a legal case needs to be looked at and comparisons made as justice is done. "SWORD- "This item symbolizes enforcement and respect and means that justice stands by its decision and ruling and is able to take action. The fact that the sword is unsheathed and very visible is a sign that justice is transparent and is not an implement of fear. A double-edge blade signifies that justice can rule against either of the parties once the evidence has been perused, and it is bound to enforce the ruling as well as protect or defend the innocent party. "BLINDFOLD- The blindfold represents the impartiality and objectivity of the law and that it doesn't let outside factors, such as POLITICS, WEALTH, or FAME influence its decisions." This is a reminder, a refresher course to those who have forgotten the meaning of equal justice.

Let me be clear, I do not condone, take part in or delight in seeing lawlessness and injustice being done. I also believe, injustice for injustice never yields a solution. I continue in reference about the article in question concerning a Georgia lawyer given no leniency by a judge who watched lawlessness, chaos, destruction of lives and property across America for almost 9 months and in some cities like Portland the violence is yet ensuing. BLM/Antifa rioting was applauded and celebrated as mostly peaceful as we watched cities burn. One mayor would call the mayhem, "A summer of love." Mind you BLM/Antifa thugs destroyed federal buildings, federal monuments, federal statues, federal vehicles, private property, private vehicles, businesses and anything in sight. They even threatened lives of police officers inside a federal building by setting the exit on fire to impede egression. Not to mention, these thugs, when arrested were given bail and released, sometimes within the same day. Again, I do not condone violence, but 1 day of riot on January 6, 2021, in comparison to what the world saw for months across the nation is massively disproportionate. Now, after almost a year of chaos ignored, Trump rallies were put under a microscope and any little thing that went wrong at a Trump march was looked at as the UNPARDONABLE SIN. I can't reiterate it enough, such hypocrisy and a double standard to say the least.

This type of grotesque injustice and disdain for conservatives, Christians and Trump supporters is blatantly obvious by the judgements rendered to these types of citizens. Case in point: This is a quote from the article in question, "You were at the Capitol on January 6, 2021, the judge said, adding that Calhoun and PATRIOTS crossed a sacred line." ARE YOU TRYING TO TELL ME IT'S A SACRED LINE DEPENDING ON WHO'S CROSSING IT? Because that's exactly what that says to me when BLM/Antifa destroyed D.C. and other cities, but were never told they crossed any lines, they were given cheers for their violence and true incitement from corrupt politicians and media. They even went into neighborhoods wreaking havoc, but a law-abiding couple from St. Louis protecting their property from these menace to society were arrested. BLM wrecked a restaurant in Rochester, NY as white patrons were dining, urging them to leave with threatening and derogatory remarks towards them. This is only a few examples of many incidents that transpired over many months of reverse racism and civil disobedience. Yet, there is silence from the: media/social giants, professional sports, justice system, academia, Hollywood, major corporations, democratic politicians, republican politicians (RINO's), big tech, governmental agencies, ie. (FBI, CIA), unpatriotic offended blacks, and unpatriotic guilt-ridden white liberals. Mind you, this disorderly conduct was all done in the name of justice for a black life. IF BLACK LIVES REALLY MATTERED, WHY NO OUTRAGE FOR BLACK-ON-BLACK MURDER THAT KILLS THOUSANDS ACROSS AMERICA EVERY YEAR?

Wealthy black enablers like: Lebron James, Ice Cube, Oprah Winfrey, and Tyler Perry to name a few, use their influence to divide and spread the cancer of racism from their own hearts. Yet, not a word about the murder rate among blacks killing one another. SUCH HYPOCRITS!!!

In conclusion, while I have your attention, with yet another example of the justice system's bias enforcement and lack of integrity. We have courts across America identified as kangaroo courts and I would say the U.S. Supreme Court would be Captain Kangaroo. It was blatantly obvious to anyone with a brain watching the elections with President Trump up hundreds of thousands in some battleground states in question with 85-95% of votes already in; Then it happened, something that has never happened in the entire history of an election, states were told to stop counting and to resume the following morning. We woke up only to find Biden up in votes. What just happened was every patriot's response? President Trump had record crowds at every one of his rallies. Biden on the other hand could not draw flies if he had dung over his entire body, but he received more votes than former President Obama? That in itself would spark the interest to at least see the evidence presented by the Trump legal team. What gross injustice, not one court across the nation including Captain Kangaroo did not want to hear or see the evidence of massive election fraud. I don't care if you love or hate Trump, or if you are a republican, democrat, independent, humanitarian or libertarian, if you knew anything about the assault on our republic, you should be enraged, because it's my vote this time and yours the next time. If we can have a domestic and international collaboration to hijack an election to get the approval of the CCP, we may as well welcome in China, North Korea and congratulate George Soros, Bernie Sanders and AOC for successfully ushering in socialism. I never thought I would see the day when a white male would be the most hated in America and patriotism would be synonymous with white supremacy. The media is complicit in the plot to destroy America from within. How else do you get unpatriotic offended blacks and unpatriotic guilt-ridden white liberals to riot? You feed them racism and you make it a steady diet!!! Malcolm X made a profound statement concerning the media, I believe why we are at a crossroad to save a nation or see it come to its demise. Malcolm's quote," The media's the most powerful entity on earth. They have the power to make the innocent guilty and to make the guilty innocent, and that's power, because they control the minds of the masses."

May God bless America,
Sonny B.

LETTER TO U.S. SUPREME COURT
(The Case for America)

Greetings to the honorable supreme court justice: Clarence Thomas; Stephen Breyer; John G. Roberts; Samuel A. Alito, Jr.; Sonia Sotomayor; Elena Kagan; Neil McGill Corsuch; Brett Michael Kavanaugh; Amy Coney Barrett

This letter is in regard to the massive voter fraud of our Presidential election and all elections in question, present and future across our nation. I am a proud black American citizen of this great nation. I tell you of my color to assure you I am not with the racist/Marxist Black Lives Matter movement. So please allow me a moment of your time, while I explain the case for America.

I am a father of (6) six awesome children with my beautiful, lovely wife of 22 years. Contrary to popular belief according to the anarchist of America, our country affords us all the freedom and opportunity to do and become whatever you set your mind to. Justice Clarence Thomas and 2 term former President Barack Obama are two examples of many thousands of blacks with like success stories because of our sovereign nation under God. However, you would never know it, if you listen to the mainstream media (enemy of the people), Lebron James, Oprah Winfrey, Tyler Perry, Ice Cube and Snoop Dog, just to name a few; With many blacks employed by the media and all just mentioned are living the American dream. However, with their plush bank accounts, they only spew negative words of anger, hate and disdain for our country, President Trump and the patriotic citizens of the U.S. Imagine if they used all of their time, energy and influence in a positive way. The impact on the lives of little black boys/girls would be priceless. Instead, they choose to use their influence to divide a nation, and project racism on others, to hide the real racism in their hearts. I like to say this to my black race from time to time: Racism comes in all colors, just because you're black, God does not give you a pass. These same people, including the media, tells us 24/7 that police brutality is vast in our country, but ignore the thousands of deaths across America every year because of black-on-black murder. There is silence on this subject from: NBA, NFL, MLB, NHL, WNBA, major corporations, BLM, colleges, Hollywood, music entertainers, Al and Jesse. Not to mention: Fatherlessness, teen pregnancy, abortion, black-on-black homicides, crime, drugs, gang violence, incarceration, illiteracy, and school dropout; Are all self-inflicted problems that has plagued the black community for decades, and the most disheartening thing is, these communities are governed by mostly black democratic officials. Did anyone notice anything? Police brutality does not make the list. The media is endangering our courageous men and women who don the police uniform, by telling the black community they should be afraid of the cops. When more deaths disproportionately to police brutality come out of the black community at the hands of blacks.

I never thought that I would see the day, when the white male would be one of the most hated in our country because of success and love of country. To me this sounds more like envy than hate, but that's just me. If a white man is rich, he is a white supremacist; If he loves his country, he is a nationalist; If he wants safety along our borders from illegals, he becomes a xenophobe. Sadly enough, this notion of discontent is pushed by white democratic liberals. Also, any blacks calling out this non-sense are ridiculed and deemed out of touch, sellout, Uncle Tom, and a coon, sadly enough the derogatory name calling is done by black democrats. I do not like politicians, and I believe I have the sentiment of most in our nation, this is why President Trump was elected in 2016, and should've been elected on November 3rd, if it wasn't for election fraud. In the past, I did not make it common ground to talk against either party, because I felt like both parties were corrupt. However, in 2020, when I see the diabolical scheme of the democratic party, mainstream media (extension of the democratic party), and foreign enemies conspiring together to induce socialism into our country, I must call out their corruption and hypocrisy.

Deplorables as Hillary would call those who support President Trump. This is how the democratic party feels about anyone who disagrees with their ideology. They don't want free speech, they one speech, and that is to fall in line their beliefs or else. Democrats and liberals say they are tolerant, until you disagree with them. They say they want unity but use identity politics to divide. They say they want dialogue, until they are hit square between the eyes with the truth. Democrats want to blow conservatives and Christians off the map. Take for example a very, very, extremely unfunny Trevor Noah, wanting Florida to be blown off the map because it went red for trump. If we had honest governors across the nation like Ron DeSantis, the whole country would be red!!! No censoring of the comment from Trevor's twitter account, but twitter censors the President of the United States of America. What? Social media did a massive censorship on conservative outlets two weeks before the election to hide the truth about Hunter Biden among other things. These radial progressives are telling us exactly who they are, and they aren't hiding it. There evil is done arrogantly in plain sight and dare anyone to question it. Well, I'm standing up to the renegades destroying our country. I am fearless, courageous and bold, I have the tenacity of the anarchist and savages without the violence; Because injustice plus injustice never equals solution.

I digress to my original point. The election between Trump/Biden will set a precedent if the grotesque corruption of obvious massive amounts of election fraud is allowed. Absolute power in the hands of the government (humans) corrupts absolutely; That's socialism in layman terms. If anyone can control and overthrow an election, our Republic is DEAD!!! We may as well welcome in North Korea and China and congratulate George Soros, Bernie Sanders and AOC on their success of transforming America into socialism. I don't care which side of the isle you're on, rather you are democrat, republican, independent or libertarian. This must be stopped!!! We have seen the blatantly obvious election fraud scam revealed by real news outlets, while fake news ignores it, as if it never happened. The media has been able to mesmerize and sway low information voters towards their agenda for decades. We come to really understand this like never before, when Trump became the primary candidate for the republican party. Malcolm X, I believe summed up the media, I quote," The media's the most powerful entity on earth. They have the power to make the innocent guilty and to make the guilty innocent, and that's power, because they control the minds of the masses." End quote.

I close with this, the way it looks, the incredible responsibility to right the wrong, will rely on the U.S. Supreme courts' decision to do so. I'm asking on behalf of millions of Americans who only want all of the legal ballots counted. In essence, a fair election. Each of you have a huge responsibility to uphold the rule of law as it is written in the Constitution. America hangs in the balance of a hostile socialist takeover or continual freedom for all, no matter your race, creed, or beliefs. The future of generations to come, depends on your decision to do the right thing. Thank you for your attention on this urgent matter.

May God bless America,
Sonny B.

EMAIL PROPHECY 12/12/2020

To publisher concierge

Good morning sir, I know you heard about the decision of the US supreme Court, very appalling. Again in 2016 everything was stacked against President Trump, but he came out on top because of the effectual and fervent prayers of the righteous availing much. I believe God likes to have this way, to remind us humans who's in charge. Psalms 20:7 talks about some trusting in chariots and in horses, but I'm trusting in the name of the Lord. An interpretation for today's time, some trust in attorneys and some in the US supreme Court, but I'm trusting in the name of the Lord. God's ways are not our ways, and His thoughts are not our thoughts. I don't understand His ways at times, but I do understand, we are always victorious no matter the situation. There is deep deep deep corruption, pedophiles, human trafficking and abortion to name a few, that must be stopped, and God intend to do it through another 4 years of Trump retaining his presidency. Sit back and watch the salvation of the Lord. It's far from over, God is exposing all of the secret, hidden corruption and letting the Patriots see who's really on our side. This is the beginning of a new revolution in America. May God bless America 🙏U

LETTER TO JU

Greetings,

I am a proud black American citizen of this great country. This letter is in regard to the Biden/Harris sign in the window of the Gooding building. I would like to start out by saying, this duo isn't dynamic at all, but they dynamically wreaked havoc on the black community in the early stages of their political careers. Which is why, I believe academia is no place for political biases where students should be educated about science, biology, math, etc, etc, to steer students in the direction to become productive citizens in society.

Academia, from grade school to the collegiate level has played a role in indoctrinating our children with propaganda of America being a racist nation; as a result, somehow, we need to cleanse our country of the constitution, republic and freedoms this country affords us all. I've had enough of the identity politics, with the underlying motive of using the black race like a school project to be completed. It's unfortunate, we fall for the rhetoric every time. All the far-left progressives have to do is, mix racism with any subject and you get an explosion of emotional outrage without all the facts, with chaos and destruction to follow. The most disheartening thing is, it doesn't have to be true, as long as the subject of the day is pushed 24/7 by the mainstream media, then it becomes the gospel. Even white liberals began to believe the falsehood, that somehow believe the lie that blacks are held down by a system. Just look at a year of riots in 2020. How else do you get blacks and whites to riot? You feed them racism and you make it a steady diet.

Case in point, George Floyd was a career criminal, which is why he came in contact with the law on that dreadful day. It was unfortunate, Floyd lost his life the way he did; However, the media would seize the opportunity to demonize all cops and purport our country as a racist nation. Simply because it was a white man killing a black man. Let me explain with a question, do black lives only matter, when a black man, kill a black man? I'll answer it for you with statistics and the real issues of the black community. In 2019, there were 7,484 black murders. In 2020, there were at least 8,600 black murders. In both years and prior to, over 90% of those said murders, were black on black homicides. Only silence from the media, professional sports, major corporations, social giants, colleges and all the black fake woke like: Colin Kaepernick, LeBron James, Gwen Berry, Oprah Winfrey, Tyler Perry, Joy Reid, Don Lemon, Ice Cube, and Snoop Dogg to name a few.

Let's talk fatherlessness in the black community, another huge problem no one is talking about. Why not? When this issue is the root of the black race undoing's. Fatherlessness leads to: Teen pregnancy, abortion, gang violence, drugs, incarceration, black on black murder, domestic abuse, school dropout and illiteracy. These are all self-inflicted problems that has plagued the black community for decades. Contrary to popular belief: Social injustice, systemic racism, oppression, white privilege and police brutality do not make the list. To add insult to injury, these communities are represented by mostly black democratic elected officials. Do you need more? This past 4th of July weekend in Chicago alone, were 80 black shootings and 14 deaths; yet, police brutality is an epidemic? This is happening in plain sight, but it's considered as the norm and of no concern; Therefore, it doesn't get the 24/7 publicity to paint a narrative of racism in America and to push a socialist agenda.

Lastly, please let your political science professors know, Biden/Harris is a part of the corrupt system destroying America. Just take an honest look at the economy, the border and everything else their hands are involved in. Then, by keeping a straight face say our nation is better off with these two. I don't care rather a candidate is republican or democrat, I look at the whole body of work of a politician. That means, I do my own research and I don't allow the media to control my decision making. Why is this? I believe this quote from Malcolm X will help you better understand. "The media's the most powerful entity on earth. They have the power to make the innocent guilty and to make the guilty innocent, and that's power, because they control the minds of the masses. "Let's just say, I will not be controlled by the media and likewise your attitude should be the same. If we all followed the truth, we all could truly unite as Americans and win back a true love and appreciation for the greatest country in the world. If you disagree with that final statement, then find a country you believe in and reside there. No one wants to take that advice, because it's easier to complain and take advantage of the leniency, prosperity and freedoms of our nation. Thank you for your attention to this matter.

May God bless America,
Sonny B.

DEAR NASCAR, LET'S GO BRANDON!!!

Greetings,

This letter is in response to the article by Fox 13 Tampa Bay's Andrew Mark Miller published on November 8, 2021, titled: "Nascar denounces 'Let's Go Brandon' trend, says it wants to stay out politics." Also, article by Beyond the flag. Com's Asher Fair published on November 14, 2021, titled: "Nascar is going after some 'Let's go Brandon' users."

I would like to start out by saying, I am a proud black American law-abiding citizen of the greatest country in the world. Anyone disagreeing with this notion, I point you to the exit door of our nation, and may I recommend the southern border? Since a tyrannical Biden regime has it open for the world to migrate here illegally; However, it's just as easy to leave as it is to come in.

I too, respect the office of the president when it is deserving. Our presidential elections in 2020 was corrupted by domestic and international interference, while the mainstream media was complicit in one of the greatest scandals to destroy our Republic. Let me explain. President Trump had a massive following with thousands unable to get inside his rallies because the crowds were too large to fit into one venue. However, on the other hand, Biden/Harris could not attract flies, even if they had cow manure smeared all over their bodies, but Biden received more votes than President Obama? President Trump had an overwhelming lead in all the states in question that are getting a forensic auditing overhaul, like Maricopa County. President Trump was on his way to a second term, and then it happened. Something that has never happened since the inception of the election, **THEY STOPPED COUNTING!!!** We would wake up to see a mysteriously Biden lead the next morning. They either think the American people are stupid or they just don't care we know they cheated. The way the media tells boldface lies, and the arrogance of so-called journalist, I'm going to say the latter. There is proof of massive election fraud and the media along with Big Tech is hiding, censoring and ignoring the proof. Why? Because they were in on it. They are thieves, they stole the election. I don't care if you are republican, democrat, independent, or a libertarian, this diabolical scheme to overthrow our Republic should infuriate every citizen in this nation. If this grotesque plot to overthrow America isn't fixed, there will no longer be a need to vote. So, no I do not respect the totalitarian rogue Biden administration destroying our freedoms under the Constitution of the United States. Not to mention, Biden is compromised and owned by China, Ukraine and Russia.

Brandon Brown was being interviewed by NBC's sports reporter Kelli Stavast after Brown's Nascar win. When the crowd broke out in the background with 'F' Joe Biden. A phrase that has caught on all across the U.S. Stavast tried to cover it up by proposing the crowd was chanting, "Let's Go Brandon" This is the disingenuous, propaganda, lies and blatantly obvious bias news coverage the American people have grown to despise the fake news media for. So, Nascar President Steve Phelps, why are you feeling sorry for Kelli Stavast, a liar who lack character and integrity?

Also, Mr. Phelps, you said in the article, Nascar doesn't want to associate with politics. I believe it's a little too late for that gesture, when Nascar allowed Bubba Wallace to adorn his car with Black Lives Matter (BLM). BLM is a Marxist and racist organization that destroyed cities across the country along with Antifa, under the guise of black lives mattering. I say under the guise, because my black race accounted for at least 7,740 BLACK ON BLACK MURDERS IN 2020, but police brutality somehow is an epidemic? Not to mention, millions were donated to this organization, but the black communities didn't see a dime of it; Instead, it went into the pockets of BLM co-founder Patrisse Cullors and the DNC. If that's not political, I don't know what is. By the way, does anyone know why Cullors resigned from BLM? That's a rhetorical question by the way. Our country is in trouble, because of identity politics, professional sports and the media bullhorn of 24/7 intentional divisive bias news coverage. They divide, we fight one another, and they conquer!!!

This is the hypocrisy of professional sports, which is why I am 5 years removed from all professional sports and ESPN. Mr. Phelps you say respect the office, I say, tell professional athletes to respect our flag and National Anthem, which is the highest degree of honor, more than any individual in this country, including the president. That's the difference between a patriot and a renegade posing as an American. I continue by saying, I think it's shameful, how Nascar is going after patriots and threatening lawsuits because citizens of our nation are expressing displeasure for a Biden administration destroying the sovereignty of our country. This speaks volumes to me, apparently Nascar is in favor of lawlessness and chaos. A year of destruction, violent crimes and disorder in 2020. Yet, Nascar helped to celebrate it by allowing a BLM race car into their competition, but you're attacking law-abiding citizens making a profit on dishonest news coverage. I called that despicable and repulsive, worthy of fans leaving Nascar behind in the rearview mirror.

Lastly, the Biden regime have become political gangsters allowed to run amok with no accountability, but what do you expect from a thief. We the people are fed up, which is why we hear chanting of "Let's Go Brandon" across the nation. The political cesspool on Capitol Hill, academia, major corporations and the lying mainstream media have failed the American people to say the least. This is the Great Awakening; we stand together against tyranny to save our country from a hostile communist takeover (Globalism, the Great reset). I fight, we fight for our children and the generations to come. I'm willing to die for our freedom, because if we lose it, then we are dead already. So, this is a message to: All corrupt politicians, academia, fake news media, Big Tech, Big Pharma, major corporations, Hollywood, professional sports, elites, Nascar and the deep state system. You either get on the train or get ran over. Mr. Phelps, Let's Go Brandon will not cease, until we get the impostor out of office. 1776 REWIND!!! LET'S GO BRANDON!!! LET'S GO BRANDON!!! LET'S GO BRANDON!!!

May God Bless America,
Sonny B.

THEY WON'T TAKE OUR FREEDOM WITHOUT A FIGHT!

I am a proud black American citizen of this great nation. I am a father of (6) six awesome children with my lovely wife of 22 years. This letter is in response to your article posted on December 21, 2020, in the Gateway Pundit by Cristina Laila, titled, "Democrats' Stimulus bill gives $600 to suffering Americans- But sends more than $2 Billion to Africa and Asia."

I want to say from the offset, thank you Gateway Pundit, because of news outlets like yourself and individuals across America debunking fake news, we become informed about what is really going on in the world. The Marxist mainstream media has done the American citizens a disservice by spreading their propaganda and divisiveness to control a narrative. It has become very obvious to those who are not mesmerized by their rhetoric and bias opinions as they push the socialist agenda. I have to be careful about singling out the democratic party because after seeing the proof of massive election fraud, I can see clear as ever, RINO's are in on America's demise as well. We realize, President Trump and a few patriots in D.C. are fighting on behalf of the people to save our constitution. Malcolm X makes a profound statement in a quote about the media, "The media's the most powerful entity on earth. They have the power to make the innocent guilty and to make the guilty innocent, and that's power, because they control the minds of the masses." In 2020, we see the catastrophic effects of mind control.

I'm literally in tears as I write this letter, because I never thought we would be in a war for our freedom in 2020. I realize what is at stake, the future of America lay in the balance because of one of the greatest scandals in history. When I say scandal, I mean election fraud. I don't care what side of the isle you're on, rather you are democrat, republican, independent, libertarian or humanitarian, you should be outraged with this grotesque assault on our election process. This isn't about President Trump, this is about our Republic, and the future of the USA. My heart aches deeply, when I cannot convince certain people of the truth; As a result of the media, they see you as the enemy. I always knew there was something diabolical lurking in the waters of the media and the government, but I had no idea how VAST.

I began to understand how VAST, as I paid attention to the treatment of Donald Trump when he announced he was running for president. To them, Trump was a farce and they spoke of him as such, until he became the primary candidate of the republican party. The media still saw him as a joke, but not a threat to defeat their candidate, corrupt Hillary. When Trump became president, we began to see the media and politicians as the vipers they are. The vicious attacks on President Trump haven't stopped through his whole first term as president. No other president in history has ever gotten so much negative publicity as President Trump. 24/7 of 99.9% negative coverage; Whereas, the only other person in these times that would get the same negative coverage is Jesus Christ, I would say Trump is in good company. It's really disheartening for me to believe that satan would get a pass from the mainstream media today. One would think since America is such a racist country (That's called sarcasm by the way), 2x former President Obama would've received the ultimate grand prize for negative media coverage in history. No, instead President Obama got a pass, just like satan would. I would say Obama is in like company.

Democrats are highlighted in the article title because democrats own the house, but RINO's are in on it as well. Tell me, how can a person like Republican Devin Nunes look at a stimulus bill with all of the pork in it, and say with a straight face, this is all we could get, before a Biden administration settles into the White House. Devin Nunes has already given up the fight against the biggest election hoax of the century, or is he a part of it? You see, this is the lackluster, lackadaisical, lethargic, cowardice, and spineless attitude of the political cesspool millions of Americans are fed up with. I could accept $600 dollars, if a 100% of the stimulus bill was dedicated to the hurting American people of our country. This is a slap in the face, can somebody tell me why and with justification of why is American tax dollars going to anything other than Americans in need? A booming economy has been wrecked by the Wuhan virus (Covid-19), purposely done to spite one of President Trump's major accomplishments to hopefully end his tenure as president. ARE YOU KIDDING ME??? THESE PEOPLE ARE SHAMELESS AND CORRUPT TO THE VERY CORE OF THEIR BEING, IS PUTTING IT LIGHTLY. These are rhetorical questions, but I'll ask them anyway. Why is $135 million going to Burma? Why is $85.5 million to Cambodia?

Why is $1.4 billion for Asia reassurance Initiative Act? Why is $130 million to Nepal? Why is $700 million to Sudan? Why is $250 million to Palestinian Aid? Why $25 million for gender programs in Pakistan? ALL OF OUR FOCUS SHOULD BE ON THE AMERICAN PEOPLE!!! Speaking of the Pakistan gender program, Republican Senator Lindsey Graham had the audacity to tell the American people, one of the reasons for this program is so women in Pakistan can have a bank account. You can't make this ridiculousness up; we are in the Twilight Zone. I am bewildered, baffled and mystified to say the least.

The American people have been BAMBOOZLED; we have been sold a bill of goods that is rotten to the core. President Trump redlined all of the pork in the stimulus bill and wants to increase the amount significantly for hurting Americans. Yet again, the president is attacked by the far-left and mainstream media, trying to make him out to being the villain once again to their ill-informed base. Yet again, President Trump is standing alone in the interest of the American people, no backing from any of the political traitors in D.C., but the patriots know the truth. Is there a wonder why Big Tech want to censor every conservative, patriotic voice and every voice that doesn't line up with the corrupt system of the DEEP STATE? There is no longer free speech, it has become blatantly obvious, there is only one speech, the speech of the CCP. One would tweet out about the politicians in D.C., he said they hate us, and I would add they also think we're stupid, remember we are a "BASKET OF DEPLORABLES." Can we get a warm welcome for the democratic party who exudes love, who is all inclusive and very tolerant, until you disagree or have a different opinion than them.

I conclude with this by saying, everyone, I do mean everyone is against the President, except the 80 plus millions of American patriots that voted for him. It was a landslide by epic proportions on November 3, anyone with eyes and a working brain could see this. I'm left shaking my head in disbelief as I see my America destroyed from within and from without. 2020 has been like the final piece of the puzzle. The image didn't make sense until all of the puzzle pieces of 2020 was set in place. Radical BLM/Antifa thugs yelling death to America, bring in Communism as they burned the American flag. When Russia said they will destroy America without ever firing a shot, I believe the CCP intercepted. I said OMG, now it all makes sense. Here are some lines from a couple of blockbuster movies to bring home my point, my feelings and I believe the sentiment of 80 million plus Americans.

Robert The Bruce, "We need the nobles (politicians). William Wallace, "Now tell me, what does that mean to be noble? Your titles give you claim to the throne of our country, but men don't follow titles, they follow courage. Now our people know you, Noble or common, they respect you. And if you would just lead them to freedom, they'd follow you and so would I." (Braveheart 1995)

This is about everyone against us. Persian, "A thousand nations of the Persian empire descend upon you. Our arrows will blot out the Sun." Stelios responds, "then we will fight in the shade." (300 2006)

Here is another line from Braveheart, a pep talk that was given to an army, because of their hesitation and reluctance to fight against a massive army of precision and strength. Well, I can tell you, there is no hesitation, no reluctance to fight as a patriotic American citizen, because I realize if we lose this war, we are dead already. Here is a message to everyone against our republic and freedom of America, both domestic and foreign, in this line. William Wallace, "Yes, fight and you may die. Run and you'll live, at least a while. And dying in your beds, many years from now, would you be willin to trade all the days, from this day to that, for one chance, just one chance, to come back here and tell our enemies that they may take our lives, but they'll never take … OUR FREEDOM"!!! (Braveheart 1995)

"IT'S ALL FOR NOTHING IF YOU DON'T HAVE FREEDOM." (Braveheart 1995)

May God bless America,
Sonny B.
WWG1WGA

I AGREE BUT RECONSIDER

Greetings Bryson Gray,

I am a proud black American citizen of the greatest country in the world, that the Marxist liberals are trying to destroy. I am an engaging and blessed father of six (6) wonderful children with my lovely wife of almost 24 years. I want to say from the offset, I love and appreciate the message in your music, your tenacity, your love for Jesus Christ and your stance on God's word. Your commitment to our country and to the kingdom of God is unparalleled to the counterfeit Mega church Christianity.

I know Trump is not God, he's not the Savior, but like MLK he has been chosen for such a time as this. Arguably, President Trump is the best president our country has ever seen. Remember he left a multi-billion-dollar empire to become president, why? For one reason, he loves this country. Moreover, he didn't take a presidential salary and the only president that left office with half of his wealth gone with no multi-million-dollar book payoff deals and no endorsements.

I remember his inaugural speech on that glorious day in January of 2017. When President Trump made this statement as he turned to everyone seated behind him and told the world, these people have failed the American people. Then he turns back to face the audience and the American people tuning in and said, but I come to give the power back to the American people. Everyone seated behind him was: Daddy Bush, the Clinton's, Son Bush, the Obama's, republican establishment, and the 1 or 2 democrats that had the decency to at least show up.

That sealed the deal, I knew at that moment, President Trump was the right candidate for the country (We the People) and wrong for the political cesspool on Capitol Hill (the swamp) and the deep state. Everyone hated him, except 'We the People' who voted for him. This is the list of all of the fake woke who hated Trump: mainstream media (Enemy of the People AKA fake news), the church, republicans, democrats, Hollywood, professional sports, Big Tech, Big PHARMA, music industry, academia, foreign foes, and the elites. They had to cheat to get him out of office, because he was actually draining the swamp, and because he became just that popular. The loyalty of his following was unprecedented, and the movement had to be stopped by any means necessary. Which is why they had to conjure up a scheme on January 6th just as treasonous as the 2020 election fraud.

I digress to the main purpose of this letter addressed to you, Mr. Gray. I saw your podcast the other day, and I agree wholeheartedly, but consider what I'm about to say. There is a huge difference between the political world and the kingdom of God. Therefore, we must act and not react accordingly in respect to these differences. I don't understand President Trump's fixation on the experimental vaccines and boosters. However, I do know that it was imperative for Trump to orchestrate operation warp speed with the vaccines to detour the plans the deep state had for our nation concerning the Wuhan China virus. The vaccines are Trump's baby, he has to own it and if he doesn't, the last five years of the media roasting Trump is going to be a walk in the park in comparison. Remember, before the vaccines, he tried to go the therapeutical way. In February 2020 Trump announced to the world about the therapeutic hydroxychloroquine to treat the virus, we saw what the deep state through the media bullhorn did with that. Not to mention, on March 23, 2020, the Trump administration wanted to introduce ivermectin initially to New Jersey, New York, who were hardest hit and then to the world, but it was struck down within the corrupt government. SIDE NOTE: Like Joe Rogan, I too contracted covid and was treated and cured by ivermectin. This "Pandemic" was purposely induced into the world and the vaccines introduced into the mix so quickly is a mystery, but time was of essence. Trump was expecting safe vaccines, but the corrupt CCP owned FDA had others plans for the vaccines (Read between the lines). With that being said, the vaccines had to come into play, or it would've been checkmate for the deep state, and years of lockdown to follow for our country. We would be seeing a mirror image of what's going on right now in Australia. We're watching a chess match for our FREEDOM and certain strategic moves must be made to end the game in checkmate, and stalemate is not an option. The deep state knows they've already lost, but they are playing the game out hoping for one wrong move. Therefore, we have to avoid the temptation of making background noises and trust the plan of the white hats, because we don't have all the facts, nor the intel. The biggest take away from all of this should be, Trump is pushing choice and not a mandate like sleepy Joe, the blue slave states, and Marxist liberals inside red states. We can't afford to bail out in this most crucial point in history, because I can tell you, the deep state has a keen focus to finish what they've started.

Let's take in consideration the body of work this man has accomplished with everything stacked against him. Furthermore, we don't have all the facts or the internal insight of the deep state, but Trump and his staff does. We have to be sober, wise and vigilant to see the big picture. There are strategic strategies the white hats must follow, because the elites are out for blood, literally. They don't care how many lives are lost as long as they obtain total control and power of America, to usher in globalism. Therefore, we have to give Trump a pass for the sake of the fight and what's at stake. The stakes are high, and the time is now to save America for our children and generations to come. LET ME EXPLAIN.

I know you know we are in a spiritual warfare of good (righteous) vs evil. Therefore, we can't afford to kill anyone on the side of good with friendly fire. Here is the difference between (republicans, conservatives and Christians) vs (democrats, mainstream media and Marxist liberals). Republicans, conservatives, and Christians air out dirty laundry for the world to see, as if we're doing some type of just deed for all of mankind. In addition, there is a time and place for exposing something we don't agree with. However, this is neither the time nor the place, as the world watches the decline of our nation crumbling in real time. Democrats and Marxist liberals on the other hand, stick together come hell or high water. The ship can be sinking, and everyone can visualize the democrats and Marxist liberals causing it, but they don't care that you saw them destroying the ship, they arrogantly deny, censor and blame the republicans, conservatives and Christians for causing the ship to sink. Furthermore, the tyrannical Biden administration wants to give 450K to illegals who recently crossed the southern border, but what does the black race get? "You ain't black if you don't vote for Joe." Not a peep!!! They fight with diabolical vigor to protect their own, but republicans are quick to throw one another under the bus to somehow think we're gaining a moral win, but in actuality we're strengthening the hand of the enemy. We have to remember, the Marxist liberals have a huge advantage, because they have the media, and Big Tech to get ahead of the narrative. Cancel culture was created to silence anyone going against their agenda to change the face of America. 2020 showed us the extreme damage they can cause with a lying tongue; All while ignoring the massive atrocities of present America.

Case in point, the tyrannical rogue Biden administration with a stolen election is a farce and total wreck to our country; Nevertheless, you don't hear a peep out of family, friends and the list mentioned earlier in this letter that supported Biden and despised Trump. For four years, there was 24/7 coverage of bashing President trump from fake news, democrats, Marxist liberals, Hollywood, Big Tech, Professional athletes with professional organizations, academia, the mega and black churches especially. They would rather see the country burn to the ground to save face for this circus transpiring right before our very eyes.

What am I saying? Again, we have to be strategic in our conversation and actions, because we are fighting for the soul of the United States of America; Consequently, we cannot look divided in anyway. We can't afford to put President Trump out on blast, especially from a well-known figure like yourself, as your platform increases in popularity because of your music. You are authentic and real in your approach to life, with a call of God upon your life; As a result, satan would love to use that at his advantage to sabotage relationships between the kingdom of God and the patriots of our country. Bryson, I respect your opinion and I tend to agree with the situation in question, but that doesn't mean it's prudent to say. In addition, I would even say it can be extremely detrimental to the fight against the evil at hand. So, ponder the words in this letter and reconsider your thoughts about President Trump on the vaccines and focus on the long battle ahead. We do the possible, as we watch the Lord do the impossible. No matter how it looks, we win!!!

Lastly, I write for eyeonJacksonville.com. I just finished up a memoir of actual letters sent out and written for the column just mentioned to be published in my first book. I'm sending you a sample of one of my writings entitled, 'Information War', to give you a better understanding for why I wrote you and why I got into this fight. Remember we're on the same team, so let's fight together. Let's Go Brandon!! 1776 Rewind!!! Masks are about as useless as Joe Biden!!! May God Bless America!!!

Your brother in Christ,
Sonny B.

WRITERS FOR TATUM REPORT

Greetings,

I listened to Tatum's podcast concerning President Trump's interview with Candace Owens about the vaccines. The vaccines are Trump's baby, he has to own it and if he doesn't, the last five years of the media roasting Trump is going to be a walk in the park in comparison. I have to say, we must learn 'The Art of War'. We are in an 'Information War', so please forward this urgent message to Officer Tatum, because he has a large following. Which means he's in a position to influence a lot of people.

I have a question for Mr. Tatum, who are you going to vote for, if it isn't for President Trump? I would like to remind him, that the first forensic audit was in his home state. There was massive evidence of election fraud (TREASON) found in Maricopa County Arizona, after three months, we're still waiting to see if Arizona will decertify their electoral. There is CCP controlled, deep state government corruption all over the country, since we know this, we have to be wise as a serpent and harmless as a dove. Needless to say, if the 2020 presidential election and the whole election process isn't fixed, our Republic is useless, and America is done. Not only will Trump not be an option in the coming election, but not any conservative candidate for that matter. Like 2020, like the recent recall election in California, 2022 mid-terms, and 2024, the candidates will be chosen by Dominion, foreign and domestic collaboration and CCP owned politicians. While, once again, the fake news media, will hide, deny and vilify massive proof of TREASON. This is World War III, just not with guns, but information. We are in a battle for the soul of this nation, our children's future is at stake and generations to come.

I have a letter with this one, addressing Bryson Gray for the same concern as Tatum, that explains in detail my stance on the vaccines. So, please forward the letters to Tatum, to prayerfully change his mind, appreciate a different perspective and reconsider his position on President Trump. All he has to do is put his name in place of Bryson Gray, because it is befitting to both patriots. May God Bless America, because we sure do need Him now, Sonny B.

$99.18 AT THE GAS PUMP

It's 11 o'clock in the morning on March 15, 2022, just over a year since the rogue Biden administration stole the election through international and domestic collaboration, while the Marxist mainstream media sat by idle watching one of the greatest scandals of the century. Matter of fact, the fake news media would deny all claims of election fraud through mail-in-ballots and Dominion machines. Someone once said, elections have consequences, but stolen elections have severe consequences. Well, Americans and even the world can see the detriment to our nation as a result of a fraudulent election.

I digress to my original point, my gas light on my dash came on the night before. Like myself, I believe most Americans dread seeing and hearing that ding. It's the sights and sounds of working families budget go down the drain. Along with inflation, the gas prices take away food out of the mouths of hard-working law-abiding citizens just trying to make an honest living. Unfortunately, in desperate times, people become desperate, like the person or persons who parked over the gas hatch at a gas station in Houston with a floorboard hatch, to syphon about a thousand gallons of gas on separate occasions. Did I say I spent $99.18 cents at the gas pump on March 15, 2022? This is one of the many atrocities being ignored by the media who are incapable of telling the truth. Love or hate President Trump, under the Trump administration we were oil independent, Biden took that all away by closing the Keystone pipeline. All the media says is, the gas prices are skyrocketing without affirming the reason for the gas hikes. I'll be the first to say that democrats and republicans have failed the American people; however, you know the media would show off their bias muscle to blame Trump or any other republican in office for the gas prices and it would be on a 24/7 rotation, making it juicy to stir up the masses, especially the black race. The media would embellish the story to cause Americans to despise a president they have no clue why. Within this book I've noted a question to blacks, why do you hate a man that has done more for the black community than any other president, especially Obama? My black race can be so gullible and so foolish. There is a corrupt Three ring circus going on in our country, but the silence is deafening from the same blacks and Marxist media that criticized President Trump during his entire tenure. SUCH HYPOCRISY!!!

False Press Secretary Jen Psaki arrogantly day by day with a straight face can say whatever she wants to say with no accountability sought by the fake news media. Want an example? She just told the American people that the Biden administration does not want to depend on foreign oil. REALLY??? So, how do we accomplish that??? That's a rhetorical question by the way. This administration say they want to move to electric cars by getting rid of fossil fuels while going green. WHAT??? Where does electric come from??? Again, that's a rhetorical question. Ok, now let's blame it on Ukraine, perfect timing, the Marxist liberals don't care if you realized the gas prices were already sky high. Here is the final example, I believe hits the nail on the head to bring home my point. The movie is 'What's love got to do with it,' the setting: Ike was bashing Tina's head in, in front of their children. Ike tells the children to leave and go play, me and your mother is just talking. That's the media, they say, are you going to believe me or your lying eyes? They don't care if you see the corruption, just put the manure on your plate and eat it with a knife and fork and love it!!! Our nation is going to pot, but we don't care, let's continue to divide the nation, destroy the country and push our global agenda by any means necessary.

The national and local media mockingbirds do a 24/7 rotation to control the minds of the masses, and if you don't think the way they do, they're going to punish you. This Communist thinking is like saying, shut up you dumb Americans, we know more than you do, so believe what we say, or be silenced. The sad part of it all, the CCP owned media has bought into this lunacy, because they are a part of the diabolical scheme to change the face of America. It's a well-planned out strategy by the CCP to takeover a nation without ever firing a shot. The Chinese government has influenced every facet of our country, especially our government and media. I'm shaking my head as my America is becoming unrecognizable as the lawless is allowed to run amok, while patriots are being treated like criminals. Jussie Smollett committed a serious crime that could have cost more lives and more mostly peaceful protest (RIOTS!!!). He gets 5 months, such a kangaroo court, they just waisted long hours and taxpayers' money when they could've just done nothing and saved everyone the trouble, because his sentencing was NOTHING!!! Not to mention, he was released from jail pending his appeal granted by the court. WHAT A JOKE!!!

Need I say, there are corrupt governments all over the world and they are interconnected. The citizens are never really the problem; however, corrupt governments allow citizens to become corrupted when consequences have double standards. In other words, 'Absolute power, corrupts absolutely.' The hard truth is, anyone can become vulnerable to power if you succumb to its temptations. Power doesn't care about your party affiliation, it doesn't discriminate and unlike the political cesspool on Capitol Hill, power is bipartisan. Where there is power, it brings money, and 'The love of money is the root of all evil.' Just take a moment and look at our government thru decades of corruption, follow the money (or should I say, follow the career politicians holding office for years) and you'll find the corruption, just ask Durham. Government, justice system, media, academia, professional sports, major corporations, Big Tech., and Hollywood are all corrupt and they need to be leveled like a wrecking ball to a building in need of demolition. Some things are not worth saving, tear it down, destroy it and start all over with American patriots with integrity that will not be bought!!!

LAWLESS

I've said it before and I'll say it again, so you don't get it confused. I do not like politicians, democrats or republicans, well just a hand full of them, because it has been said that 98% of Capitol Hill are either compromised or just plain corrupt. One is a wolf (Democrat) and one is a wolf in sheep's clothing (Republican). The democrat let you know just who they are, and they don't make any apologies and dare anyone to challenge them. However, the republican, I believe is the worst of the two because they use conservativism and Christian principles to hide behind and as a means to catapult their political careers. In other words, both use their side to get ahead and push an agenda by dividing with identity politics, but with the same goal as they point fingers at one another to distract from the real issues of America. If you think there's a two-party system, you are nowhere in the fight.

The MEDIA, the real enemy of the people, the bullhorn, the greatest manipulator, the illusionist and professional distractor away from the truth. Malcolm X said it best, "The media's the most powerful entity on earth. They have the power to make the innocent guilty and to make the guilty innocent, and that's power, because they control the minds of the masses." It's been said, without the media our country would be much better off, and may I add, the world would be much better off if they just told the truth.

Let me continue with our government. This statement was just mentioned in a conversation, I believe sums up our entire government, it was, "The justice department is where truth goes to die, never to be seen again." I believe if we had an honest mainstream media and local media throughout the country to hold the government accountable, we wouldn't see the vast amount of corruption we are experiencing today. Example, I was reading an old article published by the Washington Compost, I mean Washington Post on May 12, 2017, by Peter Whoriskey, entitled, "The labels said 'organic.' But these massive imports of corn and soybeans weren't." Here is a couple of quotes from that article, "A shipment of 36 million pounds of soybeans sailed late last year from Ukraine to Turkey to California. Along the way, it underwent a remarkable transformation." But by the time the 600-foot cargo ship carrying them to Stockton, Calif., arrived in December, the soybeans had been labeled "organic," according to receipts, invoices and other shipping records." We pay a substantially amount more for organic products, but I wonder, how much is really organic? By the way, isn't California the home state of some very prominent, vocal and nefarious installed politicians? Like: Gavin Newsom, Maxine Waters and Nancy Pelosi. Nothing surprises me anymore after the 2020 presidential election debacle, mostly peaceful protest (RIOTS), and P-L-A-N-demic, I realize nothing is off limits with these renegades posing as Americans.

That's real journalism from the Washington Post exposing the corruption. You don't ignore scandals like, Hunter Biden's Laptop from hell as Russian disinformation, because you have sided with a certain party affiliation. The NY Crimes, I mean NY Times finally admitted that Hunter Biden's laptop is real. One of the many corrupt three letter agencies of our government called the FBI new about Hunter Biden's laptop back in December of 2019, because the laptop was seized by this same corrupt agency. Almost a year later, the NY Post came out with the story of Hunter Biden's laptop in October 2020, but it was banned by Big Tech., another deadly cancerous part of the Marxist media. I believe the political cesspool on Capitol Hill saw into the future that 'Cancel Culture' would take center stage in the 'Information War;' therefore, they legislated Section 230 to protect Big Tech, which is why they're able to get away with selective censorship. Our country, even the world would be much better off without the fake news media, social giants, and corrupt politicians.

The media got caught covering up one of the greatest scandals of the century and now they are reluctantly releasing information to the public that the Hunter Biden laptop does exist. They have to be forced to be honest because the media is incapable of telling the truth. Their lies of the tongue have cost so many lives and division in our country. It has become blatantly obvious who's side they're on. The media supports the Marxist globalist pushing for the Great Reset. Therefore, the media can't be trusted, which is why most people with a brain don't tune in, because of the propaganda and rhetoric to control a narrative that America is in need of a change. This is partly true, 'We the People' see that America is in need of a complete overhaul, spiritual cleansing, an exorcism to destroy the whole deep state system controlling the media, government, academia, professional sports, major corporations, Hollywood, Big Tech., Big Pharma, healthcare, and now we know because of the scamdemic, the medical facilities.

One more example of why I despise the media. The media has plastered the 'Don't say gay' bill all over the news outlets, in which the bill clearly does not say, don't say gay, but they want to manipulate the masses to conform to an allegation built on a lie, and hold the Disney CEO Bob Chapek responsible for going silent on the issue. That's what the media is crafty in doing, creating an illusion to divert your attention from the real issue like: Four child trafficking arrest of Disney employees from a sting operation which led to 108 arrests. That's from a U.S. News article entitled, "Four Disney employees arrested in Florida human trafficking, child predator sting," published on March 17, 2022, by Minyvonne Burke. This story is hidden under the shadows of the identity political propaganda and rhetoric. The news is so disingenuous with absolutely no integrity, but the cat is out of the bag, and the gig is up. I can't be entertained by Hollywood, Disney and sports, because this is the 'Great Awakening.'

Did I say one more example? Well, this is the last one. I had to add this example because my son broke down in tears after witnessing the broken justice system while performing his civil duties as a juror. He broke down because I believe he thought he and the juror's let the little girl down after her compelling testimony on the stand as the evidence wasn't enough to convict a pedophile. Which is a lead-in to my next point. Could Biden have chosen anyone else in the world as a SCOTUS nominee? That's a rhetorical question by the way, because I think it's an impossibility for someone like Biden to make a sound and moral judgement. I believe progressive liberals in the political hemisphere takes advantage of the fragmented legal system because they have been allowed to get away with murder for so long, no pun intended. It's like second nature, lawlessness comes natural to a Marxist liberal. Of all the candidates that could've been chosen, Biden chooses Ketanji Brown Jackson for a SCOTUS nominee, known to be a pedophile sympathizer with a history of leniency on convicted pedophiles. Not to mention, she refused to define the definition of a women because she's not a biologist, this is a circus and a farce. I make no apologies; this is disgusting and if Mrs. Jackson is confirmed as a U.S. Supreme Court Justice this would validate my deep sincere concern for where our nation is headed.

Who else is much the blame for where I country is headed? The black church supporting a Marxist, racist BLM movement while the white church pandered to the identity political madness as if black vs white or black vs cop is the real issue of our nation. Pastors sold out by the 501c3 tax gift of 30 pieces of silver from the government to shut up, stay out of politics and let them handle destroying the country. It was a well-planned out strategy to take God out of everything and rip the constitution to shreds while politicians lined their pockets with dirty money. Meanwhile, the church has been too busy getting their breakthrough, going to another level, attending MEGA conferences, concerts and going to church entertaining one another, instead of getting involved with our community like: city council meetings, and school board meetings. The church would rather vote for a personality, color, and political party, instead of godly principles; as a result, elected or installed officials have been given free rein to shape our communities into the direction of evil. However, the 2020 chaos and covid lockdowns would become the school master for ushering in the 'Great Awakening,' awakening true patriots of our nation that is. The church on the other hand is either controlled by the fake news media, forgotten what the fight is about, or never knew that the fight has always been good vs evil. The real fight is evil, all others are just a distraction from the diabolical scheme of the elites to keep us divided while they conquer.

WWJD (What Would Jesus Do), I can tell you what He wouldn't do is get the covid vaccine Mr. Franklin Graham, how ridiculous and outlandish. WWJD is a phase everyone got into by making T-shirts, bracelets, bags, and bumper stickers. The church is big on cliches and acronyms; as a result, they were able to exploit the Christian psyche while making a lot of money. Just my opinion, I believe WWJD was a ploy to shut down the conservative Christian voice or should I say the gospel of Jesus Christ. To shame the conservative voice to say you're not loving but judging, cause WWJD. To make one think that Jesus was this weak and emaciated savior. When actually there were times when He showed His assertiveness towards pompous religious leaders during His time. Examples are: Calling them a generation of vipers; and you are of your father the devil. Here is a message from Jesus to the Pharisees He wanted relayed to King Herod out of (Luke 13:31-32 NLT) to send a clear message, 31) "At that time some Pharisees said to him, get away from here if you want to live! Herod Antipas wants to kill you." 32) "Jesus replied, go tell that fox that I will keep on casting out demons and healing people today and tomorrow, and the third day I will accomplish my purpose." I can tell you that Jesus would become and did become angry when religious folks made His Father's house a 'Den of Thieves' by turning over the tables of the moneychangers. This act teaches us, if you are using the church in a deceitful way, God will not be pleased. We are witnessing judgement as pastors are stepping down and arrests being made all over the country as it bleeds over into the corporate world and politics.

BLM/Antifa, committed violent/deadly assaults, destroyed cities, lives and livelihoods across the nation under the guise of a black life, all throughout 2020, but we were told by the media that the riots were mostly peaceful. The mayor of Seattle would coin the phrase, 'It's a summer of love,' as we watched the chaos transpire right before our eyes in plain sight and in real time; but somehow January 6 was an insurrection and an attack on our democracy. WHAT??? The media either thinks the American people are stupid or they just don't care that we know they are telling a bold face lie. I tend to lean towards the latter, because they go about their daily lives arrogantly without any fear of repercussions.

The only thing I like about these leftist Marxist democrats is they fight with vigor, tenacity, and passion without a care about what conservatives think even though they know they are dead wrong. They have the media bullhorn on their side, which emboldens the lie that they are invincible and incapable of being punished. On the other end of the spectrum, we have weak, emaciated, spineless, wimpy, and cowardice RINOs and Christians too afraid to fight even though we are on the side of right with all of the answers. They would rather hold on to the answer out of fear of stepping over the line of political correctness or being attacked. I've said it before and I'll say it again, this is exactly why President Trump got into office, with his fight for the American people. As a result, 'We the People' would share a foxhole with the president any given day of the week to war against evil Marxist. No, we don't idolize Trump or treat him as if he is God. We happen to believe he is one of us, a deplorable who loves his country, willing to sacrifice everything to save the soul of this nation. Now that's a real president who has all my respect, not the false resident residing presently in D.C.

Everyone sees the trend taking place right before the whole world eyes in Ottawa. Citizens are peacefully protesting for the right to choose what goes into their bodies, it's being called an insurrection, an attack on our democracy by the media and Trudeau. Yes, the same Trudeau that kneeled in solidarity to the BLM movement that wreaked havoc on America and Canada. See the trend, they are calling right wrong and wrong right. Does this look like a battle of politics, black vs white, black vs cop, vaxxed vs unvaxxed, conservative vs liberal, left vs right, elephant vs donkey, republican vs democrat, or a war of GOOD vs EVIL? These people feel they are above the law, above the Constitution, they are lawless, and they are emboldened by a rogue totalitarian Biden regime who wants to take away our freedoms under the Constitution. One Marxist liberal would call the Constitution trash, but no one on 'The View' refuted the comment, as the media as usual went silent. So, I guess you can say, his thoughts are their thoughts. We're in trouble!!! 1776REWIND!!! Let's Go Brandon!!!

MLK, A DREAM ALREADY COME TRUE

Dr. Martin Luther King Jr. was a man who truly cared about black lives and had a dream for all lives to join hands together in unity and love. I believe he would turn over in his grave if he saw the state of our nation today, especially the state of the black race. Also, I believe he would have mixed emotions, he would be proud of the progress and ashamed of how this progress is abused and squandered by the black community.

MLK was a great man filled with righteous indignation and tenacity, yet his life was encompassed about with compassion, meekness and inclusiveness of all races. Moreover, his words of wisdom and passion demanded a peaceful battle against evil regardless of revolt from the opposing forces. I believe the disloyal Americans tend to ignore, MLK was a proud black American citizen who never said or did anything unpatriotic against America. He only expressed his disdain for the conditions and treatment of black Americans desiring equal rights and the same opportunity to excel in the American dream. He never asked for handouts or special favors. Again, he only wanted the same opportunity of his white counterparts to show how blacks can exemplify hard work and work ethics to assist in a productive society. Black Lives Matter (BLM) on the other hand is a Marxist and racist movement I know MLK would openly denounce. What I have gathered over the years, blacks think just because they're black, they have a right to be enraged with anger and hate towards the white race because of slavery and the civil rights movement. MLK lead a civil rights movement under extreme conditions, yet he urged everyone to fight with non-violence. Why is this? Because he realized fighting evil for evil only breeds more evil. Cities destroyed across the country in 2020 for many months under the guise of social injustice, only validates my point. What change has it made other than a movement closer to socialism. I have a news alert fake news won't tell you; Racism comes in all colors, just because you're black, God does not give you a pass!!!

I am a proud black American citizen who loves his country, I only tell you this because patriotism is becoming a dying trait in our society and frowned upon as white supremacy. I was asked to write about MLK. I have written to the White House to the church house and everything in between to effect change for the better in our country; Ironically enough, I never gave any thought of writing about MLK. Maybe because I sometimes feel ashamed and embarrassed for where the black community has been heading for decades. I've seen and read about the major sacrifices he made for the black race while on this earth. The chaos driven by a BLM movement in 2020 is an insult to his legacy. You see, I look at my America in 2021 as I write about MLK with tears flowing from my eyes and I can earnestly say, America today is not the dream he had in mind, or was it? Just follow me, as I try and make sense of what I just said.

The I have a dream march in D.C. on August 28, 1963, was a day to remember. The dream came to fruition right there in plain sight. Check out the footage on that day, before MLK uttered a word of his famous, I have a dream speech; All God's children, black men and white men, Jews and gentiles, Protestants and Catholic's walked hand in hand against the evil of racism. We can say the same, the dream lives on in 2021 as American patriots of all backgrounds walked hand in hand with the president of the United States on January 6, 2021. Again, from the walk on D.C. in 1963 until now in 2021, the dream is alive and well. There are 100 million plus American patriots, all God's children, black men and white men, Jews and gentiles, Protestants and Catholic's standing in defiance of tyranny and treason. We are lockstep, hand in hand and shoulder to shoulder, crying out to God, asking Him to judge everyone that would want to destroy our republic and our freedom.

I can't say it enough, our present battle isn't about black vs white, Trump vs Biden, or republicans vs democrats, this fight is about good vs evil and truth vs lies. This fight is about decades of Chinese communist party (CCP) infiltration that has eroded our society from within, through: republican and democratic parties, past presidents, media, Hollywood, professional sports, academia, major corporations and churches. They use identity politics like: blacks against whites, gay against heterosexuals, and men against women, etc … endorsed by the mainstream media to incite violence and riots. They censor the conservative voices to shield the American people from the truth; As a result, producing ill-informed and low information voters. The concept of the media is one of ole, if you divide, you can conquer, we see the catastrophic effects from a 2020 year of chaos of epic proportions. If we are to thrive in the present, we must take self-preservation to seek a brighter future, learn from our past so not to repeat it and CHOOSE TO FORGIVE to restore the breach. No, the Marxist say rehash the past over and over again 24/7 to gullible offended blacks and guilt-ridden white liberals to make restoring the breach practically an impossibility; I believe this is what the fake news media had in mind all along.

MLK's efforts from the past and the effects of his sacrifices are astounding even today. Here is one of many success stories because of MLK's fight for justice. This is a recent story published by AFROTECH posted on January 14, 2021, by Shanique Yates, titled: "Meet Ashley Lamothe, the HBCU grad who became Chick-fil-A's youngest black franchise owner at age 26." May I add, she owns (2) two Chick-fil-A restaurants.

I hate to put a damper on such a great success story, but we have the media (enemy of the people) to blame why I must defend an outstanding sitting president. The media has demonized President Trump for over 4 years non-stop, 24/7 negative coverage. Every single day, we had to hear that President Trump is a dictator, racist, bigot, misogynist, homophobe, islamophobe, and xenophobe to divide a nation. Well, here's some positive news about Trump you will never hear from fake news. President Trump BROUGHT BACK the HBCU funding that directly effect in a positive way, blacks like Ashely Lamothe I just mentioned. That HBCU funding President Trump brought back, WAS ERRADICATED (TAKEN AWAY, CANCELLED, REVOKED) BY FORMER PRESIDENT OBAMA; Not to mention, President Trump added an additional 17% to the HBCU funding. Did anyone hear about this in the news? I'll answer it for you, NO!!! GO AHEAD AND FACT CHECK IT, it's in an article published by the NY Post on July 4, 2020, by Gianno Caldwell, Titled, "How Trump- NOT Biden- has helped make black lives better." A black co-worker of mine, said a very profound statement I will never forget, he said "All black people are NOT GOOD, and All white people are NOT BAD."

Ms. Ashely Lamothe proves once again that MLK's dream is alive and well. MLK has paved the way for so many blacks to live the American dream. We had a black president who served not just one but two terms in the White House. Will anyone tell me what blacks cannot do? It has to be legal though, ok I'll name one, blacks cannot change their race. Black men/ black women can drive what they want, live where they want, eat what and where they want to, travel where they want to, attend any school they want, play a round of golf and go into any profession they want to, and the list goes on and on. What am I saying? Quit complaining and enjoy the blessings of this great nation. We as black people do ourselves a disservice when we live beneath our privileges. When we allow the far- left mentality to control how we live and think, we forfeit the dream of MLK. When we harbor unforgiveness, anger and rage in our hearts because of the past, we become stagnated in self-pity and victimhood. Close your ears off to the voices of wealthy black enablers and ask yourself the question, how did they make it? Listen, as long as you see yourself as a product of the system, you'll always be dependent on a phantom solution that will never arrive. I've been told, I'm very hard on my race of people, that's because I care and I'm willing to tell you the truth. Proverbs 27:6 says, "Faithful are the wounds of a friend, but the kisses of an enemy are deceitful." (Meaning, real friends tell the truth even if it hurts, even risking losing the friendship; However, an enemy doesn't care if you get hurt, therefore they will deceive you with false benevolence to make you think they care).

One final story, my wife and I had the privilege of dining at the Cowford Chophouse for our 23rd wedding anniversary, Cowford is a restaurant comparable to the Ruth Chris steak house. Mind you, this is not a place we frequence because of the priciness, with a family of (8) eight, we have to be frugal in our spending; However, on a special occasion like our anniversary we like to splurge a little. HERE'S THE POINT OF THIS STORY, as the crowd began to pour in, my wife and I noticed something in particular, there were a lot of black people within the crowd, as if they owned the place. My wife and I were having the same thoughts as our eyes focused on one another, we whispered simultaneously and asked: Where is the systematic racism? Where is the white privilege? Where is the social injustice? Ladies and gentlemen, the CCP has planted a hoax into our society. We have been sold a bill of goods. Again, they use offended blacks and white guilt to distribute the bold face lie and is celebrated across the country by the CCP owned mainstream/social media. Please, don't be fooled by the false narrative given in the airwaves across the media scape of our country. MLK, a dream already come true. So don't let MLK's death for justice be in vain. No one can hold you back but you, the sky's the limit, SO WHAT ARE YOU WAITING FOR???

May God bless America, Sonny B.

LETTER TO DR. SIMONE GOLD

Exposing the KTLA media and Associated Press lie,

The purpose of this letter is for encouragement to Dr. Simone Gold to keep fighting on behalf of the American people, the soul of our nation and to know that there are millions of patriotic American citizens on your side. We are with you and most of all, God is with you, and He will never forsake you. Most importantly, what really inspired this letter was an article I read titled, "Beverly Hills doctor who founded anti-vaccine group pleads guilty to joining Capitol riot." Published by KTLA on March 3, 2022, from an Associated Press column. As a result, my heart was saddened, sickened, disturbed and enraged with righteous indignation and fire in my eyes. A plea deal? When you and others did nothing wrong, set-in motion in my mind that something nefarious is going on. These George Soros funded attorneys and judges are lawless, they are berating the justice system by snatching the blindfold off of Lady Justice to indict anyone going against their global agenda. It was said that the virus is the New World Order, with vaccine passports, one would have to agree. This letter is for encouragement and a response to the article, but mostly a rant all wrapped up in one.

I am a proud black American citizen of the greatest country in the world. A father of 6 awesome children with my amazing wife of 24 years. I tell you of my ethnicity to inform you that all blacks are not mesmerized and brainwashed by the Marxist mainstream media. We are not all controlled by the race hustlers who promote America as a racist nation by 24/7 coverage of police brutality antics and rhetoric. I've never seen so many radical renegades posing as Americans in my life, using identity politics to divide our nation. It's sad to say that my black race takes center stage in the theatrical display of a CCP takeover and don't even know it. We're being played in this concert of propaganda, while white socialist liberals pander to the foolery. Prime example in this article published by News4Jax on March 1, 2022, by white reporter Jim Piggott, titled, "UNF group faces backlash after posting Black History Month trivia question that some found offensive." The trivia question asked, "What is the popular drink in the African American community?" The answer was: Red Kool-Aid. There were blacks and whites protesting this non-sense, while a tyrannical, CCP owned and rogue Biden administration is totally wreaking havoc on our economy and dismantling our freedoms under the Constitution.

All throughout 2020, the Marxist mainstream media that told us the 2020 BLM/Antifa riots, destruction, violent fatal assaults and chaos were mostly peaceful as we saw in real time cities burning to ground all across America. One mayor amongst the mayhem and atrocities in her city, saw it as, "A summer of love." But somehow, January 6 was an insurrection and an attack on our democracy as patriots stormed the Capitol. When in fact, patriots were led into the Capitol by the corrupt metropolitan DC police department, and security guards the unselected committee refuse to release the damming evidence footage of. Not to mention, undercover agents were leading patriots to the slaughter while BLM/Antifa infiltrated a truly peaceful protest by disguising themselves as MAGA supporters to incriminate innocent citizens standing for truth and justice. It was a well-planned out strategy by the deep state-owned political cesspool on Capitol Hill and given 24/7 coverage by the fake news Marxist media, still talked about over a year later as the unpardonable sin, but the 2020 RIOTS conveniently just went away, SUCH HYPOCRISY!!!

I believe January 6 was the beginning of the Great Awakening, not just in the U.S., but all over the world and it's spilling into 2022 as American citizens fight for the soul of our nation. On January 6, true Americans went out to protest in defense of our republic, due to the overwhelming amount of evidence of election fraud. This was done in plain sight as they shut down the 2020 presidential election for the first time in history because they knew Biden/Harris couldn't draw flies even if they had cow manure smeared all over their bodies. We as Americans have trusted those, we thought we were electing to govern our nation, but the 2020 election exposed the whole corrupt system. We weren't electing these officials; they were being installed by a dishonest election process. Which is why democrats are for mail-in-ballots, early voting (more time to cheat) and against voter ID, while republicans sit on the sidelines cheering for the opposing team. Again, this is where blacks take center stage, all the democrats have to do is cry racism while the media bullhorn pushes the narrative of blacks being discriminated against. Blacks have been programed by the media to get outraged as soon as they hear the word racism. We're being used like a fatal covid lab specimen during every election cycle, but we continue to jump on the racial issues like a dog in heat. Will we ever learn? I've written to Governor DeSantis and several elected officials and told them our election process must be fixed, it's not an option. We must have election integrity because it is the doorway to cleaning up this mess, which is why the deep state is working overtime to destroy patriots like yourself, Dr. Gold.

Dr. Gold, they need you quiet and they want to shut up your voice by any means necessary, because I can tell you that your voice is being heard loud and clear. Your voice caused me to pursue other avenues of cures for the virus. I still remember you and the other frontline doctors in DC before your message was censored for sharing the success of hydroxychloroquine against the Wuhan China virus AKA Covid-19 or is it the Delta-variant? Omicron, or Omicron BA.2, flurona; Deltacron; stealth Omicron and the HIV-variant? I believe they close their eyes, grab a medical dictionary and point to the next fear mongering virus. This has become a collaborated three ring circus by Fauci the fraud, FDA, CDC, NIH, and WHO as the disingenuous mainstream media spread the propaganda that therapeutics like: ivermectin, hydroxychloroquine, budesonide, monoclonal clinics are either ineffective or ladened with life threatening side effects that could end your life instantly. When the deadly experimental vaccines are actually ineffective and ladened with lethal consequences. Even though there is only 1% of deaths and injuries reported to VAERS because of the vaccines, the numbers are still astounding but what's more astounding, it's being ignored and demonizing doctors like yourself as spreading medical misinformation.

If this was the greatest pandemic the world has ever seen killing millions worldwide, shouldn't they want to throw everything imaginable at this virus? No, they don't because this was a P-L-A-N-DEMIC courtesy of Fauci the frauds 'Gain of Function.' Therefore, they had to censor, block, vilify, demonize, and hide the therapeutics to destroy the economy and remove President Trump from office. Well, it didn't work, President Trump got more votes than any other sitting president. The virus was the greatest scandal of the century next to Obamagate and the 2020 presidential election fraud. So, KTLA, Associated Press, I pray that everyone that had a hand in one of the greatest crimes against humanity including the media, would either spend the rest of their lives in GITMO or be executed, anything less would be an insult to every American like Dr. Simone Gold, frontline doctors, patriots exposing the lies, innocent families who lost loved ones, livelihoods destroyed and president made mockery of 24/7 by Marxist like Elie Mystal who sees the constitution of the United States of America as TRASH!!! These renegades posing as Americans have no conscious, no morals, and no integrity; Therefore, they go about their lives arrogantly without the thought of ever being criminalized for their sinister deeds. In addition, God sees everything, and it will be judged, which is why they try to convince themselves and others that God doesn't exist. (Romans 3:3-4 NKJ) 3 "For what if some did not believe? Will their unbelief make the faithfulness of

God without effect? 4 Certainly not! Indeed, let God be true, but every man a liar. As it is written: that you may be justified in your words and may overcome when you are judged."

Dr. Gold, I'm terribly sorry our America is becoming unrecognizable because of a godless society controlled by a few elites. I love this comment by UFC fighter Bryce Mitchell in reference to Ukraine as I paraphrase, "I will not fight on foreign soil on behalf of political corruption, but I will defend any fight that comes to American soil, and I will defend it to the death." This is exactly why they have been vowing to take away our second amendment, while considering our constitution as trash to mimic the hostile Australian governmental takeover. You see, you're not on the frontlines alone, there are millions of Americans with you and again, most importantly the God of heaven is with us. We will stand together against the tyrannical evil of a rogue Biden administration that stole the oval office with a collaboration of domestic and international interference, while the Marxist media try an sale us on election integrity in 2020. Because of this regime, patriots like yourself are targeted by these three letter agency thugs (FBI, CIA, DOJ, IRS, CDC, FDA, NIH, WHO, to name a few). Our own government is used to bully American citizens by saying shut up, wear your mask and comply with the Great Reset as we suppress therapeutics like hydroxychloroquine while they push the deadly vaccines. Well, we will not comply!!! I guess you can tell by know, I'M PISSED OFF!!!

In conclusion, Dr. Gold, I know you didn't do anything wrong, but most importantly God knows you did nothing wrong. Under this false Biden administration, evil has been allowed to run amok, to make us think evil will prevail. I'm reminded of two of my favorite bible scriptures I believe is befitting for the times we're living in: 1) "For nothing is secret that will not be revealed, nor anything hidden that will not be known and come to light." (Luke 18:17). 2) "Because sentence against an evil work is not executed speedily, therefore the heart of the sons of men is fully set in them to do evil." (Ecclesiastes 8:11). I'm fighting with every fiber in my being and willing to die for what I believe in: (God; Family and Country), there are millions of patriots I believe are willing to do the same, so Dr. Gold don't you ever stop fighting because if we lose our freedom, then we are dead already. God is in control!!! Evil will not prevail!!! Let's Go Brandon!!! 1776REWIND!!! WWG1WGA!!!

May God bless America,
Sonny B.

VERBAL ADDRESS TO SCHOOL BOARD

What I would've said if I had more than 3 minutes. I wrote a letter sent to the Enemy of the People: FDA, CDC and NBC news concerning the propaganda and lies about ivermectin, and the non-essential need for a mask, because they don't work. Every school board member received that letter via email. Thank you, Supt. Greene, for the only response. It wasn't a response I wanted to hear; Then again, if you are taking your orders from a deep state-controlled Teachers Union, I completely understand your response.

Mask coverings and social distancing is a control mechanism under the guise to keep us safe. It alienates each citizen from one another and annihilates the very existence of human touch, communication, care and love. Not to mention, they don't work. Have you noticed? Socialist liberals are perfectly fine with masks and social distancing, because it means they don't have to touch, communicate, care or portray love. Why is this? Because socialist liberals have no love: No love for God, no love for family and no love for country. Liberals destroy everything good, because they have evil in their hearts. Liberals say they are the most tolerant and they exude love. Oh Yeah, just disagree with one and you will feel the wrath to collude with plan to destroy you.

There is a cure, therapeutics and treatment for Covid-19, or should we say antidote? Some may say, wait a minute- Antidote is defined as a medicine taken and given to counteract a particular poison. That is correct, because we learned that Fauci the fraud was responsible for 'Gain of Function'; Bioterrorism- a poison in the form of the coronavirus called Covid-19, or as I would say, the Wuhan virus, since it was created in China's Wuhan Institute of Virology and funded by the corrupt government controlled by the deep state. Are we seeing some similarities here?

As a result of this diabolical scheme, on October 23, 2020, the day the trajectory of my life would be changed forever along with many millions of Americans as well. The Wuhan virus caused a lockdown of our booming economy and millions loss their jobs and so did I. Like everything else made in this country by China, you can say, I was made by China, because the China virus made me a man on fire, in search of the truth and to eradicate and expose the fake news media for who they really are: Enemy of the People. So, yes, I am pissed off!!! So don't blame me for my anger, blame China, because the Wuhan virus made me.

You see, I was living the American dream this country affords us all, no matter your race, color, creed or nationality background. Which makes me a proud black American of the greatest country in the world. Anyone disagreeing with this notion, I show you the exit door of our nation and may I suggest the southern border? Since the rogue totalitarian Biden regime has it open for the whole world to migrate here illegally; However, it's just as easy to exit as it is to come in. I continue by saying, I am not oppressed by systematic racism, white privilege, white supremacy or social injustice and I vehemently disagree with the term CRT-Critical race theory, because it teaches us that white people are inherently evil and racist and black people are weak and pathetic needing help from the true oppressors killing our country: Wealthy black offended, like: Colin Kaepernick, Oprah Winfrey, LeBron James, Tyler Perry, Snoop Dogg, Don Lemon, Joy Reid, Al and Jesse, to name a few and white socialist liberals, the modern day slave masters controlling and manipulating the black race thru race hustling and race baiting, as the media bullhorn pushes the narrative that America is a racist nation, and anyone leaving the plantation is labeled as an Uncle Tom and a sell-out because we are not brainwashed by the fake news media zombie apocalypse.

Headline: "Fully vaccinated Mississippi sheriff found dead in his home after positive Covid-19 test". This article was published by Black Enterprise.com on August 7, 2021. Headline: Fully vaccinated Colin Powell dies of Covid-19 complications. Headline: Captain pilot dies mid-flight after taking second vaccine shot a few days prior of the emergency landing. A FULLY vaccinated 16-year-old student dies suddenly during a school zoom meeting. "NBA PLAYER got blood clots from Covid vaccine that ends his season and possibly his career- NBA told him to keep it quiet". Yet, KYRIE IRVING is demonized by the fake woke mob for not getting the deadly experimental vaccine.

Thousands of stories and many others like these never make the headlines. Why? Because they don't want you to know how deadly the experimental vaccines are. Maybe this is the depopulation plan the former prime minister of Malaysia DR. Mahathir Mohamad, and Bill Gates was speaking of.

There is a cure for Covid-19, and the political cesspool on Capitol Hill knows it; Which is why, they have been secretly getting the cure like ivermectin prescribed to them and their families, but they are complicit in the scandal to keep it away from the American people, by: hiding it, demonizing it, blocking it, and censoring it, and using the media to say the cures are ineffective and can cause severe side effects with deadly consequences. While Gov. Gavin Newsom has exquisite dinner parties with no social distancing and no mask during his own lockdown and as Nancy Pelosi gets her hair done at her local beauty parlor during the lockdown; And to add insult to injury, she was getting her hair done while millions of hurting Americans were waiting on her to sign off on the stimulus package to bring some relief to the citizens of this country.

There is a cure, because I contracted the Wuhan virus and was treated by the horse dewormer-ivermectin, and budesonide, both of which, hospitals will not give you; Instead, they would rather give you a drug that puts you into renal failure called remdesivir and midazolam a drug that relieves anxiety but slows down the breathing, and once the oxygen saturation decreases to an almost fatal rate, they intubate you, place you on a vent for you to die alone, because there are no visitations from family members due to covid regulations. The Hospital collects over 40K from FEMA, then hospital Executives, run to the bathroom to wash their hands of the blood money they've acquired.

Again, this is the greatest "Pandemic" the world has ever seen; Yet they are blocking it in every way through Big Tech, Big PHRAMA, Hospitals, doctors, and fake news. If they were really concerned for human lives, shouldn't they want to exhaust every possibility known to mankind to get rid of this deadly virus killing millions of people worldwide? This is the Global reset and once more Americans wake-up from the mesmerizing spell of the fake news media and realize there was no need for a "pandemic" (SCAMDEMIC!!!) nor deadly vaccines, there will be hell to pay!!! Which is why, I am here to stand in defiance of tyranny and expose the whole corrupt deep state system, to win back our country from renegades posing as Americans. Because if we lose our freedom, then we are dead already, because there would be no reason to live. Now, to the school board, if you continue on this path, you too will be complicit in the scandal to destroy our constitutional rights as Americans; But know this, I will fight to the DEATH to save our freedom!!! Because without freedom, we are dead already!!! Let's go Brandon!!! 1776 REWIND!!! And May God bless America!!! Because we sure do need Him now.

II ACTUAL VERBAL ADDRESS TO THE SCHOOL BOARD

I never thought I would see the day, where the white male would be the most hated in our country and patriotism would be synonymous to white supremacy. While the black race lead by BLM has become the new Karen. News Alert: Racism comes in all colors; Just because you're black, God does not give you a pass!!! So, let's judge one another by the content of his/her character. I believe MLK would appreciate it.

I was living the American dream before the SCAMDEMIC shut down the world. America gives us all, the freedom of life, liberty and the pursuit of happiness under the Constitution of the United States, no matter your race, color, creed or nationality background. Which makes me a proud black American of the greatest country in the world. Anyone disagreeing with this notion, I show you the exit door of our nation and may I suggest the southern border? Since the tyrannical Biden regime has it open for the whole world to migrate here illegally, but it's just as easy to exit. I continue by saying, I am not oppressed by systematic racism, white privilege, white supremacy or social injustice and I vehemently disagree with the term CRT-Critical race theory, because it teaches us that white people are inherently evil and racist and black people are weak and pathetic needing help from the true oppressors killing our country: Wealthy black offended, like: Colin Kaepernick, Oprah Winfrey, LeBron James, Tyler Perry, Snoop Dogg, Don Lemon, Joy Reid, Al and Jesse, to name a few and white socialist liberals, the modern day slave masters controlling and manipulating the black race thru race hustling and race baiting, as the media bullhorn pushes the narrative that America is a racist nation, and any blacks leaving the plantation is labeled as an Uncle Tom and a sell-out because we are not brainwashed by the fake news zombie media apocalypse.

Let's talk about Fatherlessness, the catalyst for the black community's undoing's, like: Black on black murder, teen pregnancy, abortion (Legal genocide), domestic violence, crime, drugs, gang violence, incarceration, illiteracy and school drop-out. These are all self-inflicted problems that has plagued the black community for decades. However, the most disheartening thing is, these black neighborhoods across the country are represented by mostly black democratic elected officials, while republicans sit and watch the atrocities transpire right before their eyes with their finger up their butt. Yet, there is total silence on these vitally important issues just mentioned, but Marxist, shove down our throats: CRT, police brutality, social injustice and little boys in dresses (which causes sexual assault cases like Loudoun County in public schools). The political cesspool on Capitol Hill, Pastor's cowering in a corner, too afraid to stand up to the fake woke mob, disingenuous news coverage and academia has failed the American people, to say the least. Our country has gone to pot; but We the People are here to take back our country!!! 1776 Rewind!!! Let's Go Brandon!!! May God bless America!!! Because we sure do need Him now!!!

III ACTUAL VERBAL ADDRESS TO THE SCHOOL BOARD

WHAT I WOULD'VE SAID IF I HAD MORE THAN THREE MINUTES. All lives do matter, not just black, or Asian, or Hispanics or gays and lesbians There shouldn't be a highlight or preferential treatment of any group or person. I do not announce nor advertise that I am a heterosexual; Therefore, I do not need to know your sexual preference. Furthermore, I do not condone bullying, I denounce assaults and violence towards any people or person. All criminal acts should have a swift and harsh penalty without special treatment of a singled-out case, because evil is evil, no matter who its towards. The care and safety of all children should always be the general focus, and no one group singled-out for a political agenda. Plain and simple, equal justice under the law.

I believe in traditional marriage (One man and One Woman) in holy matrimony. It is your prerogative if you are two consenting adults to have relations. As long as you are not abusing underage children sexually or emotionally there will be no problems out of me nor the law. I want to be clear, I do not hate LBGTQ, gays and lesbians, trans-gender or any other pronoun; However, I will not affirm, legitimize nor celebrate any of the lifestyles just mentioned.

The 90's Chicago Bulls, was the greatest team of all times, for only one reason MJ (Michael Jordan). Before the beginning of their second three-peat, the Bulls would acquire a fragile, and an emotional wreck in Dennis Rodman. Dennis Rodman is arguably the greatest defender and rebounder of all time, if he gave you any points at all, it would just be a bonus.

After leaving a dismantled championship Detroit Pistons, Rodman would be acquired by several NBA teams before landing with the Bulls. Outside the Bulls, no one could hon in his energy, which could sometimes become negative. He would at times get so angry, that he would go to the end of the beach and take off his shoes before the game was over. This would create a huge problem, when it was time for him to go back into the game, he couldn't because he was not dressed fully in uniform.

Those of us who know Rodman, he could be very colorful. He's been known for dressing up in a wedding gown. Well, the first time Rodman went shoeless at the end of the bench with the Bulls, he got checked by the G.O.A.T. (MJ). MJ told Rodman, we want you, but we don't need you. I don't care what you do outside this basketball arena, but when you step foot in the arena, you come to play basketball. Some might speculate that MJ said these things, let's just say, it never happened again; As a result, the Bulls would earn its 6th championship by sealing their accomplishment with another three-peat.

Let's assess the parallel between the two sources to obtain a moral common ground: Basketball and Education. When anyone is on a basketball team, you come to play basketball and nothing else. When anyone attends school, you come to get educated by curriculum like: Math, English, reading and nothing else. It is not the job of academia to indoctrinate our children with the school's ideals, that's the parent's job, it's imperative that the schools advocate teaching them skills to become productive citizens for our economy to provide for themselves and/or a family. Anything outside of this, causes confusion for impressionable immature boys and girls, that create sexual assault incidents like the one we saw recently in California's Loudoun County public schools.

3ʳᴰ ACTUAL VERBAL ADDRESS TO THE SCHOOL BOARD

All lives do matter, not just black, Asian, Hispanics, gays or lesbians. We shouldn't highlight or give preferential treatment to any group or person. I do not go around announcing I'm a heterosexual; Therefore, I do not need to know your sexual preference. Furthermore, I do not condone bullying, I denounce assaults and violence towards any people or person. All criminal acts should have a swift and harsh penalty without special treatment of a singled-out case, because evil is evil, no matter who its towards. The care and safety of all children should always be the general focus, and no one group singled-out for a political agenda. Plain and simple, equal justice for all under the law.

I believe in traditional marriage (One man and One Woman) in holy matrimony. It is your prerogative if you are two consenting same sex adults having relations. As long as you are not abusing underage children sexually, physically or emotionally there will be no backlash from me nor the law. I want to be clear, just because a person disagrees with your lifestyle does not mean we hate the LGBTQ community, pansexual or any other pronoun one might label themselves at the moment. With that being said, I will not affirm, legitimize nor celebrate any of the lifestyles just mentioned. Again, that does not mean I hate you. You have a right to be what you want to be, and I have a right to disagree. This is the definition of free speech, not hate speech.

In my opinion, the 90's Chicago Bulls was the greatest team of all times, for one reason,

Michael Jordan. The Bulls had just acquired Dennis Rodman, for his incredible defensive and rebounding ability. However, Rodman was known for his colorful personality and defiant temperament. Which generated a conversation between he and Jordan. Jordan would relay this message to Rodman, he said, we want you, but we don't need you. I don't care what you do outside this arena, but when you come to the arena, you come to play basketball. The Bulls would go on to win three more consecutive titles with Dennis Rodman.

Let's assess the parallel between the two sources to obtain a moral common ground: The Jordan Rules and Education. When anyone is on a basketball team, you come to play basketball and nothing else. When anyone attends school, you come to get educated by curriculum like: Math, English, reading and nothing else. It is not the job of academia to indoctrinate our children with the school's ideals, that's the parent's job. It's imperative that the schools advocate teaching them skills to become productive citizens for our economy to provide for themselves and/or for a family. Anything outside of this, causes confusion for impressionable immature boys and girls, that create sexual assault atrocities like the one we saw recently in Virginia's Loudoun County public schools. What is the moral of the story? Identity politics is the breeding ground for Marxism, and it's killing our country!!! 1776REWIND!!! May God Bless America!!!

4ᵀᴴ ADDRESS TO SCHOOL BOARD

Tell a big enough lie repeatedly, eventually people will believe it. We're 3 years into the Wuhan China virus (AKA: Covid-19; or is it the Delta-variant? Omicron, or Omicron BA.2, flurona; Deltacron; stealth Omicron and the HIV-variant? I believe they close their eyes, grab a medical dictionary and point to the next fear mongering virus. This has become a collaborated three ring circus by Fauci the fraud, FDA, CDC, NIH, and WHO as the disingenuous mainstream media spread the propaganda that therapeutics like: ivermectin, hydroxychloroquine, budesonide, monoclonal clinics are either ineffective or ladened with life threatening side effects that could end your life instantly. When the deadly experimental vaccines are actually ineffective and ladened with lethal consequences. Are you going to believe me? Or the Marxist media that told us the 2020 BLM/Antifa riots, destruction, violent fatal assaults and chaos were mostly peaceful as we saw in real time cities burning to ground all across America. One mayor amongst the mayhem and atrocities in her city, saw it as, "A summer of love."

What am I saying? This virus has been prostituted like a $10 dolla whore. There never should've been a "pandemic" and no need for vaccines. I contracted Covid-19 and, like Joe Rogan, the NFL secretly, the political cesspool on Capitol Hill secretly and many thousands around the world were treated and cured by ivermectin. A 40-year old safe and FDA approved medication that won a Nobel prize in 2015 for curing just about any disease it came in contact with, and in March of 2020, we would learn it cured Covid-19, but it is still being blocked, hidden, vilified, censored and demonized as medical misinformation (Just ask Joe Rogan, he is being roasted and threatened for sharing ivermectin to his over 11 million a day fan base). Dr. Robert Malone, a vaccine scientist, who invented the mRNA technology was banned by Big Tech. Can anyone tell me, for 2 whole years, where has the flu gone? Does anything I've said this far, raise any serious concern?

So, why are we pushing vaccines to healthy school age children with strong immune systems as young as 5 years old? And now the corrupt pharmaceuticals want to give the jab to infants as young as 6 months!!! I had a gentleman get angry at me for talking about the dangers of the vaccines because he and his family got the jab and were doing fine. I said, "thank God you and your family are doing well, I pray that continue to be the case down the road." "But tell that to the many thousands that have died and had life altering adverse effects from the vaccines." I continued, "just because tragedy hasn't hit your house or someone you know, doesn't mean cases don't exist. You can't see gravity, but it exists." The only 1 percent of VAERS data reported deaths (12,612) and adverse effects from the vaccines is astounding enough, but what's more astounding, it's being ignored. This is my constant prayer, that everyone that had a hand in this crime against humanity, would find themselves in GITMO for the rest of their lives or be executed, anything less would be an insult to the citizens of the United States of America, who was injured, have lost loved ones and livelihood stripped because of the 'P-L-A-N-DEMIC'!!!

IV ACTUAL VERBAL ADDRESS TO THE SCHOOL BOARD

Teachers are priceless, because we cannot put a price tag on exceptional people who are instrumental in shaping the minds of several generations. This can be very beneficial to the future of our country or can be very, very dangerous when children are indoctrinated with the wrong tools. When put into the hands of mad scientist controlled by the deep state system.

I believe Covid-19 was a blessing in disguise. Why do I say this? Because I'm here again tonight, without the virus and the 2020 chaos and lawlessness, the world would not know Sonny B. I was never interested in a school board meeting, but I guess you can say, like everything else in this country made by China, I too was made by the Wuhan, China virus. So, excuse me if I seem to be a little pissed off.

Everything was shut down because of the virus, including our means to provide for our families. Almost two years later, our corrupt three letter agencies like the FDA and CDC are still making up names for Covid-19 like: Delta variant, omicron, and omicron BA.2, how do they figure out these things with the same PCR test that has been known to give false positives. If you think I'm fabricating the truth, a relative of mine tested positive at one location, I told him to test at a different location and what do you know, he tested negative.

2020 put life in perspective for me, I always knew there was something evil lurking in the waters of our government, but I had no idea how diabolically sinister every facet of our government was, until the lunacy captivated my attention. All the three letter agencies, the political cesspool on Capitol Hill, major corporations, Big Tech, Big PHARMA, professional sports, Hollywood, and yes academia are destroying the Constitution of the United States of America, with the virus, identity politics and intentional economy sabotage. While the CCP owned mainstream media assists in our nation's divide and demise.

Has anyone ever thought, why does Hollywood stars, professional athletes and some mainstream media icons, get paid insurmountably more than teachers? Teachers that at one time would become an integral part in shaping the minds of all just mentioned. I have the answer, have you ever heard the saying, 'Send in the Clowns'? They put more emphasis on paying them well to distract and redirect your attention to things that are diminutive. They pay media icons of news outlets like: CNN, MSNBC, and FOX, as local media are the mockingbirds to feed you propaganda and rhetoric, while blocking, hiding, vilifying, censoring, and contextually fabricating of the truth. To keep citizens, ignoring, in the dark, ill-informed, ignorant, and divided, while turning our children into Marxist and hating the country they live in.

5ᵀᴴ ADDRESS TO THE SCHOOL BOARD

I support salary increase for teachers 100%, because they are instrumental in educating the bright minds of the future, as long as teachers are not forced to indoctrinate our children with curriculum that has nothing to do with education. With that being said, I have a question, where did the lottery money go? Do I want to open that pandoras box? Yes, I do!!! We were told that the lottery money would subsidize the educational budget and resolve the woes of the public school system. You have an operating budget of 2.1 billion dollars, that's about 20% more than the whole city's budget. We need an audit of where the lottery money is funneled. Since you're asking for a millage fee during a war-torn economy cause by a P-L-A-N-DEMIC. Not to mention, the Biden administration is doing an excellent job aiding in the economy's demise with mindless and reckless decisions. Why am I having a difficult time with this additional fee? Let me count the ways, but I'll give you one, I DO NOT TRUST THE GOVERNMENT, and it's unfortunate the Marxist mainstream media doesn't hold them accountable, because they are a huge part of the problem. Furthermore, about 10 years after the lottery was implemented, some public-school children with their parents came to my doorstep asking for donations for things like pencils. I was astonished, and my question was, what happened to the lottery money? Needless to say, I did not donate one penny on that day, and if this millage fee gets to the ballot, I will vote no, and encourage others to do the same, because our government cannot be trusted. In addition, where are you getting the 350K to pay Read USA? Is it part of Gov. DeSantis's recent 800-million-dollar approval to increase the teachers' salaries? If we did an investigation, would we find more indoctrination of our children through books? Or through visuals like a family reading of a book entitled, 'A Boy like you' presented by two white men, with their black adopted son on READ USA's website? This is a prime example of the identity politics that is destroying our country.

I digress back to the covid vaccines to ask the question. Why are we vaccinating perfectly healthy children with a survival rate of 99.97% to covid? Also, medical professionals say that only 1% of covid vaccine deaths and injuries get reported to VAERS. From December 14, 2020, through March 28, 2022, that's only a 15-month span, in which there were 13,637 deaths reported to VAERS from the covid vaccines. This is astounding for vaccines they call safe, but what's more astounding and sinister is that IT'S BEING IGNORED, by everyone, especially the: Fake news media, the White House, CDC, FDA, NIH, WHO, DARPA, and the political cesspool on Capitol Hill!!! Citizens of the United States, PLEASE WAKE UP!!!

VI PARENTAL RIGHTS BILL
ADDRESS TO DCSB

I'm here in support of the parental rights bill deemed as 'Don't say Gay' bill by the Marxist mainstream media. It's 7 pages long and nowhere does it say 'Don't say Gay' because I read it. However, it does give the rights to parents to govern their own children and not allow indoctrination of our children by the educational system. So, what's the problem?

I believe it's time to revisit an address to the school board several months ago. All lives do matter, not just black, Asian, Hispanics, gays or lesbians. We shouldn't highlight or give preferential treatment to any group or person. I do not go around announcing I'm a heterosexual; Therefore, I do not need to know your sexual preference. Furthermore, I do not condone bullying, I denounce assaults and violence towards any people or person. All criminal acts should have a swift and harsh penalty without special treatment of a singled-out case, because evil is evil, no matter who its towards. The care and safety of all children should always be the general focus, and no one group singled-out for a political agenda. Plain and simple, equal justice for all under the law.

I believe in traditional marriage (One man and One Woman) in holy matrimony. It is your prerogative if you are two consenting same sex adults having relations. As long as you are not abusing underage children sexually, physically or emotionally there will be no backlash from me nor the law. I want to be clear, just because a person disagrees with your lifestyle does not mean we hate the LGBTQ community, pansexual or any other pronoun one might label themselves at the moment. With that being said, I will not affirm, legitimize nor celebrate any of the lifestyles just mentioned. Again, that does not mean I hate you. You have a right to be what you want to be, and I have a right to disagree. This is the definition of free speech, not hate speech.

When a child attends school, they come to get educated by curriculum like: Math, English, reading and nothing else. It is not the job of academia to indoctrinate our children with the school's ideals, that's the parent's job. It's imperative that the schools advocate teaching them skills to become productive citizens for our economy to provide for themselves and/or for a family. Anything outside of this, causes confusion for impressionable immature boys and girls, that create sexual assault atrocities like the one we saw recently in Virginia's Loudoun County public schools. What is the moral of the story? Identity politics is the breeding ground for Marxism, and it's killing our country!!! May God Bless America!!!

ACTUAL VERBAL ADDRESS TO SCHOOL BOARD

Mask coverings and social distancing are control mechanisms under the guise to keep us safe. It alienates each citizen from one another and annihilates the very existence of human touch, communication, care and love. Not to mention, they don't work.

There is a cure, therapeutics and treatment for Covid-19, or should we say antidote? Because we learned that Fauci the fraud was responsible for 'Gain of Function'; Bioterrorism- a poison in the form of the coronavirus called Covid-19, The Wuhan virus, because it was created in China's Wuhan Institute of Virology and funded by the corrupt U.S. government.

Here are some vaccine Headlines for you to ponder: "FULLY vaccinated Mississippi sheriff found dead in his home after positive Covid-19 test". FULLY vaccinated Colin Powell dies of Covid-19 complications. A CAPTAIN PILOT dies mid-fight after taking second vaccine shot a few days prior of an emergency landing. A FULLY vaccinated 16-year-old student dies suddenly during a school zoom meeting. "NBA PLAYER got blood clots from Covid vaccine that ends his season and possibly his career- NBA told him to keep it quiet". Yet, KYRIE IRVING is demonized by the fake woke mob for not getting the deadly experimental vaccine.

Like Joe Rogan, I too was cured of Covid with ivermectin and budesonide. However, hospital protocols are prescribing a drug that puts you into renal failure called remdesivir and midazolam, a drug that relieves anxiety but slows down the breathing, and once the oxygen saturation decreases to an almost fatal rate, they intubate you, place you on a vent to die alone, because there are no visitations from family members due to covid regulations. The Hospital collects over 40 thousand dollars from FEMA, then hospital Executives, run to the bathroom to wash their hands of the blood money they've just acquired.

This is the greatest "Pandemic" the world has ever seen; Yet, they are blocking, censoring, hiding and vilifying the cures, while hiding staggering numbers of vaccine deaths and adverse effects. Think about it, if they were really concerned for human lives, shouldn't they want to exhaust every possibility known to mankind to get rid of this deadly virus killing millions of people worldwide? This is Globalism at work, the Great Reset and once more Americans wake-up from the mesmerizing spell of the fake news media and realize there was no need for a SCAMDEMIC!!! nor deadly vaccines, there will be hell to pay!!! Which is why, I am here to stand in defiance of tyranny, express my displeasure and expose the whole corrupt deep state system, to win back our country from renegades posing as Americans. Now, to the school board, if you continue on this path, you too will be complicit in the scandal to destroy our constitutional rights as Americans; But know this, I will fight to the DEATH to save our freedom!!! Because without freedom, we are dead already!!! Let's go Brandon!!! 1776 REWIND!!! And May God bless America!!! Because we sure do need Him now.

DCSB-READ USA, INC

Greetings School board members,

I have been attending school board meetings for the past 5 months. Like parents across the nation, I am concerned for the education and wellbeing of our children. Whoever controls what goes into the minds of our children at a very young age, is most likely to have them for life. There are some very bad people who are aware of this; which is why it is a constant battle for the children, because future generations can be used for political gain and power to support an agenda. They want the parents asleep and trusting, with little or no resistance as possible as they influence the children spiritually, socially, and politically to make it easy to usher in the Great Reset. Therefore, the parent(s) should be the focal point in influencing their child's education with the school system being an advocacy for what the parent(s) want for their child, and not the other way around.

I agree with Superintendent Greene, when she said it's about literacy, and I agree with board member Jones wanting to get three free of charge books each year for elementary children. Books are a wonderful tool in helping to educate our children and to rid our country of illiteracy, especially in the black community. However, I do not want to see a READ USA partnership as another form of indoctrination. It was said on record in last night's meeting, "the board wants to be transparent to the public." I can't agree more; as a result, I would like to have a full list of books that will be on display with a description of the content in each book, because having titles alone does not always translate to us the content inside of a book.

In addition, because the DCSB is partnering with READ USA, Inc, I feel your committee should have significant input and influence of what is displayed on their website on behalf of the parents. Reason being, their website is an extension of the books they are providing; therefore, all the material on their website should be scrutinized and removed if deemed inappropriate.

I made a comment on record last night of my displeasure of the content displayed on READ USA'S website, and that was, "If we did an investigation, would we find more indoctrination of our children through books? Or through visuals like a family reading of a book entitled, 'A Boy like you' presented by two white men, with their black adopted son on READ USA's website? This is a prime example of the identity politics that is destroying our country." This wasn't actually a question; I already knew what was on their website. This is not propaganda, this is just one example of what I found on their website as a tool to influence impressionable young minds, and it was disgusting to see a little boy used as a photo-op to push the LGBTQ+ agenda.

I'm going to give you a quote of mine on record from February's board meeting concerning the LGBTQ+, and any type of injustice of ALL our children, "All lives do matter, not just black, Asian, Hispanics, gays or lesbians. We shouldn't highlight or give preferential treatment to any group or person. I do not go around announcing I'm a heterosexual; Therefore, I do not need to know your sexual preference. Furthermore, I do not condone bullying, I denounce assaults and violence towards any people or person. All criminal acts should have a swift and harsh penalty without special treatment of a singled-out case, because evil is evil, no matter who its towards. The care and safety of all children should always be the general focus, and no one group singled-out for a political agenda. Plain and simple, equal justice for all under the law."

"I believe in traditional marriage (One man and One Woman) in holy matrimony. It is your prerogative if you are two consenting same sex adults having relations. As long as you are not abusing underage children sexually, physically or emotionally there will be no backlash from me nor the law. I want to be clear, just because a person disagrees with your lifestyle does not mean we hate the LGBTQ community, pansexual or any other pronoun one might label themselves at the moment. With that being said, I will not affirm, legitimize nor celebrate any of the lifestyles just mentioned. Again, that does not mean I hate you. You have a right to be what you want to be, and I have a right to disagree. This is the definition of free speech, not hate speech."

Along with the LGBTQ+, social justice, CRT, and any materials, visuals, videos and statements that causes division and isolation of a particular group or person, I ask to be removed from READ USA's website. If you want a description of the content I'm referring to, I can note it in my next email to you. However, I do ask, before you initiate a request from me, I ask that each of you go take a look for yourself, and ask yourself, is this age-appropriate material for elementary students? And why are they focusing on things that has nothing to do with education? And then let your conscience be your guide. Just like racism is taught and learned, telling a certain race that they are oppressed by another race is taught and learned, a little boy can't choose his bedtime, but he can choose his gender, this is taught and learned, and telling a little black boy that white cops are bad is taught and learned. I believe schools take advantage of the amount of time they have with the students. With this time, they are able to use the power of persuasion to create an illusion to develop curiosity or a negative thought in the mind of a child; which can become detrimental to the developmental psyche of a child. This has no place in academia, and it needs to stop.

In conclusion, this is America in a nutshell, from a quote from the Declaration of Independence, "We hold these truths to be self-evident, that all men are created equal, that they are endowed by their Creator with certain unalienable Rights, that among these are Life, Liberty, and the pursuit of Happiness." So, let's keep the identity politics out of education, please.

May God Bless America,
Sonny B.

LIVING A LIE?

I'm a simple guy, I like to wear plain standard suits, nothing flashy. I keep a cell until it's on its last leg, and I never change my number. Let's just say I'm an ole school kinda guy. Which is why, the only reason I have a Facebook account, is because my sister-in-law kept bugging the life out of me. I hate cell phones because they have become a necessary part of our lives and I hate relying on an electronic device. It has opened us up to a whole new world literally, we longer have to travel to far off lands to experience the joy of traveling or feeling, touching, and smelling the elements of another country. Just pick up your phone, tune into social media and presto, you're in a whole new world or should I say country. We used to make eye contact with another person and actually have a conversation with a person you just met in the grocery store or a subway. Now, we see the tops of everyone's heads because they are in tuned with their device with their heads down in total concentration with the world wide web. Not to mention, the fake and phony social media pages to let everyone see how many miles you ran today, as if anyone cares. We pride ourselves on having it all together, which is why humans can be the greatest pretenders, by showing the world what we wish our lives could be. It's a façade, which is one of the reasons we're in the predicament we're in, in our nation of course. We are too busy with our four and no more; as a result, we fell to see that the Roman empire is falling, or we see it, but feel we will be exempt when communism comes knocking. The virus was a foretelling of what's to come, but what did Americans do? They complied, without hesitation and without question. The media talked up the numbers of covid, posted them 24/7 on fake news to stoke fear, while killing thousands of Americans with Fauci the frauds mandatory hospital protocol across the country. The George Soros installed governors, mayors and AGs were glad to oblige with the hostile mandates to control the citizens. With the fear, came non-approved emergency use only jabs for a virus that had several cures, but they were hidden, blocked, vilified, censored and demonized as having deadly implications. Americans gave up their rights and freedoms under the constitution for the right not to choose. It is April 15, 2022, going into the third year of this scamdemic and they're still talking about cases surging. I live in Florida, and I can tell you, the citizens of Florida are out, thanks to the best governor ever. That governor would be DeSantis. I've learned, if the deep state, the political cesspool on Capitol Hill, and the Marxist media hates you, then you are doing a grand job for 'We the People.' Will someone in my circle use your brain, use some critical thinking and ask the question, WHERE DID THE FLU GO FOR TWO YEARS??? It's magically gone, this was one of the biggest hoaxes of the century. I've said it before, when those controlled by the media zombie apocalypse awake from their coma, it's going to be hell to pay. Which is why I'm here to wake you up. I like the term used, I'm like your alarm clock, you hate it when it goes off, but you eventually wake up, I'm that alarm clock!!!

I despise social media, because it is used for evil by our stellar government to spy into our lives by relinquishing our information willingly. In other words, they went through the backdoor of the constitution to pry into our lives. However, it's a wonderful thing to spread truth when it's allowed, when you're not censored. Someone, explain the bait and switch. Everyone and anyone could express their feelings or share knowledge to the world. Now, whoever goes against the Marxist agenda, is censored by Big Tech and guess what, you are not able to sue because of section 230 implemented by who? You guessed it, our corrupt politicians in DC. Yes, Big Tech would hook up with our corrupt politicians and propose a deal called social media, of course they didn't want anyone to find out about big brother watching you through all of our electronic devices. Cancel Culture has become the evil brother of the first amendment. Go ahead and give it a try, try an expose Big Pharma, Patrisse Cullors, Hunter Biden's laptop from hell and any one of the corrupt three letter governmental agencies and watch your account go dark.

We live in a Westworld. What brought me to that resolve? Two major years of my life would change the trajectory of my life forever. Yes, 2020-2022 has been an eye-opening experience, to say the least. As a result, I am questioning everything I believed was true. When you become aware of the manipulation of the whole deep state system, you cannot return to the old guard. Before 2020, I did have some trust in our government; however, during 2020 would put my trust in government at a negative 100%. Let me give you an example of why I don't trust the government. My family and I have been trying to eat healthier by eating organically without all the GMOs. It's very expensive by the way. I contacted a chicken farm to ask rather their chickens were organically certified or not. Boy did I get a wake-up call when he basically said organic is about as worthless as the dollar bill backed by the Central banks by referencing an article to read. That article was published by Washington Post on May 12, 2017, by Peter Whoriskey, entitled "The labels said 'Organic.' But these massive imports of corn and soybeans weren't." In the article, it tells the audience that the feed starts out as a regular shipment (meaning not labeled organic) when the shipment leaves Ukraine's port, makes a stop in Turkey, heading to California as its last stop. By the time it gets to California, the labels magically transform from regular feed to organic. Is this criminal or what? I was flabbergasted with my jaw to the ground. Thousands of tons of animal feed were distributed to organic farms across America that wasn't actually organic. This was Gavin Newsom's state before his scandal, along with a stellar cast starring Nancy Pelosi and Maxine Waters heading up the establishment. If you are a critical thinker and not one of these brainwashed Marxist created by the fake news media and academia, you would ask yourself the question. Are we really eating and paying for organic? It's going into the fifth year with no follow-up story and no action taken. Are you surprised? I'm not, but before 2020, I would've been shocked. Now, I can't be surprised by anything of the lunacy flooding in everyday in this country like a tsunami. Go read it for yourself, if this story isn't appalling, then you are part of the problem.

I'm questioning everything I was ever told. Who really killed Malcom X? Who really killed MLK? Who really killed JFK? And did we really land on the moon? I believe these are legitimate questions, knowing what I know now about our sinister and evil government, while the media backs them up with an onslaught of lies.

I was talking to someone the other day at a meeting to try and save the nation. When she asked me, did I have a telegram account? My response was, I don't know, I believe I do. So, I commenced to show her what I thought was telegram, and sure enough, I had it. My question, was how? Because I never added it as an app. She said it was secure, and I said to myself, oh really? Is anything really secure? So, the next question was, how did they get my information? I did easy research, I say easy because there was not an arsenal of fact checking, nor did the algorithms bury it, making it practically impossible to find, and nor was it censored. It popped-up right away, and what do you know, it's owned by Russians. Thanks to my sister-in-law, that explains why they already had all of my info, I believe from Facebook or Google, because how else would they have my information if it wasn't given? In my research, it mentioned that the app is encrypted from end to end, but the clincher is, the user has to turn on the encryption for it to be secure. Here's my conspiracy theory, because I already told you I don't trust the government. What? You don't believe that Big Tech is a part of the government? Then ask yourself this question, why would Capitol Hill give them an exemption of lawsuits by implementing Section 230? Back to my theory, I believe when you turn on the encryption, it alerts Big Tech that somebody or somebody's wants to request a secure line of communication; as a result, makes you more vulnerable to Big Brother watching you. Remember, these same social media sites did give us the ole bait and switch. At one time, anyone could post or say what they wanted to say. Now, it's common ground that Marxist get special treatment while patriots are de-platformed and censored for telling the truth and exposing the agenda of the Globalist. You can de-platform the president of the United States of America!!! ARE YOU KIDDING ME!!! Folks we are in trouble!!! This is why Truth Social was created, to have an open platform of all sides. I've said it, and I'll say it again, I standby what I believe; therefore, your argument is not a threat to me. However, when a person knows they don't have an argument and their theory is BS, they become intimidated and angry. To the point, they ghost you, never to have any more dealings with you. That's the difference between patriots and Marxist liberals; unfortunately, the church can more often than not fall into that category. The deep state can't afford truth to be unleashed without it being censored; as a result, they are already plotting on a strategy to try and take down Truth Social, because God forbid people get real news with nothing but facts without all of the propaganda and rhetoric. In the words of Forrest Gump, "and that's all I have to say about dat."

MESSAGE 355

This is kind of a response, but really a message to those who are oblivious to decades of renegades posing as Americans undermining the constitution. Willing to hand over our freedom to foreign global Communist. Not to mention, I was inspired to write about this profound and enlightening movie, because 2020 prepared me for the messages in this thriller; As a result, I would like to share my thoughts on global corruption in every government around the world. It's been said, 'Absolute power corrupts Absolutely'. This blockbuster is a prime example of wanting power leading to corruption.

Now, about this unsettling review, By Pajiba.com, titled, "I have now stared into the void, and it's called 'The 355,'" written by Ciara Wardlow and published on January 13, 2022. I will not linger on the review, but I will say, apparently Mrs. Wardlow still watches movies for entertainment based on her criticism of the movie, with her quote "A joyless script, and the only bright point in the movie was Graciela Rivera played by Penelope Cruz because she had caring emotions." She has no idea how real life the plot in this blockbuster hits close to home. Apparently, she didn't pay attention to the 2020 wake-up call. The message was clear, the deep state controls every aspect of our country, including the propaganda that goes out to control the narrative. That would be the mainstream media and Big Tech. I must admit, the plan is brilliant, if you control the narrative, you can infiltrate and indoctrinate half of America to create Civil War 2.0. In reality, we are already in an 'Information War,' World War III as I call it. If you don't believe me, just think about all of the lives that have been lost because of the Wuhan China virus. I explain in detail, in my 'Right to Try' and 'Enemy of the People' letter.

I got some wise advice from a platform that fell into the black hole of cancel culture just before the stolen 2020 presidential election to go and see 355 because it had a message in it. A message would be the only reason why I would attend a movie. 2020 destroyed the very notion of enjoying entertainment, thanks to BLM/Antifa and all of the fake woke that supported them, like: Hollywood, professional sports, academia, major corporations, Big Tech and music industry. While the mainstream media bullhorn would act as the diversion factor to conceal the corruption running rampant in our government. Do I sound pissed? Absolutely!!! Because I'm sick of the BS, I found out, we as American people have been duped, bamboozled, hoodwinked, and swindled. Notice, I said American people, not democrat or republican, right vs left, liberals vs conservatives, vaxxed and unvaxxed, but all Americans. They've used us all as pawns through identity politics. Which was one of the most important lessons in the movie that Mrs. Wardlow completely overlooked or never even noticed, because she's still distracted by entertainment. Which was, every nation represented in the movie came together as one to combat evil all over the world, a lesson all Americans must learn if 'We the People' are going to win this war.

The second lesson I learned was, the citizens around the world are never the problem, it's the diabolical elitist and tyrannical governments around the world who control the scandalous system that keeps us worlds apart. We have to be smarter than they are and understand that the people are not the enemy, but the globalist are. Those who want to strip every ounce of freedom out of society, and control what you eat, drink, where we live, and how you receive medical attention. To dictate where you eat, where you can travel, where and when you can congregate, how many feet can you leave your home and how much time, social distance without ever touching and hide your smile with a useless mask.

The third lesson, the cabal wants power by any means necessary. They will use 9/11, George Floyd, and the Wuhan China virus (Covid-19, Delta variant, omicron, omicron DA.2, flurona, deltacrom). The flu magically disappeared for two years. I have been trying to alert the masses in my corner of the world and I tell you, it is very difficult to pry them away from the control of the CCP owned fake news media. The media has the Caucasians with white guilt and the blacks offended with social injustice and vengeful for a hundred-year-old black wall street. Keep everyone at odds, while the deep state conquers the world.

This is the fourth and final lesson learned, there may be more, but these are the four I gleamed from the movie. Go see it for yourself, I promise, if you already understand CCP takeover transpiring right before our eyes, you won't be disappointed. There was a family at the very end of the movie, going about their way, safe, comfortable and enjoying life without a care in the world. The comment was made, look at that family, they don't have any idea that they almost lost everything and no idea who just save them from losing everything.

The church has much to blame for this. The church was given access to the 501c3, a huge tax benefit. I believe we call that hush money, the thirty pieces of silver. Stay in your plush Mega churches and preach to your people behind the four walls and leave the cultural changes to the political cesspool on Capitol Hill, local and state government throughout the country. It's gotten so bad, pastors are telling the people to stay out of politics, not realizing, politics frames our world and the society we are a part of each and every day. Even most of the gospel music is no longer inspirational but it's entertaining, a part of that distraction I spoke of earlier. In other words, the church is combat ineffective and powerless. 'We the People' have to join in 'The Great Awakening' to save the soul of this nation. Listen folks, there is no cavalry coming to help fight in this war, we're it. So, put on the whole armor of God and get to fighting!!!

HOW IMPORTANT IS LOCAL AND STATE GOVERNMENT?

It's been said that elections have consequences, but a stolen election has severe consequences. For everyone not brainwashed by the zombie media apocalypse, can I get an Amen? If you can see America's downward spiral into the black hole with our constitutional freedoms never to appear again in the universe, then you are a part of the 'Great Awakening.' Our country is in a wreck and if you are trying to cover for this rogue Biden regime while avoiding voters' remorse, then you are enabling the problem. Let's use the gas prices for instance. The Keystone Pipeline was shut down immediately when Biden took office that would cause gas prices to go out the roof. However, the brainwashed people listening to the media tell them the gas prices are skyrocketing because of Russia invading Ukraine are in a blue pill induced 'Matrix' coma. Remember, this is the same Marxist media that told us the 2020 RIOTS were mostly peaceful as cities burned down behind them. Should I say it? Yes, I should. If Trump was in office with this present-day disaster, there would be a 24/7 rotation of bashing news of Trump derange syndrome. We would hear it in the morning, in the afternoon, in the evening, in the nighttime and when we awake the next morning, we would hear it all over again. Some might think I'm embellishing but it's not exaggerating if it's 100 percent true. We wouldn't hear the end of it from all the democrats and mainstream media that have gone silent to all of Biden's debacles and major pitfalls, while the republicans sit on the sideline cheering in secrecy as they hide behind conservative values and Christian principles. But that's what you get when you have a Resident and not a President; with the Three Ring Circus on Capitol Hill drowning in the political cesspool with literally only a handful working for 'We the People.' Our government has the audacity to induce war on the law-abiding citizens all across the nation by using the corrupt three letter agencies like the: FBI, CIA, DOJ, NIH, CDC, FDA, and IRS as they excused, dismissed, overlooked, pardoned and applauded BLM/Antifa for creating mayhem. The selective outrage is lunacy and has a term I'm searching for, yes that's right, it's called HYPOCRISY!!!

This is a collaborated coup, so wake up and understand that your neighbor is not your enemy, your family member is not your enemy, your friend is not your enemy, your co-worker is not your enemy, and the party affiliates are meaningless without integrity. This week I realized that none of this will no longer matter. What do I mean by this? Joining organizations like CCDF-USA, and Mom's for Liberty or who we elect to our government will be null and void if we do not fight with everything within us. This message would take an unexpected detour with the knowledge of disturbing and unsettling news to say the least.

I was going to give you two recent encounters as a lead-in to how important it is for us to have constitutionalist in our local and state level government before I learned that an illegitimate president activated the son Bush's treaty in January of 2021. I'll explain later in this message, but before I do, I need to expose the critical role of how identity politics plays in deceiving the masses. It is a vital tool to keep us divided and focusing on miniscule issues while the elites live out their diabolical scheme to undermine the Constitution as Americans were being: lied to by the media, providing for our families, entertained by Hollywood, vacationing to Disney theme parks, entertained by NFL, NBA, MLB, collegiate level sports and ESPN. While democratic and republican citizens fight one another as our educational system was indoctrinating our children making them prime for Communism thru social injustice and police brutality as we lived the American dream. The media's propaganda would be instrumental in creating a mirage by continuing to 'Bring in the Clowns' to cause Americans to ignore the bloody trauma in America and focus on a paper cut.

Ladies and gentlemen, corruption has no party affiliation boundaries. Republicans have played in my opinion a bigger role in deceiving the conservatives. These two parties are lawless but the worse of the two evils are the republicans because they are the wolf in sheep's clothing. Again, they hide behind conservative values and Christian principles making us think they were on our side, when they were actually cheering for the opposition from the grandstand. Again, the republican establishment is equally at fault as the far left and the Marxist lunatics for the massive decline of our country because we thought they were running our country in the interest of the people.

My apologies, I never get the lettering in the Bush's name correct, so I distinguish the two by calling one son Bush and the other daddy Bush. Furthermore, really there isn't a difference at all, like the ole saying, 'like father like son;' In other words, they were both corrupt. Son Bush created the health emergency treaty with the World Health Organization (WHO) in 2005 during his presidency that would hand over our sovereignty to the WHO and U.N. control in another health emergency (PLAN-Demic). Do you still think 9/11 was a surprise? You would think that this act would've garnered major backlash from the media or even a leak like SCOTUS Judge Alito's draft opinion for banning Roe v Wade, no not a peep. You can see where our priorities lie, right in-line with the deep state Communist and the establishment. Only a couple of weeks left before 196 nations will vote on the treaty by May 28 to possibly seal our doom if the military doesn't step in.

How important is local and state government? Do you need air to breathe? It is the difference between a free state and a modern-day plantation. However, securing local and state level seats will become meaningless if this treaty isn't stopped. The present power that local and state officials have to defy unconstitutional mandates will be null and void if the popular vote holds up. All power will be given to the WHO coupled with force by U.N. soldiers taking control during another PLAN-Demic. In other words, Gov. DeSantis would have no authority, the RINOs and democrats can continue cheating in elections, because the Constitution will die along with the United States of America.

So, how do you like them apples? Will you continue to sit on the couch and do nothing? While your fellow citizens sacrifice their lives, families, careers, and comfortable living to save the soul of this nation!!! You do realize, if we lose our freedom, that includes you? Don't find yourself living in regret or should I say existing in regret because you did nothing to help save our country. It's called living when you're free, when you're not free it's called existing by the way. So, jocking for position, supporting the establishment, wanting your name to be recognized, seeking political stardom, wanting your name in lights or having a fat bank account backed by a worthless Central Bank system is all vanity and it will be crushed quickly under the weight of Communism. I don't know what else to tell you to make you understand the urgency of my message as I leave you with a final quote. "You will own nothing and be happy." From Klaus Schwab's 'Great Reset' (New World Order). May God bless America!!!

ELECTION INTEGRITY

Letter sent to: Gov. DeSantis; Lt. Gov. Nunez; Mayor Curry; Duval Supervisor of Elections (SOE), Mike Hogan and 32 member staff; Florida State of Secretary; Florida Supervisors of Elections; CISA; and half of Florida's SOE's, a couple of Florida Representatives and one Georgia Representative to total about 75 letters sent out. Do you think I'm serious?

Greetings,

I am a proud black American citizen of the greatest country in the world, despite the allegations towards the U.S. as being a racist nation. If you are not mesmerized by the zombie media apocalypse, I believe you would agree. **I want a fair, unmanipulated election and every American should want the same.** I don't care if you love or hate President Trump, that is beside the point nor the reason for this letter to present Trump as the 'Holy Grail.' However, this letter is about **Election Integrity** and our **Republic** on trial to be put to **DEATH,** if the 2020 elections and prior to isn't fixed. In other words, election fraud was and is massive across the country and there has never been a secure election, because how else do you get some of the worse career politicians on Capitol Hill, Ex. (**Nancy Pelosi, Maxine Waters and Mitch McConnell**). _Not to mention, Andrew Gillum a no name in the governor's race narrowly escapes_ *a victory against Ron DeSantis in 2018 (**We remember the ballots mysteriously appearing out of thin air**).* A political cesspool filled with democrats and republicans in a political position for themselves and the lobbyist who own them with Americans willing to commit treason against our elections.

Before Attorney's Sidney Powell 'Releasing the Kraken,' Rudy Giuliani, Mike Lindell, 2000 Mules, True the Vote and other evidence that the election was stolen; **I knew this was a collaborated effort domestically, and internationally, while the media was complicit in the whole corrupt scam, when I saw the elections shut down for the first time in history.** That was red flag number 1. Red Flag number 2, Biden not only got more votes than President Trump, but he would generate more votes than **President Obama. What???** Biden, an unpopular guy that lived in the basement, and the few times he arose from the dead to greet the public, he was met with a small shroud of people. However, on the other hand, President Trump had record crowds everywhere he went and still today, his popularity is enormous. I know this because I do not watch **'Fake News.'** Not even the devil himself can make me believe Biden got more votes than any other president in history. **So, don't insult the intelligence of the American people as if we are infantile schoolhouse toddlers that can be manipulated on a whim.**

The mainstream media has caused such a disdain for President Trump, citizens would rather, turn a blind eye, cheat, and risk losing our country by turning it over to a senile renegade posing as an American. **I've heard it said, elections have consequences, but stolen elections have severe consequences!!!** If you are not brainwashed by the media, look around, I believe you would see the fruits of a stolen election. My America is becoming unrecognizable, but I believe that is what some very evil elites had in mind all along. However, I will fight 'til the death, if necessary, to save the soul of our nation.

How can we fix this problem? I believe Arizona gives us a great prototype for all 50 states to follow. 1) Election holiday; 2) One day elections; 3) No drops boxes; 4) Mail-in ballots for military only and vetted convalescent individuals unable to leave their homes; 5) No early voting; 6) Voter ID of verified citizens of the United States of America (Not the illegals dropped off in states by the rogue Biden administration that were given ID's and Social Security numbers); 7) Smaller precincts with paper ballots and human counting without machines like Dominion; 8) This is my addition; as a result of **2000 Mules and True the Vote**, investigate every non-profit as an accomplice for possible election fraud. **Be a part of the solution and not part of the TREASON by saying nothing happened on November 3, 2020. I realize if we lose our Republic, America is done, and we may as well thank AOC, Bernie Sanders, Klaus Schwab and George Soros for ushering in Communism (The Great Reset; New World Order). Open your eyes and see the**

handwriting on the wall!!! *I'm a very concerned proactive law-abiding citizen that wants to know what's going on with our election process before it's too late. By the way, Communism doesn't discriminate, everyone will be ruled under the iron fist of a tyrannical government like the one we see coming forth.* **I'm willing to die for God, Family and country, because if we lose our freedom, then we are dead already!!!**

May God Bless America,
Sonny B.

CONCLUSION LEAD-IN TO MY RANT

Here is the conclusion of the whole matter in a more unorthodox way, similar to my book, or should I say memoir of actual letters written to save the soul of our nation. When I say unorthodox, I mean an ordinary Joe, characterizing the lies and deceit of the media injected into our culture and put into a book without any chapters. I hold back nothing, I come out swinging like Mike Tyson and if you are inside the ring of propaganda destroying our nation, you will be KO'd by the truth. You will feel the passion and love for God, family and my country, because I realize we are in the fight of our lives against very evil people. I believe this maybe the first book without chapters, but that really doesn't matter. I wanted to do something in defense of a very battered America, with a purpose in mind, and a goal to release my feelings and inspiration on paper towards anyone hating on my America.

I sit here typing with tears flowing from my eyes as I reminisce on the life I have enjoyed growing up as a child and now as an adult. Under the Constitution of the United States anyone can live a full life of liberty and the pursuit of happiness. For anyone trying to destroy the foundations of our freedom, this book is directed to all of those: individuals, entities, elites, media, major corporations, academia, professional sports, government, elected officials (democrat and republican), kangaroo courts, offended blacks, white Marxist liberals, (clergy, Mega Churches, evangelicals), and Hollywood renegades posing as Americans who are allowing and destroying the very fiber of our country. Also, to tell patriots to not lie idle and to get up and fight before it's too late, because losing our freedom is not an option. As I go around sounding the alarm, I try to help Americans understand that communism doesn't discriminate, the destruction it causes to humanity is equally distributed. So, you can continue to be too busy living your life, but if you allow the takeover of our nation, "you will own nothing, and you will be happy," the words from Klaus Schwab's 'Great Reset.'

Jesus said to occupy til I come, so that's what I'm doing. I will not use the lame excuse of saying the bible said it would be like this, like some lackadaisical Christians say. I remind you that Nehemiah was comfortable in a faraway country when he heard his homeland was in shambles. He got up and saved his country by building the wall under similar attacks we see today, but he had the passion and love for his country to fight in spite of the aggression. Therefore, I will not be fazed by what men may do to me, because my God the Father is in control. He inspired me, so you take it up with Him. I will fight until I die and if I die, I will die as a free man. In short, here is my book explained in under 25 minutes of how I feel and addressing the lunacy, latency and hypocrisy, in a poetic rhythmic rant entitled, 2020 School Master.

2020 SCHOOL MASTER RANT

-When I wrote this rant

It seemed like it would never end

Because I see communism right around the bend

So some might call me a doctor of dread

So listen to my rant with your mind at ease

As I dismantle the fake woke like an audible of Drew Brees

-I see so clearly now

The handwriting on the wall

So the Lord sat me down

And showed me the call

Naw Nathan McCall it makes me wanna holla

This mess we in

Makes it hard to swalla

-So don't get mad at me because you can't see

It was the China virus that would set me free

But now we know it could've been Ukraine

Truth is a word I can never refrain

-Listen to my story as it continues to evolve

March 23rd 2020 is when I lost my job

-Home for the first time in 41 years
When I saw the chaos it brought me to tears
-I was minding my own business
I was livin the American dream
As 'Gain of Function' would unveil an evil scheme

-I want peace I don't want to fight
The deep state has stirred a fire
To spread truth as I write
-The dream is for all
I don't care what you say
The KKK is now white liberals that use the black face
-2020 taught me everything I needed to know
That politicians across the nation needed to go
-Capitol Hill is where the corruption flow
And Congress is one big dog and pony show
Had us fooled for decades to no end
But the gig is up
We had enough of the pretend
98 percent of Capitol Hill is compromised
The other two work for the people
While the two parties point fingers
To distract from both of their deadly stingers
-While we were working providing for the fam
They were stoking the alters for a crucified lamb
-Professional sports all making their rounds
Combined with the media to 'Bring in the Clowns'
-Don't sleep on academia they would play a huge part
Preparing the children for a communist heart
-Democrats and republicans played us all like a fool
Made us think we had a right to choose
-Bamboozled hoodwinked man can't you see
We were chained together thinking we were free
-Covid-19 sent out to pry
Into our lives to make us all comply

-Put George Floyd into the mix
While they did the election fix
-My head is spinin
Cause I thought we were winin
They've created an illusion
With Russian collusion
President trump never once conceded
Because he knew there was a whole lotta cheatin
Trump rallies had the biggest crowds
But Biden/Harris couldn't fill a small shroud
-Sleepy Joe got more votes than Obama?
I guess a paper cut is the same as a laceration trauma!!!
-Mask and vax mandates to keep us safe
Was a sign of an early dictate
Isn't that why y'all wanted Trump impeached?
Shoe on the other foot but not one word preached
You see that's what happens when you're the one with the hate
It numbs the ability to think logically and straight
-Media told us all to hate President Trump
As they kick us all in the rump

-My black race can never see the trouble
Because we are the most gullible
Social injustice is used across the board
Exploiting your blackness while being ignored
But we hate the whites that really love us
But love the whites that continue to use us
-Some people you can't tell em
They have to be shown
Baby formula in America is all gone
But to illegals it's flown
If you didn't know
You were played like a fool
Keeping you hypnotized
By the viewing of fake news

-The black race is in the spotlight
But we blinded by the same light
As the LGBTQ get all the rights
-Enslaved in our minds thinking we are free
But escape from the modern day plantation
And you will hang from a tree

-Let me continue with my race
I'm black so I feel it's my place
Cuz at times it can be a disgrace
Y'all know we can show out
And you know I have a case
No one wants to deal wit
The fact is what we lack
When the killin is Black on Black
-What about a person who's mixed with black and white
Looks like that's gonna cause some trouble
What do you do? Do you hate yourself double?
Blacks know we hate the truth we'd rather put on a muzzle
We like an enigma and a Ten thousand piece puzzle
-Treat blacks equally always
Not different
Not worse
Cuz anything else would bring on a thirst
To think blacks are entitled to disperse
Racism it's called, but in reverse
-Racism comes in all colors
And no you don't get a pass
Just because you're black
Gives no right to harass
So live for today
And stop livin in the past

-Elections have consequences
Stolen elections have severe consequences
You know Trump was better for the nation
But you rather vote for them who hate our creation
If you didn't know, I'm talkin bout abortion

Killing black babies thru planned parenthood extortion

-Dr King wanted inclusiveness

But it came with a price

Togetherness with all

Including the whites

-So if you hate yo fellowman

Then throw it out wit the can

Cuz division of race

Was never in God's plan

-Let's take two opposing views

You know one's a fact

But the other you choose

To except the lie

And the truth you refuse

-Whoever heard protecting the vaxxed from the unvaxxed?

Does that give off any red flags?

This causes no reaction

Klaus Schwab's main attraction

One plus one still equals two

But you won't even look at a different point of view

-Covid vaccines killing people by the thousands

Vaccine injuries at a faster pace

Media hidin and censoring the truth

Of vaccines they call safe

-Why are black people so gullible?

And Marxist white liberals so terrible?

One's the slave

The other's the slave master

After hundreds of years pickin cotton

They still got blacks jockin

-A bigger plantation is a replica

And mind slavery is the new Mecca

So you don't realize you're already free

Cuz 1619 is the only thang you see

-The chains are off

Those not aborted are born as a bastard

But what we gon do, bout the man we call master?
Sounds familiar?
Blacks don't wanna leave the plantation
They'll rather have communism
Running throughout our nation
-Quit letting white liberals and Dems rule your life
By keeping you angry
And in a world of strife

-Why if I'm black
I gotta vote democrat
But if republican I choose
Then I get the abuse
Democrats know they have your vote
That's why they don't ask for your vote
That's blatant disrespect
Cuz there's no need to respect
Hilary shook a bottle of hot sauce
And the democratic vote we tossed
Obama told blacks to quit your complaining
Put your walking shoes on and go vote
Did more for the gays
But turned you off like a remote
Sleepy Joe said you ain't black
If you don't vote democrat
Man blacks ain't learned yet
The meaning of disrespect
Just yell discrimination
And they'll never leave the plantation

-How vile is the pedophile
I have one worse
A Biden SCOTUS
A sympathizer and perverse
But fake news berates
The judge that ended the mask mandate
Grab a lantern
Shine light on it

See the pattern
Borrowed words from Tyson James
So you could see the media's hypocritical claim
Mind control without any shame
One you celebrate
The other you desecrate
This is inconceivable
Pedo over a mask
That's exactly why media numbers have crashed
-Media created an illusion
When they did the collusion
What else have they lied about
Don't wanna know cuz I'm more devout
Malcolm X said it best
Media control the minds of the masses
Make the guilty innocent
And make the innocent guilty
When it's really their hands that are filthy

-Media say cases like George Floyd is extreme
But Black on Black murder happens only in our dreams
If that didn't suit your fancy
Then I got one better
Over 400 thousand black babies are murdered each year
Cuz the definition of abortion has become unclear
-Can you believe a liberal said my writings are dark?
After BLM riots but not one remark
Liberalism is a mental disorder
They lock their doors but want an open border
I'm not done yet Antifa did their part
They tore up cities like a great white shark
This duo will be remembered
Like the Pearl Harbor disaster in early December
-The NBA took a knee
To defy the country
Silly rabbit it wasn't for a black life
It was to pay Patrisee Cullors a big hefty tithe

-Big Tech use algorithms to keep from exposing the con
Had BLM founder to change her name from Cullors to Khan
Y'all think mainstream is tellin you real news
But they wanna control your political views
As y'all sit piously in church filled pews
-The Biden regime doesn't care bout yo blackness
450K to illegals paid for by your taxes
They don't have any loyalty to you
They only need you as a part of their coup

-Sprinkle it with racism
That will cause some black fervor
But nothin says overlook
Like Black on Black murder
-How do you explain someone who don't wanna hear the truth?
Lay it all out with nothin but proof
They turn a blind eye and open up to fakery
It's simple to see the effects of mind slavery
Just listen for a minute
And please don't ignore
We've all been exploited
Like a ten dolla whore
-I love my black race
But I want what's better
I want the real cow hide
But they only want pleather
-Supposed to be wise as a serpent and harmless as a dove
Powerless in the fight and misinterpreting the word love
The world would be better off if the church was alive and well
Instead pastors have their members on a road paved to hell
-Churches pick and choose
And their battles are selective
Which is why they've become combat ineffective

-Good vs evil
And there's no in between
Choose hot or cold or things could go south
Lukewarm Christians God spews out of His mouth

-Yes I'm on the church hard
Their masks are on, it's all a façade
Make you think they stand for truth
Bible principles go out the window at the election booth
-Evil was lurkin
While Christians were busy churchin
Prayer was taken out of school
While the church played the fool
-When is the black church gonna stand up and fight
And understand the fight is not white
Got the white churches believin the hype
While the Mega church preach about houses and land
And neither one is in God's plan
-Hoodwinked bamboozled wool pulled over our eyes
Including the church, is everybody compromised
-I've never seen so many Christians avoid the truth
They'll rather stay comfortable, misinformed and aloof
I don't care if it lines up with the word
I'll rather sit, watch, eat and observe

-Turn on fake news
As they see the headline
Truth just don't register
To the ones who are brainwashed and blind
If Trump's a racist
He's doing a mighty poor job
He did more for blacks
Then you show them the list
Can't handle the truth
So they storm off pissed
-Democrats use anything as a racial hoax
Haitians whipped, Jussie Smollett, and Bubba Wallace was all a joke
Racism so massive
They gotta manufacture
To make us think racism is a routine disaster
-Someone tell me how ID became voter suppression
You need it to drive

So what's the obsession
Here's a little simple suggestion
Get an ID before the next election
Don't you want an election that proves your identity
I almost forgot
The left has no integrity
-Who said Dems are tolerant and the party of inclusion
Just disagree with them and you'll experience the collusion

-Where has our country gone
And what exactly went wrong
America once on top
Now it's being dethroned
-Outside influences
Killin us from within
Riots on the streets
Has become the new trend
-Did you know chaos cannot bring order
Just like three dimes and a nickel can't make a quarter
The Big Bang proved to us that theory
It's about as real as the January 6 committee
I found there's no reasoning with the left
They enjoy destruction and identity theft
-Dems knew they didn't have a chance in hell
So they released the unholy grail
Bringing fear they knew Biden couldn't fail
With fake ballots across the country trail
Of election fraud on a massive scale
As Covid-19 would again prevail
-See you vote because of a person
And I rely on my assertion
I don't depend on fake news
To cloud up my Christian views
The lies they tell makes people react
I'm not moved by emotions
Just give me the facts
-I think John DeBarry Jr is a republican in disguise

His words about the riots came as a big surprise
Coward politicians that didn't demonize
Left cities destroyed by a criminal uprise
Go figure he was ousted by the democratic party
For speaking against the fake woke army
-Teach CRT in our colleges and throughout our schools
Dumbify them from learning
Until they all become fools
How else do you get blacks and whites to riot
You feed them racism and make it a steady diet
-Wokeness is in our sports
Can't even enjoy a game
Those who continue to watch
Are like sheep ready to be slain
-When did patriotism leave and it was okay to take a knee
I'm done with sports, but that's just me
They hate the nation but love the currency
And waving the flag has become white supremacy
Free at last, free at last, are we really free at last
Can't be, Elie Mystal called the constitution trash
-I know what's the problem
We've been blessed way too long
Even our homeless in the streets
Are better off than Hong Kong

-The Russian leader said he would take over America
But the CCP intercepted the plot
Killin America from within
Without ever firing a shot
-Lets talk Afghanistan
Biden fumbled without a ball in hand
Kinda reminds me of Benghazi
What a dog and pony show
Left Americans stranded with no place to go
-If Trump had our country in a disaster
We would hear it again and again and the morning after
Y'all know this country is in the pit

But there are only sounds of a very small cricket
Y'all are a joke, a farce and a hypocrite
Pretending like our nation is thriving and lit
-One party system ain't no need to vote
Elites got us all
At one another's throat
-Democrat, republican
They are one in the same
They are both corrupt
They just hold a different name
-One is a wolf
The other in sheep's clothing
Failed policies are the same
Cuz both are self-promoting

-We've been hoodwinked bamboozled and swindled
Government expanded
While we the people dwindled
-I don't care what you thank
Capitol Hill stank
Causing everyone to hate
Brothers and sisters can't even relate
-We fight one another because of the political gangsters
Enjoying the wheel like an overweight hamster
I try to educate to give them a clue
But they still denounce the colors of red, white and blue
-We can't rely on political rule
Too busy swimin in the political cesspool
There's only a handful that work for the people
The rest want a country full of mindless sheeple
-They downplayed the presidential election
To vow for my affection
There is no question
Election fraud was not a suggestion
The 2020 school master would teach me a lesson
The corruption is great
That's why it's called the deep state

-Look at California recall election
Like 2020 it went in the same direction
Republican votes were already cast
We gotta fix the system before we can move pass

-The problem with Marxist
Are from within
They don't care how
They just want to win
Stuff the ballots
And make sure your guy gets in
Their platform sucks, oh let me do tell
Cuz they know they don't have a chance in hell
-Maricopa County audit already done
It showed the proof how President Trump won
The 2020 election was a monumental disaster
If not fixed, we will lose the nation faster
Keystone pipeline shut down
Gas prices out the roof
Losing the nation faster, therein lies my proof
-Ahh midterms
Another four years has come around
Another election year
So send in the clowns
-Oh the virus, I didn't say it wasn't real
But we were punk'd by mass appeal
I had the virus
THERE IS A CURE!!!
All FDA approved no reason to fear

-Think about it
We're in a global PLAN-demic
But the cures were hidden
And demonized as a gimmick
-Round them all up for high treason
Families devastated for absolutely no reason
But for a Great Reset and America to be weakened
-They did it with a curable disease

And they did it with ease
The people just complied
Because they couldn't see the lie
-I tried telling them the truth
But they see you as a goof
Fake news is the only thing
Sheeple believe as real proof
-Wake-up call for those of you still in a coma
Gotta revive you with a medical stoma
Fake news please tell the truth to the people
Cuz nothing else is real to mindless sheeple
Got the power to make the innocent guilty
And calling wrong right
With persuasion from the 'Angel of Light'
-When we gon learn the media's been lyin
Maybe if they saw backward birds flyin
If there's a cure for covid then why it's not on the news
This question is laughable except it ain't even funny
Fake news making fools look like a big dummy
-15 months into the covid jabs
14,068 deaths for a vaccine they call safe
Is that not alarming to you
Because you refuse to hear the truth
That's only one percent reported to VAERS
I wonder how many more are dying in pairs
I get it, you already took their advice
Went full speed ahead like the three blind mice
So anything negative, you don't want to hear
Possible death in the future brings too much fear
-Covid hospital visits was killin people far and near
With a drug by Fauci called remdesivir
Go ahead and check the hospital record
And ask yourself why they died on a stretcher
A class action suit is a powerful thang
Can't sue Pfizer though, don't you think that's kinda strange
-SCOTUS couldn't call the election
And neither could Mike Pence

The world had to see the corruption
Before they could be convinced
To remove the media folklore
To prevent a civil war

-I have plenty more to say
But not enough time in a day
To warn those gone astray
With Biden, our nation is not okay
I don't care what the news is trying to relay
The bottom line is, we need to pray
For our country's in disarray
2020 School Master, showed us Communism is underway
To wake-up the masses, before it's too late